Tobacco Control

Comparative Politics in the United States and Canada

Donley T. Studlar

broadview press

NATIONAL LIBRARY OF CANADA CATALOGUING IN PUBLICATION DATA

Studlar, Donley T.
  Tobacco control : comparative politics in the United States and Canada

Includes bibliographical references and index
ISBN 1-55111-456-9

  1. Smoking—Government policy–Canada. 2. Smoking—Government policy—United States. 3. Tobacco habit—Prevention—Government policy—Canada. 4. Tobacco habit—Prevention—Government policy—United States.
I. Title.

HV5735.D65 2002   362.29'66'0971   c2001-903862-3

BROADVIEW PRESS, LTD.
is an independent, international publishing house, incorporated in 1985.

North America
Post Office Box 1243,
Peterborough, Ontario,
Canada K9J 7H5
Tel: (705) 743-8990
Fax: (705) 743-8353

3576 California Road,
Orchard Park, New York
USA 14127

customerservice@broadviewpress.com
www.broadviewpress.com

United Kingdom
Thomas Lyster, Ltd.
Unit 9, Ormskirk Industrial Park
Old Boundary Way, Burscough Rd.
Ormskirk, Lancashire L39 2YW
Tel: (01695) 575112
Fax: (01695) 570120
books@tlyster.co.uk

Australia
St. Clair Press
P.O. Box 287, Rozelle, NSW 2039
Tel: (612) 818-1942
Fax: (612) 418-1923

Broadview Press gratefully acknowledges the financial support of the Book Publishing Industry Development Program, Ministry of Canadian Heritage, Government of Canada.

Cover design by Zack Taylor. Typeset by Zack Taylor.

Printed in Canada

For Susan, Carl, and Ross

Contents

List of Tables and Figures

9

Acronyms

ACF	Advocacy Coalition Framework
ACIR	Advisory Commission on Intergovernmental Relations (US)
ACS	American Cancer Society
ADM	Assistant Deputy Minister (Canada)
AHA	American Heart Association
AI	Advocacy Institute (US)
ALA	American Lung Association
AMA	American Medical Association
ANR	Americans for Nonsmokers' Rights
ASH	Action on Smoking and Health (US, Alberta in Canada–unaffiliated organizations)
ASSIST	American Stop Smoking Intervention Study for Cancer Prevention
ASTHO	Association of State and Territorial Health Officers (US)
BAT	British American Tobacco
BATF	Bureau of Alcohol, Tobacco, and Firearms (US)
BQ	Bloc Québécois
CCS	Canadian Cancer Society
CCSH	Canadian Council on Smoking and Health
CDC	Centers for Disease Control and Prevention (US)
CFNR	Californians for Nonsmokers' Rights
CMA	Canadian Medical Association
COMMIT	Community Intervention Trial for Smoking Cessation (US)

COSH   Coalition on Smoking OR Health (US)

CTMC   Canadian Tobacco Manufacturers Council

CTRI   Canadian Tobacco Research Initiative

DOL   Department of Labor (US)

DHEW   Department of Health, Education and Welfare (US)

DHHS   Department of Health and Human Services (US)

DOC   Doctors Ought to Care (US)

ETS   Environmental Tobacco Smoke

FCC   Federal Communications Commission (US)

FCTC   Framework Convention on Tobacco Control

FDA   Food and Drug Administration (US)

FTC   Federal Trade Commission (US)

FTCS   Federal Tobacco Control Strategy (Canada)

GASP   Groups Against Smoking Pollution (mainly US)

GATT   General Agreement on Trade and Tariffs

HEW   Health, Education and Welfare

HPP   Healthy Public Policy

HSFC   Heart and Stroke Foundation of Canada

IDRC   International Development Research Centre (Canada)

IMPACT   Initiatives to Mobilize for the Control and Prevention of Tobacco Use (US)

INFACT   Infant Formula Action Campaign (US)

INGCAT   International Non Governmental Coalition Against Tobacco

JAMA   *Journal of the American Medical Association*

JTI   Japan Tobacco Inc.

MSA   Master Settlement Agreement (US)

NAFTA   North American Free Trade Agreement

NCI   National Cancer Institute (US)

NCTH   National Clearinghouse on Tobacco and Health (Canada)

NDP   New Democratic Party (Canada)

NGO   Nongovernmental Organization

NIOSH	National Institute for Occupational Safety and Health (US)
NPR	National Public Radio (US)
NSRA	Non-Smokers Rights' Association (Canada)
NSRTU	National Strategy to Reduce Tobacco Use (Canada)
NTCP	National Tobacco Control Program (US)
NTCS	National Tobacco Control Strategy (Canada)
OCAT	Ontario Campaign for Action on Tobacco
OSH	Office on Smoking and Health (US)
OSHA	Occupational Safety and Health Administration (US)
OTRU	Ontario Tobacco Research Unit
PQ	Parti Québécois
PSFC	Physicians for a Smoke-Free Canada
RCMP	Royal Canadian Mounted Police
RJR	R.J. Reynolds Tobacco Company
RWJ	Robert Wood Johnson Foundation (US)
SCARC-NET	Smoking Control Advocacy Resource Center (US)
SES	Socio-economic status
SHAF	Smoking and Health Action Foundation (Canada)
STAT	Stop Teenage Access to Tobacco (US)
TDRS	Tobacco Demand Reduction Strategy (Canada)
TFI	Tobacco Free Initiative (WHO)
TPCA	Tobacco Products Control Act (1988) (Canada)
TSYPA	Tobacco Sales to Young Persons Act (1993) (Canada)
UICC	International Union Against Cancer
UNICEF	United Nations Children's Fund
USSTR	United States Special Trade Representative
WCTOH	World Conference on Tobacco or Health
WHO	World Health Organization
WTO	World Trade Organization

Acknowledgments

In addition to those named individually and collectively below, this research especially benefited from comments by Colin Bennett, Raymond Tatalovich, Rob Cunningham, Kenyon Stebbins, L. Christopher Plein, Rebecca Klase, Lou Fintor, Jeffrey B. Freyman, George Hoberg, and Jeffrey Worsham. Previous work containing some of the material in this book has been published in *Canadian-American Public Policy, Annals of the American Academy of Political and Social Science*, the *Occasional Papers* series of the Canadian Studies Center, Bowling Green State University, the *West Virginia Public Affairs Reporter*, and *The Politics of Pain: Political Institutions and Loss Imposition in Canada and the United States*, edited by Leslie A. Pal and R. Kent Weaver. Parts of this work were previously presented in several different forums. These include the Middle Atlantic and Northeast Conference on Canadian Studies, University Park, Pennsylvania; the University of Texas School of Public Health, Houston; the Political Studies Association of the United Kingdom, Belfast, Northern Ireland; the American Political Science Association, Washington, D.C.; the Canadian Political Science Association, Sherbrooke, Quebec; the Association for Canadian Studies in the United States, Pittsburgh and San Antonio; the Political Science Department of Wittenberg University, Springfield, Ohio; the Political Science Department of the University of Toronto; the School of Public Administration of Carleton University, Ottawa; the Centre for Addiction and Mental Health, Toronto; the Health Policy Forum, Health Canada, Ottawa; the World Conference on Tobacco or Health, Chicago; the Political Science Department, West Virginia University; and the Western Political Science Association, Las Vegas.

Various parts of the research were supported by grants from the Canadian Embassy in Washington through its Faculty Research Program, the Faculty Senate of West Virginia University, the Eberly College of Arts and Sciences, a sabbatical leave from West Virginia University, and the Fulbright Exchange Program of Canada and the United States, which allowed me to serve as a Senior Fulbright Scholar at the University of Toronto. Thanks to Robert Vipond, Chair of Political Science at Toronto, and the members of the Ontario Tobacco Research Unit, especially Mary Jane Ashley, Joanna Cohen, Nicole de Guia, Roberta Ferrence, and Diane Van Abbe, for providing such a hospitable work environment during my stay. Cathy Anderson, a student in the School of Law at U of T, presented the stimulus of a fresh mind doing work in the same area. Melissa Haussman provided information on controversies over tobacco control in Massachusetts. Al Olivetti, Kevin Cox, Justin Harrison, Mark Dennison, and Jennifer Mesich of the WVU Political Science Department have served as research assistants in various capacities during the course of the research. Heather Starsick performed minor miracles with the computer, as did Mary Hapel and Bryan Shanahan of the Research School of Social Sciences, Australian National University during copy-editing. Allan Hammock, Chair of Political Science at WVU, facilitated completion of the book by providing that most valuable and overlooked of all resources, time. At the University of Toronto, Hyla Levy performed a number of chores which helped launch the manuscript in written form. At WVU, Elizabeth Yost typed and retyped the manuscript until she could recite it practically verbatim.

I thank all of the people who consented to interviews on this topic. They are listed in the Appendix. Obviously I am responsible for all interpretations. This work would have been much poorer without the assistance of the staff at the Canadian Clearinghouse on Tobacco Control in Ottawa and its immense depository of materials on tobacco matters in both Canada and the United States, a treasure for researchers which needs to be maintained and enhanced.

1

Introduction: The Problem of Tobacco-Control Policy

"The cigarette was, and still is, the most profitable consumer product ever sold legally." (Stoffman 1987: 20)

"Smoking represents the most extensively documented cause of disease ever investigated in the history of biomedical research." (1990 US Surgeon General's report, as quoted in Davis 1992: 1)

"There can be no question that if cigarettes were a food or drug or being newly marketed, their sale would have to be prohibited or strongly regulated on the basis of evidence now available…" (Isabelle 1969: 9)

Introduction

Tobacco control is both an old and a new public policy issue. In recent years tobacco control has engaged governmental and public attention on a regular basis in both Canada and the United States. Battles over regulation, taxes, and litigation against tobacco companies have made headlines and generated political conflict.

Yet an examination of the historical record shows that a restrictive tobacco-control policy, especially focussed on cigarettes, has appeared on the political agendas of both the general public and the government periodically in the past. This occurred especially around the turn of the twentieth century, largely on moral grounds, and again mid-century based on rising concerns about the health effects of cigarettes. In both previous instances, concern about restricting cigarette usage receded after a time, and the politics of tobacco returned largely to one of promoting tobacco as an economically profitable product for growers and companies, society at large, and government tax coffers. For our purposes, even tobacco promotion can be considered part of tobacco-control policy since it involves an active role for the government. There are various degrees of tobacco-control policy, ranging along a continuum from promotional to restrictive.

The late twentieth-century political controversy over cigarette production and usage appears to be increasing rather than receding. The conflict has become widespread, covering many countries and levels of government. The stakes are high: the few multinational tobacco companies are some of the largest and most profitable business corporations on earth. The largest one, Philip Morris, has an annual worldwide economic output of all products, tobacco and otherwise, greater than the individual gross national product of all except approximately the largest 20 countries in the world; in other words, its annual output is about the same as the GNP of Australia.

On the other hand, the death toll resulting from tobacco usage is also immense. Even with tobacco usage in decline for a third of a century, most estimates of tobacco-related deaths in Canada and the United States consider them to be a contributing cause of at least 20 per cent of the total (see Table 1-4). On a global basis, the World Health Organization (WHO) has estimated that by the year 2030 tobacco will be the leading cause of death in the world, rising to ten million from four million in 2000. Unlike some other dangerous products, such as alcohol, in which problems result from overuse, there is no such thing as a safe level of cigarette consumption. It is now widely recognized that the cigarette is the only readily available consumer product which, when used regularly, *as intended*, results in death in one out of two cases.

The globalization of the political conflict over tobacco will be examined in the last chapter of the book. The major focus, however, is on Canada and the United States, two countries sharing the North American continent who have similar histories of the impact of tobacco but who have, at times, responded differently to these challenges. What might explain the patterns of convergence and divergence in tobacco-control policy in these two countries over the past 40 years is the major question of this study.

In both countries, tobacco control has two broad dimensions: (1) regulation through laws, orders, and agreements concerning individual and corporate behaviour and (2) finance, especially taxation and subsidies. Both of these can be used for either restricting or promoting tobacco production and consumption. For instance, regulations can be drafted in

ways that promote tobacco use, as in some US state "preemption" statutes that prevent local governments from enacting more restrictive tobacco-control laws. At times, the regulatory and revenue functions may come into conflict. This has been the case especially when tobacco taxes account for a large portion of the revenues raised by governments. The Canadian federal government traditionally has placed higher taxes on tobacco than the United States and has had a greater dependence on such revenues, although many provincial governments did not tax tobacco products until the 1960s (Friedman 1975). Even today, when more restrictive regulations have been passed in many jurisdictions, both federal and provincial/state governments in Canada and the United States continue some financial policies favourable to tobacco growing, manufacture, and consumption. More recently, some states that had received money from the tobacco industry in the Master Settlement Agreement took steps to protect their revenues from the potentially huge punitive damages in the *Engle* class action lawsuit against the industry. This has led some anti-tobacco activists to become reluctant about allowing governments to become dependent on the financial contributions of tobacco companies, through either taxation or settlements of lawsuits.

This study analyzes the political conflicts over tobacco that have emerged in Canada and the United States, especially since the landmark Report of the Advisory Committee of the United States Surgeon General on tobacco in 1964. Although there were earlier official expressions of concern about the health effects of cigarette smoking by both the US Surgeon General and Health and Welfare Canada, the 1964 Surgeon General's Report is almost universally accepted as a watershed for tobacco-control policy in shifting the political agenda from one of indifference to and promotion of tobacco usage to one that incorporated some governmentally endorsed attempts at tobacco-use reduction. There was a flurry of activity in both Canada and the United States in the years immediately after the Surgeon General's Report and a gradual decline in tobacco consumption in both countries, from approximately half of the population in each country to about a quarter, with somewhat higher rates in Canada. Yet, in terms of the demonstrated severity of the problem, the governmental response at all levels was minimal until about the mid-1980s.

A short list of the major policy decisions, primarily legislation, executive action, and court decisions, at various levels of government from the mid-1960s to the present day, based on innovation as well as breadth, is presented in Table 1-1.

Table 1-1: Major Decisions on Tobacco Control, Canada and US, 1964-2001

A. Situation Normal: US Takes the Lead, 1964-1984

1964 (US) Surgeon General's Report on the health effects of cigarette smoking

1965 (US) Federal *Cigarette Labeling and Advertising Act of 1965*

1967 (US) Federal Communications Commission issues equal-time ruling

1970 (US) Federal *Public Health Cigarette Smoking Act of 1969*

1971 (C) Voluntary agreement by cigarette industry to end TV and radio ads, place warning labels on packages

1974 (US) Minnesota passes comprehensive indoor anti-smoking legislation

1981 (C) Federal and provincial taxes on cigarettes made *ad valorem* and increased

1982 (US) First federal tax increase on cigarettes since 1950

B. The Mouse that Roared: Canada Becomes a World Leader, 1984-1994

1984 (US) Federal warning labels strengthened and increased to four

1985 (C) Major federal tax increase on cigarettes

1986 (US) US Surgeon General's Report on the effects of second-hand smoke

1988 (C) Tobacco Products Control Act (TPCA)

(C) *Non-Smokers' Rights Act*

(US) Surgeon General's report on cigarettes as addictive

(US) California *Proposition 99*, tobacco taxes for health promotion

1989 (C) Major federal tax increase on cigarettes, explicitly for health purposes

1991 (C) Another major federal tax increase on cigarettes

(US) ASSIST program

1992 (US) Massachusetts passes referendum for tobacco tax, partially devoted to anti-tobacco programs

(US) Environmental Protection Agency report on dangers of second-hand smoke

1993 (C) *Tobacco Sales to Young Persons Act*

1994 (C) In wake of smuggling crisis, federal and provincial taxes in five provinces reduced

(C) Ontario *Tobacco Control Act*

(US) Tobacco company executives testify before House Subcommittee

---

C. International Leapfrogging: Policy Convergence, 1994-2001

1995 (US) Food and Drug Administration proclaims intention to regulate tobacco

    (C) Supreme Court of Canada overturns TPCA

1997 (US) State National Settlement with tobacco industry over Medicaid costs

    (C) Federal *Tobacco Act*

1998 (C) *Amendment to Tobacco Act*, delaying sponsorship ban

    (C) British Columbia passes legislation enabling it to sue tobacco companies

    (C) Quebec *Tobacco Act*

    (US) Senate rejects National Settlement

    (US) Minnesota settles out of court with tobacco companies

    (US) 46 states and tobacco companies reach Master Settlement Agreement

1999 (C) British Columbia sues tobacco companies; imposes licensing fees

    (C) Federal government sues tobacco companies in US courts for conspiracy in smuggling

    (US) Justice Department sues tobacco companies over Medicare costs

2000 (C) Federal government adopts new, graphic cigarette warnings

    (US) Supreme Court overturns FDA authority

    (C) Federal government suit disallowed in US court

2001 (C) Federal Tobacco Control Strategy

More detailed although somewhat varying chronologies of government policy in Canada and the United States are available elsewhere (Cunningham 1996; Nathanson 1999; Fritschler and Hoefler 1996).

Within this broadly similar tobacco-control policy agenda, the question arises, why did governments take particular actions? Why have some levels of government been more restrictive in tobacco control in each country? After almost 40 years of activity in tobacco control in both countries, what are the similarities and differences in policies, timing, and levels of government involved? Although the study is not primarily quantitative, it attempts to explain what statistical studies call both "within-group" variance, e.g., why policies have changed over time within a single country, and "between-group" variance, that is, how policies compare across the two countries. In the process, it tests the relative value of several competing explanations of tobacco-control policy, usually developed from less far-ranging studies in time and space, as discussed in Chapter Two.

A major question to be answered emerges in the division of periods in Table 1-1. For approximately the first twenty years after tobacco restrictions became an issue on the governmental agenda, the United States was the leader between the two countries, and at least initially in the world. This is not unusual because in many matters of product regulation for health, Canada tends to follow the agenda and often the contents of US policies closely (Hoberg 1991; Harrison and Hoberg 1994). In 1965 the US legislated the first health warnings on packages in any country. However, beginning in the mid-1980s, for about a decade Canada became not only the leader in tobacco-control policy between these two countries, but even a world leader. In the mid-1990s, the US began to take more restrictive action in tobacco control, and since then the two countries have engaged, when all levels of government are considered, in a pattern of leapfrogging, employing similar policies and each innovating in some areas. A more detailed description of these periods is contained in Chapters Three and Four. What explains these patterns is the major question to be answered in an extended comparison of the two countries.

The Phases of Tobacco Control

Legislative attempts to restrict tobacco usage, especially cigarettes, through regulation and taxation began in the late nineteenth and early twentieth century and have continued sporadically ever since. One way to understand these phenomena is to divide them into stages corresponding roughly to the rise and decline of restrictions, especially on cigarettes, as a political issue in the United States and Canada. Restrictions have been a periodic rather than a regular part of the political agenda, broadly considered, in both countries, at least until recently. Scholars of tobacco policy have offered several different "wave" analyses, depending on their focus. The economist Richard McGowan (1995) presents an analysis of government regulation of the US cigarette industry in three waves, based on the principal concern in each: (1) 1911-1963: The Structure of the Industry; (2) 1964-1985: The Health of the Smoker; and (3) 1985 to the present: The Rights of the Nonsmoker. From a legal perspective, Kelder and Daynard (1997) have developed a widely accepted threefold division of tobacco litigation in the United States: (1)1954-1973, when individual plaintiffs were hampered by a lack of medical evidence acceptable to the courts; (2)1983-1992, when such lawsuits had better medical backing but were rebutted on the basis that the health warning on packages made smokers responsible for their own plight and even initially successful suits faced insurmountable legal expenses; and (3) 1992-to the present, when, in addition to individual lawsuits, class action and medical reimbursement suits brought not only new arguments but also greater financial resources to bear on plaintiffs, resulting in some significant losses for tobacco companies. Although analyses of litigation have now been extended to other countries, the "wave" analysis has not (Daynard, Bates, and Francey 2000), which suggests its limitations. Nathanson (1999) analyzes the recent development of smoking control movements in the United States in terms of three overlapping waves: (1) 1950-1964: Making the Health Connection; (2) 1965-1996, The Struggle for Regulation; and (3) 1971-1995, The Discovery of Innocent Victims. She also suggests there is yet a fourth overlapping wave, "Demonizing the Tobacco Industry," stemming from 1988. Like the litigation phases, this is based only on recent US experience and more on events than on any theoretical foundation, as exemplified by having two and possibly three phases which exist almost simultaneously.

One can combine and extend these analyses into a division of historical periods useful for examining tobacco control in Canada and the United States, as seen in Table 1-2.

Table 1-2: The Phases of Tobacco-Control Policy, 1884-2001

Phase 1: 1884-1914	Consolidation of the Cigarette Industry and Early Controversies
Phase 2: 1914-1950	Era of Good Feeling; Cigarettes Promoted by Governments
Phase 3: 1950-1964	The Gathering Storm of Health Concerns
Phase 4: 1964-1984	Regulatory Hesitancy
Phase 5: 1984-2001	Tobacco as Social Menace

The dates are only approximate because phases do overlap, especially if one considers more specialist professional and interest-group concerns which eventually become part of the governmental and public agenda. Nevertheless, when considered as a whole, the political debate over tobacco policy for an extended period does have noticeable beginnings, even if they are not always as self-evident as the 1964 Surgeon General's

Report. The first period stems from the mass production of cigarettes in North Carolina by James B. Duke and the growth of the American Tobacco Company, a monopoly extending into Canada, until the outbreak of World War I (Canada fought from 1914, the US from 1917). The second phase marks the governmental decisions in both countries that tobacco was essential to the war effort and the resulting decline of anti-tobacco groups until the first four definitive "retrospective" health studies documenting that smokers had higher death rates from cancer, published in 1950; one could just as well note the end of this period as December 1952, when *Reader's Digest* brought the issue to the attention of a wider public with its edited article from a smaller publication, "Cancer by the Carton" (Sobel 1978; Cunningham 1996). The third phase is from the early 1950s until the Surgeon General's Report in 1964. The fourth phase of limited regulatory attempts proceeds from that time until the early and mid-1980s, when a confluence of circumstances raised concern over broader medical and social effects of tobacco, epitomized by the Surgeon General's Report of 1986, *The Health Consequences of Involuntary Smoking*. This moved the debate from one of individual choice and governmental education programs to the restriction of the political and social power of the tobacco industry, both through financial and regulatory means. This fifth phase, initiated in the mid-1980s, has continued into the twenty-first century.

While the major part of this book will focus on phases four and five, it is worthwhile to give some attention to the earlier phases, to show how the issue has evolved and the elements at work in making it a matter of political controversy. As Schattschneider (1960) and Bachrach and Baratz (1962) contend, an analysis of public policy must consider not only the political agenda, but also how some issues are organized into controversy and others are not (non-decision-making). What makes tobacco control a suitable issue for such an analysis is the fact that it has existed for a long time, has been on the agenda at times and off at others, has operated at different levels or jurisdictions of political systems (municipal, state/ provincial, federal), has taken different forms, and has led to different outcomes, both over time and between two comparable countries. The rest of this chapter will give a broad overview of the policy content of these five phases, followed by basic social and economic comparisons of tobacco in these two countries, a description of political institutions in the two countries potentially relevant for tobacco-control policy, and an outline of the rest of the book.

PHASE 1

1884-1914 – EARLY CONTROVERSIES AND THE
CONSOLIDATION OF THE CIGARETTE INDUSTRY

Until the late nineteenth century, cigarettes were only a small share of the tobacco market, and it was not until the middle of the twentieth century that they completely overshadowed other forms of tobacco consumption. Through the technical inventions of the mass production machine and the portable safety match, changing social circumstances, and government policies, cigarettes became ever more popular, eventually emerging as the dominant form of tobacco usage. The portability of manufactured cigarettes and eventually matches were an asset in increasingly mobile, urbanized societies. The fact that cigarettes were inexpensive and in small packages, usually of ten, encouraged working-class consumption, as did immigration from parts of Europe where cigarettes were better established than in the New World. In contrast, chewing tobacco, with its accompanying spittoon, was largely a rural phenomenon and went into decline.

In 1884 James B. Duke began producing cigarettes to complement his company's other tobacco products in North Carolina, using a near-exclusive agreement to employ the Bonsack cigarette-making machine rather than more expensive, slower hand labour. The gamble was immense, for two reasons. First, the machine was initially unreliable. Second, previously machine-made cigars had not found favour with the public. Other critical ingredients for Duke's success in what became the American Tobacco Company included the invention of reliable packaging for cigarettes and extensive advertising to promote the new product (Goodman 1998). Within a few years Duke's business in cigarettes was booming, and he approached other companies about dividing up the market.

In 1890, Duke incorporated the other companies into the "Tobacco Trust" through which American Tobacco came to dominate the fledgling US cigarette market and extended itself into other tobacco products as well. Duke's goal was no less than world domination of the tobacco market. In combination with British Tobacco, Duke formed the British-American conglomerate and expanded into Canada, where the two companies soon controlled over 80 per cent of the market. This monopoly was ended after a Royal Commission investigation and parliamentary action to ban the "exclusive contract" system of marketing that American Tobacco had employed (Cunningham 1996: 33-34). The Tobacco Trust's similar monopoly position (over 80 per cent) in the US was ended by a US

Supreme Court decision in 1911 which declared that it constituted a violation of the *Sherman Anti-Trust Act* of 1886. American tobacco was broken
into 14 different companies, of which three originally made cigarettes—
American Tobacco Company, with a 37-per-cent market share, Liggett and
Myers, 28 per cent, and Lorillard, 15 per cent. Eventually they were joined
by a fourth cigarette maker, Reynolds, already making other tobacco products. The net result was that an oligopoly replaced a monopoly (Kluger
1996).

Over the years, three companies emerged in Canada. American
Tobacco's holdings in Canada were sold to BAT, which established
Imperial Tobacco Ltd. as its outlet in Canada. An old Canadian manufac-
turer, Macdonald, eventually merged with RJ Reynolds from the US and
later JTI from Japan; these became RJR-Macdonald Inc. and later JTI-
Macdonald Inc. The separate companies Rothmans and Benson and
Hedges, the latter with support from its partial owner Philip Morris,
became major players in the 1950s and merged in the 1980s into
Rothmans, Benson and Hedges, Inc.

Thus the fundamental pattern of business ownership in the tobacco
market was established for the rest of the century in both countries.
Through changing fortunes, business mergers, and renaming, the identity
and market shares of the cigarette producers varied, but an oligopoly of
between three and six major companies continued in both countries.

In terms of the share of the tobacco market as a whole, cigarettes had
made persistent but less-than-spectacular gains (Tate 1999; McGowan
1995). In the medium term, before World War I, the most important
feature of the tobacco market was the precipitous decline of chewing
tobacco—half the tobacco products sold in the US in 1880, but only a
quarter in 1914. Cigars and pipe tobacco as well as cigarettes cut into this
market. The relative market shares of tobacco products in the US in this
era are presented below (Tate 1999):

> 1880: cigarettes, 1%, pipe tobacco, 19%,
>   chewing tobacco, 58%, cigars, 19%

> 1914: cigarettes, 7%, pipe tobacco, 34%,
>   chewing tobacco, 29%, cigars, 25%

By 1920 cigarettes comprised 20 per cent of the market, rising to 30 per
cent by 1925, and 40 per cent by 1930 (Tate 1999). Cigarettes would

constitute over 85 per cent of total tobacco sales by the mid-1960s (McGowan 1995). The Canadian data are less complete, but, judging by a study of the diffusion of cigarette smoking in Canada back to the 1920s, the pattern was probably broadly similar (Ferrence 1989).

There is some disagreement about how cigarette smoking spread in the United States and Canada. Tate (1999) argues that opposition to cigarettes represented to some degree class and ethnic biases as well as genuine concern about the effects of cigarettes. She claims that working-class, recent immigrant communities in the cities of the Eastern seaboard of the United States were the first major consumers of the "little white slaver." Ferrence's (1989) quantitative study of the spread of cigarette smoking in Canada and the United States, however, indicates that, by the 1920s, the activity was diffusing from the higher socio-economic status (SES) groups to the lower. Perhaps the practice spread from lower-class ethnic groups into the middle and upper classes through the effects of World War I, and then more broadly into longer established working-class groups.

Government policy has often affected tobacco usage. Historically, governments have supplied tobacco products in some form to troops in wartime. The profitability of James B. Duke's mass-produced cigarettes was facilitated by a drop in the US federal tax on cigarettes due to a continuing surplus of government revenue in the early 1880s. When the federal government increased the tax later, cigarette consumption fell (Tate 1999). Government policies favourable toward cigarettes in both world wars would transform the marketplace and facilitate the dominance of the cigarette within that market. In contrast to cigars, moreover, the less expensive cigarettes have proved to be relatively resilient to general economic downturns.

The US Congress eschewed regulating tobacco in the late nineteenth and early twentieth century, leaving the issue to the states. The US Supreme Court in 1900 refused to hear a challenge to a Tennessee law regulating cigarettes, rejecting an argument that the law constituted a violation of interstate commerce, a federal responsibility. Beginning with the state of Washington, 15 states banned cigarette sales to adults between 1893 and 1921, but the laws were sometimes quickly repealed and only laxly enforced (Tate 1999: 159-60). Other restrictive laws on cigarettes and smoking were adopted by states, and bans on sales to minors under the age of 16 were nearly universal (Tate 1999; Sobel 1978; Wagner 1971). In a pattern to be repeated much later, the federal government rather than the provinces passed the major restrictive legislation in Canada, the *Tobacco Restraint Act* of 1908, banning cigarette sales to those under 16.

As their share of the market grew, cigarettes provoked considerable opposition from social reformers, especially for what were thought to be their deleterious health and moral effects on youth. Although always taking a back seat to the fight against alcohol, anti-tobacco messages were part of the platform of the Women's Christian Temperance Union and other reformist groups on both sides of the border. The most vehement was the Anti-Cigarette League, founded by Lucy Page Gaston in 1899. In the early part of the twentieth century, Page was second as a social reformer in the United States only to the formidable Carrie A. Nation (Tate 1999). Both the WCTU and the Anti-Cigarette League had branches in Canada as well, although their activities there have not been well documented.

Gaston and others singled out cigarettes as a particular danger. Although there were complaints about the health effects of cigarettes, the main opposition was based on morality and efficiency grounds. Cigarettes were considered a sign of moral degradation, especially for women and the young, and a "gateway drug" for other immoral behaviour such as drinking, gambling, and loose sexual relations. Some business entrepreneurs, such as Thomas Edison (a cigar smoker) and Henry Ford, objected that cigarette users were less capable workers. In Canada the retailer Timothy Eaton refused to sell tobacco in his stores (Cunningham 1996: 32).

When the predecessor of the US Food and Drug Administration (FDA) was created in 1906, tobacco was not among the products listed under its jurisdiction, a rather curious oversight considering that it was listed as a drug in the 1890 edition of *US Pharmacopoeia*, an official federal list. Former Senator Maurine Neuberger of Oregon claims that dropping tobacco from this official list of drugs, and thus from the oversight of the FDA, was a political deal to get tobacco-state representatives' support for the 1906 legislation (Wagner 1971: 74).

In Canada, the *Tobacco Restraint Act* and several provincial and territorial laws, some dating to the 1890s, prohibited sales to minors (Grossman and Price 1992: 3, 48-51). However, more restrictive measures, including prohibition of sales to adults, were debated several times in the federal House of Commons but ultimately rejected. The last consideration was by the House of Commons Select Committee on Cigarette Evils, in 1914 (Cunningham 1996: 37-38). Government encouragement of tobacco as a useful agricultural and manufactured product increasingly dominated regulatory inclinations. In fact, in the 1904 federal election campaign,

Liberal prime minister Wilfrid Laurier, who had voted against prohibition of cigarettes in a free vote in the House of Commons the previous year, ran on a platform which included a provision stating "Tobacco Industry Promoted" (Cunningham 1996: 34; A History of the Vote in Canada 1997: 53).

PHASE 2

1914-1950 – THE ERA OF GOOD FEELING:
CIGARETTES PROMOTED BY GOVERNMENT

At the onset of World War I, cigarette usage was still decidedly a minority persuasion even among tobacco users, as noted above. Government policies in both countries during the war expanded the cigarette market by associating cigarettes with patriotism. Military leaders, especially General John J. Pershing, Commander of the US Expeditionary Force once the US joined the war in 1917, called for cigarettes to alleviate the stresses and boredom of troops. This was a major impetus for making cigarette smoking socially acceptable, at least for men. During World War I the US government became the largest purchaser of cigarettes, included them as one choice of tobacco with soldiers' rations, and sold them at deep discounts at military stores. Cigarettes were also supplied by other organizations, several of whom had opposed tobacco use before the war (Tate 1999). In contrast, liquor was banned from military posts, a precursor to prohibition being enacted in the US in 1919. The other major vice appealing to soldiers, prostitution, was also banished from military camps. Thus cigarettes were considered the least of these three evils, and it became a patriotic duty to support the troops with tobacco. Similar sentiments were prevalent in Canada. In contrast to European forces, whose soldiers received a stiff drink before battle, US troops got cigarettes. While prohibition was in force in Canada during the war, Canadian forces at the front had access to drink as well as tobacco (Smart and Ogborne 1996).

The role of cigarettes in the war gave the industry a stronger domestic foothold, through both increased consumption and favourable social associations. The industry was to enhance this position for a half-century and yield it only begrudgingly thereafter. Tate (1999) has documented how Hollywood films of the 1920s began to feature tobacco in a better light, associating its usage with heroes and heroines rather than, as in the past, with villains and demimondes. Cigarettes were considered part of individual freedom, encouraged by advertisers attempting to attract women customers first in the 1920s and later, more successfully, in the 1960s. Although Duke had promoted cigarettes through advertising and other promotional schemes, in the 1920s advertising wars in the expanding cigarette market in the US began in earnest.

In the wake of the adoption of nationwide alcohol prohibition through the Eighteenth Amendment to the US Constitution in 1919, some thought that a potential Nineteenth Amendment would be a prohibition on tobacco, or at least cigarettes. Within a short period of time, however, policy moved in the opposite direction. The remaining US state bans on tobacco sales to adults were repealed in the 1920s, although prohibitions on sales to minors were retained. From then until the 1960s, cigarettes were little regulated, except through special excise taxes on their purchase, which varied considerably from state to state. These grew in popularity from the 1920s (Warner 1981), initially in states that had previously banned cigarette sales or were searching for a non-property basis of taxation (Friedman 1975: 17-18) and perhaps also as a replacement of the missing revenues from alcohol sales, which remained prohibited until 1933. After a last gasp in the 1920s, the anti-cigarette groups and propaganda died out by the early 1930s. Tobacco restrictions by government were largely ignored in favour of tobacco promotion.

The legislated absence of alcohol may have increased the popularity of cigarettes as a substitute device for sociability (Tate 1999). Since prohibition was also tried in Canada on a province-by-province basis, except during World War I when it was countrywide, a similar relationship may have occurred there. Cigarette smoking continued to spread throughout the public of both countries, undaunted by the arrival of the Great Depression. Growth continued, until over 40 per cent of the US population (and a majority of males) and more than half of the Canadian population smoked in the 1960s (Ferrence 1989).

Government again came to the aid of tobacco, in several ways. The first, in the United States, was the treatment of tobacco as an agricultural product under the New Deal *Agricultural Adjustment Act* of 1933. The federal government would provide price supports for tobacco in return for farmers limiting their acreage under production (Johnson 1984; Badger 1980). While there were several false starts in the program in the 1930s due to court decisions, by the late 1930s it was in place and the fundamental contours of the program resisted change until the mid-1980s; in other forms US federal support for tobacco growing remains today. In Canada, there was no special federal marketing program for tobacco, but it was covered under general farm assistance programs. The two leading provincial growers of tobacco, Ontario and Quebec, developed tobacco marketing boards, to allow tobacco producers to obtain higher prices through cooperative sales (Laroche 1992; Cunningham 1996). In both countries the dominant cabinet-level department concerned with tobacco until the 1960s was not Health or Finance (Treasury in the US) but Agriculture. In Canada, there were at least five separate official legislative investigations into marketing questions in the industry between 1927 and 1962 (Tait 1968: 126). Research was conducted by both governments to improve tobacco varieties. In the United States, tobacco exports were facilitated by their inclusion first in the Marshall Plan and later in the Food for Peace program (Friedman 1975: 20). Eventually, in both countries, the departments of Commerce (Trade and Industry in Canada) and State (External Affairs in Canada) helped tobacco agriculture and manufacturing find foreign markets.

World War II proved to be another major boost for the spread of tobacco consumption. Once again cigarettes became a valued commodity of relaxation, a symbol of patriotism, and, in occupied zones, a form of currency (Sobel 1978). In the United States, tobacco farmers received deferments from service because they grew an "essential product" (White 1988). When a major US brand, Lucky Strike, changed its package colour during the war from green to white, it announced "Lucky Strike Green Has Gone to War." Not only did more males smoke, but data indicate that it was World War II, not the advertising of the 1920s, that led to large-scale smoking among women (Tate 1999; Ferrence 1989). The horizon for cigarettes seemed limitless.

While promoting tobacco, governments did little to restrict or tax it. As McGowan (1995) points out, aside from supporting tobacco agriculture and manufacturing, the major concern of the US federal government about tobacco during the first half of the twentieth century was the concentrated structure of the industry. In addition to the Supreme Court decision breaking up the Tobacco Trust in 1911, a second Supreme Court decision in 1946 ruled that the reconfigured tobacco industry was an oligopoly in violation of the *Sherman Anti-Trust Act*, but little corrective action was undertaken (Tennant 1950; White 1988).

In the United States, a semi-independent regulatory agency, the Federal Trade Commission (FTC), which was provided with enhanced powers to protect consumers from deceptive advertising in 1938, did take steps on nearly 100 occasions between 1938 and 1968 to check questionable tobacco company claims, but the outcome of these actions varied because of slowness, lack of enforcement powers, and interference by Congress (Friedman 1975: 37-41; Fritschler and Hoefler 1996: 67; Kluger 1996). In Canada, the tobacco companies were expected to be self-regulating, with perhaps an occasional quiet word from the government, in the tradition inherited from the British of informal regulatory arrangements between governments and industry rather than commands and litigation (Vogel 1986). The concentrated economic power of the cigarette industry was less of a concern in a country as small as Canada. In the immediate aftermath of World War II, tobacco restrictions were off the political agenda in both countries. But they were soon to return.

PHASE 3
1950-1964 – THE GATHERING STORM
OF HEALTH CONCERNS

Just when tobacco agriculture and manufacturing had achieved an unchallenged dominance in the councils of government and among the mass public, matters began to change, largely due to health concerns. Although the increase in lung cancer, especially among men, had not gone unnoticed, it was often attributed to other factors such as a longer life span and industrial pollution. Despite scattered studies as far back as the 1920s finding some relationship between smoking cigarettes and lung cancer (Sobel 1978; Tate 1999), these had not been assimilated into mainstream medicine or the popular consciousness. These studies were based on case histories or small-scale statistical studies rather than the laboratory studies favoured by the existing medical model. The science of epidemiology, based on biostatistics, was in its infancy and not completely accepted by the medical profession or the public at large (Brandt 1992). More extensive documentation of the tobacco-cancer link done in Germany, largely under the Nazis in the 1930s and 1940s, was insufficiently recognized in the outside world (Proctor 1999). From 1950, however, studies published in prestigious medical journals linked cigarette ingredients with the production of cancer in laboratory settings, and large-scale epidemiological findings demonstrated relationships between smoking and disease. Industry and governments, however, took no action until the implications of these findings became more widely known.

Popular alarm resulting from this research was largely aroused by the article "Cancer by the Carton," published in December, 1952 in the most widely read US magazine, *Reader's Digest*. The financial success of most US and Canadian magazines was heavily dependent on advertisements, many from the free-spending cigarette companies. In contrast, *Reader's Digest* accepted no advertising from tobacco companies but depended on its monthly compendium of brief articles, often reprints, for its appeal. During the 1940s it had been a lonely popular voice against the spread of tobacco. "Cancer by the Carton" was an edited version of a longer article under a different title by anti-smoking crusader Roy Norr, which had first appeared two months earlier in the little-known *Christian Herald*. The *Reader's Digest* version received widespread attention, and other popular magazines followed with their own stories (Sobel 1978: 167-69). This bad publicity, along with the gathering medical evidence of the dangers of tobacco use, threw the cigarette companies into a panic. As a result, smoking rates temporarily declined and filter-tip cigarettes were brought onto the market; claims for "healthier smokes" abounded, keeping the FTC in the US busy (Kluger 1996; Fritschler and Hoefler 1996; Cunningham 1996).

In the 1950s Canadians absorbed US media reports both directly from the sources themselves and also through Canadian media, which reported on some of the scientific and popular controversy in the US. With no semi-independent regulatory commissions in Canada, there was less emphasis on regulating tobacco-company claims.

In 1954, cigarettes suffered a further blow. Of all charitable, professional, or public-sector bodies in the United States, the American Cancer Society was the most committed to combating tobacco usage prior to 1964. The ACS and other health groups officially endorsed findings linking smoking and cancer such as those found in the famous Hammond-Horn "prospective"study, which followed individuals over a number of years and recorded their causes of death. Smokers tended to die younger (Troyer and Markle 1983; Kluger 1996). Reflecting the growing concern about the health effects of cigarettes, the tobacco industry in both countries began to sponsor its own research. Health concerns had begun to disturb the comfortable position of tobacco.

Yet these medical, social, and economic problems left the political realm largely unmoved. Attempts to get tobacco restrictions on the governmental agenda in both countries were unsuccessful. A resolution to hold hearings on the issue of cigarettes and health in the Canadian House of Commons in 1951 failed; the Minister of Health and Welfare spoke against it as being premature. In 1954 the Minister of National Health and Welfare, Paul Martin, Sr., announced a research program into the causes of lung cancer, partly funded by the tobacco industry. The ministry also undertook its own prospective study of the relationship between cigarette smoking and disease among Canadian veterans, later to be cited as one of the seven major studies in the 1964 US Surgeon General's Report (Cunningham 1996).

In the United States, the initial government response was equally tepid. By 1957, a report sponsored by two federal research agencies, the National Cancer Institute and the National Heart Institute, identified cigarettes as contributing to lung cancer; this was supported by the chief medical officer of the US, Surgeon General Leroy G. Burney, who announced that "excessive smoking" was a cause of lung cancer (Kluger 1996: 200-01). In 1958, Democratic Congressman John Blatnik of Minnesota chaired hearings on tobacco, in which Burney testified that it was premature to place a warning on cigarette packages. In 1959 the Surgeon General spoke out more strongly on the subject, indicating that smoking was the "principal cause" for the increase in lung cancer. Yet no legislative or executive regulatory action was taken. Meanwhile, the FTC continued to confront questionable health claims about cigarette advertisements, and, despite frustrations in the courts, often obtained consent decrees from the industry (Neuberger 1963; Fritschler and Hoefler 1996).

As concern mounted, especially in those parts of the health-care community concerned with public health and among the public at large, the FTC was the only government agency in either country actively engaged in regulation of the tobacco industry. As far as both countries were concerned, the gathering storm of medical evidence on the dangers of smoking, especially as it related to lung cancer, was only enough to move tobacco restrictions from "non-decision" to a low place on the governmental agenda. Similarly, after a decline during the "health scare" of 1952-53, cigarette smoking increased among the publics of both countries until the mid-1960s (Kluger 1996; Cunningham 1996).

Taxation began to lag behind inflation and cigarette price increases in both countries. In the United States, the last federal tax increase before the 1980s occurred in 1950 and took effect in 1951, making cigarettes more affordable with every passing year. In Canada most provinces did not even have special taxes on cigarettes until the 1960s. An attempt to raise Canadian federal taxes on cigarettes in 1951 led to an increase in smuggling, which in turn prompted a two-pronged reduction of the tax in 1952 and 1953, bringing it below the 1951 level (Thompson and McLeod 1976).

Neuberger (1963: xii) quotes a British journalist about this period: "Future historians will have views on our failure to find even a partial solution to the problem of smoking during the first ten years after its dangers were revealed. The enormous and increasing number of deaths from smoker's cancer may go down in history as a strong indictment of our political and economic ways of life."

PHASE 4
1964-1984 – REGULATORY HESITANCY

By the early 1960s, tobacco, especially in the form of cigarettes, had weathered a decade of adverse publicity with remarkably few governmental attempts to regulate it, but this was soon to end. Professional health and medical organizations began to endorse expert reports on the dangers of cigarette usage, especially in relation to lung cancer. In 1961 the Canadian Medical Association (CMA) supported findings of a connection between smoking and cancer. In 1962 the British Royal College of Physicians concluded that smoking was responsible for a large number of premature deaths. Late in 1963, Canadian Minister of Health and Welfare Judy LaMarsh called a conference, including the tobacco companies, to deal with the problem. Her department later published a report summarizing the evidence on the problem of smoking and health (Cunningham 1996; Health and Welfare Canada 1964).

Despite these earlier official expressions of concern, the report that publicly certified internationally that cigarette smoking was a serious danger to health, and one worthy of attention from political leaders, was that of the Advisory Committee of the US Surgeon General in January, 1964. Such an investigation had been urged on President John F. Kennedy in 1961 by professional health groups—the American Cancer Society, the American Public Health Association, the American Heart Association, and the National Tuberculosis Association, but not the American Medical Association, a consistent laggard on tobacco control, especially in comparison to other professional health associations and its counterpart in Canada. Senator Maurine Neuberger, the leading legislative tobacco-control advocate in Congress at the time, had also demanded an executive inquiry (Kluger 1996).

President Kennedy set up an investigatory committee under Surgeon General Luther Terry. The members were carefully selected for their public neutrality on the questions to be examined. The tobacco industry, along with other interested groups, had input on the panel's composition. The committee undertook no new research, but considered some 7,000 studies on the subject from around the world and interviewed hundreds of witnesses. Of seven major prospective studies carefully pooled and reviewed, one was of Canadian veterans, begun in 1956 and ending in 1963 (Health and Welfare Canada 1964). After Kennedy's successor as President, Lyndon Johnson, declined to label it the "Report of the President's Advisory Council" or to call his own press conference on the matter, the Surgeon General announced the results. The committee's conclusions, endorsed by the Surgeon General, were dramatic: "Cigarette smoking is a health hazard of sufficient importance in the United States to warrant appropriate remedial action.... Cigarette smoking is causally related to lung cancer in men; the magnitude of the effect of cigarette smoking far outweighs all other factors. The data for women, though less extensive, point in the same direction" (US Department of Health, Education and Welfare 1964; Wagner 1971: 130-31).

Yet the political responses, analyzed in more detail in the following chapters, were relatively anodyne. The Federal Trade Commission was ready to impose a warning label on packages and advertisements which would read either "Caution: Cigarette Smoking Is Dangerous to Health. It May Cause Death From Cancer and Other Diseases" or "Caution— Cigarette Smoking Is a Health Hazard. The Surgeon General's Advisory Committee Has Found That Cigarette Smoking Contributes to Mortality From Specific Diseases And to the Overall Death Rate" (Whelan 112). Some states and local governments also considered advertising restrictions. The cigarette companies countered with a voluntary code of conduct.

Congress, with White House acquiescence, blocked stronger actions and passed the *Cigarette Labeling and Advertising Act* in 1965, followed by the *Public Health Cigarette Smoking Act of 1969*, both of which mandated a relatively weak warning label on the side of cigarette packages. The 1965 label was "Caution: Cigarette Smoking May Be Hazardous to Your Health." In 1967, the FTC report to Congress stated, "there is virtually no evidence that the warning statement on cigarette packages (required by Congress) has had any significant effect" (Friedman 1975: 43). In 1970 the label became "Warning: The Surgeon General Has Determined That Cigarette Smoking Is Dangerous to Your Health." The states were barred from stronger warning labels. In 1972 the FTC managed, through a consent decree with the tobacco companies, to extend the warning to other print advertising. Under pressure from the FTC and the Federal Communications Commission (FCC), in the second major piece of legislation Congress required that cigarette advertising be eliminated from the airwaves.

Canada was slower to act. Despite cabinet deliberations, legislative hearings, and a bill introduced to ban all cigarette advertising and place health warnings on packages, the Liberal government in 1971 finally accepted a written voluntary code produced by the cigarette companies addressing many of these issues. The major provisions of this voluntary code were cessation of advertising on radio and television, a health warning on packages, maximum tar and nicotine yields, advertising expenditures restricted to 1971 levels, and limitations on free distribution and billboard advertising near schools. Since the code was voluntary among the companies rather than by formal agreement with the government, they could and did amend it unilaterally later (Cunningham 1996: 59-62). Government agencies responsible for health in both countries engaged in educational campaigns about the dangers of smoking, as did some private organizations.

After a flurry of restrictive activity in both countries in the mid-1960s and early 1970s, tobacco control was largely off the governmental agenda in most jurisdictions, especially the federal one, for over a decade. In the wake of the federal actions in both countries, most states and provinces were reluctant to address tobacco control. British Columbia did legislate warning labels and also passed an advertising ban in 1971, but, despite a favourable court ruling, replaced it with a partial ban in 1972 (Cunningham 1996). Little action occurred in other Canadian provinces. Arizona passed the first state legislation limiting environmental tobacco smoke in public facilities in 1973, followed by Minnesota's more comprehensive law in 1974 and others. Attempted statewide limitations on environmental tobacco smoke through the initiative and referendum process were defeated twice in California, in 1978 and 1980. The US and Canada had some of the lowest tobacco taxes in the industrialized world. Even though Canadian taxes had crept up from one and a half times the US level in 1970 to twice the US level in 1980, both had declined in terms of real income during a period of 100-per-cent inflation in consumer prices (Sweanor 1991: 25).

By the early 1980s, Peter Taylor's book *The Smoke Ring* (1984) summarized the situation: the international tobacco industry had survived the impact of the Surgeon General's Report and attempted restrictions by various jurisdictions with amazingly few political losses. Cigarettes were more affordable than ever, but regulation was minimal. The decline in smoking rates since 1964 was significant, but those who continued to smoke were purchasing more cigarettes than ever before, making Canada and the United States the first and third countries in the world by this measure (see Table 1-4).

But in the same year, the title of another book indicated that a major transition was taking place. Elizabeth Whelan's *A Smoking Gun: How the Tobacco Industry Gets Away with Murder* (1984) was among the first volleys signalling a new phase of tobacco control, one that would engender a greater amount and intensity of conflict, on various levels, than ever before. A short three years later, *Fortune* magazine asked, "Does the US cigarette industry have a future? Could *any* with so many enemies have a future? How bullish can you get about a business whose customers are starting to look like pariahs?" (McGowan 1995: 3).

PHASE 5
1984-2001 – TOBACCO AS SOCIAL MENACE

This new phase of tobacco-control policy featured new medical evidence, reinvigorated anti-smoking social movements and interest groups, and increased governmental activity on both regulation and taxes. Its most potent symbol was the 1986 US Surgeon General's Report, *The Health Consequences of Involuntary Smoking* (US Department of Health and Human Services 1986). This report documented that smoking was not merely a problematic choice for individuals, but also a concern for those exposed to second-hand smoke. The smokers' choice could also imperil other people's health. Environmental tobacco smoke had been of increasing concern among professional researchers for several years, as indicated by a less well-known but prescient report from the Ontario Council of Health (1982). A later report from the US Environmental Protection Agency (EPA) in 1993 further established these dangers by finding tobacco smoke a human carcinogen. The 1988 Surgeon General's Report (US Department of Health and Human Services 1988) emphasized the addictive properties of cigarettes, another blow for the idea that smoking was an individual choice.

Another major element of this new phase was the rise of more aggressive tactics against the industry by new, radical groups or newly energized coalitions of older, professional groups, as described below. These groups were either singularly focussed on combating tobacco use or emphasized it as an issue of high priority. Tobacco restrictions were now firmly on the political agenda, not only at the federal level in each country, but also at the state and local levels, as indicated by the increasing number of bills introduced and legislation enacted. Eventually the "tobacco war," as it came to be called, also developed in the legal realm, through what has been termed the second- and third-wave lawsuits in the United States and, somewhat surprisingly, also in Canada. As Nathanson (1999) points out, if the industry is the enemy, who better than attorneys, skilled advocates at characterizing their opponents in the worst possible light, to take the lead against the economically powerful, well-lawyered tobacco companies?

As described more extensively in Chapter Two, Baumgartner and Jones (1993) contend that the tone of a debate is important in public policy agenda-setting. Over the past two decades the tobacco industry has been on the defensive in both countries. Although some analysts (Tate 1999) wonder whether a backlash against anti-tobacco reformers will occur, there is skepticism about cyclical theories of history and agenda-setting. The new concerns about tobacco, promoted by dramatic stories considered film-worthy (*The Insider*), are focused on individual and public health as well as tobacco industry behaviour. Some anti-tobacco activists have openly advocated "denormalization" of the industry as well as of the product as a goal. The former would associate the public image of the industry with that of an outlaw.

Irrespective of the acceptance of denormalization of the industry as a desirable goal, there has been more legislative, executive, and judicial policy activity concerning tobacco control in the fifth phase, as presented in more detail in Chapter Three. Beginning in the mid-1980s, both Canada and the US undertook more restrictive action on regulations and taxes, on a variety of levels. Tobacco industry and agriculture had become more politically vulnerable even though they still possessed considerable economic and political resources.

Tobacco restrictions became a more prominent issue on the federal executive, legislative, and judicial agendas. The Canadian federal government under Prime Minister Brian Mulroney adopted comprehensive tobacco-control legislation in the *Tobacco Products Control Act* (TPCA) of 1988. President Bill Clinton became the first avowedly anti-tobacco president in US history and attempted to control tobacco through the regulatory authority of the Food and Drug Administration. Through extraordinary initiatives of US state attorneys general, a National Settlement was attempted in 1997-1998 and, when that failed in Congress, a reduced version, the Master Settlement Agreement (MSA), replaced it. Victories by industry forces in the Supreme Court of Canada in its 1995 challenge to sections of the TPCA and in the US Supreme Court in its lawsuit against FDA authority in 2000 did not remove the issue of tobacco restrictions from the agenda but only rechannelled it into other venues. The Canadian federal government replied to its Court defeat by passing the *Tobacco Act* in 1997.

No longer were supporters of tobacco agriculture and industry the predominant players; increasingly opponents were politically organized as well. These ranged from anti-smoking and consumer groups to public-health charities and medical groups, which began to take stronger anti-tobacco positions. Tobacco control had become a regular, maintained part of the political agenda. Policy outcomes, however, were more variable.

The Social and Economic Context of Tobacco Politics

Overall there are considerable similarities between Canada and the United States in the social and economic context of tobacco-control policy. Each country is the other's most important general trading partner, and there is also considerable population contact between the two countries through travel, media, and other forms of communication. Furthermore, their proximity and shared use of a dominant language mean that events in one country are readily transmitted to the other, although there is more attention to the United States in Canada than vice versa. (The border between the two countries has been called "the longest one-way mirror in the world.") It is relatively easy for policy communities, both governmental and non-governmental, to communicate with each other across the border.

In health care, a comparison reveals considerable similarities as well as some differences. While the private role in health care is very limited in Canada, in the United States the private sector remains dominant. Since 1971 Canada's health-care system has been based on universal public health insurance (referred to informally as medicare) financed and generally supervised by the federal government, although the provinces decide

Table 1-3: Economics of Tobacco: Canada and the United States

		Canada		United States
Arable Land in Tobacco (hectares)	1995	31,140 (0.1%)	1996	277,630 (0.1%)
	1985	39,893	1985	278,430
Employment in Tobacco Manufacturing	1990	5,000 (0.4%)	1990	49,000 (0.4%)
Annual cigarette production	1994	49,000M	1994	725,600M

Sources: World Health Organization 1997;
Gregory N. Connolly; Non-Smokers' Rights Association

what procedures will be covered. For example, not all provinces cover nicotine replacement therapy for smokers attempting to quit. Furthermore, no drug requiring a prescription, such as nicotine replacement therapy, can be publicly advertised in the Canadian popular media. The United States relies on a mixture of financing but primarily on private insurance, increasingly administered through health-maintenance organizations to control costs. What procedures are covered depends on the plan. Prescription drugs can be advertised. US Medicare, adopted in 1965, provides public health insurance coverage for those 65 and over; Medicaid, passed at the same time, is a federal program of cost-sharing with the states to finance the needs of the "medically indigent" at any age. Yet in the US there are upwards of 40 million people without either public or private health insurance coverage.

Despite these differences in basic structure, health problems, spending, and outcomes are largely similar in the two countries (Lemco 1994). In addition, over the past quarter-century both countries have increasingly moved toward preventive health measures, including tobacco restrictions (Leichter 1991). Many epidemiological studies based in the United States have Canadian components. At least one US National Cancer Institute program designed to encourage effective community development to combat tobacco use has had a Canadian element. In 1986-1995 the US-based study COMMIT (Community Intervention Trial for Smoking Cessation), consisting of eleven matched communities, included two

Ontario communities: Brantford as a test site and Peterborough as a control site (Taylor et al. 1994; Mitchell and Garcia 1995).

Canada's population (approximately 30 million) is about one tenth as large as that of the United States. Although US tobacco production and consumption dwarf those of Canada in absolute terms, there are remarkable similarities in terms of tobacco's share of agriculture and manufacturing in each country, as well as in consumption rates. As a share of the economy, tobacco agriculture and manufacturing are of about the same importance in both countries, with one notable exception: the relative importance of the export market in manufactured products.

Tobacco agriculture plays a similar role in the economies of the two countries. In the United States, there are 17 tobacco-producing states, but growers are concentrated in the six largest (North Carolina, Kentucky, Tennessee, South Carolina, Virginia, and Georgia), which produce 94 per cent of the total. In Canada, 90 per cent of tobacco agriculture is concentrated in the province of Ontario, with small amounts in Quebec, New Brunswick, and Nova Scotia (and formerly in Prince Edward Island). Ontario is the third-largest tobacco producer among states and provinces in North America. Nevertheless, in Ontario tobacco is only the eighth leading cash crop in an agricultural economy that is less than two per cent of the total provincial Gross Domestic Product (Dyck 1997: 28).

Unlike the situation in the United States, no Canadian province is heavily dependent on tobacco for its economic livelihood. The major analysis of agricultural policy in Canada (Skogstad 1987) does not even mention tobacco as a product. For example, tobacco accounts for six per cent of agricultural receipts in Ontario, compared to 24 per cent in Kentucky, 15 per cent in North Carolina, 13 per cent in South Carolina, and 12 per cent in Tennessee (Dyck 1997; Centers for Disease Control and Prevention 1996). There has been less public sympathy for tobacco farmers and more governmental attempts to move them into other crops in Canada than in the US. A substantial tobacco-agriculture electoral constituency does not exist on the provincial or federal level in Canada, in contrast to the United States where such a constituency holds impressive sway in many municipal governments, a few states (as reflected in the disinclination of major growing states to raise cigarette taxes or have restrictions on tobacco usage), and even in Congress.

Tobacco farming, while historically subsidized by the government, mainly through research and export promotion, has not received any price supports in Canada since 1990. Since 1987, there has been an active

Canadian government program of assistance in developing alternatives to tobacco agriculture, which has had some success in reducing the number of farmers dependent on tobacco (Cunningham 1996; see Table 1-3). In the United States, market forces, especially the actions of tobacco companies in buying ever-increasing amounts of foreign leaf, have led to a decline in tobacco agriculture, but only in the late 1990s did the federal government even begin studying the transition problems of tobacco growers (US Department of Health and Human Services 2000b).

Considering both agriculture and manufacturing, there is a strong regional dimension to tobacco politics in both countries. In the US, tobacco manufacturing is concentrated in the same states as tobacco agriculture, with North Carolina, Virginia, Georgia, and Kentucky accounting for 90 per cent of the total. Tobacco production plays a significant role in the economies of the two most populous provinces in Canada. Three of the four major manufacturing plants in Canada are in Montreal and Quebec City, with the additional one in Guelph, Ontario. In Quebec, especially, tobacco has proved to be a sensitive political issue because of the presence of a large concentration of smokers as well as industry and agriculture.

Both tobacco agriculture and manufacturing are on a far larger scale in absolute terms in the US (see Table 1-3). In the mid-1980s, the US was the second-largest tobacco leaf-producing country, just below China and with over twice as much output as the third producer, India. Canada was ninth in rank, with about one-tenth of the US output. The US was the largest exporter of tobacco leaf by far, with approximately three times that of Brazil, the second-ranking country. By the mid-1990s the US had dropped to third in leaf production, behind China and India, and to second in exports behind Brazil (US Department of Health and Human Services 2000b: 296-97). Canada produces over half of its agricultural tobacco for the home market and is an insignificant exporter by world standards, even though tobacco has often been its second-ranking agricultural export, after wheat (Kinney 1981; Collishaw and Rogers 1984; Wilson 1991).

The tobacco industry is almost unimaginably rich both in assets and profitability, with all the accoutrements of power that money can buy. Tobacco sales are a $50-billion-per-year business in the US, $8 billion in Canada. Year in and year out, tobacco companies remain highly profitable, with annual profits of over 10 per cent common. Tobacco companies are part of multinational conglomerates, with some companies owning substantial shares in others. The five major multinational tobacco companies are Philip Morris, RJ Reynolds, British-American Tobacco, Japan Tobacco, and Rothmans International Tobacco Ltd. Considering the whole business and not just the tobacco parts, Philip Morris is the fourth-largest company in the world. In some years it has been the largest taxpayer in the United States (Rosenblatt 1994). In each country, manufacture of tobacco products is dominated by a few producers. In the United States, today these producers and their approximate market share in recent years are Philip Morris (49 per cent), RJ Reynolds (34 per cent), Brown and Williamson (16 per cent), Lorillard (5 per cent), and Liggett (3 per cent). In Canada, all three major companies have their headquarters in Quebec. These producers and their approximate shares of the market are Imperial Tobacco Ltd. (sister company of Brown and Williamson in the US and British-American Tobacco in the United Kingdom), with 67 per cent, Rothmans Inc. (40 per cent of its shares are owned by Philip Morris in the US), with 20 per cent, and JTI-Macdonald Inc. (formerly RJR-Macdonald, Inc.), with 12 per cent.

In short, the economic resources of tobacco companies are what one might expect if there existed an oligopoly of producers making a drug to which a lot of people were addicted (Plenary Session 1996). Famed US investor Warren Buffet views cigarettes as an excellent investment: "I'll tell you why I like the cigarette business. It costs a penny to make. Sell it for a dollar. It's addictive and there's fantastic brand loyalty" (Marotte 1997). In both countries, the decline in smoking rates has not damaged tobacco-company profits to an appreciable extent. Instead, companies have diversified into other products and extended their operations abroad. The US provides only about four per cent of smokers worldwide, Canada even less. The part of the tobacco economy in Canada and the US in major decline has been the agricultural base. Especially in the US, cigarettes overall now consist of less tobacco and more additives.

Internationally-affiliated tobacco companies can shift resources to different markets to reduce expenditures and increase profits as well as to avoid regulations and/or taxes. Increasingly they have done this in both tobacco-leaf purchase and product sales. If tobacco consumption in both Canada and the United States disappeared overnight, the companies would still be profitable and have a growing market (LeGresley 1998b). The principal new consumer markets for tobacco are in Eastern Europe and Asia. This is facilitated by the United States government through Section 301 of the *US Trade Act of 1974*, which mandates that there be no discrimination against US products in countries enjoying Most Favored

Nation (MFN) status with the US, as well as by the World Trade Organization (WTO) rules concerning "fair competition." With the US Senate approval in 2000 of permanent MFN trading status for China, US-based tobacco companies are expecting easier access to this lucrative cigarette market, previously a monopoly of the government-owned company there.

Despite other similarities, in neither US nor Canada has the population acquired a taste for the other's cigarettes; US cigarettes are milder in taste than Canadian brands. Only a small portion of each country's consumption, less than five per cent normally, is imported from the other country. The tiny Canadian market for US brands was clear when Canada became the first country in the world to mandate that the ingredients of cigarettes be printed on the packages in 1988: Philip Morris simply refused to export to Canada, and RJ Reynolds changed some of its formulas (Wilson 1991).

Table 1-4: The Consequences of Tobacco Use: Canada and the United States

Estimated Annual Per-Capita Cigarette Consumption, 15 years+		
	Canada	United States
1970-72	3,910	3,700
(Rank)	(1)	(3)
1980-82	3,800	3,560
(Rank)	(1)	(2)
1990-92	2,540	2,670
(Rank)	(13)	(11)

Age-Standardized Annual Death Rate per 100,000 (early 1990s) Lung Cancer		
Males	82.9	85.9
Females	31.5	36.9

Total Deaths Attributed to Smoking (1995)		
	46,000	529,000
	(23% of total)	(24% of total)

Sources: World Health Organization;
Gregory N. Connolly; Non-Smokers' Rights Association

Estimates of smoking rates vary, depending on the source of the data and the various definitions of smoking prevalence used (frequency as well as amount). But by any measure, tobacco consumption in Canada has a strikingly similar history to that in the United States. Even though cigarette smoking spread somewhat later in Canada (Ferrence 1989), by mid-century a larger percentage of the Canadian public smoked than did those in the United States, especially in francophone Quebec (see Table 1-4). After the Surgeon General's Report in 1964, smoking began to decline more rapidly in the US than in Canada. In fact, by 1982 Canada was first among major industrialized countries in per-capita consumption of cigarettes (Collishaw and Rogers 1984). Despite more stringent taxes and federal regulations on cigarettes since the mid-1980s, Canadian tobacco consumption is still somewhat higher than in the United States (Pechmann, Dixon and Layne 1998). In both countries, cigarette smoking varies somewhat across provinces/states (see Chapter Four).

As the scientific evidence of the health hazards of smoking and other tobacco product use has accumulated since the 1964 US Surgeon General's Report, smoking has declined substantially in the upper- and middle-income groups, much less so among lower-income groups. This trend has probably been aided by the manufacture of discount brands in the early 1990s and, in the US, by selective tobacco-company price reductions, such as that initiated by Philip Morris in 1993 (Kluger 1996). In both countries, women, who took up smoking later than men and were subjected to the 1960s campaigns associating smoking with freedom, have had more stable smoking rates while the rates of men have declined.

Lung cancer was so rare in the early twentieth century that most physicians had never seen a case; it was not codified in the *International Classification of Diseases* until 1923 (Kluger 1996; Tate 1999: 139). Since lung cancer takes about twenty years to develop in a person who smokes regularly (Rachlis and Kushner 1989), the first clusters of this disease began to appear soon after World War I in the US (Tate: 139). Subsequently it has reached epidemic proportions; tobacco is usually estimated to be involved in at least 80 per cent of lung-cancer deaths (Rachlis and Kushner 1989).

At the turn of the millennium, tobacco is a leading known cause of death in both countries, an estimated 20 per cent or more of the total number of deaths, mainly through lung cancer, respiratory diseases, and cardiovascular problems. The toll is approximately 500,000 in the United States and about one-tenth that number in Canada, proportional to the population and smoking rates. Because of the later increase in women's smoking rates, lung cancer in men has declined considerably while lung cancer now exceeds breast cancer as a cause of premature death among women (Rachlis and Kushner 1989; Corrao et al. 2000). For the past decade, in both Canada and the United States, deaths resulting from direct consumption of tobacco (even excluding second-hand smoke) have been higher than the total for alcohol, cocaine, heroin, homicide, suicide, car accidents, fire, and AIDS *combined*—in fact, nearly twice as many (Corrao et al. 2000).

Political Institutions in Canada and the United States

Canada is a federal cabinet/parliamentary system with a fusion of legislative and executive power but an expanding scope for the judiciary in policy formation. The United States is a federal presidential/congressional system, with separation of powers and checks and balances. These same framework institutions are largely reproduced in the ten provinces and 50 states, respectively. One exception is that in many US states, several executive officers are elected rather than being appointed by the chief executive of the state, the governor. In Canada all provinces and territories now have unicameral legislatures, while in the US all states except Nebraska are bicameral. On the federal level as well, the US has a strong bicameral system with nearly equivalent powers for the two houses, except that the Senate must approve most presidential appointments. Canada has a version of weak bicameralism (Lijphart 1984), with the members of the Canadian Senate being appointed by the Prime Minister although the seats are apportioned roughly according to the populations of the different provinces. The Canadian Senate rarely contravenes the House of Commons. Various attempts at creating a "Triple E" Senate in Canada— equal (for provinces), elected, and effective—have foundered. Considering the executive, legislative, and appointment powers as well as party leadership role of the Canadian prime minister, this office is one of the most formidable concentrations of power in Western democracies (Savoie 1999).

The federal court systems in the two countries, especially at the highest level, have increasingly converged in behaviour (Manfredi 1990). The US Supreme Court, whose members are appointed by the President with the approval of the US Senate, have final appellate powers of interpretation of

US law as well as the power of judicial review. Within the US political culture, they are generally recognized as the ultimate interpreters of the US Constitution. Canada's traditional status as a member of the Commonwealth under the Queen meant that supreme judicial power was exercised by the judicial committee of the Privy Council in the United Kingdom. Under the repatriation of the Canadian Constitution in 1982, final interpretative power was invested in the Supreme Court of Canada, although that power was balanced against parliamentary sovereignty through the "notwithstanding" clause. This provision allowed any parliament, including those of the provinces and territories, to override Supreme Court decisions by invoking the notwithstanding clause for a five-year term, indefinitely renewable. Few instances of this have occurred, however, and none on the federal level; instead, court interpretations through judicial review have become predominant. In Canada the Prime Minister appoints the nine Supreme Court judges, who must retire at age 75.

Both countries have central-level bureaucracies under political direction. Although both the US and Canadian bureaucracies have grown over the years, the administrative capacity of central-level agencies for research and policy recommendations has traditionally been greater in the US. Canada has expanded its central government relatively late, with the accession to power of the Liberal party, first under Lester Pearson and later Pierre Trudeau in 1965. Despite this greater administrative capacity, in the US the bureaucracy is more closely monitored and readily opposed by the legislative branch on politically controversial topics. The United States has, in addition, semi-independent regulatory commissions, not entirely under the jurisdiction of the elected political executive. The President, with the advice and consent of the US Senate, appoints members of these commissions for long, staggered terms of office not coinciding with his/her own. Congress can override proposed rule-making by these commissions, however, as it did with the FTC on tobacco in the mid-1960s (Fritschler and Hoefler 1996).

Both countries also have extensive health-care bureaucracies. In the United States, responsibilities for health care are divided both horizontally and vertically. Within the federal government, the major omnibus department is Health and Human Services (DHHS), a cabinet-level position, formerly the Department of Health, Education and Welfare (DHEW). Within this giant department lie the Centers for Disease Control and Prevention, US Surgeon General, US Public Health Service,

National Institutes of Health, the Food and Drug Administration, and other agencies with various responsibilities for protecting and promoting public health. These often work with state health agencies, which vary considerably in structure. Many health policies are pursued either through federal mandates or financial incentives for states to join as well as through individual states initiating policies on their own. The US Medicaid program, for instance, provides services for the poor through matching state financing.

The most prominent public-health official in matters of tobacco regulation is the Surgeon General of the United States, who is the country's chief medical officer, subject to presidential nomination and Senate confirmation. His authority is largely limited to agenda setting and public information, however, because his directive powers are limited to the Public Health Service. The Centers for Disease Control and Prevention (CDC), based in Atlanta, contains the Office on Smoking and Health (OSH) to conduct research and make policy recommendations to higher officials. The Food and Drug Administration (FDA) is the agency within DHHS dealing with testing and approval of pharmacological products. The FDA Commissioner is also subject to presidential nomination and Senate confirmation. The National Institutes of Health (NIH) within DHHS is the major sponsor of biomedical research in the world, but its spending priorities are subject to political pressures and sometimes at odds with the actual mortality rates of different illnesses. For instance, in 1996 cancer and heart disease, two tobacco-related problems, were second and first in terms of number of deaths, but only fifth and sixth, respectively, in terms of research dollars spent per death by NIH. Research on HIV infection and AIDS led the list, at over four times the spending per death for cancer and over 40 times that for heart disease (Pear 1998). The National Cancer Institute is the principal agency responsible for cancer research within DHHS, but prevention receives a relatively low priority in that bureau (Proctor 1995).

The US Department of Labor, another cabinet-level position, is responsible for monitoring and improving conditions for workers, a duty which impinges on health matters. Within the DOL, the major agency responsible for the health of workers is the Occupational Safety and Health Administration (OSHA), with enforcement powers. NIOSH, the National Institute for Occupational Safety and Health, is a research subunit of CDC but also advises OSHA.

In Canada there is a more straightforward division of authority. Federalism again plays a role, as the major responsibility for health-care delivery is provincial rather than federal through Canada's medicare system. The federal government establishes framework laws, provides funds, and monitors health outcomes. The major federal executive agency responsible is Health Canada, the successor agency to Health and Welfare Canada. The Minister for Health is the key player in the Cabinet responsible for policy initiatives and general administration of the agency. He has responsibilities similar to those of the Secretary of DHHS and the Surgeon General in the US. Within Health Canada, the Canadian Institutes of Health Research is the equivalent of the National Institutes of Health in the United States, but it has no branch especially responsible for cancer research. The National Cancer Institute of Canada is part of a private organization, the Canadian Cancer Society (CCS). Until recently it had never funded any tobacco-related research except in cooperation with the tobacco industry in 1954. In partnership with Health Canada, in 1997 it began to support a limited amount of such research under the Canadian Tobacco Research Initiative (CTRI).

Within Health Canada, pursuit of tobacco control has grown substantially since the late 1970s when there was only one person working full-time on tobacco, responsible for both tobacco research and policy recommendations to higher levels. As interest grew, the Bureau of Tobacco Control and Biometrics gradually expanded and eventually was divided into two sections, one for research and one for policy. These two functions became housed in different agencies. Health Canada also contains the Occupational Health and Safety Agency to deal with workplace issues, although these are largely the preserve of Departments of Labour in the provinces (Harrison and Hoberg 1994). In 1999 a new, reintegrated Bureau of Tobacco Control was created within Health Canada, integrating tobacco policy, research, regulation, compliance monitoring, and public education functions into one unit. Every province also has a Chief Medical Officer for diagnostic health matters.

Finances, including taxation of tobacco products, are the preserve of other cabinet ministers in both countries, although health ministers may make recommendations. Again, authority in the United States is more complex, with the Office of Management and Budget, part of the Executive Office of the President with a Director subject to Senate confirmation, preparing the budget. The Secretary of the Treasury provides policy direction on taxation, and this department is responsible for revenue collection. Within the Treasury, law enforcement is the particular responsibility of the Bureau of Alcohol, Tobacco, and Firearms (BATF). However, the duties of this agency are focussed mainly on its other two subjects. A recent book on the agency (Vizzard 1997) barely mentions tobacco, although the bureau has played a role in combating smuggling (Advisory Commission on Intergovernmental Relations 1985). In Canada, the Finance Minister is responsible for the preparation and administration of the country's financial affairs, including tobacco taxes. Law enforcement on smuggling matters is the responsibility of the Royal Canadian Mounted Police (RCMP), a federal police force.

One critical difference is that budgeting in Canada is purely executive; that is, acceptance of the budget as a whole in Parliament is a matter of confidence in the executive and is routinely passed by a unanimous governing-party vote. In the United States, budgets can be, and often are, changed dramatically by legislators who add and delete substantial sums of money for purposes often at variance with the original executive budget proposed.

Other federal governmental agencies in both countries have also been involved in tobacco policy over the years, notably Agriculture and Trade (Commerce in the US). The latter has acted largely as an advocate for export markets for tobacco products. The Department of Foreign Affairs (State in the US) has also facilitated these activities. The United States Special Trade Representative was especially active in attempting to get "fair play" for US tobacco companies in Asian markets under rules of the General Agreement on Tariffs and Trade (GATT) and Section 301 of the US Trade Act of 1974 (Mintz 1996; Frankel 1996; Vogel 1995). Such tobacco promotions by government continued into the 1990s in the US until passage of the Doggett Amendment in 1998 forbidding the departments of Commerce, State, and Justice from using government funds to promote tobacco products abroad and prohibiting government employees from opposing tobacco-restrictive measures in other countries (Bloom 1998). This made US policy abroad more congruent with the regulation of tobacco at home, although DHHS does not have a role in the process. Furthermore, the opening of foreign markets to US tobacco companies under free-trade legislation is still allowed, as with the lucrative Chinese market in 2000. With a much smaller export market for tobacco, Canada has not been as concerned with this issue although its export promotion efforts still include tobacco.

Federalism also functions somewhat differently in the two countries. Canada has become one of the most decentralized federations in the world, perhaps justifying its official title, "confederation." As noted above, in health policy the provinces are the main jurisdiction responsible, with the federal government providing the framework that enables the Canadian medicare system to function on a countrywide basis. There are periodic meetings of Canadian provincial health ministers, sometimes with the federal minister present as well, to discuss problems and act in a coordinated fashion when possible. These joint federal-provincial meetings constitute the core of what has come to be called "executive federalism" in Canada. In the United States, health care responsibility is shared as well. Coordination of state health programs often occurs through federal agencies and financial incentives, notably through OSH in the CDC. Coordination among the states themselves is less institutionalized in the US and often occurs through professional organizations, individual contacts, and policy emulation rather than meetings of leading state health officers (Klase 1999).

Canadian political parties are cohesive while US parties lack internal discipline. Nevertheless, in recent years there has been more ideological polarization of legislative parties in the US. In Canada the two traditionally major parties, the Liberals and the Progressive Conservatives, have been considered "brokerage" parties lacking major ideological differences, and even the New Democratic Party (NDP) has moderated its professed socialism over the years. But the two new parties first represented in the federal parliament in the 1990s, the Bloc Québécois (BQ) and Reform (now the Canadian Alliance), are more ideological as well as more regionally based. US legislators use their individual constituency profile, often only loosely affiliated to party, to help achieve a high re-election rate, irrespective of countrywide electoral trends (Mayhew 1974). On the other hand, Canadian federal legislators, bound by party identity, have re-election prospects that ebb and flow with partisan tides. Altogether the US has one of the highest re-election rates for legislators in the Western democratic world, Canada one of the lowest (Matland and Studlar 1995).

The two countries share the single-member district, simple plurality electoral system, but since the 1920s Canada continuously has had three to five parties represented in the federal House of Commons, often on a regional basis, while in the United States the two major parties have withstood all challengers since the Civil War. In Canada the party systems and even the identities of the parties vary on the provincial level, again reflecting the intense regional differences in the country. In the US, however, the two major parties are also dominant in all states except Nebraska, which has an officially nonpartisan legislature.

As in all democratic polities, interest groups play a role in the politics of the two countries. In the United States, pluralism, the existence of many groups competing for power and influence and variously successful depending on the issue, is the dominant view. On particular policy issues, however, what are generally called "policy subsystems," originally consisting of members of the relevant Congressional committees, executive agencies, and major lobby groups but now extending to a broader array of interest groups and think tanks, are widely acknowledged to exist. These policy subsystems may change over time.

In Canada, traditionally interest groups have been considered less aggressive than in the more fragmented, pluralistic United States. This is what is usually called "elite accommodation" in Canada (Presthus 1973; Pross 1992). Over the past two decades, however, this situation has changed. The encouragement of broader participation by the Trudeau Liberal governments, including government funding for "public interest" advocacy groups (Ondrick 1991; Pal 1993), the advent of the *Charter of Rights and Freedoms* in the 1982 Constitution, and the rise of "new social movements," such as environmental, women's, and other human rights groups, has helped fuel a proliferation of lobbies in Ottawa. Increasingly lobbying has become public as well as private.

Since individual legislators in Canada remain under party discipline, they are less subject to influence by groups than are those in the United States. The major aim of Canadian interest groups remains to have access to the governing party, both through the party caucus and, even better, through the Cabinet. Thus it is not unusual for major interest groups to recruit former government ministers to be on their executive committees. But groups increasingly have attempted to alter or even stop legislation, especially through delaying tactics, by public lobbying of parliamentary committees, and even media campaigns (Pross 1992). Thus there has been a convergence of interest-group behaviour in these two countries over the past 20 years.

The financing of political parties, especially for election campaigns, is an especially important part of group lobbying efforts. Such matters are more transparent but less controlled in the United States. In Canada, financial support goes to parties rather than to candidates. Canada limits election expenses by both candidates and parties, a policy that is designed to avoid reliance on the financial contributions of a few wealthy sources; "issue advocacy" spending by other groups and individuals, however, is allowed (Smith and Bakvis 2000). Cunningham (1996) contends that tobacco companies are the second largest contributors as a group to Canadian parties, trailing only banks, but this cannot be documented from studies of political finance in Canada.

The US system of federal political finance, backed by a US Supreme Court decision equating financial contributions with free speech, enables large contributors to gain enhanced access to elected decision-makers. Although the US approach to campaign finance has been to limit contributions rather than spending, this has been undermined by loopholes allowing "party-building" contributions (soft money) which do not count against campaign contributions to candidates, as well as a broad interpretation of what constitutes "issue advocacy" spending. Presidential candidates are allowed to avoid spending limits if they refuse federal matching funds. Large contributors with much at stake politically, such as businesses and labour unions, have more obvious advantages in the US system of campaign finance. Despite recent legislative attempts at a more egalitarian system of campaign finance, the system benefits incumbents, who are reluctant to change it substantially. US tobacco companies are among the largest contributors to political parties and candidates, especially during election campaigns (Lewis and the Center for Public Integrity 1998; Abramson 1998). Increasingly that support has gone to Republicans, as Democratic electoral strength in the South has eroded and their longtime dominance of Congress has also declined.

The Tobacco Industry Network

The political power of tobacco is not based solely on its economic importance in agricultural and manufacturing. As Taylor (1984; 1985) puts it, the "Smoke Ring" incorporates several other organizations connected to large-scale tobacco production and profits, including governments, unions, sports, the arts, charities, and various commercial enterprises such as advertising, publishing, convenience stores, the hospitality industry, and gambling. Since the 1950s, tobacco companies have diversified their holdings through takeovers and mergers, a process accelerated in the 1980s (Miles 1982). In several instances, they have ceased using "tobacco" in their corporate names. The tentacles of these huge and multifaceted corporations extend practically everywhere, giving them many possibilities for political alliances based on either mutual interest or trade-offs in the legislative process (Pertschuk 1997; Advocacy Institute 1998). For instance, it has been estimated that 25 per cent of convenience-store sales in the US are tobacco products. Vendors thus have interests in opposing increased tobacco restrictions and taxation. Similarly, proprietors in the hospitality industry, restaurants and especially bars, have resisted stringent restrictions on smoking in their establishments. Since this is usually a local or perhaps provincial/state issue, their argument is that they will lose trade from smokers to nearby venues without such restrictions. This has resulted in some of the most ferocious local and state/provincial battles, as in British Columbia and California. Another commercial industry, and an increasingly powerful one, connected to tobacco is gaming. Gambling and smoking, like drinking and smoking, are hard to separate. Nevada, the traditional US gaming state, has the highest rate of smoking, and gambling interests usually resist smoking restrictions (MacLeod 1996).

As noted above, from early days advertising has been intimately intertwined with tobacco. The man who is sometimes considered the founder of modern advertising and Madison Avenue, Edward Bernays, created many of the major cigarette campaigns of the 1920s, including having women march down the street demanding the right to smoke (Kluger 1996; Tate 1999). Subsequently, with the growth of media, tobacco, especially cigarette advertising, became a staple of radio and television fare. After bans on broadcast advertising, print-media cigarette advertisements increased, especially those in magazines and newspapers ostensibly devoted to the public interest. Only slowly and reluctantly did major print media give up such a lucrative source of revenue, and there is some evidence that coverage of the dangers of tobacco was compromised by this economic connection (Warner, Goldenhar and McLaughlin 1992).

The tobacco industry became sponsors of charities, the arts, sports, and civil rights organizations, gaining political allies in the process (Pertschuk 1997; Advocacy Institute 1998). In recent years, regulation or elimination of tobacco sponsorship activities has become one of the most difficult and embarrassing issues for ostensibly anti-tobacco governments, especially those in Canada, because of the obvious needs that tobacco donations meet. On questions of First Amendment freedoms in the United States, the American Civil Liberties Union has sometimes sided with the tobacco industry (Pertschuk 1997). Starting in the 1950s, tobacco companies in both Canada and the United States also sponsored research into the relationship between tobacco and disease, some of it under the auspices of reputable organizations. In one episode, tobacco companies financed a study of the relationship between smoking and lung cancer by the American Medical Association, which delayed the latter organization from endorsing the conclusions of the 1964 US Surgeon General's Report until 1978 (Wolinsky and Brune 1994).

The tobacco companies and their allies can maintain well-financed lobbying organizations. The Canadian Tobacco Manufacturers' Council (CTMC) has formally existed since 1971. However, it has functioned informally since 1963 as a political lobby for the tobacco industry, ever since they were invited to the initial conference on tobacco called by the Health Minister (Callard 2000). In recent years some strains have appeared in the CTMC as tobacco companies have struggled to cope with an increasingly restrictive environment. In the United States, the Tobacco Institute was founded in 1958 to produce research and lobby for tobacco manufacturing interests (Kluger 1996). The disbanding of the Tobacco Institute by the MSA in 1998 hardly ended the lobbying efforts of the industry. Individual companies also maintain a bevy of lobbyists at federal, state, and provincial levels (Goldstein and Bearman 1996; Cohen et al. 1998).

In the United States as well as in Canada, it is common for such organizations to employ former federal executive and legislative officials as lobbyists (Kluger 1996; Freeman 1999). Some of them have surprising backgrounds. Former Canadian health minister Marc Lalonde, former US Senator Howard Baker, whose first wife died of lung cancer, and Carter Askew, a longtime aide to Democratic vice-president Al Gore, have all worked for the tobacco industry, an indication of its financial attractiveness on both sides of the border. Although Smokers' Rights organizations exist in both countries, they are heavily financed by the tobacco industry and do not constitute a strong social movement, in contrast to their opponents (Nathanson 1999).

More generally, over the years tobacco became woven into the culture of Western societies. It was often considered an essential prop in many scenes on stage and screen (Klein 1993). In short, the social legitimacy and consequent residual political power of tobacco were great. Tobacco company denials and obfuscation on health questions meant that opponents had to be well organized to have an impact. In recent years, tobacco's social legitimacy has declined dramatically even if not as far as anti-tobacco campaigners might have wished. Whistle-blowers and documents revealing a pattern of tobacco-company duplicity and cover-up of the dangers of smoking have enabled critics to make the argument that not only their product but their lack of credibility makes tobacco companies a social pariah (Wilson 1991). In response, the tobacco companies have attempted to cultivate a new public image of responsibility and reasonableness (Brookes 2000). Meanwhile, the companies continue to pursue lawsuits against many forms of federal or state/provincial government regulation and also have been accused of complicity in illegal smuggling activities on the US-Canada border (Marsden 1999).

Anti-tobacco Interest Groups

Several of the groups organized for more restrictive tobacco control in each country have been active for some time. In Canada, such groups have been continuously organized since 1974 with the advent of the Non-Smokers' Rights Association (NSRA) and the Canadian Council on Smoking and Health (CCSH), the latter an umbrella organization for public-health and professional groups combating tobacco use, ranging from the local to the federal level. Only in 1987, however, did CCSH hire a full-time executive director. CCSH also maintains the Canadian Clearinghouse on Tobacco Control, a library in Ottawa, to assist the anti-tobacco community. The Non-Smokers' Rights Association was organized specifically to combat tobacco usage through political action and has benefitted from Canadian government grants that finance much of its operating budget, to the chagrin of the tobacco industry. Some charitable health organizations such as the Canadian Cancer Society, the Heart and Stroke Foundation of Canada, and Canadian Lung Association were traditionally reluctant to move from the "medical model" of individual treatment for disease, but became more active in attempting to influence government policy in the mid-1980s. The CCS hired an experienced professional lobbyist, Ken Kyle, in 1986, and he has subsequently played a prominent role in political conflicts around tobacco in Canada and more widely.

In contrast, the Canadian Medical Association's reluctance to take concerted political action against tobacco, despite pronouncements on the smoking-disease connection since 1959, led some disgruntled members to form the Physicians for a Smoke-Free Canada (PSFC) in 1985. Along with the NSRA, PSFC has acted as a "ginger group," willing to confront the tobacco industry aggressively and take political action. On the provincial level, however, the strength of tobacco-control groups varies, with Action on Smoking and Health (ASH) in Alberta being one of the most active.

In the United States, the anti-tobacco coalition has changed more over the years. The pioneer in the field, the American Cancer Society (ACS), combined forces in 1981 with two other charitable organizations active against tobacco, the American Heart Association and the American Lung Association, under the umbrella of the Coalition on Smoking OR Health (COSH). The Association of State and Territorial Health Officers (ASTHO) has also been a strong advocate of tobacco restrictions.

The American Medical Association (AMA) has a more compromised history on tobacco. It was slower than its Canadian counterpart to condemn tobacco use; its reluctance to endorse the findings of the 1964 Surgeon General's Report was previously noted. An official history of the AMA in the mid-1980s does not even mention tobacco (Campion 1984). Over the years the AMA and state medical associations have proven to be unreliable allies for anti-tobacco groups. The AMA often subordinates tobacco-control advocacy to political causes closer to the immediate interests of its members, such as opposing Medicare in 1965 and limiting liability claims later (Wolinsky and Brune1994; Glantz and Balbach 2000). Despite these priorities, the *Journal of the American Medical Association* (JAMA) has continued to be a major source of research on tobacco-generated problems and has taken strong editorial stands in favour of tobacco restrictions.

In the mid-1980s the Advocacy Institute was formed under the leadership of Michael Pertschuk, a veteran of Washington tobacco struggles as a former Senate Commerce Committee staffer and chairman of the Federal Trade Commission. Since 1987 the Advocacy Institute has supported community anti-tobacco advocacy through its government and private contracts for training programs and administration of the Smoking Control Advocacy Resource Center (SCARC-Net), including GlobaLink as an Internet information service for tobacco control. Ralph Nader's Public Citizen has also played a role (Forster and Wolfson 1998: 219).

Other older, smaller, but more radical groups in the US include ASH (Action on Smoking and Health, unaffiliated with the Alberta ASH) and GASP (Groups Against Smoking Pollution, with two chapters in Canada). ASH, led by Washington lawyer John Banzhaf, scored an early success when it sued under the FTC's Fairness Doctrine to get anti-smoking commercials on the airwaves in the late 1960s. This eventually led to the US broadcast ban on cigarette advertising, but thereafter the effectiveness of their publicity-conscious campaigns has been minimal (Wagner 1971; Troyer and Markle 1983). In California, GASP transformed itself first into Californians for Nonsmokers' Rights (CFNR) and eventually into Americans for Nonsmokers' Rights (ANR), focusing on local-level restrictions (Nathanson 1999). Doctors Ought to Care (DOC) was founded in 1978 along similar lines as PSFC in Canada, by physicians unhappy with the conservative stance of the major national medical association on tobacco issues. Later, other radical groups such as STAT (Stop Teenage Access to Tobacco) and INFACT (Infant Formula Action Campaign, named for its initial battle, against Nestlé's merchandising of infant formula in poor countries) were formed in the United States.

During the 1980s, the anti-tobacco coalitions in both countries, the Canadian Council on Smoking and Health (CCSH) and the US Coalition on Smoking OR Health (COSH), began to think in terms of political advocacy as well as health promotion and education. In Canada, the more radical and publicity-conscious groups, NSRA and PSFC, took more prominent leadership roles against tobacco. In the US, the effort at the federal level was more muted, largely because the strongest radical group in the US, the Americans for Nonsmokers' Rights, was far from the seat of central power and preferred to concentrate on the state and local levels. But the1985 International Summit of Smoking Control Leaders in Washington helped US community-based coalitions to form and grow (US Department of Health and Human Services 2000b: 382-83).

In 1997 COSH ceased to exist. In its place, however, there arose a new, well-financed organization devoted solely to combating tobacco: the National Center for Tobacco-Free Kids. This has provided a more focussed lobbying effort against tobacco. The MSA established the American Legacy Foundation as a national organization to operate media-based programs discouraging underage smoking. The social movement against tobacco has been active in many areas since the early 1970s, growing larger on the state and local level from the late 1970s (Nathanson 1999).

Plan of the Book

Tobacco control has moved from being a low profile, intermittent issue on the political agenda in both Canada and the United States to a more persistent, at times highly contentious issue. Not only has the issue engaged the executive, legislative, and judicial branches on the central level in both countries, but it has also become more important on the state/provincial and local levels as well. What has influenced tobacco-control policy in these two countries? Have these influences changed over time? How convergent have policies in the two countries been? Why? What theories best explain the course of tobacco-control policy at various levels in the two countries over the past 40 years?

The rest of the book examines and evaluates the evidence for answering these questions. Chapter Two outlines different political science explanations which might be applied to tobacco-control policy. Chapter Three sets out a more elaborate description of federal-level tobacco policy in both countries in phases four and five, noting the major policy developments in comparative perspective. Chapter Four performs a similar task for states, provinces, and municipalities, covering some general patterns and developing trends in regulation and taxation as well as identifying patterns of variation in both countries. Chapter Five evaluates different explanations of tobacco-control policy, with the exception of lesson drawing, in a comparative analysis. Chapter Six analyzes lesson drawing/policy transfer as a particular explanation of comparative tobacco-control policy. Does this theory help explain similarities and differences in policy in the two countries, especially changes over time, that would not be explained adequately by the other theories? Chapter Seven summarizes the findings, suggests some possible developments for tobacco-control policy in the two countries in the near future, and puts Canadian and US tobacco-control policy into a global context, a process made more evident by their participation in the discussions over the Framework Convention on Tobacco Control in the World Health Organization.

2

Theories of Tobacco-Control Policy
Across Space and Time

"Health promotion policies involving individual life-styles inspire greater personal passions and produce more political conflict than other areas of public policy because they impinge more directly on personal freedom, choice, intimacy, and morality." (Leichter 1991: 261-62)

"What the smoker does to himself may be his business, but what the smoker does to the nonsmoker is quite a different matter. This [the nonsmokers' rights movement] we see as the most dangerous development to the viability of the tobacco industry that has yet occurred." (Roper Organization, 1978, in a report to the Tobacco Institute, as quoted in US Department of Health and Human Services 2000b: 46)

"Let me say that it should not be surprising if these policies in many instances either reflect or take into account the proximity of the United States. Living next to you is like sleeping with an elephant. No matter how friendly and even-tempered the beast, one is affected by every twitch and grunt." (Pierre Trudeau, Prime Minister of Canada, at the National Press Club, Washington, D.C., 1969)

Introduction

Despite the growing importance of tobacco control and a burgeoning literature on many dimensions of the tobacco problem, especially public-health ones, there have been surprisingly few analyses of the *politics* of tobacco control, especially from social scientists. The previously published work is predominantly journalistic in nature, focussing on a single country, usually the US. Earlier work tended to be more historical (Neuberger 1963; Wagner 1971; Whelan 1984; White 1988; Kluger 1996), while recently more specific episodes of policy have been described and sometimes analyzed (Doron 1979; Troyer and Markle 1983; Hilts 1996; Pringle 1998; Mollenkamp et al. 1998; Orey 1999; Kessler 2000). Work from public-health activists has been more analytical but also tends to focus on a single country or state (Cunningham 1996; Glantz and Balbach 2000). Lacking a domestic tobacco agriculture although not a domestic tobacco industry, British journalists such as Taylor (1984; 1985) and Wilkinson (1986) have tended to adopt a more international perspective, as has the Australian-based political philosopher Goodin (1989). The five editions of a US political science textbook on tobacco control (from Fritschler 1969 to Fritschler and Hoefler 1996), mainly concern the active role of the federal bureaucracy in policymaking, specifically on the question of cigarette labelling and advertising. Recent political science work has examined state and local actions in the US, often in a quantitative manner (Licari and Meier 1997; Spill, Licari and Ray 2001; Chard and Howard 2000; Hager and Gabel 2000; Hays et al. 2000a, 2000b). Similarly, most political science studies of tobacco control policy outside the US also usually focus on a single country (Pross and Stewart 1994; Read 1996; Sato 1999). Comparative empirical studies of tobacco-control policies among industrialized countries are still relatively rare and largely dated (Friedman 1975; Kagan and Vogel 1993; Roemer 1993, but see Licari 2000a).

Political science research in health policy more broadly has almost completely ignored tobacco (Rushefsky and Patel 1999; Weissert and Weissert 1996; Tuohy 1999). Despite the prominent roles of US agencies in tobacco policy, general studies of regulatory policy barely mention it (Harris and Milkis 1996; Eisner, Worsham and Ringquist 2000). Similarly, despite the many studies of state and provincial politics in the two countries (Dunn 1996; Gray, Hanson and Jacob 1999), none has analyzed tobacco control as a policy issue in any detail.

This has left much of the scholarly analysis of tobacco-control policy to researchers in public health, who have provided several valuable but limited studies on such topics as social movements against tobacco (Nathanson 1999), legislator perceptions and attitudes (Flynn et al. 1997; Goldstein et al. 1997; Cohen et al. 1997; De Guia et al. 1998), state and provincial policies on tobacco (Warner 1981; Jacobson, Wasserman and Raube 1993; Shultz et al. 1986; Alciati et al. 1998; Chriqui 2000; de Groh and Stephens 2000), implementation of tobacco policies (Jacobson and Wasserman 1996; Jacobson and Warner 1999) and, more recently, analyses of the implications of the Master Settlement Agreement (Jacobson and Warner 1999; Bloch, Daynard and Roemer 1998). In summary, there are few comparative, general studies of the process of tobacco-control policy in Canada and the United States.

This chapter will outline the major theories that might be applied to comparative tobacco-control policy and briefly summarize how they have been used in previous examinations of that policy, usually in one country and for a limited time period. The nature of the evidence that would be needed to support comparatively a persuasive version of each explanation of tobacco-control policy will be described as well. Chapters Three and Four will offer an empirical examination of how the actual process of policymaking functions at several levels of government in Canada and the United States. An evaluation of the applicability of the theories will be considered in Chapters Five through Seven.

Policy Convergence

In addition to attempting to explain the development of tobacco-control policy in each country over time, this study is also interested in the question of convergence. To what degree have US and Canadian tobacco-control policies converged? What factors have encouraged and inhibited convergence? Traditionally, the study of convergence has focussed on the existence of similar policies rather than closely examining their content and paths of inheritance (Kerr 1983). Bennett (1992: 6), however, notes that convergence is a process rather than a condition. Persuasive evidence of this phenomenon must demonstrate that it takes place across both time and space (Waltman 1987; Bennett 1991b, 1992, 1997; Rose 1993; Seeliger 1996). For two countries to be deemed "convergent" in their policies, one must find "change in difference over time" (Seeliger 1996: 289). In order to establish convergence, a reference point for policy in each country and a time frame are essential. Otherwise, as Seeliger (1996: 298) points out, claims for "policy convergence" may be no more than indications of which jurisdiction was first to introduce certain policies. Furthermore, it must be shown that, over an extended period of time, their policies have, overall, moved closer together rather than moving in parallel, away from each other, or back-and-forth over shorter periods of time. Policy developments can also be divergent (moving away from each other), synchronous and identical (changes of the same magnitude *and* same direction), or indeterminate. It is also important to look at several dimensions of policy rather than narrowing the research to specific and limited policy choices. The diversity of policy possible in federal systems such as the US and Canada adds a further complication to establishing convergence in comparative policy research (Seeliger 1996:302-03).

There are many sources potentially inhibiting convergence, such as different political institutions, political cultures, socioeconomic conditions, interest groups, and partisan ideologies, as well as ignorance of what is occurring abroad on an issue. Of course, similarities in all of these factors except the last one could also act to facilitate convergence. Knowledge of what is occurring elsewhere on a policy could facilitate convergence. This is where lesson drawing may occur. In order to demonstrate lesson drawing as an explanation for convergence, as opposed to more general processes such as socioeconomic modernization, technological determinism, democratization, or the growth of government, it must be shown that changes in policies in a country were, to some degree, based on knowledge of policies adopted or attempted in another country (Bennett 1997). Whatever the tendencies toward convergence from general sources, the demonstration of policy transfer needs explicit evidence of influence, even negative, from abroad.

Theoretical Approaches to Tobacco-Control Policy

What are the implications of various general explanations of public policy for tobacco-control policy in Canada and the United States over time? The "stages" approach to policy analysis provides a guide to the process since it has been widely applied, even to tobacco control (Ripley 1985, Harrop 1993; Ryder 1998). The utility of the stages approach is that it analytically distinguishes the different parts of the policy-making process, however mixed they might be in practice.

Analyses of the policy process vary somewhat but usually have five stages, setting out a logical series of steps through which policies can be analyzed. A five-step process is (1) agenda-setting, (2) policy formulation, (3) policy adoption, (4) policy implementation, and (5) policy evaluation. Several studies of tobacco-control policy have focussed especially on stages three and four. Much of the literature on tobacco control, especially in the discipline of public health, consists of evaluations of the impact of public policies—for instance, on the success of cessation, prevention, and protection, three widespread goals of policy.

This study will concentrate on the first three stages. It is, however, sometimes difficult to separate the stages (Jacobson and Wasserman 1997). For instance, the broad historical phases of policy set out in Chapter One could be considered relevant to all five stages, although more to stages 1-3 than to the others. One criticism of the "stages" perspective is that it assumes more rationality in the policy process than really exists. Accordingly, while focussing on policy activities in the first three stages, this study will not assume that policy necessarily operates entirely through a sequence of stages.

The major explanations of what influences tobacco-control policy can be summarized as (1) agenda-setting theory, (2) interest group/social movement theory, (3) partisan/ideological/electoral politics theory, (4) institutional theory, (5) political culture theory, (6) policy typology theory, and (7) lesson drawing/policy transfer theory. As tobacco control becomes an issue suitable for concerted international action, as described in Chapter Seven, these theories will need revision. Theories focussed on domestic policy processes will have to incorporate theories of global public policy, especially variations of what is called "global society" theory, but some of the same explanations may be applicable on that level, too. Nevertheless, this study primarily concerns theories and evidence of how domestic tobacco-control policies have arisen and been addressed in Canada and the United States.

AGENDA SETTING

Agenda setting is usually considered the first of the stages used in categorizing and analyzing the public policy process. Agenda setting as a stage is defined as the process through which political institutions and actors confront political issues and consider making policies to cope with them. But that stage must be distinguished from agenda-setting *theory* used to explain why governments act as they do on policy issues. Agenda-setting theory argues that getting an issue to be considered seriously is the critical stage for achieving any policy goal. If so, then the major questions to be answered are how issues get on the political agenda and how they are defined. As Schattschneider (1960: 68) puts it, "the definition of the alternatives is the supreme instrument of power; the antagonists can rarely agree on what the issues are because power is involved in the definition."

Theorists have made various distinctions within the process of agenda setting. There is general recognition of a difference between a formal (governmental) agenda and a systemic (public) agenda (Cobb, Keith-Ross and Ross 1976; Nelson 1984; Ripley 1985). In addition, Kingdon (1995) refers to "specialized" or "professional" agendas among members of policy communities and the attentive public, issues which may not have reached either the governmental or public agendas. The struggle is not only to recognize problems, but to define them on the governmental agenda in ways favourable to particular groups. It is often difficult to separate the problem itself from alternative policies that might be employed to address it. Sometimes a preferred policy is embedded in the very definition of the problem itself. Walker (1977) presents a typology of agenda items in the US Senate as varying between two poles, required and discretionary. Some issues are routinely maintained on the formal agenda; others appear less frequently due to spillovers from other issues, or to discretion or randomness (Howlett 1998). Others may not appear on the agenda at all, irrespective of conditions in society which suggest they are worthy of consideration (Bachrach and Baratz 1962). Downs (1972) argues that issues can best be conceptualized in terms of an agenda-setting cycle.

The state of public opinion is an important part of all agenda-setting theories in democracies, even if that opinion is indifferent to the issue or is ignored. Public sentiment about the significance of an issue and, among those who think the issue important, the division of opinion about what policies should be enacted, need to be considered. The public can be actively interested in an issue, indifferent, or "permissive," that is, leaving political leaders wide leeway in what policies to follow on the issue. When sections of the public become "intense minorities," actively pushing particular issue definitions and polices, then social movements and interest groups are formed (Dahl 1956).

Broadly, the agenda-setting literature can be divided into two major theoretical approaches, which resemble the pluralist and elitist schools of thought derived from interest-group theory. The pluralist approach emphasizes the role of the public, interest groups, and the media in developing the governmental agenda (Cobb and Elder 1972; Downs 1972). In contrast, the elitist approach to agenda setting sees the major initiatives coming from government officials connected to policy communities; other elements are secondary (Walker 1977; Kingdon 1995; Nelson 1984). Cobb, Keith-Ross and Ross (1976) provide a bridge across these two approaches by positing three models of agenda setting: outside initiative, mobilization, and inside initiative. The first is mass to elite, the second elite to mass, the third elite to elite only.

Kingdon (1995) presents a provocative analysis of agenda setting, policy formulation, and policy adoption on the central level in the United States, sometimes referred to as the "multiple streams" approach (Zahariadis 1999). Kingdon's argument is that the policy process does not proceed in as logical a manner as some infer from "stages" analysis, but instead depends on the interaction of three factors, which he labels the problems, policy, and politics "streams." At any particular time, a potentially large number of public-policy problems exist that could be addressed by government. There also are many advocacy groups with ready-made "solutions" for these problems, what Kingdon (1995) terms the "policy primeval soup." In order for problems to reach the governmental agenda and perhaps eventually policy adoption, there must exist a "policy window" in which potential solutions, also known as policy alternatives, can be joined to the problems in such a way as to impel serious consideration. But the "politics stream," meaning the context of institutions, political parties, media attention, and policy entrepreneurs, may be the most influential of all in determining which problems reach the governmental agenda, which are adopted into policies, and in what forms. Policy entrepreneurs are especially important because they are politically accountable figures, either in the executive or legislature, who sponsor particular issues and attempt to provide solutions. This theoretical orientation has been found to be applicable in other countries as well (Zahariadis 1999).

The other major development in agenda-setting theory in recent years has been "punctuated equilibrium" (Baumgartner and Jones 1993). Their argument is that, on the federal level in the US, various policy subsystems are created which allow particular groups of actors—executive; legislative and interest group, e.g., a policy network or subsystem—to dominate a particular issue by imposing their definition on it. These subsystems can be successfully challenged by outsiders, but not without an insurgent group developing a competing definition of the agenda, one that resonates to some degree with the public, as indicated by media portrayal of the issue. However, it is not only the number of media stories, but also their tone that is critical in helping the challenging groups to shift the agenda of discussion, and thus the subsystem.

Recently, Howlett (1997, 1998, 1999; see also Soroka 1999) has subjected the agenda-setting theories of Downs, Kingdon, and Baumgartner and Jones to empirical tests over time with Canadian data on six different issues, but not tobacco-control policy. He finds the greatest amount of support for Kingdon's version of agenda-setting theory, but little evidence for those of Downs and Baumgartner and Jones.

Although it is not their main focus of attention, Baumgartner and Jones (1993) briefly discuss US tobacco politics. Overall, this policy fits their theory in that there was greater media coverage and that the tone of coverage was more negative as the Congressional policy subsystem moved from dominance by agricultural and production concerns in the 1950s to consideration of health effects as well. Congressional activity trailed behind public mobilization (as measured by articles in *Reader's Guide to Periodical Literature*) in both frequency and tone, becoming more critical of tobacco only in the 1970s despite the publicity over the Surgeon General's Report in 1964 and a later decline in media attention. In short, it took time for concerns over the health effects of tobacco to move from the systemic (public) agenda to the formal (governmental) one. In Congress, the venue of the hearings on tobacco issues also moved from agriculture, foreign trade, and taxation committees to health committees, indicating a breakup of the old policy subsystem through a changing definition of the issue (Baumgartner and Jones 1993: 90-93; 209-10). They argue that the policy subsystem for agricultural promotion was a well-entrenched one, apparently established even before the twentieth century. This suggests that Neuberger (1963) may be correct that tobacco interests dating from as far back as that period managed to keep tobacco out of the 1906 *Pure Food and Drug Act*.

Almost all of the research on this topic assumes that over the past four decades tobacco-control policy has moved onto the political agenda through a process of what Cobb, Keith-Ross, and Ross (1976) call "outside initiative," with nongovernmental professional expertise and social movements playing a major role (see Pross and Stewart 1994; Nathanson 1999). The role of policy entrepreneurs (Mintrom 1997a; 1997b), however, has tended to be ignored until recently (Studlar 1999b; Spill, Ray and Licari 2001).

In comparing the course of tobacco-control policies across countries, it is especially important to distinguish when tobacco control is on the political agenda (especially the governmental or formal agenda), for how long, and under what circumstances. In Walker's (1977) typology of agenda setting, tobacco control has become a periodically recurring problem since the mid-1980s, whereas previously it was only sporadically recurring. At one time it was part of the discretionary agenda, but more recently it has been maintained on the agenda although not always with the same priority. In Durant and Diehl's (1989) typology, policy agenda change is usually gradualist, that is, transformative and protracted. This is complicated by the ability of groups on each side to change venues, not only at the same level, for instance from legislative to judicial, but also at different levels, from federal to state or provincial.

A persuasive explanation of tobacco-control policy through agenda-setting theory, depending on the version, would emphasize multiple streams, windows of opportunity, issue definitions, venue shifts, and entrepreneurs in getting the issue on the governmental agenda or changing the definition of the issue. Once it is on the governmental agenda, an explicit decision of some sort would need to be made, even if it involved a rejection of government regulation. In either case the issue would be likely to return to the agenda, although not necessarily immediately, because established groups and entrepreneurs would be alert to take advantage of favourable circumstances to revisit it. Comparisons between the two countries would be on the basis of the similarity of the streams—problems, policy, and politics—leading to agenda setting. If groups were frustrated in their preferred policy in one venue, they would be likely to pursue it in alternative venues, at either the same level or a different one. Thus an agenda-setting explanation of tobacco control in Canada and the United States would have to encompass several different institutions involved in policy.

INTEREST GROUPS / SOCIAL MOVEMENTS

Organized groups and their relationships with government constitute the core of this theory. It is not just actors within the political institutions that are important; policy is also influenced by groups of people outside the formal institutions. Those inside government depend on those outside, and vice versa. For instance, perhaps the leading theorist of Canadian interest groups, Pross (1992: 268), says, "The policy community dominates its policy field and is itself dominated by its sub-government; it is by no means impervious to change but experiences constant internal tensions as competing groups—especially those in the active public—challenge established policy paradigms."

A number of related terms have been used by interest-group theorists, including "iron triangle," "subsystem," "issue network," "policy network," "policy community," and "advocacy coalition." While these debates are of interest to specialists, for our purposes subtle distinctions need not be closely observed. Eisner, Worsham and Ringquist (1999) argue that the major interest group-subsystem theories can be categorized into three types: dominant coalitions (classic iron triangles with static membership serving the interests of narrow, politically effective groups), transitory coalitions (issue networks, with a large number of highly fluid actors with varying degrees of commitment), and competitive coalitions (an increased diversity of interests, including well-organized, long-term players but fewer shared interests and more competition for limited resources). The latter resembles what Sabatier and his colleagues (1999) call the advocacy coalition framework (ACF) but with two additional categories: actors at all levels of government (especially subnational); and journalists, researchers, and policy analysts (as germinators of ideas). Actors form coalitions based on a shared set of beliefs and engage in coordinated activity over time. The policy subsystem will consist not only of a small number of coalitions but also of actors unattached to a particular coalition, at least for a period of time.

Social movements are a looser form of interest group, not usually tied specifically to a subsystem. They constitute an attentive public that can be mobilized to support policy actions in some circumstances. The concept is linked especially to the rise of less organized, more spontaneous, and sometimes short-term groups since the 1960s, especially civil-rights, environmental, and women's movements. Members of these groups do not necessarily pay dues, have an explicit organizational structure, attend meetings, or carry out regular political action as one might expect from classic interest groups, but as a section of the public subject to mobilization on particular policy concerns they are, in effect, an interest group. The major theorist of social movements influencing tobacco-control policy is Nathanson (1999), who treats them largely as if they were diffuse interest groups lobbying governments. For this reason, social movements will be treated as part of the broad category of interest-group theory.

Several studies of tobacco-control policy in each country have considered it to be influenced strongly by interest groups, policy networks, and social movements (Friedman 1975; Troyer and Markle 1983; Doron 1979; Pross and Stewart 1994; Nathanson 1999; Read 1996; Cunningham 1996; Glantz and Balbach 2000; Daynard, Bates and Francey 2000). Without such involvement, policy would be in the hands of institutionalized elites, who are likely to be susceptible to economic arguments from tobacco industry and agriculture. What accounts for the changes in tobacco control over the past 40 years? It may be that there is now an organized movement beyond specialist scientific and health groups to advocate for more restrictions on tobacco (Nathanson 1999). If tobacco control is largely an outside-initiative issue, it is one stimulated by attentive subsets of the public, whether they are called interest groups, social movements, or advocacy coalitions.

A considerable change has occurred over the past two decades in the strategy and tactics of Canadian interest groups, especially in the area of tobacco control. Such groups have been more organized, aggressive, and publicity-conscious on both the federal and provincial levels. They have also been given a large share of the credit for more restrictive tobacco-control policies. But in a more pluralistic environment, some defeats, such as the tax rollback in 1994, are possible due to the superior efforts of more pro-tobacco groups (Pross and Stewart 1994). Some observers have argued that this is part of a more general change in interest-group behaviour in Canada stemming from the politics surrounding the repatriation of the Canadian Constitution in 1982, especially the addition of a *Charter of Rights and Freedoms* enshrining a stronger role for individual and group rights. This allowed the courts to become more politically significant bodies as federal and provincial laws became subject to Charter challenges (Knopf and Morton 1992). Several advocacy groups, including those involved in tobacco-control policy, have been the beneficiaries of federal subsidies to carry out their activities on the grounds that it was in the public interest to encourage a variety of non-traditional groups in developing a more pluralistic Canada (Pal 1993).

Kagan and Vogel's (1993) comparative study of the United States and Canada argues that interest-group theories cannot adequately explain the change in federal policy leadership between Canada and the United States over time. They also consider it a problem for this theory that in the US there are more stringent regulations on smoking on the state and local levels while Canada has more comprehensive tobacco regulation at the federal level. Their alternative explanation emphasizes political institutions, political culture, and agenda setting.

A successful explanation of tobacco-control policy emphasizing interest groups would show that changes in the configuration and/or goals of social movements/interest groups are responsible for the policies in both countries over time. Similarities and differences between the two countries would be attributable to a comparison of the relative power of interest groups, especially their connections to institutional policy-making mechanisms through subsystems.

PARTISANSHIP / IDEOLOGY / ELECTIONS

Another possible set of explanations for differences in tobacco-control policy is concerned with partisan and ideological differences in policy-makers, especially if these might be related to tobacco control as an issue in elections. The importance of partisanship, ideology, and elections in shaping public policy is a highly contested area in comparative public policy (King 1973; Klingemann, Hofferbert and Budge 1994; Rose 1982; Castles 1998). As Rose and Davies (1994) point out, many of the policies of governments are inherited, and usually new governments emphasize continuity rather than changes in practice, whatever their rhetoric beforehand. But some studies do find indications that both left-wing and right-wing governments pursue policies one might expect from their ideological orientation. In the case of tobacco-control policy, the question would be whether more restrictive policies on regulation and taxation are introduced, adopted, and supported by left-wing governments or legislators. Since more restrictive tobacco regulation has been increasingly accepted by the public, tobacco control also might be an issue on which elections could be fought. On the other hand, political parties in Canada, especially, tend to take a "brokerage" form in government, and, in the US, the system of shared powers and lack of party discipline leads to party disunity on some issues.

Previous research has found ideology and partisanship to have some utility in explaining tobacco control policy outcomes. Ideology may be important for legislators in voting on tobacco issues, but this would occur mainly where party discipline is loosened, as in the United States (Moore et al. 1994; Wright 1998). Perhaps more remarkable is the degree of consensus about tobacco-control policies found in several attitudinal studies of US state and Canadian federal and provincial legislatures (Goldstein et al. 1996; de Guia et al. 1998). The degree of continuity observable in tobacco-control policy also suggests that partisan effects are limited, at least once policies are established. On the other hand, studies of state government actions in the US (Chard and Howard 2000; Spill, Licari, and Ray 2001; Chriqui 2000; Alciati et al. 1998) indicate that there is partisan influence, in the expected direction, on policy. Over the years in the United States, on the federal level there has been a substantial shift in tobacco-company financial support from Democrats to Republicans as the latter began to win more legislative seats in tobacco-producing states. All parties seem to have internal divisions about how to deal with tobacco, and even those that might seem to be more favourable toward the industry, such as Republicans in the United States and Liberals in Canada (Callard 1997), often do not want to admit these connections publicly, particularly in recent years as the industry has come under increasing attack.

If ideology and party are important in tobacco-control policy, then parties of the left, such as the NDP in Canada and the Democrats in the US, should be more likely to introduce and support restrictive tobacco-control policies. If elections are important, then parties favouring greater tobacco control should make this a campaign issue and be rewarded at the polls, especially in recent years, given the generally supportive public attitudes for tobacco control. On the other hand, parties of the right should be resistant to more restrictions and be supported by tobacco constituencies. Comparatively, the country with more consistent leftist control of governments should have more comprehensive tobacco-control policies.

POLITICAL INSTITUTIONS

Institutional explanations of political phenomena have recently received renewed attention in academic research. The "new institutionalism" argues that too much attention has been devoted to factors outside government *per se* in attempting to explain policies. The structural properties of governments themselves make a difference in policy outcomes. While the implications of some structural differences, such as those between presidential and parliamentary systems, federal versus unitary forms of rule, and different types of electoral systems, have long been investigated, others are of more recent vintage. These include the effects of bicameralism, the role of the judiciary, and "policy styles" in the bureaucracy (Weaver and Rockman 1993; Richardson and Jordan 1982). Some institutional theorists would also include the role of "policy legacies" as part of the institutional framework of government (Weir and Skocpol 1985; Waltman 1987).

The major difference among constitutional democracies, of course, is whether the system is parliamentary/prime ministerial or congressional/presidential. Legislators are usually more important in policy-making in separation-of-powers systems and the executive is more powerful in parliamentary systems, especially those based on single-party majorities. The fragmentation of political institutions, both horizontally and vertically, in the United States enables policy-making to occur at different levels and encourages venue switching, while making policy coordination more difficult.

Other institutions can also play a role in policy. In Canada, the dominant bureaucratic policy and enforcement style has changed somewhat from the British one of negotiated, often informal arrangements between government and industry, toward more command and control (Vogel 1986; Harrison and Hoberg 1994). As noted previously, the role of Canadian courts in policy has expanded over the past two decades.

The few political scientists who have studied tobacco control comparatively have disagreed about how important institutional factors are in influencing policy differences (Friedman 1975; Kagan and Vogel 1993; Studlar 2002). Friedman finds that the supposed Canadian advantage of single-party majority government at the central level led to less government action on tobacco control by the mid-1970s than did the more fragmented system in the United States. He attributes much of US federal policy leadership to the role of the semi-independent regulatory agencies such as the FTC and FCC. Later analyses, however, see the central executive and legislative institutions in the two countries performing more as expected theoretically, but moderated by the increasing power of the judiciary in Canada and competitive federalism in both countries.

An explanation based on political institutions would emphasize their role as the foundation for policy differences and similarities, across both time and space. Differences might be explainable with reference to either the structures of presidential and parliamentary systems, or other institutional variations such as bureaucratic practices, the strength of bicameralism, the power of legislative committees, or how federalism is practised. Even though political institutions tend to change only slowly over time, such alterations, for instance in the Canadian judiciary and bureaucracy, might help account for changes in policy.

POLITICAL CULTURE — GENERAL

Another possible explanation of tobacco-control policy in Canada and the United States is the general political culture of the two countries. On the surface, it would seem that these two predominantly English-speaking democracies occupying the same continent clearly would constitute part of a "family of nations" (Castles 1993) with congruent policies in many areas based on historical and cultural influences. Yet because of longstanding constitutional and cultural ties, in some policy areas Canada has more closely followed British domestic policy rather than that of the United States (Studlar and Tatalovich 1996).

Kagan and Vogel (1993) contend that the Canadian federal government initiated a more restrictive tobacco-control policy in the 1980s because Canada, in comparison to the United States, has both more communitarian values and more concentrated power in the federal cabinet and parliament. Since Hartz (1964), cultural arguments have been offered that political values help account for differences in political behaviour and policy between the two countries. Probably the best known of its proponents is Lipset (1990), although Canadian analysts (Thomas 1993, 2000) also employ it. Historically, loyalists who chose not to challenge the King's authority fled to Canada during the American Revolution. Canada received its independence from Great Britain without a revolution and, even after, continued to maintain strong political ties to the United Kingdom. It is still a member of the British Commonwealth, with Queen Elizabeth as its nominal Head of State. The motto of Canada is "peace, order and good government," not "life, liberty, and the pursuit of happiness." Famously, the Royal Canadian Mounted Police (RCMP) specifically and the Canadian government more generally largely controlled Western settlement, without the widespread tradition of armed frontier rivalries and lawlessness which obtained in some parts of the United States.

Although attenuated over time, these differences in historical development supposedly have contemporary manifestations in values, which in turn have an impact on policy (Lipset 1990; Thomas 1993, 2000). Overall, Canadians are more collectivist, Americans more individualist. Canadians are more deferential to authority and more willing to trust government; Americans are less trusting and more suspicious of government. In terms of specific policy differences, the two most common examples offered are the Canadian form of nationalized health insurance and a more stringent gun-control regime than in the United States.

Yet the continuing differences in political culture may be neither as great nor as influential on policy as its advocates claim. Even Lipset's (1990) extensive use of public opinion surveys relies on the consistency of relatively small differences in opinion between the populations of the two countries to make its case. Furthermore, even he admits that such value differences are not as great as they once might have been. This suggests that even more exposure to cross-border influences may erode remaining differences, a prospect that many Canadians fear (Rosenau et al. 1995).

Other systematic studies (Banting, Hoberg and Simeon 1993) have found greater policy differences between the two countries than differences in values, which suggests that factors other than mass political culture explain policy distinctions between the two countries.

From a broader global perspective, Canada and the United States are similar in values and, if anything, are becoming even more convergent (Inglehart, Nevitte and Basanez 1996; Nevitte 1996). This is not solely the result of Canada "catching up" to the United States. According to this perspective, both Canada and the United States are part of a worldwide shift toward postmaterial values, and in some respects Canada is ahead of the United States.

POLITICAL CULTURE CHANGE — HEALTHY PUBLIC POLICY

One change in political culture, especially elite political culture, over the past quarter-century which may have influenced tobacco-control policy in both countries is the development of a perspective on health policy called "healthy public policy" (HPP). This perspective is based on health policy not as curative (the traditional medical model) but as preventive. As the population in Western democracies has aged and medical care costs for treatment have escalated, increasing emphasis has been placed on the prevention of illness, including not only what government and health professionals can do, but also what people, both individually and with community support, can do for themselves. In Canada and the United States, the foundation for this new emphasis was the "Healthy People" government publications of the 1970s, which set out a new philosophy of health policy. In Canada, Liberal Health and Welfare Minister Marc Lalonde issued *A New Perspective on the Health of Canadians*, specifying four elements of health—human biology, environment, lifestyle, and health care organization. In response to criticism that this was a "blaming the victim" approach that simply allowed governments to issue public-service announcements advocating prevention through appropriate individual behavioural changes, proponents of the approach increasingly emphasized a second element, namely that the environment influences behaviour (Health and Welfare Canada 1974). Subsequently improving this environmental structuring of behaviour became part of the public-health agenda, to be promoted through community support and even legislated by governments (Wilson 1991). The 1978-79 *Canada Health*

Survey was the first attempt at comprehensive documentation of the health practices of the Canadian population.

In 1983, Health and Welfare Canada issued a document on its tobacco-control policies, *Canadian Initiatives in Smoking and Health* (1983), which explicitly linked the Lalonde Report to policies discouraging smoking. In 1986, Canada hosted the first International Conference on Health Promotion in Ottawa, supported by Health and Welfare Canada, the Canadian Public Health Association, and the World Health Organization (WHO). WHO subsequently issued the *Ottawa Charter for Health Promotion*, with five principles for promoting health: (1) building healthy public policy, (2) creating supportive environments, (3) strengthening community action, (4) developing personal skills, and (5) reorienting health services. In a Canadian government document of the same year, *Achieving Health for All: A Framework for Health Promotion* (Health Canada 1986), Health Minister Jake Epp recommended a three-pronged strategy for promoting health: (1) fostering public participation, (2) strengthening community health services, and (3) coordinating healthy public policy (Rachlis and Kushner 1989). He also pointed out that supporting tobacco production while at the same time promoting nonsmoking was an example of policies needing better coordination under the auspices of HPP (Wilson 1991). This presaged the federal tobacco-control bill, introduced the next year.

Health monitoring and health promotion have continued to be a major activity of Health Canada and its provincial/territorial counterparts. This trend accelerated in the 1990s, with the first comprehensive official report appearing in 1996, followed by a second in 1999 (Statistics Canada 1999). Recent reports have included information on smoking, nicotine dependence, restrictions on public smoking, exposure to environmental tobacco smoke (ETS), knowledge of the health impact of smoking, and knowledge of the health effects of ETS.

Even though it was borrowed from Canada, in the United States there has been even closer, more regular monitoring of this broader, more preventive approach to health (McEwen 1979). In the *National Consumer Health Information and Health Promotion Act*, 1976, Congress required the Secretary of Health, Education, and Welfare to develop a strategy for health education and promotion, including research grants to private, non-profit organizations working in the area to conduct periodic surveys and the establishment of the Office of Health Information and Health Promotion. "To encourage a second public health revolution," two documents were issued in quick order: *Healthy People: The Surgeon General's Report on Health Promotion and Disease Prevention* (US Department of Health, Education and Welfare 1979) and *Promoting Health, Preventing Disease: Objectives for the Nation* (US Department of Health, Education and Welfare 1980). The latter publication included a section on smoking, among other environmental health hazards and lifestyle-related problems (Leichter 1991: 92-95). Subsequently the CDC periodically assessed the "National Health Promotion and Disease Prevention Objectives" set out in 1980 for achievement by 1990. In that year, further objectives were set out and periodically reassessed for 2000. Most recently these have been updated in *Healthy People 2010* (US Department of Health and Human Services 2000a), which includes a section on smoking-reduction goals. The name of a major federal agency with responsibilities in tobacco-control policy as well as other aspects of public health was changed in 1992 to the Centers for Disease Control and *Prevention*, to reflect its broader purposes.

In a comparative analysis of the United States and Britain which acknowledges the leading public-policy role of the Lalonde Report, Leichter (1991) argues that government involvement in encouraging healthy individual behaviour inevitably generates conflict with those espousing the individual's right to choose unhealthy behaviour in such areas as alcohol consumption, drug use, sexual behaviour, seat-belt and motorcycle-helmet usage, and tobacco consumption (see also Mills 1993). Sullum's (1998) broadside against government discouragement of tobacco use is an example of what Leichter predicted.

One should not overestimate the degree to which views on the politics of health care have changed. The medical model of treatment for individual diseases and other health problems still dominates discussion of health policy. Nevertheless, the preventive nature of healthy public policy has made significant inroads in both Canada and the United States.

Even though tobacco-control policy has arisen as an issue in practically all advanced industrial democracies over the past 20 years, and many similar actions have been taken (Roemer 1993), countries have differed in both specific policies and the speed with which these policies are adopted (Licari 2000a). Thus political culture may still play a role in how countries react to common problems. An explanation based on political culture would show that either traditional or emerging differences in political values are related to differences in policy. If similar shifts in values occur, such as incorporation of HPP, then greater policy similarities should emerge. Changes in political culture also may have an indirect effect through generating shifts in public opinion on tobacco-control policies.

POLICY TYPES

Although theories based on how different types of policy influence the policy process have been popular in recent years, a fully-developed effort at explaining tobacco control using this perspective has never been attempted. Based on investigations of US federal policy, Lowi (1964) argued that policy could determine politics, as well as vice versa, and provided the classic political science classification of policies into distributive, regulatory, and redistributive. Distributive policies were log-rolling, "something for everyone" policies decided out of the general public view in Congressional committees. Regulatory policies were conflicts over the relative roles of sectors in private business and government, generating more controversy and settled on the floor of Congress. Redistributive policies were the rarest, amounting almost to class conflict over policies that involved broad economic reallocations and required executive as well as legislative involvement. While his categories have been reformulated many times by others and extended into comparative analysis (Smith 1975; Freeman 1986), in none of these versions is it clear where tobacco-control policy lies.

Tatalovich and his associates (Tatalovich and Daynes 1988; 1998; Smith and Tatalovich 2002) contend that there is a second form of regulatory policy, called "social regulatory policy," which deals with questions of individual rights versus social morality rather than with conflicts over material issues. Included are issues such as abortion, the death penalty, homosexual rights, language laws, and many religiously-oriented questions.

Meier (1994) argues that "sin politics" really represents a case of redistribution of values rather than material resources, normally leading to discouragement of the undesirable behaviour through special taxes as well as regulation and possibly even prohibition. But he does not present a full-scale analysis of tobacco to complement those for alcohol and illegal drugs.

Leichter (1991; see also Nathanson 1999) argues that tobacco-control policy has an unusual nature, namely that it is not just regulatory over economic production and consumption but has elements of moral controversy. Policy discouraging or restricting tobacco usage involves regulation of individual behaviour which might be considered threatening to that particular person's values. These moral dimensions of tobacco use were apparent in the early twentieth century and, even if not as the dominant dimension, have recently reappeared. Resistance to tobacco-control regulations has often been argued in terms of individual freedom of choice; people resent government intrusion into their personal habits, however harmful.

Some observers argue that portraying tobacco companies as a social menace involves a return to moral arguments for tobacco-control policy. Tate (1999) wonders whether the current anti-tobacco movement risks inducing a backlash as the early movement did. But this is not the first time that a public-health question also has been interpreted as a question of morality. The controversy over fluoridation of the water supply in several local communities in the United States and Canada in the 1950s and 1960s became entangled with moral concerns and led to what some called "rancorous community conflict" (Coleman 1957; Hahn 1968).

Nevertheless, over the past century arguments for restrictions on tobacco have moved from being largely morality-based to having a more scientific and health basis, with the economic aspects always present. Even today, as developments in the United States have shown, governments have a vested interest in the financial health of the tobacco industry; it has been described as a "cash cow" for governments because of its reliability as a revenue source through taxation.

Baumgartner and Jones (1993) argue that, in the US, health concerns have moved tobacco from its traditional position as a distributive (low-level, promotional) policy. Expanding the number of actors involved and the scope of conflict has moved the issue into the regulatory category (higher profile, health and economics as major concerns); or, if one considers morality as an important dimension of the debate, perhaps even a redistribution of material resources and values (Sullum 1998). This analysis may be applicable to the past half-century of tobacco control policy in Canada as well. If phases two and three were distributive, in phase four tobacco control became more regulatory as conflict expanded. In phase five the issue became even more conflictual and a regular part of the political agenda, with hints of redistribution involving a denormalization of the tobacco industry. A successful delegitimization of the tobacco industry would certainly be a redistributive outcome, but this is far from being achieved. Facile comparisons of tobacco control with alcohol prohibition often ignore the fact that in both Canada and the United States the liquor industry was composed of a number of small producers, not the oligopoly that has existed in tobacco for a century.

If policy typology theory is to help explain similarities and differences in tobacco control, it must be demonstrated how different policy categories account for institutional behaviour and policy outcomes. Tobacco-control policy would most likely be of the same type of policy in both countries, although not necessarily simultaneously. Policy might move from distributive to regulatory and even to redistributive at a different pace in the two countries, depending on the dominant actor perceptions of the issue.

LESSON DRAWING

A seventh possible explanation for Canadian and US tobacco-control policies goes under several different names: diffusion, lesson drawing, policy borrowing, policy transfer, emulation, and policy copying. Although distinctions can be made among these concepts, basically they all involve political jurisdictions, usually countries or states/provinces, learning policy from other jurisdictions, usually either at the same level or at different levels within the same country. This policy is then imitated or adapted by the host jurisdiction to deal with a similar problem.

Policy transfer has developed from two distinct lines of investigation: diffusion studies from comparative US state politics and lesson drawing across countries by comparative politics specialists. Gray (1994) argues that diffusion studies are quantitative while emulation (lesson drawing) studies involve qualitative analyses of how policies are passed from one jurisdiction to another. There have been relatively few attempts to cross-fertilize these two research orientations (but see Mossberger 2000).

Diffusion studies are concerned with the spread and adoption sequences of similar, innovative policies in US states (Walker 1969; Gray 1973, 1994; Eyestone 1977; Welch and Thompson 1980; Savage 1985; Jacob 1988; Glick and Hays 1991; Glick 1992; Berry and Berry 1990; Mooney 2000), occasionally Canadian provinces (Poel 1976; Lutz 1989; Gow 1994), and infrequently comparatively across countries (Collier and Messick 1975). The approach is largely quantitative in nature, relying on several instances of adoption for its generalizations about speed, socioeconomic and political influences, and geographic patterns. Drawing its inspiration from the classic work of Rogers (1995), it often finds adoption patterns resembling an S-curve, which are then used to demonstrate policy diffusion and the presence of leaders and laggards. Aside from broad institutional and cultural variables that help account for patterns of policy adoption, these studies normally contain very little specific information about how one jurisdiction comes to emulate the policies of others, or indeed even how closely the policies resemble each other in content. Even though some studies are concerned with "reinvention" of policies in the diffusion process (Glick and Hays 1991), only in rare instances have such studies shown how policy is transferred from one jurisdiction to another (Klase 1999; True and Mintrom 2001).

Comparative country studies, however, have focussed more on the social learning mechanisms through which policies spread, no matter how innovative the policies may be. Although lesson-drawing studies originated after diffusion research (Waltman 1980; Hall 1989; Rose 1991, 1993; Studlar 1993; Gray 1994; Robertson and Waltman 1993; Wolman 1992; Bennett 1992, 1997; Dolowitz and Marsh 1996, 2000; Dolowitz 1998; Mossberger 2000), they have considerable potential to explain the conditions that lead to policy convergence and divergence among governments. The first widely-cited systematic study of "policy copying" was Waltman (1980), which examines how the income tax and old-age pension were transferred from the United Kingdom to the United States. Other policies studied have included Keynesian economics, enterprise zones, urban development policies, race relations, welfare policy, data protection, freedom of information, the ombudsman, youth employment training, and education.

Research in lesson drawing is difficult for several reasons. It involves in-depth knowledge of the content of policy and policy development in two or more countries. As Hall (1993: 290) notes, "Like subatomic particles, ideas do not leave much of a trail when they shift." The problem becomes more difficult with research into the formation of policies further in the past since the number of participants and observers shrinks and memories fade.

Thus, even if one can document that policy-makers in one country were searching for lessons from abroad, how can one discern what lessons were learned and how influential they were in policy formulation, especially over an extended period of time? There can also be hidden policy transfer, whereby governments unconsciously engage in lesson drawing by relying on analyses not overtly linked to other countries but through what Seeliger (1996) calls (general) diffusion of knowledge. For domestic appeal, policies often are constructed in ways that make them seem homegrown even if they borrow heavily from abroad. For instance, a recent document advocating government restrictions on tobacco in the province of Alberta surveys a wide array of evidence and policy, including from WHO and the US, and then concludes by referring to the policy recommendations derived from them as "made in Alberta" (*Tobacco Policy Options* 2000).

Even if they are hard to trace, policy ideas usually come from somewhere else. Policy learning is facilitated by the amount of high-level political, economic, and bureaucratic contacts among countries, especially advanced industrial democracies; by the availability of cross-national data on a variety of topics; and by increasing communication through international organizations. The appearance of similar problems on the political agendas of countries generates a search for alternatives to deal with the problems. One relatively easy place to look is in the political experience of similar countries: "A lesson is thus a political moral drawn from analyzing the actions of other governments" (Rose 1991: 7). But policies are not necessarily readily transferred from one country to another. Differences of conceptualization, institutions, political cultures, policy styles, previous policy commitments, and international position, among others, may inhibit successful policy borrowing (Neustadt 1966; Rose 1974, 1993; Waltman and Studlar 1987; Richardson and Jordan 1982). Nevertheless, lesson drawing can help set agendas, specify alternatives, and influence policy adoption, the first three stages of the policy process (Mossberger 2000).

Policy transfer is concerned with how governments attempt to use both time and space to improve their policy-making. The space dimension involves looking at the policies that other governmental units, domestically or abroad, have adopted to deal with similar problems. As Rose (1993) points out, if a government adopts a policy because it seems to work well elsewhere, then the borrower is betting that its future will resemble the other government's past or present, a time calculation. The governmental units analyzed are usually countries, although there is no reason why one could not develop similar analyses of other jurisdictions. Rose (1993) puts forward four steps that governments follow in drawing a lesson: searching elsewhere, developing a model of how a program operates, creating new programs of its own, and evaluating transfers prospectively.

The existence of common problems does not mean that policies in dealing with them will be similar. As Dolowitz (1998) points out, policy transfer is a complicated and problematic process, subject to a variety of considerations. Dissatisfaction with current policies encourages policy-makers to search elsewhere, in both time and space, for policies that might work better. The existence of international bodies and the relative ease of international transportation and communication today facilitate the exchange of information about how countries deal with similar problems. Some problems, such as environmental and trade issues, have obvious externalities that make them prime candidates for more coordinated policy-making. Increased economic interdependence generates both more opportunities and more urgency for lesson drawing. But knowledge of policies in other countries is a two-edged sword; opponents may be able to mobilize opinion against a policy that has had, from their perspective, undesirable consequences elsewhere. Thus lesson drawing can be negative as well as positive.

Rose (1993) argues that lesson drawing has both normative and empirical components. Normatively, policy-makers search for lessons that are compatible with their values. The empirical study of lesson drawing is even more complex, however, because policy-makers have to draw up models of how policies work elsewhere, what elements could be transported to their own polity, and what the likely consequences would be. Rose (1993) develops a number of general hypotheses about the processes facilitating and inhibiting lesson drawing, including the role of more powerful countries, ideological propinquity, partisanship, geographical proximity, social-psychological closeness, value similarity, the breadth of focus of the policy, technological capability, and the nature of the issue (whether more technical or value-laden).

Less populous and internationally powerful states tend to draw lessons from more populous and powerful ones, especially those close regionally and/or linguistically (Castles 1993; Rose 1993). Other conditions facilitating lesson drawing include an issue that is unfamiliar domestically, and a similar cultural heritage. International credibility is also important; for this reason, the experience of hegemonic countries, at least within their "family of nations," is likely to be closely scrutinized by others (Castles 1993).

Diffusion and lesson-drawing studies often examine policies on a horizontal basis, that is, among jurisdictions (states or countries) at the same level. When vertical diffusion is studied, it has usually been on a top-down basis, examining the federal incentives for similar state programs in the US (Welch and Thompson 1980). But, as Gray (1994) suggests and Mossberger (2000) amplifies, vertical lesson drawing can be bottom-up as well as top-down. A more complex conceptualization of policy transfer recognizes the multiple sources of lessons, both governmental and nongovernmental, and across the boundaries of jurisdictions. This is what Mossberger (2000) calls "polydiffusion." Federal systems are especially suitable for analyzing the possible multiple sources of policy transfer. Countries with similar socioeconomic and political institutions, and sharing an advanced system of linkages through language, transportation, and communication, would be more likely to have such polydiffusion.

The roles of interest groups, think tanks, and social movements in lesson drawing is now receiving increased attention (McAdam and Rucht 1993; Stone 2000). For instance, the protest strategy of the civil rights movements in the United States in the 1960s had profound repercussions abroad (Morris 1993). Application of these lessons did not necessarily have the same outcomes in different contexts, as demonstrated in Northern Ireland (Rose 1976), because of differences in political institutions and cultures in the two countries. Keck and Sikkink (1998) have demonstrated how, even in an earlier era with less well developed forms of international communication, the anti-slavery and women's rights movements were international in nature. Studies of transnational social movements have demonstrated the capacity for nongovernmental actors to spread their ideas and tactics across countries, but thus far this literature has tended to focus on movement-to-movement rather than movement-to-government transfers (Ayres 1998; Della Porta, Kriesi and Rucht 1999).

Several of the most significant theoretical and empirical works in policy transfer have been produced by Canadian scholars (Bennett, 1990, 1991a, 1991b, 1992, 1997; Bennett and Howlett, 1992; Manfredi, 1990; Hoberg, 1991). Canadians are sensitive to the influence of larger, more powerful countries, especially the United States, on their affairs, most memorably captured in the mouse-and-elephant comments of Pierre Trudeau cited earlier.

Canadian studies confirm that the dominant path in lesson drawing runs from the United States to Canada. They document and attempt to explain why the example of the United States was accepted or resisted in the development of Canadian public policy; i.e., how and why either positive or negative lessons predominated. In his meticulous study of comparative environmental policies, Hoberg (1991) indicates that in nine out of ten cases involving pesticide regulation, Canadian policy was influenced by the United States to some degree; the last case showed coterminous policy development rather than policy borrowing. More generally, Hoberg (1991: 125) concludes, "these case studies demonstrate that American influence over Canadian environmental, health and safety regulation is pervasive." Subsequently, however, Harrison and Hoberg (1994) found other cases in which Canada did not follow US practices. Other studies have found Canadian policy emulation from the United States in civil liberties (Manfredi 1990; Bennett 1990), urban policy (Sancton 1998), women's rights and affirmative action (Backhouse and Flaherty 1992), and various economic matters (Brooks 1993). At least one scholar (White 1999) has suggested that Canada could benefit from the US experience, properly understood and modified, even in a social welfare policy, namely childcare. On the other hand, with its size, resources, and sense of distinctiveness, the United States appears relatively resistant to lesson drawing from other countries (Bennett 1992). Even when it occurs, US public officials may be less likely to acknowledge it.

Although Friedman (1975) and Leichter (1991) mention policy transfer briefly as a possible influence on tobacco-control policy, they largely ignore it theoretically and do not assess it empirically in a systematic fashion. Only recently has this explanation been applied to tobacco control, through diffusion studies at the level of US state lawsuits (Spill, Licari and Ray 2001; Chard and Howard 2000) and lesson drawing among municipalities (Hays et al. 2000a, 2000b).

One would expect whatever lesson drawing occurred on tobacco-control policy between the US and Canada to follow patterns previously established for other issues. The dominant influence would be from the US toward Canada, as in most other health policies. US influence over Canadian tobacco-control policy through lesson drawing might be expected because of several possible factors, including population size, proximity, language, hegemonic position within a similar family of nations, research dominance, economies of scale, greater familiarity with the issue, and media dominance.

Aside from the usually greater resistance of an international or regional leader to lesson drawing from other countries, US reluctance is likely to be abetted by a political culture emphasizing distinctiveness and superiority to other regimes, the "city on the hill" mentality. Bennett (1992) finds that the US is more reluctant to study the experiences of other countries even in a newly developing policy area than are other advanced industrial democracies. Nevertheless, even if the US may be uniquely resistant to lesson drawing because of its double disinclination (from international and cultural factors), it may be more susceptible to policy borrowing from Canada than from other countries because some factors may assist Canadian influence. These include geographic propinquity, language, ease of communications, socioeconomic circumstances, and health conditions. Nevertheless, on balance, one would consider the predominant theoretically supported pattern of lesson drawing, if it existed at all, to be from the United States to Canada rather than the reverse.

Since tobacco control operates on different levels, one might expect some policy transfer to be bottom-up as well as top-down, at least within the same country. Any cross-border transfer involving jurisdictions other than federal ones is more likely to occur from the United States to Canada, because of greater Canadian attention to the US than vice versa. Since nongovernmental groups have played significant roles in tobacco control in both countries, one would expect there to be lesson drawing between some of these groups, tobacco companies as well as anti-tobacco groups, across the border.

One of the major shortcomings of several previous studies of policy transfer in public policy has been the failure to compare it against other possible explanations for the same phenomenon. There is a tendency to assume that any evidence of lesson drawing in policy establishes its explanatory power. This research will evaluate policy transfer more critically, as one possible explanation among others. Even if policy transfer is found to exist, how important is it compared to other factors influencing policy?

Methodology

The methodology employed here is that of the theoretically relevant comparative case study. This follows the approach of such previous work as Heidenheimer, Heclo and Adams (1990) and Bennett (1992) in attempting to evaluate different explanations of public policy in light of the evidence of how Canada and the United States have confronted and dealt with tobacco-control policy since 1964. The approach is primarily qualitative and controls for the different variables cannot be applied in a statistical manner. Nevertheless, one can attempt systematically to evaluate how different factors contribute to the adoption of policy. Where appropriate and available, quantitative data on some questions, such as cigarette taxation, tobacco growth, production, consumption, and expert ratings of tobacco-control policies, are utilized.

The empirical conditions affecting development of policy in different countries over an extended period of time need to be carefully delineated in a theoretical context. This research was carried out through examination of relevant written records, published and unpublished, statutes, legislative hearings, debates, executive and legislative reports, documents from interest groups, newspaper stories, academic research reports, and journalistic commentaries, as well as interviews with people concerned with tobacco control in both countries. A list of the persons interviewed is contained in the Appendix. Based on a critical weighing of this evidence, the persuasiveness of different explanations of tobacco-control policy in these two countries over a nearly 40-year period will be evaluated.

Summary

Several different theories either have been offered or could be presented which might explain tobacco-control policy. Few of these of these have been examined at length, however, especially in comparative perspective. The following chapters examine which of these competing explanations, or which combination of them, provides the most convincing explanation of tobacco-control policy in both Canada and the United States over time.

3

Tobacco Control: A Federal Case?

"From a regulatory perspective, the principal conundrum is how to regulate a product that is lethal when used as intended but remains legal for people over 18 years of age." (Jacobson and Wasserman 1993: 2)

"I remember when we were doing public opinion surveys on smoking back in the early sixties and shortly after the Surgeon General's report, a very frequent comment that people would make.... 'if they were really bad the government would do something about it.' There was very little positive action you could point to that the government had done something about it, and it is the fact that the government has required something that serves as a symbol of this kind of concern." (Daniel Horn, Director of US National Interagency Council on Smoking and Health, appearing before the Canadian House of Commons Committee on Health, Welfare, and Social Affairs, November 20, 1969.)

Introduction

This chapter examines in some detail federal government action on tobacco in both countries since 1964, including how tobacco control has waxed and waned on the governmental agenda. The focus will be on comparisons of policy through the years in the two countries. Both regulation and financial matters, primarily taxation but with some consideration of agricultural subsidies, will be covered. As the discussion will demonstrate, increasingly regulation and finance have become intertwined as governments, both state/provincial and federal, have used litigation in attempts to get tobacco companies to pay directly for some of the costs incurred through smoking. This chapter will concentrate on developments within the two countries in phases four and five of tobacco control, as outlined in Chapter One. More detailed comparisons will be presented in theoretical context in Chapters Five and Six.

Phase Four: United States, Regulation

The landmark Surgeon General's Report of 1964 brought widespread and intense media attention to the question of tobacco control, although the quality of discussion was not necessarily high (Kluger 1996). Apparently the commercial nature of the US media inhibited criticism of a major advertiser (Warner, Goldenhar and McLaughlin 1992). The two leading media crusaders against tobacco use before the 1980s were *Reader's Digest* and *Consumer Reports*.

Increased Congressional attention resulted in little legislation (Baumgartner and Jones 1993; US Department of Health and Human Services 1990). The legislation that did pass in 1965 and 1970 hobbled the tobacco regulatory initiatives of the semi-independent regulatory agencies and the states, and was compromised by exemptions for tobacco from some federal laws and regulations (Fritschler and Hoefler 1996). Congressionally-mandated exemptions for tobacco from regulatory laws had previously occurred in 1906, as noted in Chapter One, and again in 1938, when new legislation created the present FDA (Rienzo 1998). Even after the dangers of cigarette smoking became widely recognized, Congress specifically excluded tobacco from regulation under the *Fair Packaging and Labeling Act* (1966), the *Controlled Substances Acts* (1970), the *Consumer Product Safety Act* (1972), the *Federal Hazardous Substances Act* (1976), and the *Toxic Substances Control Act* (1976). Federal agencies such as the FDA and OSHA declined to regulate tobacco even when the relevant federal statutes suggested they might be able to do so (Kluger 1996: 375).

In addition to legislating mild health warnings on cigarette packages, the first federal anti-tobacco legislation in 1965 mandated annual reports from the Surgeon General on the problem, including legislative recommendations. These reports became an effective mechanism for agenda setting and general learning (see Chapters Five and Six) even as their recommendations for legislation were being neglected or emasculated (Kluger 1996; Nathanson 1999). The FTC and the Secretary of Health, Education and Welfare pressed for health warnings on printed advertising as well, and with the expiration of a five-year Congressional ban on further FTC rule-making on cigarettes, the major cigarette companies agreed to include the Surgeon General's warning in 1972.

The broadcast ban on advertising was initiated when the Federal Communications Commission in 1967 acted on a petition by Washington attorney John W. Banzhaf III. This petition claimed that tobacco smoking was a controversial issue, so cigarette advertisements should be balanced by free broadcast time for those opposed to smoking. The FCC agreed to invoke the fairness doctrine to allow free broadcast and telecast "public service" announcements on the dangers of cigarette smoking in a ratio of one anti-smoking presentation for every three paid cigarette advertisements. These anti-smoking announcements were considered so effective that by 1970 the tobacco manufacturers and their Congressional allies were willing to agree to federal legislation banning cigarette advertising on radio and television, which also eliminated the mandate for counter-advertising (Fritschler and Hoefler 1996; Doron 1979). Until 1998, advertising through other means such as newspapers, magazines, and billboards continued unabated. Although an increasing number of newspapers and magazines refused tobacco advertising, billboards and convenience stores remained prolific outlets. The 1997 National Settlement and 1998 Master Settlement Agreement promised the virtual elimination of billboard advertising, at least as far as the major tobacco companies were concerned.

Within the executive branch, there was some attempt at coordination of antismoking efforts, but this was frustrated by the refusal of Congress to grant adequate funding and by opposition from other executive agencies which promoted tobacco. The National Clearinghouse for Smoking and Health within HEW was initially responsible for health research, information, and promotion designed to reduce smoking; much of its work was on a contractual basis with other national and local organizations (Friedman 1975: 70). It was eventually rejuvenated in 1978 as the Office on Smoking and Health within the Centers for Disease Control. Yet the National Cancer Institute, a separate organization within HEW, provided the bulk of the funding for research. Initially the National Interagency Council was also formed; this was composed of government and voluntary health organizations to coordinate anti-smoking education and promotion. After lobbying by the American Cancer Society, the National Interagency Council sponsored the First World Conference on Smoking and Health in New York City in 1967 and the first National Conference on Smoking and Health in 1970 (Friedman 1975: 66). This began a process of public-private cooperation on tobacco-control matters (Hall 1969) which later took new forms through Canadian government grants to public advocacy groups and US federal aid for local capacity-building in tobacco control. In the mid-1980s a reformulated National Interagency Committee on Smoking and Health was established as a coordinating committee within government to advise the Secretary of Health and Human Services on issues within this realm (US Department of Health and Human Services 1989: 51-59).

When the Secretary of DHEW, Joseph Califano, embarked on an anti-tobacco campaign in 1978, his efforts were not welcomed by the Secretary of Agriculture or by President Jimmy Carter, seeking tobacco-state support for his forthcoming re-election effort in 1980 (Califano 1981). Although this effort probably contributed to Califano's dismissal in 1979, his abortive campaign against the social acceptability of tobacco was unusual for a public official before the mid-1980s.

After a plateau of federal government action on tobacco control for over a decade, the ascendancy of an anti-regulatory conservative Republican administration led by President Ronald Reagan in 1980 might have been expected to herald no further change. But some of the currents manifesting themselves more clearly a few years later had already begun to stir.

In 1981 the surprisingly aggressive anti-smoking campaigner, Surgeon General C. Everett Koop, declared that "cigarette smoking is clearly identified as the chief preventable cause of death in our society." A 1981 report from the Federal Trade Commission concerning the need for improved cigarette package health warning labels eventually led to the *Comprehensive Smoking Education Act of 1984*, discussed below. Also, at the end of 1981 the major US anti-tobacco organizations on the national level—ACS, AHA, and ALA—pooled their efforts into an umbrella lobbying organization, the Coalition on Smoking OR Health.

In summary, by the early 1980s, health education and promotion had led to a decline in smoking, but the defeat of Secretary Califano's foray against tobacco and the rise of an anti-regulatory administration did not augur well for tobacco-control efforts. Anti-tobacco forces were mobilizing, however, in ways which would lead to more success in the mid-1980s.

Phase Four: Canada, Regulation

The 1964 US Surgeon General's Report received considerable attention in Canada, as did the earlier 1962 Report of the Royal College of Physicians in the United Kingdom. The earlier report was little noticed in the United States, except in specialized professional circles. Health Minister Judy LaMarsh issued a statement to the House of Commons in 1963 expressing her belief in the association of tobacco use with various diseases and called a national conference on the topic. The participants included tobacco companies and growers as well as professional health and volunteer organizations and provincial health ministers. Health and Welfare Canada began some modestly-funded smoking education programs, mainly directed at health workers as intermediaries to carry the message to the public (Health and Welfare Canada 1964: 7-9; Health and Welfare Canada 1983). Thus the Canadian federal government actually acted officially on this issue somewhat earlier than did its counterpart in the United States.

By the time that Health and Welfare Canada (1964) issued *Smoking and Health*, the US Surgeon General's Report had been released. The Canadian book acknowledged the superior status of the British and US reports by including extracts from both of them (10 pages and 25 pages, respectively) in a section entitled "Summaries and Conclusions from Authoritative Reports," along with six pages of an excerpt from a 1963 American Cancer Society report. Together these three reports took up almost a quarter of the book. This was followed by some Canadian studies, including two papers on the study of Canadian veterans. In addition to its education programs, Health and Welfare Canada began internal deliberations about possible government action on tobacco. In 1967 Minister of Health Allan MacEachen received cabinet approval to prepare legislation prohibiting misleading advertising and requiring tar and nicotine information on cigarette packages and advertising, but it was never introduced. This began the 20-year-long Canadian odyssey of executive deliberations but no legislative action on tobacco control.

In Canada, private members' bills, introduced without government support and with little chance of passage, sometimes stimulate a government to put forward its own legislation on a subject after hearing the arguments and gauging public support. In the late 1960s there were six Private Members' bills seeking to regulate cigarettes or cigarette advertising. Issues arising from these bills and the general concern about smoking and health were considered in hearings conducted by the House of Commons

Committee on Health, Welfare, and Social Affairs over a year-long period, 1968-69, culminating in a unanimous all-party report. The hearings were begun with testimony from the Minister of Health and Welfare, John Munro, and continued with other Canadian witnesses, mainly from professional associations and research organizations. Although some members requested testimony by foreign experts, the only one appearing was Daniel Horn, Director of the Interagency Council on Smoking and Health in the United States. Other than domestic evidence, scientific findings and government regulatory actions in the United States and the United Kingdom (in that order) were of most interest to the committee, which was provided with a considerable amount of written material on actions in these countries (House of Commons Standing Committee on Health, Welfare and Social Affairs 1968, December 19: 127). As Friedman (1975) indicates, the committee's review of possible government actions on tobacco was remarkably well-rounded, including examination of the economic contributions of tobacco, government support of tobacco agriculture and export promotion, taxation, advertising, scientific evidence on health effects, and warning labels. The report of the committee urged restrictions on the advertising and promotion of tobacco products, including warning labels on packages, advertisements, and vending machines; a phased-in ban on advertising, restrictions on vending machine placement, an end to coupon schemes and free distribution, increased education programs, and coordination of national, provincial, and local activities (Isabelle 1969).

The Liberal cabinet deliberated several times in 1970 and 1971 over how to deal with tobacco control. The examples of the US and British governments, public opinion, the recommendations of the Isabelle Committee, and Canada's reputation as an international health leader pushed it to take action. But there were also concerns about effects on the tobacco industry and getting too far ahead of other countries in limiting tobacco advertising, as well as fears of more immediate political repercussions. Various options were surveyed, including putting tobacco under the *Hazardous Products Act* through an executive Order in Council, as well as legislation banning or restricting tobacco advertising in various media, prescribing maximum constituent levels, and ending promotional schemes (Cabinet Memoranda and Minutes 1970, 1971).

In 1971 the Liberal government finally put forward legislation to ban advertising of tobacco products, not only in broadcasting but also in newspapers, magazines, and billboards, and to assume broad regulatory authority over tobacco. Before debate could take place on the bill, however, the government accepted a written but informal voluntary industry code which took tobacco ads off the airwaves as of January, 1972. The tobacco companies placed the following warning on cigarette packages: "Warning: Health and Welfare Canada advises that danger to health increases with amount smoked." In 1976, "avoid inhaling" was added to the end of the phrase. Both of these warnings, but without an attribution to Health and Welfare Canada, had originally been recommended by the government in its abortive legislation (Friedman 1975: 92). Various other unilateral industry amendments were made to the voluntary code over the years including adding a health warning to billboard advertising in 1984 (Cunningham 1996: 68-69). A private member's bill to regulate smoking on common carriers passed second reading in 1974 but went no further (Cunningham 1996: 194).

As the Liberals continued governing on the federal level for all but ten months until 1984, there was periodic official concern, especially within Health and Welfare Canada, that greater governmental control of tobacco might be necessary (Cunningham 1996:121-22). Starting in the mid-1970s, repeated requests by government ministers and civil servants to the tobacco industry to display health warning and contents labels more prominently on packages and advertisements and to include carbon monoxide levels in the descriptions of contents were ignored (Morrison 1977; Callard 2000). The issue of greater regulation of tobacco was discussed in at least two meetings of federal and provincial health ministers. In Canada an interagency council consisting of private as well as public agencies to combat smoking had also been established, similar to the US. In 1974 Health and Welfare Canada turned this into a separate organization, the Canadian Council on Smoking and Health, with initial three-year funding. By 1980 Health and Welfare Canada, in cooperation with the provinces and with voluntary and professional organizations, decided to engage in a new, long-term educational program called "A Generation of Non-Smokers" (Health and Welfare Canada 1983). The Non-Medical Use of Drugs Directorate even commissioned an internal study on the use of taxation as an instrument to combat tobacco use rather than as a revenue mechanism (Health and Welfare Canada 1979). But the voluntary code of the tobacco industry continued to be the *de facto* regulatory policy.

As in the United States, there was some movement for federal action on tobacco control in Canada the early 1980s after years of dormancy. This began within Health and Welfare Canada when Monique Bégin was Health Minister. The role of preventing tobacco usage within the "healthy public policy" concept began to gain adherents in the department. A federal/provincial health ministers' conference in 1983 identified smoking as a health issue requiring national attention. *Canadian Initiatives in Smoking and Health* (Health and Welfare Canada 1983) was released in conjunction with Canada's hosting of the fifth World Conference on Tobacco and Health in Winnipeg. At that conference, Bégin advocated substantially greater taxation of cigarettes without first clearing this position with the Minister of Finance. Although subsequently this was characterized as a "personal lobby," her department had been investigating tax questions as a possible element in tobacco control for some time (Cunningham 1996: 121-22). Clearly there was growing opinion that the regime of voluntary tobacco control in Canada was not meeting public-health objectives.

Phase Four: United States, Finance

There were few attempts to control tobacco through use of economic measures in the US in phase four. The federal agricultural price-support program for tobacco continued without major change until 1982. One of the few subsidies to come to an end was the tobacco ration to US soldiers. This was removed in 1978.

Federal taxes as a share of the price of tobacco continued to drop, as no increases to offset inflation occurred between 1950 and 1982. Finally, in 1982, taxes were slightly raised in a response to the growing deficit. A federal tax increase of eight US cents was imposed, beginning in 1983. Unlike in Canada, this was not the beginning of a concerted federal tax effort on cigarettes (see below), but several US states also began increasing taxes during the latter portions of this period, as described in Chapter Four.

Phase Four: Canada, Finance

As in the United States, government actions in regard to financial matters on tobacco were stable for most of this period, but in the latter part there was some recognition of the power of taxation to influence tobacco consumption. Federal tobacco taxes, while higher than those in the United States at the time and constituting a larger share of federal tax receipts than in the US (Ontario Council of Health 1982), remained relatively low in comparison to other countries. The Canadian federal government continued to support agricultural research and seek foreign markets for Canadian tobacco.

The first major Canadian federal tobacco restrictions were through the financial sector, although not apparently motivated by health concerns. Because of lagging revenues in an era of high inflation, beginning in 1981 the Canadian federal government began to raise taxes on tobacco products as well as on alcohol (Cunningham 1996). Also for the first time, taxation of cigarettes was switched to an *ad valorem* basis (price rather than units). Several provinces followed suit in raising taxes, also *ad valorem*. This created a cigarette taxation spiral as taxes began to increase rapidly on both levels (Cunningham 1996: 122; Sweanor 1991). By 1985 the government decided to heed tobacco company protests and end *ad valorem* federal taxation. The implications for public health of this increase in cigarette taxation were not fully assimilated at the time, however (Sweanor 1991).

In both regulation and finance, then, tobacco control in Canada entered a period of stability once the 1971 voluntary agreement of the tobacco industry was adopted and accepted by the federal government. Although anti-tobacco groups were formed, their activities were, if anything, less visible than in the United States. There were some stirs of change in the bureaucracy, but, except for Monique Bégin's short-lived campaign at the end of the last Liberal government of the era, there were no highly visible figures like the US Surgeon General or HEW Secretary Califano publicly urging greater restrictions on tobacco.

In summary, during phase four, 1964-84, the US was clearly the policy leader and Canada the follower, except for taxation at the end of the period. Friedman's (1975:155) similar conclusions from his study of tobacco policy in the two countries through the early 1970s were still valid a decade later.

Phase Five: United States, Regulation

As the fourth phase ended and the fifth began, US federal government skirmishes with the tobacco industry continued, but no concerted attempt at comprehensive regulation occurred until the mid-1990s. After a protracted struggle and considerable compromise, four new, stronger, and slightly larger warnings on cigarette packages were mandated by the

Comprehensive Smoking Education Act of 1984. All preceded by "Surgeon General's Warning," they are as follows (Pertschuk 1986):

"Cigarette Smoke Contains Carbon Monoxide."

"Smoking Causes Lung Cancer, Heart Disease, Emphysema, and May Complicate Pregnancy."

"Smoking by Pregnant Women May Result in Fetal Injury, Premature Birth and Low Birth Weight."

"Quitting Smoking Now Greatly Reduces Serious Risks to Your Health."

A general list of ingredients included in cigarettes also was required to be filed by all manufacturers to the Office on Smoking and Health, CDC. But federal agenda setting on tobacco control continued to outpace policy adoptions by a large margin. As the *Tobacco Products Control Act* was passing through the Canadian Parliament in the late 1980s, similar legislation was introduced in the US House of Representatives by Democrat Mike Synar, but it, like other bills introduced regularly by such anti-tobacco legislators as Democratic Senator Edward Kennedy and Democratic Representative Henry Waxman, got nowhere (Stoffman 1987; US Department of Health and Human Services 1990). These bills were not backed by the President or the Executive branch, then controlled by the anti-regulatory Reagan and Bush Republicans. In fact, the Reagan-appointed chairman of the Federal Trade Commission, Daniel Oliver, appeared before a Congressional committee to argue against a proposed advertising ban on cigarettes (Oliver 1987). In addition, there was an expanded drive by the Commerce Department and the US Special Trade Representative to open up foreign markets for US tobacco products (Mintz 1991; Frankel 1996).

Nevertheless, some anti-tobacco groups and legislators called for further federal restrictions on tobacco advertising from the mid-1980s, and the Reports of the US Surgeon General, especially in 1986 on Involuntary Smoking (second-hand smoke) and in 1988 on Nicotine Addiction (US Department of Health and Human Services 1986, 1988), served as beacons for the anti-smoking movement. Cautionary reports on the health effects of environmental tobacco smoke led to a series of measures restricting smoking in government buildings and on common carriers under federal regulation, including an airline treaty with Canada and Australia in 1994 and support for a global agreement for nonsmoking flights. As shown in Chapter Four, however, the major regulatory action as well as taxation in this period was at the state and local level. In early 1994, the largest US anti-tobacco group, the Coalition on Smoking OR Health, issued a report card on 30 years of federal efforts at smoking prevention which gave Congress, the White House, and most federal agencies grades of D or F. Only the Environmental Protection Agency and the Veterans Administration managed a grade as high as B (Leary 1994), the former for its 1993 report on the dangers of second-hand smoke. US Presidents, Congress, and federal agencies, including DHHS, had largely avoided the issue, afraid to tangle with tobacco and its powerful patrons on Capitol Hill (Nathanson 1999). But as in Canada a decade before, matters had already begun to change.

The federal government, in cooperation with states and sometimes private organizations, had initiated programs for "capacity building" at the community level to encourage tobacco regulation. These were inspired by analyses of the importance of building social support for HPP (US Department of Health and Human Services 1991). The mid-1980s saw a blossoming of state-based tobacco-control coalitions of private and public organizations with local policy components (US Department of Health and Human Services 2000b: 383). The federally-financed programs began with the National Cancer Institute's experimental COMMIT (Community Intervention Trial for Smoking Cessation), 1985-93, which included a Canadian component. This was followed by the same organization's ASSIST (American Stop Smoking Intervention Study for Cancer Prevention) program in 17 US states, 1991-98, financed by the National Cancer Institute and the American Cancer Society. The Centers for Disease Control and Prevention supplemented ASSIST with a lesser-financed program, IMPACT (Initiatives to Mobilize for the Prevention and Control of Tobacco Use), for the other 33 states. The ASSIST and IMPACT programs were eventually incorporated into the National Tobacco Control Program (NTCP) of the CDC on an ongoing basis. One observer characterizes ASSIST as "the most important anti-tobacco public health effort ever undertaken by the US Government" (Pan-American Heath Organization 1992: 6) and the impact of this program are generally viewed more favourably than those of its predecessor, COMMIT (US Department of Health and Human Services 2000b). The Synar Amendment to the *Alco-*

hol, Drug Abuse and Mental Health Agency Reorganization Act of 1992 gave financial incentives to states for substantially reducing teenage tobacco usage.

In 1994 the House Subcommittee on Health and the Environment, chaired by Democratic Representative Henry Waxman, held hearings in which tobacco company executives were questioned about their knowledge of the toxic and addictive properties of cigarettes. Revelations about the internal knowledge and decision-making of tobacco companies, often from company documents themselves, as in The Cigarette Papers (Glantz et al. 1996) and in court cases, especially the state of Minnesota lawsuit against tobacco companies, have encouraged public support for tobacco-control measures and given credence to the necessity for government regulatory actions (Hilts 1996; Pringle 1998; Mollenkamp et al. 1998). After years of lobbying from anti-tobacco groups, in February, 1994, FDA Commissioner David A. Kessler, a Republican appointee holdover from the Bush Administration, indicated that he supported COSH's claim that the FDA had the authority to regulate tobacco as a drug. In August 1995, President Clinton publicly directed the FDA to propose tighter restrictions on cigarette advertising and tobacco availability to minors. The year-long period for written commentary on the proposed regulations led to 700,000 submissions, more than on any previous federal rule, indicating the mobilization capacities of those closely involved with this issue. In August 1996, the President announced that the FDA would begin to regulate cigarettes as drug (nicotine) delivery devices in an attempt to combat underage tobacco use, along with other tobacco regulatory measures. The specifics of the regulations, also known as the FDA Rule, are listed in Table 3-1.

By claiming that the FDA had such authority over tobacco products, no legislation was necessary. The tobacco companies immediately challenged the legal basis of such broad, previously unclaimed regulatory authority in federal courts (Rienzo 1998). Eventually the US Supreme Court, in a 5-4 decision in March, 2000, disagreed with the claim that the FDA already had authority to regulate tobacco; it would need explicit Congressional legislation to do so. The majority opinion asserted that tobacco was so dangerous that, under current FDA rules, the FDA would have to ban rather than regulate it.

The final decision still rests with the legislative and executive branches. A properly written law would give the FDA authority over tobacco, but Congressional Republicans, such as their leader in the Senate, Trent Lott of Mississippi, have been disinclined to allow the FDA to do this. Without

Table 3-1: Major Provisions of
US Food and Drug Administration Regulations, 1996

1. FDA claims authority to regulate tobacco products because they are "drug-delivery" devices (nicotine is a drug) and FDA has authority to regulate medical devices
2. No sales to anyone under 18, photo identification required
3. Free samples banned
4. No vending-machine sales except in locations where those under 18 cannot enter
5. No sales of "kiddie packs" of less than 20 cigarettes
6. Packages must bear warning "Nicotine delivery devices for persons 18 or older"
7. Outdoor advertising banned within 1000 feet of public playgrounds, elementary and secondary schools
8. Billboard advertising restricted to black text on white backgrounds; no photos
9. Full-colour advertising and photos allowed in adult-oriented publications, defined as those having less than 15-per-cent readership of people 18 years of age or younger and read by fewer than two million young people
10. No non-nicotine products may display tobacco company logos
11. No free gifts for purchasing cigarettes or smokeless tobacco products
12. No sponsorship of social or cultural events or teams under brand name of tobacco product, but corporate sponsorship is allowed if it does not include a brand name
13. Tobacco companies must pay into fund for health warnings about cigarettes

such authority, the United States lacks a federally-legislated comprehensive tobacco-control policy.

Despite the defeat over FDA authority, President Clinton is generally recognized as the first anti-tobacco US President. He banned smoking in the White House in 1993 and later in federal buildings through executive orders. Yet proposed OSHA rules restricting smoking in the workplace across the United States, the subject of hearings even before he took office, have never been issued. Both business and labour have reservations about strong rules, and health groups are unwilling to settle for weak ones.

Organized labour, a redoubt of blue-collar smokers and a major Democratic campaign supporter, has been reluctant to have OSHA act (Delducci 1996; Nathanson 1999). Although supposedly the Labor Department under Secretary Robert Reich was working to bring about a strong federal standard (Pertschuk and the Advocacy Institute Staff 1994), Reich's (1997) memoir does not even mention the topic. In recent years federal workplace smoking rules have been very low on the political agenda. Their fate shows the limits of the Clinton Administration's proclaimed toughness on tobacco.

Tobacco control also became a campaign issue in the 1996 presidential election because of the anti-tobacco stance of the Clinton Administration and the maladroit public pronouncements of Republican candidate Bob Dole (Kaplan 1996). Although tobacco control was not a major issue in the 2000 US presidential election, there was little doubt that the tobacco companies favoured George W. Bush, whose record as governor of Texas was lukewarm on tobacco control (Chartier 2000).

The US penchant for making policy through litigation also came to the forefront in the 1990s. As a growing number of US states sued tobacco companies to recover the smoking-related costs of state public health care programs, mainly the jointly federal-state shared cost program of Medicaid, many of them joined a "National Settlement" with the industry to provide a comprehensive resolution, one involving regulation to complement the FDA Rule as well as financial compensation (see Table 3-2). Although it assumed only a supporting role in the negotiations, mainly through White House Adviser Bruce Lindsey and Matthew L. Myers of the Campaign for Tobacco-Free Kids, the Clinton Administration supported this agreement (Pringle 1998; Mollenkamp et al. 1998). Since the agreement included a specific legitimation of the disputed FDA authority over tobacco as well as limited protection for the companies from further lawsuits, it required approval by Congress for enactment.

Once it reached the US Senate, however, public-health groups, encouraged by the White House, managed to change provisions of the bill to the disadvantage of the tobacco industry (*Final Report of the Advisory Commission on Tobacco Policy and Public Health* 1997; Bloom 1998). The major legislation became known as the McCain Bill after its main sponsor, Republican Senator John McCain of Arizona. The financial payment from the tobacco companies was increased from US$369 billion to $517 billion, and some of the liability protections were weakened. Declaring that the price was too high, the tobacco companies turned against the deal

Table 3-2: Comparison of US National Settlement and Master Settlement Agreement

	June 20, 1997 Agreement	McCain Bill (Managers Amendment)	1998 State Attorney General Tobacco Industry Agreement
Authority of the FDA	Authority of the FDA to oversee the tobacco industry and tobacco products as Drugs/Devices	Authority of FDA to oversee the tobacco industry and tobacco products in a separate tobacco chapter	Not addressed
	Authority to regulate harmful constituents including nicotine	Authority to regulate harmful constituents, including nicotine	Not addressed
	Authority to require safety testing and disclosure of ingredients	Authority to require safety testing and disclosure of ingredients	Not addressed
	Authority to revise health warnings	Authority to revise health warnings	Not addressed
	Authority to require tobacco industry to disclose health research	Authority to require tobacco industry to disclose health research	Not addressed
	Authority to restrict marketing and sales practices to protect children recognized	Authority to restrict marketing and sales practices to protect children recognized	Not addressed
	Imposed procedures greater than for other products	Did not impose procedures greater than for other products	Not addressed

Table 3-2 continued: Comparison of US National Settlement and Master Settlement Agreement

	June 20, 1997 Agreement	McCain Bill (Managers Amendment)	1998 State Attorney General Tobacco Industry Agreement
Health Warnings	New stronger health warnings on cigarette and smokeless tobacco packages and ads	New stronger health warnings on cigarette and smokeless tobacco packages and ads	Not addressed
	New, more visible warning format	New, more visible warning format	Not addressed
	Authority of FDA to revise warnings	Authority of FDA to revise warnings	Not addressed
Youth Access Restrictions	Comprehensive Enforcement plan	Comprehensive Enforcement plan	Not required
	Requires proof of age	Requires proof of age	Not required
	Limit vending machines to adult-only facilities	Limit vending machines to adult-only facilities	Not required
	Bans self-service displays	Bans self-service displays	Not required
	Free sampling banned	Free sampling banned	Free sampling limited to adult-only facilities
	Licenses retailers	Licenses retailers	Not required
	Minimum pack size	Minimum pack size	Minimum pack size
Youth Targets and Penalties	Requires youth tobacco-use reduction targets	Requires youth tobacco-use reduction targets	None set

	Industry-wide penalties	Combination of industry-wide and company-based penalties	None
Funds – Tobacco control programs	Funds for tobacco efforts at the federal level, i.e. community-based programs	Funds for tobacco efforts at the federal level, i.e. community-based programs	None
other than public education	Funds for tobacco-control efforts at the state level	Funds for tobacco-control efforts at the state level	Agreement does not require that funds states receive be used to reduce tobacco use
Cessation	$1 to 1.5 billion a year provided	Annual funding beginning at $680 million	Not addressed; no guaranteed funding
Research	$25 billion trust fund, plus more than $100 million annually	$850 million annually (1/3 of total research allocation)	$25 million annually to a national foundation for both tobacco and substance abuse
Public Education – Counter Ads	$500 million a year indefinitely	$500 million a year indefinitely	$300 million a year guaranteed for 5 years, with contingency for longer funding
	No limit on content	No limit on content	No criticism of tobacco companies or officials
Restrictions on Marketing to Children	Not addressed	Not addressed	General prohibition of youth targeting

Table 3-2 continued: Comparison of US National Settlement and Master Settlement Agreement

	June 20, 1997 Agreement	McCain Bill (Managers Amendment)	1998 State Attorney General Tobacco Industry Agreement
Transit	Bans transit ads	Bans transit ads	Bans transit ads
Cartoons/ Human Images	Bans cartoon and human images, like the Marlboro Man	Bans cartoon and human images, like the Marlboro Man	Bans cartoon and human images, like the Marlboro Man
Print Media	Limits ads in newspapers and magazines with large youth readership to black and white text only	Limits ads in newspapers and magazines with large youth readership to black and white text only	Newspaper and magazine ads not limited
Brand Name Merchandise	Bans all tobacco brand name merchandise	Bans all tobacco brand name merchandise	Bans all tobacco brand name merchandise, except at tobacco sponsored events
In Store Advertising	Black and white text only; limited number and size	Black and white text only; limited number and size	No limits
Use of Non-Tobacco Items or Gifts Based on Proof of Purchase	Banned	Banned	Banned to children

Use of Non-Tobacco Brand Name on Tobacco Products	Banned	Banned	Banned
Internet Tobacco Ads	Banned	Banned	Not addressed
Tobacco Product Placement in Movies, TV	Banned	Banned	Banned
Brand Name Sponsorships	Banned	Banned	Prohibited for concerts, events in which any contestants are under 18, or in football, baseball, soccer or hockey; except for Kool Jazz Festival or GPC Country Music Festival; Otherwise limited to one event or series (like the Winston Cup Race Tour) annually

Table 3-2 continued: Comparison of US National Settlement and Master Settlement Agreement

	June 20, 1997 Agreement	McCain Bill (Managers Amendment)	1998 State Attorney General Tobacco Industry Agreement
Tobacco Industry Organizations	Dissolves Tobacco Institute, Council on Tobacco Research; CTR may not be reconstituted	Dissolves Tobacco Institute, Council on Tobacco Research; CTR may not be reconstituted	Dissolves Tobacco Institute, Council on Tobacco Research; CTR may not be reconstituted
Environmental Tobacco Smoke Protections	Set nationwide minimum standards	Set nationwide minimum standards subject to right of a state to disapprove	Not addressed
Farmers	Not addressed	Conflicting provisions to fund and assist farmers	Not addressed; except to require industry to meet with farmers
Payments	$368.5 billion over 25 years, of which $196.5 billion is for the states	$506 billion over 25 years, of which 196.6 billion is for the states	$206 billion over 25 years to settle state cases; federal government has a claim on a portion of the funds

Federal Tax Restrictions – Offset	None	None	Industry gets deduction on payments to the states if federal government imposes a payment or a new tax on the tobacco companies and returns the money to the states unrestricted, for health care or tobacco control
Tobacco Industry Liability	Limits on punitive damages for past wrongdoing and on class actions	No limits on punitive damages or class actions	No limits on punitive damages or class actions
	Annual liability cap	Annual liability cap	No annual liability cap
	Settle state Medicaid cases and addiction class actions	Settle state Medicaid cases and addiction class actions	Settle state Medicaid cases, but not addiction class actions. State settlement covers cities and countries and private attorneys general cases for all claims the states brought or could have brought

and waged an expensive public campaign against the bill (Kurtz 1998). The legislation failed to pass for lack of a 60-per-cent majority to cut off extended debate in the Senate.

As Table 3-2 indicates, the successor agreement between the state attorneys general and the tobacco companies, the MSA , was significantly different and in many respects less stringent than its immediate predecessors, the original National Settlement as negotiated by the state attorneys general and the McCain Bill, which reached the floor of the US Senate. If either version of the National Settlement had passed, US and Canadian tobacco-control policies now would resemble each other even more closely than they do, as discussed in Chapter Six. The major differences between the US and Canada would have been greater limits on executive authority over tobacco and on tobacco company liability in the United States. Either version also would have provided greater tobacco-company financial compensation for health care costs than did the MSA.

In the wake of the collapse of the McCain Bill, four individual states— Mississippi, Florida, Texas, and Minnesota—made individual out-of-court settlements worth US $41 billion with the tobacco companies, and in November 1998 the MSA included the remaining 46 states for $206 billion, along with limitations on tobacco advertising and lobbying activities (see Table 3-3).

Since these agreements did not include FDA authority or litigation limits, they did not require Congressional approval. With the refusal of the Supreme Court to uphold the FDA Rule, the MSA has become the *de facto* comprehensive *federal* tobacco regulatory policy in the United States, even without formal legislative or executive action. The MSA is discussed further in Chapter Four.

Jurisdictional squabbling emerged over whether the federal government should receive a share of the MSA funds since it provides some of the funding for state Medicaid programs. The US Congress settled the issue by forbidding the federal government from sharing in the proceeds. The US Justice Department then filed its own lawsuit against the tobacco companies for recovery of health-care costs in the major federally-financed health care program, Medicare. Under its new Republican attorney general, however, in 2001 the Justice Department indicated a willingness to settle the suit out of court (Lichtblau and Levin 2001). In short, during the fifth phase the United States federal government has moved more aggressively and with some modest success

Table 3-3: 1998 Master Settlement Agreement (United States)

1. Tobacco companies pay US $206 billion over 25 years to 40 states to cover health-care costs of sick smokers on US Medicaid, plus a total of US $41 billion to Mississippi, Florida, Minnesota, and Texas

2. After 25 years, payments to continue indefinitely based on inflation and health-care costs

3. Tobacco companies fund US $1.45 billion nationwide anti-smoking campaign over 10 years

4. Tobacco companies pay US $250 million over 10 years for foundation to prevent teen smoking

5. Smokeless tobacco companies pay $400 million for health-care costs

6. Tobacco Institute and Council for Tobacco Research, industry promotion and research organizations, disbanded

7. Cartoon characters banned in tobacco advertising, labelling, packaging, and promotions

8. Outdoor advertising on billboards, public transportation, sports arenas, and shopping malls banned; in-store ads allowed but limited in size

9. Tobacco brands on non-tobacco merchandise banned

10. Free samples banned except in adult-only facilities

11. Product promotions in movies, theatre productions, live performances, music videos, and video games banned

12. One brand-name sponsored sporting event per year allowed; no sponsorship of events with underage participants. No limits on sponsorship in adults-only facilities

13. Any successful local government lawsuits against tobacco industry are deducted from the amount paid to the state in which the municipality is located

toward greater regulation of tobacco, but policy has been not been centrally coordinated.

Phase Five: Canada, Regulation

In Canada in the mid-1980s, a change of government, the stimulus of a private member's bill in the House of Commons, and the advent of a more aggressive lobbying effort spearheaded by NSRA allowed a window of opportunity to open for a two-pronged "inside-outside" strategy which led to the adoption of the *Tobacco Products Control Act* in 1988. Health Minister Bégin's 1983 attempt at raising the issue of increased tobacco restrictions was continued by other officials in the ministry even after the government changed in 1984. The Bureau of Tobacco Control and Biometrics in Health and Welfare Canada began to make public some of its research on tobacco, cigarette smoking, and the health effects of tobacco consumption. These papers became widely cited sources of the dimensions of the tobacco problem in Canada. They often cited comparative data on tobacco production and consumption in order to put the Canadian situation in world perspective and invoked WHO standards (Collishaw and Rogers 1984; Collishaw and Mulligan 1984; Rogers, Myers and Collishaw 1985; Collishaw 1986a; Wigle et al. 1987). More direct policy reconsiderations were also under way. The lack of enforceability of the tobacco-industry voluntary code began to bother Neil Collishaw, the chief tobacco researcher, and he advised the Minister of Health and Welfare to consider a wider range of options, ranging from a written agreement with the industry to legislative action.

The 1985 National Strategy to Reduce Tobacco Use (NSRTU) began a concerted government attempt at public education on the dangers of smoking (McElroy 1990). Three goals were posited: smoking prevention, smoking cessation, and protection from ETS (Cunningham 1996: 198). The strategy also provided for public-health voluntary organizations to work closely with both federal and provincial health ministries. Yet 1985 legislation, especially the *Hazardous Products Act*, did not cover tobacco despite such advocacy by NGOs (Grossman and Price 1992: 3-24-27). Meanwhile, anti-tobacco groups were taking more assertive political action, starting with the campaign against tobacco-company sponsorship of Canadian amateur skiing in 1984-85 (Cunningham 1996: 68). Early in the next year NSRA (1986) presented to Conservative Health Minister Jake Epp a critique of tobacco industry self-regulation, entitled *A Catalogue of Deception: The Use and Abuse of Voluntary Regulation of Tobacco in Canada*. Legislative controversy over tobacco was further stimulated in 1986 by the introduction of a private member's bill by avid anti-smoking New Democratic Party MP Lynn McDonald. This bill proposed to ban all tobacco advertising and mandated smoke-free zones in all areas under federal jurisdiction, including common carriers. Although the bill was initially not welcomed by the government, it generated considerable support, especially from public-health organizations. After negotiations

Table 3-4: Major Provisions of Tobacco Products Control Act, 1988 (Canada)

1. Restrictions on tobacco-company sponsorship
2. No tobacco names or trademarks on non-tobacco products
3. Free samples, discounts, and prizes banned
4. No kiddie-packs (less than 20 cigarettes) allowed
5. No advertising of tobacco products other than at point of sale
6. Health warnings on packages more prominent (front of package) and in stronger language
7. Toxic content information required
8. Tobacco companies not allowed to use warning labels on packages as a liability defence in lawsuits

with the tobacco industry over a new voluntary arrangement stalled, the government introduced its own legislation in 1987, Bill C-51, providing for a comprehensive policy of tobacco regulation. This eventually became the *Tobacco Products Control Act.* This legislation prohibited the advertising of tobacco products in Canada, special promotions for tobacco products (free distribution, discount coupons, gifts, or lotteries), and the use of tobacco trademarks on other products. It also mandated health warnings and lists of toxic constituents on packages, but did allow use of tobacco-company corporate names (but not brand names) in sponsoring entertainment events (see Table 3-4) (Gray 1988).

A titanic struggle ensued to get the bill passed, which some observers (Ondrick 1991; Pross and Stewart 1994) have seen as the apotheosis of the decline of old-style Canadian "elite accommodation" (Presthus 1973) into a newer form of competitive group politics. The tobacco companies were confident that the old-style politics of quietly settling matters behind the scenes would continue and were surprised that the bill was actually introduced. They were forced to engage in defensive public lobbying against the aggressive anti-tobacco movement, which showed itself adept at the new techniques of generating mass support, coalition management, media access, and publicity (Ondrick 1991). While the Conservative government had a large majority, a delay until the next parliamentary election, expected in 1988, would have killed the bill, at least temporarily, or it could have been withdrawn by the government, as had happened in 1971. Tobacco interests had well established ties with the Liberal party, now in opposition (Stoffman 1987). But they quickly hired Bill Neville, formerly a top aide to Conservative leader Joe Clark; his first mission was to stop Bill C-51 (Sawatsky 1989). The pro-restrictions coalition, led by NSRA and CCS, turned to some controversial public lobbying, including full-page advertisements, to expose Neville's role as well as other tobacco industry tactics (Wilson 1991; Cunningham 1996).

Although some members of the health lobby considered it was their job to reign in the more radical NSRA and PSFC (Wilson 1991), the coalition stayed together and was able to celebrate victory with the passage of two bills. The government legislation did not address the nonsmoking provisions in McDonald's bill. Despite government reservations, her bill, the *Nonsmokers' Health Act*, became law as well. (Kagan and Vogel 1993; Pross and Stewart 1994). Furthermore, unlike in the United States, federal regulations did not pre-empt stronger provincial action, and package health warnings could be altered on the basis of administrative discretion without the need for further legislation, thus avoiding the periodic struggles that occurred in the US. The tobacco industry immediately sued in a Quebec court, claiming that the elimination of advertising interfered with guarantees of freedom of expression.

In 1993, the *Tobacco Sales to Young Persons Act* raised the minimum age for purchasing tobacco products to 18 and limited locations for vending machines (see Table 3-5). Yet the number of health inspectors to enforce the *Tobacco Products Control Act* was so limited that more had to be borrowed from other departments.

Table 3-5: Major Provisions of Tobacco Sales to Young Persons Act, 1993 (Canada)

1. Legal age set at 18 for tobacco purchases in Canada
2. No cigarette packages of less than 20 allowed to be sold
3. Vending machines allowed only in bars

Although the Canadian government mandated health warnings on packages relatively late, by 1993 Canada had, at the time, the strongest health warnings in the world (Cunningham 1996). They were larger (25 per cent of the package, on both front and back, one side for each of the official languages), more easily read, and more direct than their US counterparts. From 1993-2000, Canada had eight rotating warnings:

"Cigarettes are addictive."

"Tobacco smoke can harm your children."

"Cigarettes cause fatal lung disease."

"Cigarettes cause cancer."

"Cigarettes cause strokes and heart disease."

"Smoking during pregnancy can harm your baby."

"Smoking can kill you."

"Tobacco smoke causes fatal lung disease in non-smokers."

In 2000, Canada moved further on health warnings with approval of a government proposal to provide 16 multi-coloured, graphic pictorial warnings taking up 50 per cent of cigarette packages, front and back, in French and English, plus various other strengthened warning information. These new, graphic warnings have garnered international attention.

Just as substantial US federal regulatory efforts were being initiated in the mid-1990s, however, Canadian efforts to reduce tobacco use suffered two serious setbacks. One was the lowering of federal and provincial taxes in the smuggling crisis of 1994, discussed below. The second blow occurred in the Canadian Supreme Court decision of September 21, 1995, which overturned parts of the *Tobacco Products Control Act* dealing with advertising, trademarks, and labelling. The Court, in a narrowly argued 5-4 decision, held that such regulation was, in principle, within federal jurisdiction. It nevertheless found that some provisions of the TPCA—those concerned with banning advertising, the use of tobacco trademarks on non-nicotine products and services, and the unattributed health warnings—violated freedom of expression because they were too broad. The Court also found that there was inadequate government justification of the likely effectiveness of some provisions (Hiebert 1999). Canada suddenly found itself without a comprehensive tobacco-control policy although the TSYPA was still in force. The tobacco companies indicated that in the short term they would continue observing the disputed provisions of the TPCA, but this ended in a few months with the announcement of an industry "voluntary advertising code," which did include retaining health warnings on packages. There were, however, several documented violations of this code (Mitchell 1996).

In December 1995, Health Canada issued a blueprint for new comprehensive legislation on tobacco regulation and invited comment from interested parties. The blueprint went beyond the TPCA of 1988, including treating tobacco products similarly to hazardous products and

Table 3-6: Major Provisions of Tobacco Act, 1997 (Canada)

A. Restricting Youth Access
  1. Prohibiting of self-service displays
  2. Banning vending machine sales
  3. Banning mail-order distribution
  4. Requiring photo identification to confirm age

B. Limiting Marketing and Promotion
  1. Prohibiting advertising on radio and television, billboards, kiosks, buses, and displays at point-of-sale; information about products and brands permitted in print ads in publications with primarily adult readership (no more than 15% youth) and in direct mailings; signs pertaining to availability and price permitted at retail outlets
  2. Prohibiting misleading advertising on packages
  3. Prohibiting use of tobacco brand names or logos on non-tobacco products that are youth-oriented
  4. Sponsorships will be allowed, but limited to display of brand names and logos to bottom 10% of surface; broadcasting of events allowed; sponsorship promotions allowed in adult-readership publications and direct mailings and on site; latter subject to size and duration restrictions

C. Increasing Health Information on Packages, especially information about toxic substances and their health impacts

D. Establishing Executive Powers to Regulate Tobacco Products as science and the market evolve

drugs, a total ban on advertising, a ban on the use of tobacco trademarks on other goods and services, severe restrictions on sponsorships, a ban on mail-order and vending machine sales, restrictions on product displays, control of package designs, and authority eventually to regulate tobacco product constituents and emissions. The transfer of control over tobacco into a framework similar to that of the *Hazardous Products Act* and the *Food and Drugs Act* would be especially significant because it would put regulation of tobacco into Orders in Council, or executive orders, to meet changing conditions rather than the government having to bring forward legislation for debate. The new health minister, David Dingwall, strongly supported the legislation, and promised that the governing Liberals would pass legislation before the next election (Winsor 1997). Objections by Bloc Québécois and some Liberal MPs, especially from Quebec, about the stringency of the restrictions on sponsorship slowed the process, but the *Tobacco Act* became law in April 1997.

The final legislation (see Table 3-6), though somewhat modified, was still generally satisfactory to public-health advocates because it retained most of the provisions of the blueprint. Thus the Canadian government seemed poised to regain its former position as a leading tobacco-control regime. But other problems arose which led some observers to question how committed the federal government was to tobacco control (Callard 1997). The government was slow to announce the regulations necessary to enforce the *Tobacco Act*. Furthermore, it delayed the restrictions on sponsorship and then amended the *Tobacco Act* to exempt motor sports from some of the provisions. By 2003, however, all tobacco-company sponsorships must end. The tobacco companies again challenged the act in court.

In 1999 the federal government introduced a new plan for tobacco control: the National Tobacco Control Strategy (NTCS). This plan involves coordination of federal and provincial activities through health ministers, deputy ministers, and assistant deputy ministers (ADMs) in a public-private strategy involving the CCS, CMA, and Canadian Dental Association (CDA) as well. A steering committee of recognized experts was also created under this strategy to help develop a framework of baseline data, monitoring, and priorities in order for an annual report on progress in tobacco control. Specific goals of the NTCS include the traditional three — prevention, cessation, protection — and, for the first time, denormalization, although the latter goal was temporarily suspended in 2000. In 2001, the new Federal Tobacco Control Strategy (FTCS), provided revenues to implement four goals — prevention, cessation, protection, and harm reduction rather than denormalization.

Phase Five: United States, Finance

Despite the federal deficit problems of the 1980s and 1990s and various proposals to increase cigarette taxes dramatically, in the United States federal taxation has continued to lag far behind both the rate of inflation and

Table 3-7: Global Cigarette Taxes and Prices, March 2000

Average Retail Cigarette Price and Total Taxes per Pack
(US Dollars/Pack), Selected Countries, March 1st, 2000

Country	Price	Total Taxes	Tax Incidence
United Kingdom	5.32	4.58	86%
Ireland	4.54	3.63	80%
United States (Highest – New York)	4.17	1.67	40%
Sweden	4.14	2.90	70%
Denmark	3.91	3.20	82%
Canada (Highest – Newfoundland)	3.68	2.76	75%
Finland	3.59	2.73	76%
United States (Lowest – Kentucky)	2.88	0.58	20%
France	2.87	2.18	76%
Germany	2.61	1.85	71%
Belgium	2.54	1.90	75%
Netherlands	2.36	1.70	72%
Austria	2.25	1.67	74%
Canada (Lowest – Ontario)	2.19	1.25	57%
Greece	1.89	1.38	73%
Italy	1.85	1.39	75%
Portugal	1.69	1.35	80%
Spain	1.63	1.16	71%

Notes: All figures given in US dollars, for equivalent of 20-cigarette pack in
most popular price category. Tax incidence refers to the portion of the total
retail price made up of applicable taxes and fees, including excise, sales,
VAT, etc. Exchange rates as of March 1st, 2000. *Sources:* Smoking and
Health Action Foundation, European Union, Tobacco Institute, Canadian
Department of Finance (estimate).

the taxes imposed by other industrialized countries. Since 1951 there have
been only three modest federal tax increases on cigarettes, two of them
involving delays in implementation: 8 cents in 1982 (begun in 1983), 8
cents again in 1989 (phased in at 4 cents each in 1991 and 1993), and 15
cents in 1997 (10 cents in 2000 and 5 cents in 2002). Altogether, federal and
state taxes in the US accounted for only 30.5 per cent of the price of cigarettes in 1997, compared to 48.7 per cent in 1955 (Tobacco Institute 1997:

259). Even if one considers the cost of the Master Settlement Agreement as a disguised tax increase, the US continues to tax cigarettes at a relatively low rate, as Table 3-7 shows. Proposals for substantial increases in federal cigarette taxes, notably the 75-cent-per-pack increase as part of President Clinton's National Health Security Plan in 1993 and an increase of $1.25 per pack in the National Settlement, have foundered with the collapse of those bills. In both instances, these plans were portrayed by their opponents as major tax increases that would fuel wasteful government projects. Therefore, attempts by anti-tobacco groups since the early 1990s to increase US federal taxes to anywhere near world levels have largely foundered, although more modest tax increases have occurred.

US federal agricultural policy traditionally has subsidized farmers to grow tobacco at a guaranteed price as long as they stick to their federal quota allotment. Despite changes in the program in 1982 designed to reduce the cost to the federal government (White 1988), the basic policy has continued even in the wake of more recent agricultural reforms (Lugar 1998). US tobacco farmers have been losing ground to foreign-grown leaf, a process that has accelerated in recent years. Not only has the percentage of tobacco in US cigarettes been reduced by approximately one-third since 1960, but imported tobacco now accounts for almost half of the tobacco in US-produced cigarettes. In 1993 the US lost its position as the leading exporter of tobacco leaf to Brazil. Because of these developments, tobacco acreage shrank by almost 25 per cent in the late 1990s (US Department of Health and Human Services 2000b: 296). Tobacco farmers have been reduced substantially in numbers and increasingly have become disgruntled with the industry on which they have depended for their livelihood. In fact, one of the major concerns of tobacco-producing states and their representatives in Congress has been to get the industry to provide transitional assistance to tobacco farmers. The National Settlement was modified during Senate consideration for such aid (see Table 3-2) and, although not part of the original MSA, was later added to that agreement ("Tobacco Fund for Farmers" 1999). Some tobacco-growing states have used their MSA money for this purpose as well (Gibson 2000). Nevertheless, some farmers have sued the industry for price collusion in buying leaf from growers.

While the US government has continued to subsidize tobacco farmers, some observers argue that the subsidies both raise the price of tobacco and limit the amount grown; removing them might have the opposite effects, thus making cigarettes more affordable (White 1988). Nevertheless, most anti-tobacco advocates continue to demand an end to public subsidies of tobacco growing, hoping that its elimination would lead to a weakened political constituency for tobacco (*Final Report of the Advisory Committee on Tobacco Policy and Public Health* 1997; US Department of Health and Human Services 2000b: 306). While here has been no major federal government attempt to find substitute crops or employment for tobacco growers, in the latter stages of his administration President Clinton did appoint a Commission to Protect Tobacco Farmers and Their Communities to Promote Public Health. The Commission's major recommendation in its 2001 report was a federal cigarette tax increase of 17 cents per pack to fund a federal buyout of tobacco growers ("Panel Urges Tobacco Regs, Cigarette Tax Hike," 2001).

Phase Five: Canada, Finance

By 1985 the Non-Smokers' Rights Association was making other Canadian public-health groups aware of US research on the effect of price elasticity on the demand for tobacco. These groups began a successful lobbying effort at both the federal and provincial levels for increases in taxation as a way to reduce cigarette consumption. Even though the *ad valorem* system was ended in 1985, federal tobacco taxes were increased substantially. Major tax increases on cigarettes also occurred in 1989 and 1991, raising federal taxes by 60 and 80 per cent, respectively. Despite the several major tax increases on tobacco in the 1981-93 period, when adjusted for inflation and disposable income tobacco still was cheaper in 1993 than in 1949 (Cunningham 1996: 121). Nevertheless, the tobacco companies did not view a rapid federal tax increase of 360 per cent (from C$0.42 to C$1.93) from 1985-93 favourably and expressed those views to the government on several occasions (Cunningham 1996). The Mulroney government, however, was more concerned with deficit reduction and, eventually, with reducing teenage smoking than with placating the industry. By 1994 Canadian federal and provincial taxes accounted for an average of almost 70 per cent of the cost of cigarettes. Canada had also experienced impressive reductions in smoking, largely attributed to the rapid increase in taxation (Kaiserman and Rogers 1991).

By early 1994 the average price of a package of 20 cigarettes was over twice as high in Canada as in bordering states in the US. Even though Canadian-blend cigarettes have only a small share of the market in the

United States, they could be exported legaly there without incurring Canadian domestic taxes. As prices rose in Canada, exports of Canadian cigarettes to the United States rose from less than three billion in 1990 to seven billion in 1991, ten billion in 1992, and 18 billion in 1993, constituting fully one third of the total Canadian output (Cunningham 1996:126). Supposedly the bulk of these cigarettes was to be shipped to markets in Eastern Europe. Actually, however, these Canadian cigarettes were being smuggled back into Canada through Native reserves, especially the Mohawk Akwesasne reserve on the border between New York state and the two most populous Canadian provinces, Ontario and Quebec. These cigarettes were eventually resold at about half the legal, taxed price. It was estimated that up to two thirds of the cigarettes sold in Quebec in early 1994 were contraband. Public health had become intertwined with questions of tax revenues, law and order, treatment of aboriginal peoples, and Quebec politics.

By February 1994, the problem had reached a crescendo, and the new federal Liberal government headed by Prime Minister Jean Chrétien, urged on by a Quebec Liberal government expecting a tough provincial election against the secessionist Parti Québécois later in the year, decided to combat the smuggling problem. The federal government rejected calls from several provincial health ministers, the public-health community, and anti-tobacco activists for the reimposition of a severe but short-lived cigarette export tax that the previous Conservative government briefly had employed to combat smuggling in 1992. The widespread suspicion was that the federal Liberals did not want to take action that might cost tobacco-related jobs in Quebec during the period before the provincial election. Instead, the two Liberal governments, federal and Quebec, formulated a complicated plan to lower overall tobacco taxes substantially through matching federal and provincial tax cuts, which put pressure on other provinces vulnerable to smuggling to do the same. Over vehement protests in the provincial cabinet, Ontario and all other provincial governments eastward grudgingly agreed to lower taxes (Newfoundland lowered taxes only in the part of Labrador near the Quebec border). A small export tax was also included to placate health-conscious interests, along with other measures to combat smoking. Effectively, this was a 50-per-cent cut in the price of cigarettes in the participating provinces. This led to a plateau in smoking reduction and, by some estimates, an increase in smoking, especially among youth (see Figure 3-1) (Cunningham 1996:16; Callard 1997; Hamilton et al. 1997).

Figure 3-1: Smoking Prevalence, Canada and the United States

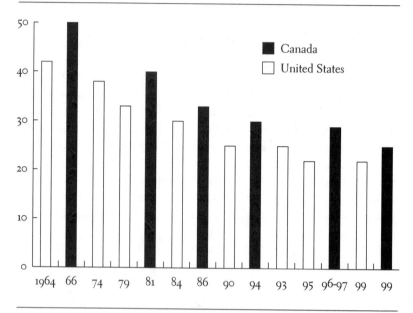

Sources: World Health Organization 1997; Nathanson 1999; National
Population Health Survey 1999, Centers for Disease Control and
Prevention 1997; Canada Tobacco Use Monitoring Survey 1999

In subsequent years, in sharp contrast to the situation in 1994, the cost
of cigarettes in Ontario and Quebec became lower than in any other
province or any US state, due to increases in prices and taxes in the United
States, even though some of the 1994 reductions were restored. In the wake
of the Master Settlement Agreement leading to price increases on US
cigarettes (an average of 33 per cent in the first year alone), the price gap
between the eastern provinces of Canada and their US neighbours
widened (see Figure 3-2). A major stumbling block to effective corrective
action has been the attitude of the Conservative government of Ontario,
which, unlike its federal counterparts in the 1980s, sees tobacco taxes not
as a "cash cow" but as just another form of taxation, to be avoided if
possible.

In an attempt to mollify anti-tobacco forces, at the same time as the
1994 tax reduction was announced the Chrétien government introduced
the Tobacco Demand Reduction Strategy (TDRS), a three-year program
of legislation, research, and public education designed, with the help of

Figure 3-2: Cigarette Prices Along the US-Canada Border, April 2001

Average price of a carton of 200 cigarettes
Provinces and US border states (in CAN $) April 2001.

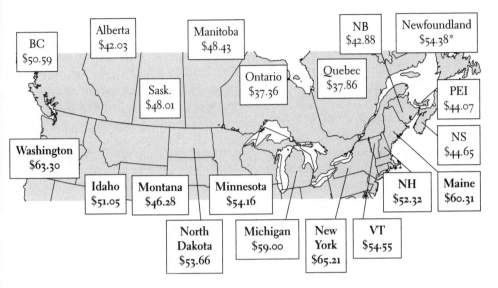

Notes: Canadian data based on federal estimates. US data taken from *The Tax Burden on Tobacco,* 1997, adjusted for price increases due to litigation settlement and subsequent tax increases. At April 4, 2001 exchange rate: $1 US = $1.5694 CAN. Prices include all state, provincial, and federal taxes. Local sales taxes and tobacco taxes in the US are excluded.
* Lower taxes are in effect in part of Labrador.
Source: Smoking and Health Action Foundation, Ottawa.

provincial and local governments and health voluntary organizations, to reduce smoking in Canada. In order to finance these programs, a profits surtax was levied on the Canadian tobacco companies. The revenue from this surtax, which was renewed in 1997 for three additional years, originally generated a plethora of programs; subsequently, however, the revenues for the TDRS were cut substantially in the interests of deficit reduction (Pechmann, Dixon and Layne 1998).

As part of a coordinated program of tobacco control announced in April 2001, the new Federal Tobacco Strategy is to provide C$480 million over five years to fund anti-tobacco campaigns. At the same time, federal and provincial taxes were raised in Ontario, Quebec, and the Maritimes, a two-tiered export tax based on volume was introduced, the surtax on tobacco-company profits was raised from 40 to 50 per cent, and Canadian cigarettes in duty-free shops were taxed.

The Canadian Senate twice has passed bills, sponsored by Senator Colin Kenny, explicitly modelled on US precedents in California and Massachusetts, for a fund to combat teenage smoking, financed by a levy on tobacco company sales (Kenny 1999). The first, Bill S-13, was ruled out of order by the Speaker of the House of Commons in 1999 because all revenue bills must originate in the Commons, not the Senate. A recrafted bill, S-20, passed the Senate in 2000 but died when the federal election was called for November, 2000. In early 2001, Senator Kenny introduced the third version of this bill, S-15, in the new parliamentary session. Some observers have seen these bills as "stalking horses" to put pressure on the federal government to increase its financial commitment to tobacco control, which was finally announced, as noted above, in the FTCS in early 2001.

In late 1999 the federal government announced it was going to take RJR-Macdonald (now JTI Macdonald) and the Canadian Tobacco Manufacturers' Council to court in the United States, where damage awards can be much larger, for complicity in illegal smuggling activities that cost the government revenue in the early 1990s. Previously, some officers of an offshoot of RJR in the United States, Northern Brands, had been found guilty in US courts of criminal activities in smuggling Canadian cigarettes back across the border at that time (Marsden 1999). This suit was disallowed in the US federal court on technical grounds in 2000, and an appeal was rejected. It may be re-filed in a Canadian court.

As part of the government's comprehensive tobacco-control policy and to assist passage of the *Tobacco Products Control Act*, the Tobacco Diversification Plan was announced in 1987 to provide financial compensation to farmers exiting tobacco production and to aid in developing alternatives to tobacco agriculture. These programs have had some success in reducing the number of farmers dependent on tobacco (see Table 1-3) (Cunningham, 1996). While there is no concerted effort to drastically reduce tobacco agriculture in Canada, there is little indication of substantial public support for continued economic subsidies to tobacco growers, in contrast to the United States where their problems generate more sympathetic government policies at both federal and state levels.

The Course of Federal Policy on Tobacco: A Summary Comparison

In comparing Canadian and US federal policy on tobacco control over the past 40 years, there are three distinct eras within the two general phases, as noted in Table 1-1. In the first, 1964-84, Canada followed its usual proclivities for taking leads on health matters from the United States; it also followed a traditional British and Canadian preference for voluntary arrangements if possible as an enforcement mechanism. This is what might be termed "Situation Normal." There were two distinct but related periods during phase five. In the first, 1984-94, Canada, contrary to the usual relationship described in Chapter Two, became "the mouse that roared," a policy leader in tobacco control not only in North America but also in world terms through increased regulation, substantial tax increases, and even the encouragement of alternatives to tobacco farming. Despite there being a large impact on agenda setting, and some policy being enacted, US federal policy adoption was relatively circumspect in comparison to its northern neighbour. As will be seen in Chapter Four, however, US states and localities took considerably more action during this period. In the third period, 1994-2001, the two countries converged in their policies at both the federal and lower levels, with both having achievements and failures. If Canada's previous international leadership role in tobacco control has been compromised somewhat, the position of the United States in tobacco control has risen, despite some setbacks such as Congressional rejection of the National Settlement and the Supreme Court overruling FDA authority. Although overall Canada may have a more comprehensive policy currently, increases in cigarette prices (even if mostly not incurred directly through taxation), continued legal assaults on the industry's position, and local capacity-building have given the US a more prominent profile in tobacco control. Thus the two countries have converged in tobacco-control policies in recent years while still not being identical. The process became one of "leapfrogging" between the two countries in tobacco-control matters, especially when the different jurisdictional levels are considered.

4

Tobacco Control in States, Provinces, and Municipalities: The California Effect?

"Our record in defeating state smoking restrictions has been reasonably good. Unfortunately our record with respect to local measures ... has been somewhat less encouraging.... Over time, we can lose the battle over smoking restrictions just as decisively in bits and pieces—at the local level—as with state or federal measures." (Pritchard 1986, as quoted in US Department of Health and Human Services 2000b: 52)

"We are here to announce what we think is ... the most historic public health agreement in history." Mike Moore, Attorney General of Mississippi, June 20, 1997 (Mollenkamp et al. 1998: 231)

"A total of 41 states have sought the anti-smoking advice of California's Department of Health Services, which also counsels Ireland, Australia and Canada. The World Health Organization has used California's work as a model of anti-smoking propaganda elsewhere around the globe." ("Smoking: Just Say No," Economist, December 9, 2000)

Introduction

In Canada and the United States, tobacco control, both regulation and taxation, is a multi-level issue. Actions by US state attorneys general in the National Settlement and Master Settlement Agreement with tobacco companies for recovery of state health care costs, the decisions of US juries in state court lawsuits by individuals against tobacco companies, local controversies over ETS requirements on both sides of the border, and restrictive tobacco-control policies pursued by the Ontario, Quebec, and British Columbia governments in Canada are examples. Authority is divided not only between the federal government and the state or provincial governments, but also between the states or provinces and local governments.

States and provinces differ in size, economic dependence on tobacco growing and manufacturing, smoking rates, susceptibility to smuggling activities, tax rates on tobacco products, and the nature of regulations on tobacco. There are considerable similarities in the political processes used to enact tobacco control within each country, as outlined in Chapter One. There is, however, one major political difference in the authority of lower levels of government in the two countries. Unlike the United States (Fritschler and Hoefler 1996), Canadian provinces are not constrained by a pre-emptive federal law for health warnings on cigarette packages. Instead, Canadian federal law has remained permissive; provinces can undertake any legislation or regulation that is more stringent than federal actions.

The focus of this chapter is on comparative state/provincial/local analysis of two dimensions of tobacco policy: taxation and non-tax regulations. States, provinces, and local governments have been particularly active in tobacco control in taxes, sales regulations (especially minors' access to tobacco products), advertising, and regulation of environmental tobacco smoke. There is wide variation among the 50 states and District of Columbia in taxation and other regulation of tobacco products, which will continue for the foreseeable future. Variation among the ten Canadian provinces and their municipalities is more limited. This chapter describes and analyzes, in general terms, the policy adoptions and trends in tobacco control that have occurred across US states, Canadian provinces, and local governments in both countries. In addition to broad coverage of comparability and trends, some consideration will be given to which jurisdictions are leaders and laggards at each level. Although some attention is given to possible explanations for these findings, most of this analysis will occur in Chapters Five and Six. More specific information on the policy process, adoption, implementation, and evaluation of the success of tobacco-control policies in particular states and provinces is available elsewhere (Glantz and Balbach 2000; Studlar 1998, 2000; National Cancer Institute 2000).

Table 4-1: Cigarette Smoking by States
Among Adults Aged 18 and Older, 1999

State	Prevalence	State	Prevalence
Alabama	23.5	Missouri	27.1
Alaska	27.2	Montana	20.2
Arizona	20.1	Nebraska	23.3
Arkansas	27.2	Nevada	31.5
California	18.7	New Hampshire	22.4
Colorado	22.5	New Jersey	20.7
Connecticut	22.8	New Mexico	22.5
Delaware	25.4	New York	21.9
District of Columbia	20.6	North Carolina	25.2
Florida	20.7	North Dakota	22.2
Georgia	23.7	Ohio	27.6
Hawaii	18.6	Oklahoma	25.2
Idaho	21.5	Oregon	21.5
Illinois	24.2	Pennsylvania	23.2
Indiana	27.0	Rhode Island	22.4
Iowa	23.5	South Carolina	23.6
Kansas	21.1	South Dakota	22.5
Kentucky	29.7	Tennessee	24.9
Louisiana	23.6	Texas	22.4
Maine	23.3	Utah	13.9
Maryland	20.3	Vermont	21.8
Massachusetts	19.4	Virginia	21.2
Michigan	25.1	Washington	22.4
Minnesota	19.5	West Virginia	27.1
Mississippi	23.0	Wisconsin	23.7
		Wyoming	23.9

Median   22.8

Source: Behavioral Risk Factor Surveillance, Centers for Disease Control and Prevention

Table 4-2: Cigarette Smoking by Provinces, Ages 15+, 1996-97

British Columbia	26
Alberta	29
Saskatchewan	30
Manitoba	27
Ontario	26
Quebec	34
New Brunswick	29
Nova Scotia	33
Prince Edward Island	33
Newfoundland	32

Source: National Population Health Survey (1996-97)

The Context: Tobacco, Economics, and Health Across States and Provinces

As indicated in Chapter One, tobacco consumption has declined by about 50 per cent nationally in both Canada and the United States since 1964. While the decline has been broadly proportional across states and provinces, differences remain. Table 4-1 shows recent smoking indicators across states and Table 4-2 across provinces. The US Centers for Disease Control and Prevention (US Department of Health and Human Services 2001) has documented adult smoking rates in the country, ranging from 13.9 per cent in Utah to 31.5 per cent in Nevada.

Recent smoking rates across the provinces are indicated in Table 4-2. Despite the reputation of residents of Quebec as "champion smokers," perhaps the most striking feature of this table is the relatively low variation in smoking rates among Canadian provinces, especially compared with those in the United States. There is only an eight-per-cent difference in smoking rates between the lowest (British Columbia and Ontario) and the highest (Quebec). Furthermore, Quebec is barely above Nova Scotia, Prince Edward Island, and Newfoundland. Generally, the provinces east of the Ottawa River (separating Quebec and Ontario) have higher rates than the Western provinces, but the differences are not stark.

As noted previously in Chapter One, tobacco agriculture is heavily concentrated in both the United States and Canada. Table 4-3 shows, as of 1997, the 17 tobacco-producing states in the US (cash receipts of at least $1

Table 4-3: US State Tobacco Agriculture, 1997 (US dollars)

State	Cash Receipts From Tobacco (millions)
Alabama	1.7
Connecticut	13.9
Florida	32.3
Georgia	158.4
Indiana	26.0
Kentucky	730.1
Maryland	18.1
Massachusetts	4.3
Missouri	10.9
North Carolina	1,193.2
Ohio	28.9
Pennsylvania	25.2
South Carolina	213.3
Tennessee	227.7
Virginia	190.8
West Virginia	3.3
Wisconsin	7.5
Summary	2,885.6

Source: Economic Research Service, U.S.D.A.

million). The six leading producers—North Carolina, Kentucky, Tennessee, South Carolina, Virginia, and Georgia—accounted for 94 per cent of total agricultural receipts, with the first two alone comprising 66.7 per cent (see Table 4-3). US tobacco companies have increasingly relied on cheaper foreign production of crop in recent years.

The major profits in tobacco are not in cultivation but in the manufacture of tobacco products (see Table 4-4). There are 19 states engaged in some form of manufacturing. Only one state, New York, is high in manufacturing without having a substantial agricultural sector, and only one state with a large agricultural sector, South Carolina, is not important in manufacturing. The five largest manufacturing states—North Carolina, Virginia, Georgia, Kentucky, and New York—have 96.7 per cent of this sector in the United States.

Table 4-4: US State Tobacco Manufacturing, 1996 (US Dollars)

State	Cash Receipts From Tobacco (millions)
Alabama	41.0
California	3.0
Connecticut	105.0
Florida	116.0
Georgia	3,038.0
Illinois	84.0
Indiana	5.0
Kentucky	2,692.0
Missouri	2.0
Nevada	4.0
New Jersey	1.0
New York	1,520.0
North Carolina	9,754.0
Pennsylvania	46.0
South Carolina	2.0
Tennessee	337.0
Texas	11.0
Virginia	6,132.0
West Virginia	34.0
Summary	23,927.0

Source: Economic Research Service, U.S.D.A.

In Canada, tobacco agriculture and manufacturing are concentrated in the two largest provinces, but each has its own specialization. Tobacco agriculture is dominant in Ontario, but manufacturing is a more important part of the economy in Quebec. The part of southwestern Ontario near Lake Erie is the major tobacco-growing region in Canada, with over 90 per cent of the national total produced there (Cunningham 1996: 180). Not unexpectedly, Ontario tobacco-belt MPs have been some of the most critical of federal tobacco-control legislation, even of their own parties.

The three major Canadian tobacco companies—Imperial Tobacco Ltd., Rothmans, Benson & Hedges, Inc., and JTI-Macdonald, Inc. (formerly RJR-Macdonald, Inc.)—maintain their major manufacturing facilities in Quebec rather than Ontario although they also have offices in Toronto. Imperial also has manufacturing capacity in Guelph, Ontario, although the number of employees there is dwarfed by the number in Quebec.

Thus there are six southern US states that, because of the relatively high share of their economy in tobacco agriculture and, with one exception, industry, constitute what is often called "the tobacco states." Yet neither Ontario nor Quebec can be characterized as a tobacco province because tobacco does not play a major role in the Ontario economy and Quebec lacks a significant agricultural sector.

Regulating and Taxing Tobacco in the States and Provinces: An Overview

As noted in Chapter One, many US states made some attempt to control tobacco consumption around the turn of the century. Not only bans on sales to minors, but also prohibitions on manufacturing and sales to adults were common. This was a time in which other personal vices with social effects such as drinking and gambling were under concerted attack as well (Meier 1994). By the 1920s, however, the forces for increased tobacco usage, especially cigarettes, were winning, and states moved from the attempt to ban tobacco, even for adults, toward taxing it. State and local regulations, insofar as they existed, were largely concerned with issues of fire safety and contamination of food. In Canada, the provinces had never entered into regulation except on these limited grounds, and even taxing cigarettes, a substantial federal revenue source, was delayed in a majority of the provinces until the 1960s. As on the federal level in both countries, however, that passive orientation changed with the Surgeon General's Report in 1964, but more quickly in the US than in Canada.

One can divide phases four and five of tobacco-control policy into three rough eras on the state and provincial level, which overlap but do not coincide in all respects with the eras outlined on the federal level in Chapter Three (see Table 4-5). In each of these eras, there was considerable variation among the states, provinces, and municipalities in both regulation and taxation, but the general descriptions hold.

Immediately after the Surgeon General's 1964 report, some US states and municipalities were poised to take action against tobacco advertising (Kluger 1996), but they were frustrated by the federal pre-emption provisions in the 1965 *Cigarette Labeling and Advertising Act.* Thereafter, states

Table 4-5: Eras of State, Provincial, and Local Tobacco Control

1964-1973	States Frustrated, Municipalities and Provinces Lag
1973-1986	States and Municipalities Increase Regulation; Provinces Increase Taxation
1986-2000	Intensification of Tobacco-Control Struggle in States, Provinces, and Municipalities

engaged in educational campaigns but few regulations on tobacco use were passed until Arizona and Minnesota passed the first laws concerning environmental tobacco smoke in 1973 and 1974, respectively. Because of lack of enforcement, previously legislated youth access provisions were sometimes repealed (US Department of Health and Human Services 2000b: 34). In taxation, however, the decade after the report of the Surgeon General's Advisory Committee saw "an unprecedented flurry of excise tax activity" (Warner 1981: 142), averaging 12 increases per year from 1964 to 1972. The gap between the low-taxing tobacco-producing states and others, already growing in the 1950s, widened, producing a smuggling problem that temporarily halted the tax increases (Warner 1981: 141-43). Only one Canadian province, British Columbia, took major regulatory action against tobacco in this era; others were just catching up to the well-established US practice of special taxes on tobacco products, mainly cigarettes. Provincial taxes in Canada remained low, although by 1974 all provinces and territories had such taxes.

The Arizona and Minnesota ETS statutes led into a second era of greater policy activity on the state and local level in the US, especially restrictions on smoking in public places (Warner 1981). But even more activity, especially in the form of ETS restrictions, occurred on the local level in the US. Anti-smoking groups, especially GASP in California, found that level of government more congenial because tobacco company political influence was less likely. Berkeley passed the first major local ETS restrictions in 1977 (Nathanson 1999). Similar movements elsewhere gave local governments a reputation as the strongest anti-tobacco jurisdictions in the US, followed by the states. The relatively weak efforts of the US federal government in regulation and taxation out it in third place. State taxation efforts slowed in this period although they began to be reinvigorated in the mid-1980s (Warner 1981: 142-43; US Department of Health and Human Services 1990: 74).

Meanwhile, in Canada some provinces and a few scattered municipalities, led by Ottawa in 1976, began to take minimal regulatory actions, but in this dimension of policy there was still general deference to federal leadership in Health and Welfare Canada, which focussed on educational policies. In taxation the provinces also followed the federal lead, but this led to substantial tobacco tax increases beginning in the early 1980s. Overall this era showed accelerating state and local leadership in tobacco control in the US with continued federal leadership in Canada.

Growth of the healthy public policy orientation and the 1986 Surgeon General's Report on the effects of second-hand smoke gave renewed impetus to tobacco-control movements (US Department of Health and Human Services 2000b: 19; *Tobacco Use: An American Crisis* 1993: 3-6). In 1985, there were approximately 800 state and local tobacco-control measures; two years later there were over 1,500. In 1986 there were some 400 state laws in effect; one year later there were almost 600 (US Department of Health and Human Services 1990: 7).

In the third era, 1986-2000, states, provinces, and municipalities assumed more prominent roles in tobacco control, but not without considerable struggle and some setbacks. Building on the achievements of the previous era, US states and municipalities consolidated and in some respects advanced their previous policies although there was increasing variation, especially in taxation and in local-level regulations. California and Massachusetts led the way with comprehensive tobacco-control programs funded through dedicated tax revenues adopted in statewide referenda. The formulation of the National Settlement and the MSA showed the degree to which tobacco-control policy leadership in the United States was dependent on the states rather than on the federal government. In Canada, both the provinces and municipalities belatedly began to take advantage of the opportunities afforded them, especially in regulation. Yet there still remain wide variations. In both countries a few states, provinces, and municipalities have emerged, mainly in this era, as exemplars for "best practices" in tobacco control. In some instances these practices have spread not only to other municipalities, states, and provinces, but also to the federal government, sometimes on both sides of the border.

STATE AND PROVINCIAL
TOBACCO CONTROL: REGULATION

State regulations on tobacco sales and cigarette usage vary widely. Even in those states where public officials have been reluctant to join the anti-tobacco crusade, however, there are some laws limiting tobacco sales, advertising, or environmental tobacco smoke. For example, 49 states have enacted at least one law on ETS, 46 have some form of vending machine restrictions, 36 states restrict product samples, 36 have a retail licensing requirement to sell cigarettes (but four have no penalties for violations), 33 states have tobacco-related school health programs, 18 restrict out-of-package sales in some fashion, and 11 have advertising restrictions (Shelton et al. 1995; Fishman et al. 1999; Chriqui 2000). This does not include these administrative initiatives aimed at reducing tobacco usage which do not need legislative approval. Thirty states have pre-emption provisions of some sort preventing local laws stronger than the state law, a major means for tobacco companies to combat restrictive local laws (US Department of Health and Human Services 2000b: 55).

US state regulations on tobacco have become more frequent and more restrictive, especially over the past quarter-century. Laws restricting minors' access have a long history. Early legislation also limited smoking in the interests of fire protection and food safety. Even before the 1964 Surgeon General's Report, there were laws restricting smoking in certain areas; in 1970, 14 states had such laws. The movement for more restrictive laws to protect the safety and comfort of nonsmokers accelerated in the 1970s and 1980s. By 1986, when the US Surgeon General's Report *Effects of Involuntary Smoking* was released, the number of states with laws restricting smoking in some public places had increased to 42, from five in 1972, and the average restrictiveness of laws had increased by 2.5 times in a 15-year span (Warner 1981; US Department of Health and Human Services 1986: 26). While less extensive, regulation of smoking in the workplace in the US also grew from Minnesota's pioneering statute in 1974; by 1985 nine states had such laws. Under the impetus of state laws and public opinion inimical to smoking, more private employers also enacted restrictions (US Department of Health and Human Services 1986: 27-28). By 1998, the cumulative number of state laws and amendments on ETS in public places had reached almost 300, but similar legislation for workplaces and restaurants has been stagnant since the early 1990s (US

Department of Health and Human Services 2000b: 200). Four US states—California, Vermont, Maine, and Utah—ban smoking in restaurants.

Despite the early twentieth-century laws on youth access, by mid-century enforcement was lacking and licensing of tobacco vendors was mainly a revenue measure. In the late 1980s, however, local attempts to enforce youth access laws and some associated research demonstrated that underage youth could make purchases in an overwhelming majority of attempts (Forster and Wolfson 1998). The 1989 US Surgeon General's report concluded that there were fewer youth access laws than in the previous quarter-century, and in 1990 the Office of the Inspector General found little enforcement among the 44 states with such provisions. Prompted by the increasing focus on youth access issues, states as well as the federal government and localities began to undertake further actions (US Department of Health and Human Services 2000b: 34). This represented a shift from the previous demand-side strategies to a supply-side strategy, and one which tobacco companies found difficult to oppose, at least initially.

Because of the preemption provisions of the 1965 and 1970 federal cigarette labelling and advertising laws, states have been reluctant to become involved in advertising restrictions. Nevertheless, state and local laws in this area have sometimes been upheld by the courts, especially if it can be demonstrated that they were adopted on grounds other than the relationship of smoking to health. Utah's 1973 law banning most forms of tobacco advertising has never been challenged in court. Massachusetts has been perhaps the most aggressive state in pursuing labelling and advertising restrictions. It was the first state to require warnings on smokeless tobacco products (1985), the second state to require cigar warnings (1999), the first state to limit advertising near schools (1999), and the first state to require disclosure of cigarette additives (1999). The latter two policies were challenge in federal courts, and in 2001 the US Supreme Court overturned the advertising ban. In 1997, 13 states had some form of advertising restrictions (Fishman et al. 1999). The MSA contained various forms of advertising restrictions, as outlined in Tables 3-2 and 3-4, but also allowed several loopholes.

In the 1995-98 period, five states strengthened their ETS regulations, 11 states added teeth to minors' access laws, eight made vending machines inaccessible to minors, and four passed laws restricting advertising (Fishman et al.1999). These initiatives reflected the continuing trend toward an emphasis on youth access questions, also found in federal

Table 4-6: **Summary of Canadian Provincial Tobacco Regulations, 1999**

	BC	AB	SK	MB	ON	QC	NB	NS	PE	NF
Age Restrictions (Sales)	19	18 (F)	16	18	19	18	19	19	19	19
Signage on sales age	■	F	F	F	■	■	■	■	■	■
Signage on health warning	■	F	F	F	■	■	■	■		■
Vending Machines banned					■		■			
Vending Machines restricted	F	F	F	F		■	F			
Self-service displays banned	F	F	F	F		■	■	■	F	F
Counter-top displays banned					F		■	■	F	F
Minimum # in cigarette package	20				20	20	15	20	15	15
Pharmacy sales banned					■	■	■	■		
Ad restrictions	■					■				
Sponsorship restrictions	■					■				
Reporting requirements (various)	■				■	■				
Manufacturer licensing	■									
Manufacturer fee	■									
Health care cost recovery lawsuit	■					■				
Price controls	■									

Table 4-6 continued: Summary of Canadian Provincial Tobacco Regulations, 1999

	BC	AB	SK	MB	ON	QC	NB	NS	PE	NF
Smoking restricted, private workplaces	■				■	■				■
Smoking restricted, public places	■		■	■	■	■				■
Smoking banned, government workplaces	■		■	■	■	■	■	■		■
Smoking restricted, government workplaces		■		■		■			■	
Smoking banned, restaurants						■				
Smoking banned, bars	■									
Smoking banned, schools	■			■	■	■				■

F = Federal

Sources: Cunningham (1999); National Clearinghouse on Tobacco and Health (1999).

programs and the 1996 founding of the National Center for Tobacco-Free Kids.

In response to increased tobacco regulation at the US state and local levels in the 1980s, tobacco companies began a strategy of pre-emption through weak state statutes. With tobacco consumption under political challenge at all levels of government in the United States, many municipalities have passed more stringent tobacco-control measures. If a state adopts a pre-emption statute, however, local governments cannot exceed the state-mandated standard. Thirty states have pre-emption laws of some variety, usually in regard to indoor air or youth access. Pre-emption has become a major strategy for the industry, leading to some acrimonious state legislative battles (Mintz 1996). Although achieving considerable success in the first decade, more recent pre-emption attempts have been stymied (National Cancer Institute 2000: 52-56).

Despite the Surgeon General's 1964 report and growing concerns about the health consequences of tobacco use, until the 1990s most Canadian provinces simply followed the federal lead in regulation. The provinces were consulted about possible federal legislation in 1970-71 and endorsed it. When no federal legislation emerged, however, only British Columbia responded with its own legislation—on advertising, health warnings, and sales to minors—in 1971 and 1972. Documents from Health and Welfare Canada (1977, 1983) indicate that the federal government continued to consult the provinces, along with professional and voluntary organizations, about policy and strategy, but there was general deference to federal leadership. Only at the time of the TPCA did some provinces began to enact regulatory legislation, but most did not become active until later.

As in the United States, provincial laws regarding tobacco vary considerably, but now some have moved beyond federal requirements. Table 4-6 shows that the minimum age for purchase in Canadian provinces is normally higher than in US states. Six provinces have a minimum age of 19, one year more than the federal government. Only two US states have a minimum age of 19, despite a federal DHSS recommendation for such a requirement in 1990; subsequently two states have reduced their ages from 20 and 21 to 18. Limiting minors' access to cigarettes through signage and restrictions on product size and placement are popular in Canada, with a majority of the provinces engaged in such activity. Two provinces ban vending machines. As in the US, retail compliance rates for not selling to minors vary considerably across the provinces; a recent study found rates from 42 to 83 per cent (Nielsen 1999).

There are bans on pharmacy sales in five provinces, reporting requirements in three, advertising and sponsorship restrictions in two, and price controls in two. Recently British Columbia embarked on a unique regime combining reporting requirements, manufacturer licensing fees, and legal action for medical care cost recovery, which finances an anti-smoking campaign based on the California and Massachusetts models. Quebec's 1998 law provides more stringent terms for the phasing out of tobacco company event sponsorship than those of the federal government.

ETS restrictions also vary considerably by province. Smoking is banned or restricted in government workplaces in every province. Six provinces restrict smoking in public places, but only five ban it in schools, four restrict it in private workplaces, and two have attempted to ban it in restaurants. British Columbia's attempt to prohibit smoking in bars was overturned by a court decision in 2000 but is being reformulated.

Based on the number of policies in Table 4-6, overall British Columbia would probably qualify as the leading tobacco regulatory province. Some provinces, notably Ontario and British Columbia, have been very active in pursuing greater restrictions on tobacco in recent years; others have done little, apart from increasing taxation, since the 1970s. The three other Western provinces—Alberta, Saskatchewan, and Manitoba—are notable for their relatively few province-wide regulations. Despite the small number of provinces, a permissive federal law, and federal leadership through the processes of executive federalism, there is still relatively little coordinated regulatory action among the provinces, in contrast to taxation. Attempts by British Columbia and the Atlantic provinces at provincial agreement in pursuing lawsuits against tobacco companies for recovery of health care costs, after the manner of the states in the US, foundered because of opposition from the other provinces, especially Alberta. Nevertheless, Newfoundland is slowly following British Columbia's lead; Ontario sued US companies as well as those based in Canada; and Quebec and Manitoba have contemplated their own litigation against domestic tobacco companies.

STATE AND PROVINCIAL TAXATION OF CIGARETTES
AND THE SMUGGLING PROBLEM

The most persistent dimension of tobacco control has been taxation. From the perspective of both producers and consumers, making tobacco more expensive through taxation may decrease consumption, depending on the amount of the tax and related practices of producers and sellers. From the point of view of government, increased cigarette taxes normally enhance revenues, even in the face of a consumption decline. But some of this potential revenue may be lost through smuggling (contraband, bootlegging) of cigarettes from nearby jurisdictions that have lower taxes. From a public-health perspective, decreasing tobacco usage through increased taxes is desirable, whatever the effects on revenue.

"Sin taxes" are usually relatively popular since they are both selective and perceived as discouraging, or at least making people pay for, morally questionable activities (Meier 1994). But from a revenue standpoint, sin taxes have the disadvantage of not producing as large and as predictable amounts as more broadly-based taxes. Since it is a sin tax, states and provinces could more readily pursue increases in the tobacco excise tax, even in periods and areas in which general anti-tax moods prevail.

The growth in the number of states imposing an excise tax on cigarettes proceeded by increments in the United States (Warner 1981). Iowa enacted the first such tax in 1921. By 1932, 14 states had them; by 1941, 26 states; by 1951, 41 states; by 1961, 48 states and by 1969, all 50 states and the District of Columbia (Tobacco Institute 1997: 7). Except for North Carolina, the last state to enact a tax, all of the major tobacco-growing states instituted excise taxes early, an indication that the initial impetus was revenue rather than reducing consumption. Furthermore, the tobacco-growing states' tax rates did not substantially diverge from others until the 1950s (Warner 1981: 141-42). Although the nominal rates were low, the relative share of state taxation in the price of cigarettes was high, averaging nearly 50 per cent of the price until it began to drop in the mid-1970s (Warner 1981; Tobacco Institute, 1997: 259). Forty-four of 51 states (including the District of Columbia) also have an excise tax on smokeless tobacco products.

In Canada, provincial taxation of cigarettes started later and spread more slowly. It was not until 1941 that the first province, Prince Edward Island, levied a special tax on cigarettes, and other provinces were slow to follow. By 1959 only a minority of provinces had such taxes. By 1970, however, all provinces were taxing cigarettes (Friedman 1975: 79), but at a rate averaging only 50 per cent of the average in US states (Sweanor 1991: 14). In 1977 only one province, Newfoundland, taxed cigarettes at higher than the federal rate. Having tobacco taxes as a nearly exclusive resource at the time, the Canadian federal government relied on tobacco taxation for seven per cent of its receipts, versus less than two per cent of federal revenues in the US (Health and Welfare Canada 1979). Canadian provinces soon realized the potential of cigarette taxes, however, first to keep up with inflation in the 1970s and then for health purposes in the 1980s. This led to the provinces having 30-per-cent higher average cigarette taxes in 1988 than did the federal government (*Tobacco Tax Policy in Canada: A Health Perspective* 1989).

Only in 1970 did state revenue from cigarette taxes in the US surpass federal revenue, but aside from a limited impact of the federal tax increase in the mid 1980s, this relationship continued until the late 1990s (Tobacco Institute 1997: 1). While US state governments in earlier times relied heavily on cigarette and other tobacco taxes, their share of state revenues has been dropping over the years. In 1978 there were 20 states taxing tobacco products other than cigarettes; by 1996 there were 44 states imposing such taxes. Nevertheless, in those states that have other tobacco excise taxes, the cigarette tax still consistently accounts for 95 per cent of total tobacco tax revenue (Tobacco Institute, 1997).

As anti-tobacco sentiment was rising in the states in the 1980s and 1990s, tobacco tax increases accelerated. Of the 51 jurisdictions, only six states, all tobacco producers (five of them major ones), have not raised the excise tax at all since 1978—Kentucky, Virginia, Georgia, South Carolina, Tennessee, and West Virginia. The 45 others have raised taxes a total of 160 times through 2000, or an average of 3.5 times per state. In 1979 the overall average state tax was 12.9 cents, ranging from 2 cents in North Carolina to 21 cents in Massachusetts and Florida . In 2000, the average state cigarette excise tax was 41.9 cents, ranging from 2.5 cents in Virginia to $1.11 in New York. While inflation was approximately 40 per cent in the US during the 1979-2000 period, overall state cigarette excise taxes increased by over 200 per cent. If one considers the tobacco company monies paid to the states under the MSA as a tax (the companies increased prices on cigarettes to recover the costs), then the increase in tobacco taxation at the state level has been even greater. But the variation among states also has become greater over time, with tobacco-producing states extremely reluctant to tax their own product since the 1950s. Thus, despite substantial tax increases in some states, these excise taxes as a share of nominal cigarette prices decreased slightly overall from 18.8 per cent in 1960 to 17.6 per cent in 1997 before the MSA (Fishman et al. 1999: 34; *The Erosion of Federal Cigarette Taxes Over Time* 2000).

Comprehensive data on tobacco taxation in Canadian provinces exists only since 1977 and more consistently since 1984, after the coordinated

Table 4-7: Provincial Taxes on 20 Cigarettes, 1984-1999 (Canadian dollars)

Province	1984	1989	1993	1994	1999
Alberta	$0.30	$0.96	$1.40	$1.40	$1.40
British Columbia	$0.45	$1.15	$2.20	$2.20	$2.20
Manitoba	$0.52	$1.56	$1.95	$1.90	$1.93
New Brunswick	$0.59	$1.74	$1.91	$1.00	$1.02
Newfoundland	$1.19	$1.28	$2.77	$2.69	$2.60
Nova Scotia	$0.40	$1.21	$1.91	$1.00	$1.08
Ontario	$0.63	$1.01	$1.66	$0.51	$0.67
Prince Edward Island	$0.42	$0.94	$1.96	$1.04	$1.27
Quebec	$0.46	$0.90	$1.78	$0.46	$0.80
Saskatchewan	$0.54	$1.34	$2.04	$1.99	$2.00
Mean	**$0.55**	**$1.21**	**$1.96**	**$1.42**	**$1.50**

increases in federal and provincial taxation had begun (see Table 4-7). In 1977, the average of provincial-based taxes, both specific and general sales, on a package of 20 cigarettes was 14 cents, ranging from 6.4 cents in Alberta (with no provincial sales tax) to 24 cents in Newfoundland. By 1984, after the sales tax increases had begun, the average was 55 cents, ranging from 30 cents in Alberta to $1.19 in Newfoundland. Yet only three provinces had general sales taxes on cigarettes. By 1991 eight of the ten provinces had general sales taxes as well as more specific ones on cigarettes (Sweanor 1991: 23). By 1989 the average of all provincial sales taxes was $1.21, ranging from 90 cents in Prince Edward Island to $1.74 in New Brunswick. This represented a tax increase on cigarettes of over 100 per cent in just five years, on top of the huge federal tax increase, but more was to come.

By 1991 the price of a pack of cigarettes in Ontario was C$4.80, almost double the price in 1985; two-thirds of the price was due to federal and provincial taxation. After the 1991 federal tax increase, cigarette manufacturers and retailers encouraged tobacco purchasers to send pre-printed protests about taxation to their federal and provincial governments. Tobacco prices in Ontario were considerably higher than in nearby US states such as Minnesota, Michigan, and New York, where average prices ranged from C$2.19 to C$2.48 (US $1.86 to $2.12 at 1991 exchange rates), due largely to lower US state and federal taxes on tobacco (Tobacco

Institute 1997: 117). From 1984 until 1991, overall Canadian tobacco taxes had quadrupled while US taxes had increased by less than 50 per cent, resulting in Canadian taxes averaging about seven times the US level (Sweanor 1991: 25). The growth of smuggling across the Canada-US border that led to the coordinated federal-provincial tax reductions of 1994 has already been described in Chapter Three.

In the wake of the 1994 tax reductions, average provincial taxation fell from $1.96 in 1993 to $1.42 in 1994, but the disparity between the tax-cutting Eastern provinces, with the exception of Newfoundland, and the stand-pat Western provinces was evident. Even with reducing taxes in lightly-populated Labrador, Newfoundland had provincial taxes of $2.69, but the five other Eastern provinces through Ontario had an average of $0.80 while the four Western provinces had an average over twice as high, $1.87. The reductions were especially sharp in the two most populous provinces, with Ontario going from $1.66 in 1993 to 51 cents in 1994 and Quebec from $1.78 to 46 cents. Provincial government revenues from tobacco taxes, already in decline since 1991 because of massive smuggling, especially in Ontario and Quebec, were initially reduced by a further two-thirds in those two provinces, but later recovered somewhat throughout the Eastern provinces. By 1999, the average provincial taxation was $1.50 overall, with Newfoundland at $2.60, Western provinces at $1.88, and the remaining Eastern provinces at 97 cents. Ontario had risen to 67 cents and Quebec to 80 cents, still less than half of their 1993 rates.

Although there are regional patterns of taxation in both countries, in Canada this has developed only since the 1994 tax reductions. Since then tobacco taxes have been substantially higher from Manitoba westward, with the exception of Newfoundland. Nevertheless, the drop in federal and provincial taxes in the Eastern part of the country in 1994 effectively placed a ceiling on tax increases in the Western part as well. In the United States, the pattern is more complicated, but, generally, tobacco taxes are substantially lower in tobacco-growing states and, even considering this, in the South. Ironically, the highest state taxes on tobacco in the US in 2001 are in those states bordering the US-Canada border, especially in the Northeast and Midwest, precisely the area where federal and provincial taxes in Canada are lowest. Furthermore, the variation in tax rates among US states is getting larger as some states legislate large increases, with the Northeast becoming a region of substantially higher taxes in the 1990s (Fishman et al. 1999). Figure 3-2 presents the average retail price of cigarettes in the provinces and bordering US states as of April 2001.

Irrespective of what taxes are legislated, how effective is collection? There is little consensus about this question among scholars. Tobacco products, especially cigarettes, are highly susceptible to smuggling because they are small, easily transported, cheap, readily sold in small quantities, potentially highly profitable, and also obtainable in duty-free shops. The problem of tax avoidance through bootlegging is that residents of a state may systematically buy cigarettes from outside the state, either through cross-border shopping (casual bootlegging) or smuggling (organized bootlegging), and then resell them. Bootlegging is raised as an objection to an increase in tobacco taxes in states bordering or near low-tax states in the US, especially since the mid-1970s as the range of taxation has widened.

The actual impact of bootlegging is difficult to demonstrate because of its illegal nature, the differential impact of population locales, and the transaction costs of seeking tobacco products outside the state. On the latter point, for instance, obviously there is likely to be more bootlegging with a large tax differential than with a small one. The limited number of systematic attempts to estimate the effects of bootlegging across states has come to varying conclusions (Advisory Commission on Intergovernmental Relations 1977, 1985; Fleenor 1996; Licari and Meier 1997). The first ACIR study in the mid-1970s found that bootlegging was a major interstate problem. After passage of a federal law prohibiting large-scale cigarette shipments across state lines in 1978 (the *Contraband Cigarette Act*) and active enforcement by the Bureau of Alcohol, Tobacco and Firearms, bootlegging activity, especially of the organized variety, declined substantially by the early 1980s (Johnson 1984: 129).

Since then, however, the rush to raise cigarette taxes in many states has led to an even greater range of state taxation. As the variation in excise taxes among states has grown, there are indications that overall bootlegging has increased. Nevertheless, bootlegging may also decline in specific states once the "shock effect" of a sharp tax increase wears off (Fleenor 1996). Licari and Meier (1997) rank the 48 contiguous states according to "bootlegging capacity" based on a measure of their cigarette excise tax rates versus those of all bordering states. They argue that bootlegging begins to affect a state's revenue once its cigarette excise tax is 5.43 per cent higher than the surrounding states' average.

As long as cigarette prices were relatively similar across the Canadian provinces, from the 1960s until early 1994 (see Table 4-7), cross-provincial smuggling was not a major problem. Instead, as in 1952-53, the major

Table 4-8: Prices and Taxes on 200 Cigarettes,
Provinces, July 2000 (Canadian dollars)

	Prov. Tobacco Tax	Fed. Excise Tax	Fed. Excise Duty	Retail Price Before Sales Tax*	PST/ GST	Final Retail Price
Newfoundland	22	5.35	5.5	46.35	8%/7%	53.30
PEI	13.25	4.00	5.5	36.25	0%/7%	38.79
Nova Scotia	9.64	5.25	5.5	33.89	8%/7%	38.97
New Brunswick	8.3	5.05	5.5	32.35	8%/7%	37.20
Quebec	8.6	2.85	5.5	30.45	0%/7%	32.58
Ontario	5.3	3.25	5.5	27.55	8%/7%	31.68
Manitoba	17.2	5.35	5.5	41.55	7%/7%	47.37
Saskatchewan	17.2	5.35	5.5	41.55	6%/7%	46.95
Alberta	14	5.35	5.5	38.35	0%/7%	41.03
BC	22	5.35	5.5	46.35	0%/7%	49.59

*Assumes a product cost of $13.50 for each province

smuggling problems involved the US-Canada border. But since the dramatic reduction in federal and provincial taxes in the Eastern provinces in 1994, there has been an East-West smuggling problem. The remaining higher-tax provinces, especially in the West, have put more resources into interdiction of contraband cigarettes. The key point is the Manitoba-Ontario border since this is dividing line between the higher tax and lower tax provinces.

In July 2000 the contributions to provincial tobacco prices were as set out in Table 4-8. In a far contrast from 1991, the cost of cigarettes in Ontario was lower than in any province or bordering state, due to increases in prices and taxes in the United States as well as the Canadian tax reductions, despite some of the 1994 reduction being restored (see Figure 3-2). Continuing discussions between the federal government and the Eastern provinces about a coordinated increase in taxes have resulted in only small increases, ostensibly because of reservations by some provinces about rekindling large-scale smuggling.

TOBACCO CONTROL AT THE LOCAL LEVEL

The major changes in tobacco control often have occurred at the local level, through different councils and agencies depending on the jurisdiction. While slow to start, by the early 1980s such legislation had gained momentum, especially in California. By 1989 California had nearly all of the local statutes restricting smoking in public and private places (US Department of Health and Human Services 1990).

The major issue of local regulation has been the problem of second-hand smoke in restaurants and public facilities. In 1980 there were only a handful of local ETS restrictions, but the increasing evidence of the dangers of second-hand smoke, especially the 1986 Surgeon General's report, had a substantial policy effect. By 1988 there were 400 ordinances on ETS, but almost none of them was comprehensive enough even for a particular site such as restaurants or workplaces. There was a second surge of such legislation, especially in certain states, in the immediate aftermath of the 1993 EPA Report, previewed three years earlier; in fact, the peak year for such adoptions was 1993. By 1998 local ordinances were both over twice as numerous and increasingly restrictive; nonsmoking had become the norm rather than the exception in many localities. By number of statutes in place, they covered, in order, (1) restaurants, (2) workplaces, and (3) public places, perhaps partially because more state laws had been enacted for public places (US Department of Health and Human Services 2000b: 202). California and Massachusetts, aided by the revenues available to local coalitions through their dedicated state tobacco taxes in the early 1990s (see below), continued to provide the majority of statutes, 286 and 124 respectively (US Department of Health and Human Services 2000b: 22, 71). Apparently public opinion was ahead of legislation, and government action encouraged private restrictions as well (US Department of Health and Human Services 2000b: 27-28).

Youth access was the second area in which local governments became active, starting in the late 1980s, accelerating in the early 1990s, and continuing at similar levels thereafter. Again, local action was not completely independent, but was stimulated by the 1989 Surgeon General's report on the decline of such laws, the 1990 model statute offered by DHHS, the Synar Amendment to the *Alcohol, Drug Abuse, Mental Health Administration Reorganization Act of 1992* (discussed below), and the growing focus on youth issues by anti-tobacco groups. In 1992 there were 161 communities with youth access provisions. By 1998 there were 764 local youth access laws of one variety or another, including restrictions on self-service displays, free samples, single cigarette sales, licensing of vendors, and vending machines. Of these 764 statutes, California had 156, New Jersey 153, Massachusetts 109, Minnesota 95, Illinois 36 and Michigan 36; the other 45 states had a total of 159 (US Department of Health and Human Services 2000b: 139).

Local restrictions on advertising were slower to emerge and spread but have nevertheless been of some importance. The first, banning tobacco advertising on public transit, occurred in Amherst, Massachusetts, in 1987, and that state has continued to be a centre for this type of local restrictions. Altogether, as of 1998 there were 68 restrictive ordinances on tobacco advertising in municipalities across the US, covering public places, public transit, and retail stores (US Department of Health and Human Services 2000b: 41-46). Of these, Massachusetts had 24 and California 14; no other state had more than six (US Department of Health and Human Services 2000b: 167).

Although most taxation of cigarettes and other tobacco products occurs on the federal and provincial levels, some cities and counties across the US do impose taxes (Warner 1981; Tobacco Institute 1997). This is often a function of state laws. Two states, Missouri and Alabama, have accounted for over 75 per cent of these local taxing jurisdictions since 1963 and the otherwise low-tax state of Virginia has had a growing number of them since 1974. Together, these three states contained 86 per cent of the municipalities taxing cigarettes in 1997. There is also an upward trend in such adoptions over time. After the 1964 Surgeon General's report, there was an increase in local jurisdictions taxing cigarettes from 226 in 1963 to 318 in 1968, a 41-per-cent increase in four years. Subsequently, due to changes in state laws, especially in California and Colorado, the number fell back to 300 in 1974, jumped to 365 in 1975, and then stayed relatively stable until 1984 when it began an incremental rise to 451 local jurisdictions in 1997 (Tobacco Institute 1997).

Canadian local government structure resembles that in the United States more than the other two levels do (Sancton 1998). Even so, Canadian local governments were slower to pursue tobacco-control policies than those in the United States. With few exceptions, Canadian municipalities did not take action until the 1990s, and most of these laws have concerned ETS. As in the US, earlier laws were more concerned with fire protection and food safety than with the effects of cigarettes on the consumer. Although the Isabelle Committee noted the need to consider the rights of nonsmokers, other sources for these laws in Canada were similar to those in the US, namely the US Surgeon General's reports, especially in 1986, research appearing in the early 1980s about the dangers of ETS, and local activist groups. Ottawa passed the first bylaw restricting smoking in public places in 1976, followed by Toronto in 1977 (Cunningham 1996: 109-13). By 1981, there were only eight Canadian cities with bylaws on ETS (Gloeckler, 2000). In 1986, Vancouver passed the first law restricting smoking in workplaces, and Cunningham (1996: 113) estimates that by 1991, almost 300 municipalities had bylaws restricting smoking to some degree. The 1990s saw relatively little growth in the number of laws restricting public smoking. The three provinces that had the largest percentage of the population covered by such laws were Ontario, British Columbia, and Alberta, with others, especially the sparsely-populated Atlantic provinces, lagging (Statistics Canada 1995). Even in this area, however, the more stringent legislation for applicable places was the federal *Nonsmokers' Health Act* of 1988. Indications are that private employers' protection of employees from ETS are not as extensive as in the United States (Cunningham 1996: 109; US Department of Health and Human Services 2000b).

Recently Canada has experienced more restrictive local anti-smoking initiatives. Prominent among them have been the decisions of municipal governments in the Vancouver, Toronto, and Ottawa areas to ban smoking in all indoor facilities. Local ETS ordinances, especially concerning restaurants and bars, continue to generate controversy when they are considered. Despite the permissive nature of Canadian federal legislation and the lack of provincial pre-emption laws, local anti-tobacco initiatives have largely been restricted to ETS and have generally lagged behind similar developments in the US.

Federal Incentives for State, Provincial and Local Tobacco Regulation

There have also been several programs involving federal-provincial cooperation in both countries. In Canada, as noted in Chapter Three, provinces and territories have been part of most national tobacco reduction strategies. Except in the short-lived Tobacco Demand Reduction Strategy of 1994 and more recently in the Federal Tobacco Control Strategy of 2001, however, these have not involved major federal financial aid even though this level controls most public finance in Canada and uses this clout to shape provincial policies in many dimensions of health care.

In the United States, however, there have been several programs involving federal financial aid and incentives, including public-private cooperation. These follow the well-established coalition models for other federal public-health programs established by the National Cancer Institute and the Centers for Disease Control and Prevention (Swan and Goss 1994). Seventeen states received awards under the ASSIST program, begun in 1991 by the National Cancer Institute, in cooperation with the American Cancer Society. State health departments were to coordinate these grants in order to help develop local coalitions to combat tobacco usage. The primary goal of the ASSIST program was to reduce tobacco use by 47 per cent from the 1985 level; in pursuit of this objective, it encouraged a variety of community tobacco-control activities, including information gathering, public education, smoking cessation, coalition building, and policy change. While ASSIST was in progress, the other 33 US states received more modest IMPACT grants, begun by the CDC in 1993. Funds for these programs ended in 1998, but evaluation of the goals of the programs have been continued under the joint supervision of NCI and CDC-OSH (US Department of Health and Human Services 2000b: 385). In 1999 OSH started a replacement program, the National Tobacco Control Program (NTCP) to provide all states and other jurisdictions with substantial funding for five years to continue and supplement their tobacco-control programs.

The US federal government provided a further spur to state action by passing the Synar Amendment to the federal *Alcohol, Drug Abuse, and Mental Health Administration Reorganization Act of 1991*. The final DHHS regulations for enforcement of this amendment were not promulgated until 1996, however, and enforcement mechanisms were left to the states. These rules mandated a series of graduated goals of reducing the illegal underage (18) purchase of tobacco products, eventually culminating with a goal of 20 per cent or less by 2003, as assessed by random, unannounced inspections. The penalty for failure to meet these goals is that states could lose part of their federal allocation, amounting to millions of dollars, under the Annual Substance Abuse Prevention and Treatment Block Grant. The Synar Amendment was designed to improve implementation of state youth access laws, but some have questioned its effectiveness (National Cancer Institute 2000: 36; Forster and Wolfson

1998; DiFranza 1999). Although all states managed to meet the interim goal by cutting illegal purchases to an average of 40 per cent by 1997, nine states failed to reach their goals for 1999 (National Cancer Institute 2000: 36).

Beginning in 1994, the private Robert Wood Johnson Foundation, in cooperation with the American Medical Association, undertook a major initiative, the SmokeLess States Program, to reduce tobacco usage through competitive grants to statewide coalitions working with community groups in tobacco-control efforts, which include public education and advocacy components. These grants have gone to an increasing number of states (Forster and Wolfson 1998). A more recent national private program established by the MSA is the American Legacy Foundation, which has engaged in activities directed at combatting youth smoking, including countermarketing activities, some of which could be labelled "denormalization."

These are examples of the use of private and federal seed money to leverage private-public cooperation in social programs. Coalitions for tobacco control, consisting of both public and private organizations as well as individuals interested in combatting tobacco use, existed in most states prior to the federal grants (Centers for Disease Control and Prevention 1990). Health professional and voluntary organizations, historically reluctant to become involved in policy advocacy, also have become more engaged in state and local programs. This growing public-private cooperation on tobacco control through policy networks has appeared at all levels of government.

Canada has also attempted this kind of multi-level, public-private tobacco-control effort, but on a more modest and less coordinated scale. The Tobacco Demand Reduction Strategy of 1994 provided federal money for community-building tobacco-control efforts at local levels, although they were subject to federal budget cuts in subsequent years (Pechmann, Dixon and Layne 1998). Furthermore, upon the abrupt announcement of this program as part of coping with the 1994 smuggling crisis, there was a scramble for revenue among affected groups, old and new. Altogether, even though there was a large amount of funds committed initially, the results were less than what might have been expected from a more long-term, better coordinated program. Whether the results of the Federal Tobacco Control Strategy will be superior remains to be seen.

Extraordinary State Policymaking: State Lawsuits, the National Settlement, and the Master Settlement Agreement

The state lawsuits against tobacco companies leading to the attempted National Settlement of 1997-98, the Master Settlement Agreement of 1998, and the settlement of separate lawsuits by Florida, Mississippi, Texas, and Minnesota involved extraordinary processes for the making of national public policy. The usual institutions for policy-making were bypassed in order to achieve greater regulation of tobacco. Individual and state lawsuits were combined, negotiations were encouraged by the President, and, when the first attempt was defeated in Congress, the MSA settled for a "national" tobacco-control policy which did not need formal approval by Congress. Although vertical policy-making is usually considered to be from the federal government to the states (Gray 1994), in this case it was in the reverse.

The rise and fall of the National Settlement is discussed in Chapter Three. With individual state lawsuits against the tobacco companies proceeding, it was no surprise that another general out-of-court settlement to satisfy both states and tobacco companies would be attempted. There were substantial differences in the MSA from the original National Settlement and McCain Bill (Table 3-2). Major ones included the following: (1) FDA authority was not addressed; (2) there were no federal tax increases; (3) there were no limits on individual liability suits; and (4) no goals were provided for reduction of teenage smoking and financial penalties for not meeting them. The tobacco companies did get protection from suits by local governments in the states, another case of pre-emption. Within one week, all 46 states, even those that had not participated in the negotiations, signed the agreement. Subsequently the federal Department of Health and Human Services claimed a share of the settlement revenue since it provides some of the funds for state Medicaid programs, but Congress resolved this issue in favour of the states.

The cost to tobacco companies of the MSA was a maximum of $206 billion over 25 years, depending on sales of cigarettes, plus a later separate agreement of $5 billion to 14 states to compensate them for harm to their tobacco-growing communities. The reservations of health organizations about the MSA were largely swept aside in the rush to accept a time-limited offer. From the perspective of anti-tobacco activists, there are at least four problems with the agreement: (1) the lack of enforcement mechanisms beyond complaints to the attorneys general makes the MSA largely a voluntary agreement; (2) the educational programs financed through the agreement are not supposed to vilify the industry, which inhibits denormalization; (3) the payments are not designated directly to tobacco prevention and cessation programs, but are simply made to the states for their discretionary spending; and (4) the payments are not guaranteed and may be reduced, either through reductions in cigarette sales or the complicating factors of other lawsuits (Godshall 1999). Within the first two years all of these problems had manifested themselves.

For instance, by January, 2001, less than ten per cent of the revenues received thus far from the MSA and associated lawsuits had gone into state tobacco-control programs (Begos 2000; De Barros 2001) although 45 states set aside some money for this purpose. According to a report issued by the Campaign for Tobacco-Free Kids, the American Cancer Society, the American Heart Association, and the American Lung Association (*Show Us the Money* 2000), only six of the 45 states that had made decisions met the minimum spending levels necessary overall (including using other state, federal, and private revenues) for comprehensive, effective smoking prevention and cessation programs, as suggested by the US Centers for Disease Control. A later report from the CDC indicated that, overall, states spent only about 60 per cent of the recommended minimum and that only seven states (Arizona, Indiana, Maine, Massachusetts, Mississippi, Ohio, and Vermont) are meeting or exceeding the minimum recommended funding levels (US Department of Health and Human Services 2001; see Table 4-9). This state spending pales in view of the size of the problem and the much larger amounts, estimated at seven times as much, spent by tobacco companies on advertising. Instead, state legislatures had engaged in a "feeding frenzy" to divert the money to other state programs (Begos 2000). States have varied widely in how they have used tobacco settlement monies. Non-tobacco related health programs, support for tobacco farmers, cancer research, and a variety of other initiatives have also been funded by settlement revenue (Chriqui et al. 2000).

There also were bills passed in five states—four of them tobacco producers but the fifth one of the leading litigious states, Florida—to protect tobacco company assets by limiting the amount of bond they would have to put up in appealing the *Engle* class action verdict. If upheld on appeal, the $145-billion award for punitive damages would be the largest in US history and could have possibly ruinous effects on the tobacco industry.

Table 4-9: Per-Capita State Spending for Comprehensive
Tobacco Prevention, Fiscal Year 2001 (US dollars)*

State	Per Capita Funding	% CDC's Low Recommendation	State	Per Capita Funding	% CDC's Low Recommendation
1. Ohio	$20.82	383	27. South Dakota	$ 4.09	36
2. Massachusetts	$10.22	184	27. Virginia	$ 1.98	36
3. Maine	$15.08	172	29. Alaska	$ 4.31	33
4. Arizona	$ 7.32	135	30. Rhode Island	$ 3.03	32
5. Mississippi	$ 7.90	120	31. Nevada	$ 1.93	29
6. Indiana	$ 5.99	105	32. Wyoming	$ 3.79	25
6. Vermont	$13.63	105	32. New Mexico	$ 1.89	25
8. Hawaii	$ 8.75	98	34. Idaho	$ 1.60	19
9. Minnesota	$ 4.71	81	35. Oklahoma	$ 1.13	18
10. Wisconsin	$ 4.37	75	36. Kentucky	$ 0.90	15
11. California	$ 3.44	71	37. District of		
11. New Jersey	$ 3.80	71	Columbia	$ 1.67	13
11. Maryland	$ 4.05	71	37. North Dakota	$ 1.71	13
14. Nebraska	$ 4.83	62	37. South Carolina	$ 0.78	13
15. Florida	$ 2.81	57	40. Michigan	$ 0.66	12
16. West Virginia	$ 4.28	55	40. Texas	$ 0.59	12
17. Colorado	$ 3.10	54	40. Kansas	$ 0.83	12
17. Washington	$ 3.08	54	43. Utah	$ 0.67	10
19. Iowa	$ 3.52	53	44. Alabama	$ 0.53	9
20. Montana	$ 4.85	47	44. Arkansas	$ 0.58	9
21. New York	$ 2.27	45	46. Missouri	$ 0.43	7
21. Illinois	$ 2.35	45	47. North Carolina	$ 0.32	6
23. Oregon	$ 2.71	44	47. Louisiana	$ 0.36	6
24. Georgia	$ 2.19	42	49. Connecticut	$ 0.30	5
24. Delaware	$ 4.61	42	50. Tennessee	$ 0.24	4
26. New Hampshire	$ 3.29	37	51. Pennsylvania	$ 0.10	2

*Rankings represent total specially designated tobacco-control allocations,
whether from MSA funds or elsewhere, including federal, state, and private
sources (grants to states). California and New York funds are from MSA only.
Source: US Department of Health and Human Services 2001

It was the Minnesota lawsuit, however, that proved particularly troublesome to the tobacco industry. The strong consumer protection laws in that state made it difficult for the companies to mount a defence. When the case was on the verge of going to the jury, an out-of-court settlement was reached with some far-reaching national implications, such as elimination of tobacco product placements in films. The decision of the Minnesota state court judge presiding over the trial to establish depositories of internal tobacco company documents, open for ten years, as part of the "discovery" process also proved to be a bonanza for anti-tobacco advocates and governments. One depository was established in Minnesota, but since US defendant Brown and Williamson Tobacco had sent many of the relevant documents to its parent company BAT, a second depository was established in Guildford, England. Subsequently the Canadian federal government and the province of British Columbia travelled to Guildford to examine tobacco company documents for their lawsuits against the companies.

As on the federal level, policy in regard to tobacco issues has been somewhat contradictory in many US states. On one hand, there has been encouragement, fuelled by federal funds and private grants, of local and state-level tobacco-control coalitions consisting of both private and public organizations. Offices of state attorneys general have also been major players in state suits against tobacco companies. On the other hand, tobacco interests have been able to defend their positions against taxation and regulation through state legislatures and the governor's office, even in states considered as anti-tobacco as California (Glantz and Balbach 2000) and through preemption statutes. No matter what happens on the federal level, however, there will still be room for significant state action in this area.

Overall Evaluation of Tobacco Control: State/Provincial Comparisons

In Canada, taxation and regulation levels among the provinces have not been strongly associated. The only exception is that, prior to 1998, Quebec was notably recalcitrant on both dimensions. Otherwise, the provinces in the West, both those with high regulation (B.C.) and those with low regulation (Alberta, Saskatchewan, Manitoba), along with Newfoundland on the far eastern side of the country, have maintained the most consistent

Table 4-10: Provincial and Federal Rankings on Tobacco Control, 1994

Score by Jurisdiction (Maximum 100%)	Combined Fed./Prov. Score (Maximum 100%)	Score with Tax Excluded (Maximum 100%)
Federal 26.9%	Federal 26.9%	Federal 20.7%
1. Newfoundland 21.2%	1. Newfoundland 38.9%	1. Newfoundland 11.1%
2. British Columbia 12.8%	2. British Columbia 32.0%	2. Ontario 9.7%
3. Ontario 11.7%	3. Manitoba 30.2%	3. Manitoba 3.6%
4. Manitoba 11.2%	4. Saskatchewan 28.9%	4. Nova Scotia 3.5%
5. Saskatchewan 9.4%	5. Ontario 27.5%	5. New Brunswick 3.2%
6. Alberta 7.6%	6. Alberta 27.3%	6. British Columbia 3.0%
7. Nova Scotia 7.1%	7. New Brunswick 24.5%	7. Quebec 3.0%
8. New Brunswick 6.8%	8. Nova Scotia 24.2%	8. Prince Edward Island 2.0%
9. Prince Edward Island 6.4%	9. Prince Edward Island 23.5%	9. Saskatchewan 1.6%
10. Quebec 4.9%	10. Quebec 22.1%	10. Alberta 1.4%
	28.6% Weighted Average	
	28.0% Provincial Mean	

Source: Cunningham (1995)

line on taxation and, in some cases, have backed this up with enhanced enforcement against smuggling. The provinces within and nearer the population centre of the country, whether they have taken action against tobacco (Ontario, Nova Scotia, and, most recently, Quebec) or have done little (Quebec until 1998, PEI), were the most willing to cut taxes in concert with the federal government to reduce smuggling in 1994. The Western provinces and Newfoundland are not only far from the population and smuggling centres of Canada, but also from low-tax states in the United States. The mix of strategies thus differs by province.

After the wave of nationwide province-level tobacco-control initiatives in the mid-1990s, Cunningham (1995) rated the ten provinces as well as the federal government in terms of how closely they matched an ideal, comprehensive tobacco-control policy through regulation and taxes (see Table 4-10). As Cunningham (1995) admits, however, it is impossible to weigh the components of tobacco control in any precise manner. In his view, taxation is so important that it accounts for 33 per cent of the index. Thus, when federal and provincial taxes from Ontario eastward were lowered to combat smuggling in early 1994, the rankings changed substantially. Table 4-10 indicates that, if the federal government is considered separately, even after the 1994 tax reductions, it rated as the strongest tobacco-control jurisdiction in Canada. This is further evidence of the federal leadership role. Newfoundland, due largely to its taxation, was also consistently high, as were British Columbia, especially on those measures including taxation, and, somewhat surprisingly, Manitoba. Quebec's taxes kept its score low although, without taxes included, three other provinces dropped below it. If this rating were brought up to date, the rankings would probably change substantially, to the benefit of British Columbia and, to a lesser degree, Quebec, in light of the laws passed in these two provinces in recent years. In fact, British Columbia might become, as the government there has often claimed to be, the "leader of the pack."

Recognizing that tobacco control is affected by all three levels of government, de Groh and Stephens (2000) studied the relative effectiveness of changes in taxation (federal and provincial) from 1988 to 1998 and the strength of ETS bylaws (mainly a municipal responsibility but with provincial influence) in 1995 across the ten Canadian provinces. They found that on the ETS bylaw index, the provinces ranked from Alberta with the strongest at 8.50, to Newfoundland and PEI at .10. Basically there were two groups of provinces: the Western ones through

Ontario, with scores from 6.50 to 8.50, and the ones east of Ontario, with scores from .10 to 2.90. Changes in taxation, especially in 1994, gave British Columbia, Newfoundland, and Saskatchewan the highest scores, Ontario the lowest.

To date there have been no similar overall ratings for tobacco-control policies in the states. As noted above, states range widely in terms of their regulations, taxes, and financing of tobacco control. Alciati et al. (1998) rated states annually in the 1993-96 period for nine dimensions of their laws (not executive regulations) on youth access only. States were given discounted scores if they had preemption provisions that prevented even stronger local laws from being passed, depending on the strength of the preemption. In 1993, the leading states on youth access regulation, with their scores, were Connecticut (18), New York (17), Oregon, Vermont, Florida, and Georgia (all with 15). The lowest was Virginia, with a score of 0. By 1996, the leading states were New York (21), Connecticut (20), and California (19). The lowest was North Carolina (1), the only state that managed to reduce its score over the period, and Wisconsin (2). Twenty-two states improved their scores over this four-year period, ranging from one point (Illinois, Mississippi, and South Carolina) to 11 (California and Virginia). Reflecting the political battle in the states, while overall scores went up slightly, the number of states with preemption reducing their scores doubled, from 10 to 20. The states that are often invoked as leaders in tobacco regulation—California, Massachusetts, and Florida—are not necessarily the ones that have high scores on youth access. While California improved its score in the mid-1990s to become a leader, Florida stood pat (15) and Massachusetts improved from 6 to 9. But if local ordinances on youth access as well as state laws were included in this ranking, then California and Massachusetts would clearly reclaim their leadership positions (National Cancer Institute 2000: 139).

Chriqui (2000) provides an updated and somewhat different estimate of state rankings on eleven youth access provisions, to 1998. The highest ranking states in terms of total provisions passed into law were Idaho with 9, Maine and Texas with 8, down to North Carolina with 0. Fishman et al. (1999) note those states which have met CDC Healthy People 2000 objectives in various categories of tobacco control. The standard for ETS, met by completely banning indoor smoking or limiting it to separately ventilated areas, was met by only one state, California. Twenty states (including D.C.) met the objective of limiting vending machines to adult-only venues. Four states (Florida, Maine, New Hampshire, and Washington) met the objective of 20 per cent or less sales to minors in compliance inspections. No state met the Healthy People goal of taxes as 50 per cent of the purchase price of cigarettes unless one also considers price increases resulting from the MSA as part of "tax" (see Table 3-4).

Even this very limited comparison of states on tobacco-control regulations indicates that rating the overall performance of states on tobacco control is a complicated process, even more so since there is controversy over the relative effects of taxes and regulations, either informational or ETS, in reducing smoking (Warner 1981; Licari and Meier 1997; Showalter 1998; de Groh and Stephens 2000). Some economists and public-health officials contend that taxation is the most effective method of combatting tobacco usage, with an estimated drop in consumption of four per cent for every ten-cent rise in taxation, assuming that other price factors remain constant. Increased taxation may also have greater effects on purchasing by youth since they are less addicted to tobacco and also have less money (National Cancer Institute 1993; Warner et al. 1995). Both US and Canadian studies indicate that taxes are more effective in reducing smoking than are regulations (ETS restrictions, advertising bans, and package health warnings in the US, local ETS bylaws in Canada), especially for younger people. However, there is an interaction effect in the US studies, and the Canadian one suggests that ETS regulations have greater effects on older adults than on younger ones (Licari and Meier 1997; de Groh and Stephens 2000). These studies involving both categories of policy agree that a combination of the two policy instruments will have more effects than either alone, even though they serve as partial substitutes for each other (see also Licari 2000b).

A more comprehensive rating system would need to consider a wider range of state regulations and taxes over a longer time span, and the relative amounts spent per capita on tobacco control. In recent years California spent more per person on combatting tobacco than did the US federal government, and Massachusetts spent the most (Biener, Harris and Hamilton 2000). Table 4-9 shows data indicating that per-capita funding in some US states, based on receipts from settlement lawsuits, has now surpassed that of Massachusetts and California (Ontario Tobacco Research Unit 2000a: 12). Funding in even the best-financed Canadian provinces, Ontario and British Columbia, is considerably lower, but Canadian tobacco-company spending on advertising and promotion does not reach US levels either. The 2000-01 budget for Ontario, the best-funded province, indicated C$1.71 (about US$1.20) per capita, the highest ever for a province, but well below most US states and below the C$8.00 recommended by an Expert Panel (Ashley *et al.* 1999). Previously, the highest spending was in British Columbia, with $1.61 per capita in 1999-2000, when Ontario's spending was $1.16. Some Canadian government officials content that having a more comprehensive tobacco-control policy overall, especially in federal regulation, means that they do not need to approach US levels of per-capita spending to combat tobacco consumption effectively.

LEADERS AND LAGGARDS

The process of policy leadership, or innovation, in tobacco control is complex and dynamic among both Canadian provinces and US states. In Canada, British Columbia undertook the first provincial regulatory actions against tobacco, has had higher than average taxes on tobacco products since 1992, and more recently has been in the forefront of attempts to imitate US states in legal actions against tobacco companies for health care costs. Quebec passed the first law limiting ETS in 1986, but thereafter took little action to combat tobacco use until 1998. Ontario undertook several substantial tobacco-control initiatives in the mid-1990s, including the first legal ban on sales of tobacco in pharmacies, followed by other provinces. New Brunswick, otherwise a laggard in tobacco control, was the first to have warnings at point of sale.

Until the tax reduction essentially forced on the province by the federal government and Quebec in 1994, Ontario was the leading tobacco-control province in Canada. The provincial NDP government of the early 1990s adopted several tobacco-control measures, first the Ministry of Health's Ontario Tobacco Strategy in 1992 and then the *Tobacco Control Act, 1994.* Following the guidelines of the Premier's Council on Health Strategy in 1991 and modelled after the US National Cancer Institute's ASSIST program, the Ontario Tobacco Strategy was designed to provide a comprehensive program for reducing tobacco use, including three major objectives: (1) to prevent the onset of smoking, (2) to protect nonsmokers from ETS, and (3) to help smokers quit (Ontario Tobacco Research Unit 1995b). Among the administrative measures were youth-oriented anti-smoking commercials, funding for local public-health units, and support for smoking-related research (Cunningham 1996: 203). In 1993 the Ministry of Health established the Ontario Tobacco Research Unit at the University of Toronto with a twofold mission: (1) to monitor the implementation of the Ontario Tobacco Strategy, and (2) to conduct research and disseminate information on effective tobacco-control endeavours (Ontario Tobacco Research Unit 1998a).

The Tobacco Control Act, 1994 was at the time the most comprehensive provincial/state tobacco-control legislation in North America. Ontario was the first jurisdiction in North America to forbid tobacco sales in pharmacies when it did so on December 31, 1994. Raising the legal sales age to 19 from 18 occurred in the same year that the higher age was also implemented in British Columbia, New Brunswick, Nova Scotia, and Newfoundland (Cunningham 1996: 299). Other provisions included signage for tobacco sales, banning vending machine sales and kiddie packs, regular reporting of sales by wholesalers and distributors to the Ministry of Health, banning smoking on school and daycare property, restricting smoking and having appropriate signage in some public places, allowing municipalities more authority to pass smoking bylaws, and enforcement and penalties (Cunningham 1996: 203; National Clearinghouse on Tobacco and Health 1995). However, in the late 1990s British Columbia and possibly Quebec moved ahead of Ontario in some aspects of tobacco control, especially smoking in public places, recovery of health care costs through lawsuits against tobacco companies, and sponsorship bans.

Although all provinces in Canada had more tobacco-control policies by 2000, no one province was leading on all dimensions (Cunningham 1995; de Groh and Stephens 2000), which suggests a process of leapfrogging whereby different provinces would take the lead in tobacco control through new measures (Studlar 1999a). Some policies, such as packaging and labelling, were left to the federal government alone. Nevertheless, the Ontario *Tobacco Control Act, 1994* gives the government regulatory authority to enact plain packaging and to add its own health warnings to those of the federal government if it chooses.

Federal-provincial conferences have resulted in less coordination of policies than in enhanced awareness of where other provinces stand and why. Provincial health ministers' conferences have not resulted, as some had hoped, in a coordinated plan of support for British Columbia's legal assault on the tobacco companies, but they did enable others to follow B.C.'s lead once that province had taken the initial steps.

California and Massachusetts are often considered to be the overall leaders in state tobacco control due to their early establishment of cigarette taxes for tobacco control through referenda (California in 1988, Massachusetts in 1992) and other measures implemented in aggressive tobacco-control programs through this dedicated funding. California's large-scale tobacco-control program is the oldest, having been established in 1989, and its goals have been closely monitored. In 1997 California became the first state to eliminate all smoking in public places, even bars and restaurants. Massachusetts has engaged in several regulatory measures rare among states, including advertising restrictions, health warnings on non-cigarette products, and stock divestiture. Arizona and Minnesota, however, were the early innovators in ETS, even if on a less extensive basis, in the 1970s. Minnesota also was the first state to ban self-service displays other than vending machines and is, along with California, one of only two states completely banning free samples (Forster and Wolfson 1998). Chriqui's (2000) innovation scores for states on youth access restrictions, based on when such laws were enacted, rates Maine, Washington, and Minnesota as the highest, with Wyoming and North Carolina being the two lowest. California was twelfth, followed by Massachusetts. As states decide how to spend their continuing tobacco lawsuit revenues, the relative positions of leaders and laggards among states and provinces may alter considerably over time, further evidence of leapfrogging. But there is no doubt that California's long and largely successful record in this field will continue to make it the focus of attention not only in the United States, but also Canada and even internationally.

Explanations for Tobacco-Control Policies

Although a more extended examination of competing explanations for tobacco-control policies across different jurisdictions in both countries will be the subjects of Chapters Five and Six, a brief summary of what appear to be the *prima facie* conditions for more restrictive tobacco-control policy across states, provinces, and municipalities is in order. The optimal circumstances for a jurisdiction to have a strongly restrictive tobacco-control policy would appear to be wealth, a relatively large percentage of health-conscious middle-class people, a pre-existing low consumption of tobacco products, no internal tobacco agriculture or industry, organized anti-tobacco activists with significant links to public health providers and government bureaucracies, and a left-leaning party in office.

In Canada, British Columbia and Ontario had most of the above conditions in the 1990s when tobacco control expanded and thus, with the exception of taxation since 1994 in Ontario, have the strongest provincial tobacco regulation regimes at present. If one considers taxation as well, then overall British Columbia has the highest rank. Among municipalities, again these two provinces have had both pioneers and a large total number of jurisdictions restricting ETS. Alberta, however, is a significant exception. With a generally conservative, individualistic political culture, this province nevertheless has a considerable number of municipalities with ETS restrictions, perhaps because the social conditions are favourable and there is a strong anti-tobacco interest group, ASH.

In the US, the greater complexity of political institutions makes the optimal formations for a restrictive tobacco-control policy slightly different. Social conditions and interest group conditions may be similar to those in Canada, but instead of having a Democratic governor or legislature, having a Democratic attorney general willing to launch a lawsuit for state health care costs (Spill, Licari and Ray 2001) or having citizens' groups undertake a successful binding statewide referendum on tobacco control, as in four states—California (1988), Massachusetts (1992), Arizona (1994), and Oregon (1996) (Pierce-Lavin et al. 1998)—appear to be more important factors.

Local tobacco-control measures also are distributed unevenly across the US states; a majority of them have been passed in California and Massachusetts. As in Canada, however, there may be other compensating factors in local community policy-making. The ASSIST program seems to have been a factor in successful local advocacy in some states (Jacobson and Wasserman 1997; Forster and Wolfson 1998: 217), even ones where social conditions are not amenable to stronger tobacco control, such as West Virginia and, until state pre-emption was passed, North Carolina (US Department of Health and Human Services 2000b: 19, 23). Hays et al. (2000a; 2000b) suggest that local entrepreneurs are a key ingredient in the US.

Provinces obviously learn from each other's experiences, both positively and negatively. It was remarkable that five provinces in one year, 1994, raised the legal age for tobacco sales for minors to 19, followed later by Prince Edward Island. The ban on pharmacy sales, initiated by Ontario, has now been adopted by New Brunswick, Quebec, Nova Scotia, and Newfoundland as well. The negative experience of Nova Scotia in attempting to legislate a province-wide ETS ban in 1994 (MacLeod 1996) probably reinforced caution over this issue in the other provinces, but eventually British Columbia and Quebec took some action. Vending machine prohibitions or their limitation to adult venues have also spread.

With only ten provinces and limited diffusion of some policies, it is difficult to generalize about regional patterns of policy diffusion, a favourite topic of researchers in the United States (Mooney 1998). The federally-induced coordination of taxes, of course, is distinctively regional, with all provinces east of Manitoba coordinating their tax policies with the federal government to some extent. Pharmacy bans on tobacco sales so far have occurred only in contiguous provinces in the eastern part of the country. Raising the age for tobacco sales has been, with the exception of British Columbia, a phenomenon from Ontario eastward. As noted earlier, aside from tax imposition and enforcement against smuggling, the three Prairie provincial governments, especially Alberta and Saskatchewan, have been reluctant warriors in the provincial tobacco wars. Most recently, the British Columbia attacks on tobacco companies through lawsuits has gradually spread eastward.

At the local level, there is also evidence of policy diffusion, mainly from within the same country. In the United States, Hays et al. (2000a; 2000b) found that youth access laws proposed for adoption in the communities they studied were sometimes based on the model of Woodridge, Illinois, an example which has also spread to Canada. On ETS regulations, however, local governments tended to look to states with restrictive policies, especially California.

An Evaluation of State, Provincial, and Local Tobacco-Control Policies: Competitive Federalism

The concept of "competitive federalism," as developed by Grodzins (1966) suggests that states or provinces, by having legislative authority in the same areas as the federal government, provide more opportunities to deal with policy problems in a country. This is one of the "multiple venues" indicated by agenda-setting theory. Only in recent years, however, has there been evidence of competitive federalism in Canada on tobacco control. While it has developed in fits and starts, there has generally been more competitive federalism on tobacco control in the United States. This may perhaps be a function of there being 50 states in the US, compared to ten provinces in Canada.

It is generally recognized that locally-based tobacco control has been more effective in the United States. This level of control originated in the 1970s when the Nonsmokers' Rights Movement was successful, especially in California, first at the local level, expanding to achievements at the state level later in the 1980s and 1990s through referendums (Nathanson 1999). Americans for Nonsmokers' Rights, based in California, works only at the local and state levels, not at the federal level. Their leading public activist, Stanton Glantz, extols the need for tobacco-control movements to be based on mass rather than elite action because the latter will compromise major tobacco-control interests (Glantz and Balbach 2000). Thus Glantz has been a major critic of the National Settlement and MSA agreements as being insufficiently restrictive.

Nevertheless, studies suggest that both states and municipalities are stimulated in their tobacco-control efforts by federal initiatives, and not only the financial ones exemplified by ASSIST, IMPACT, and the Synar Amendment. The US Surgeon General's reports, especially those of 1986 and 1988, led to a surge in regulation of ETS and other state- and local-level restrictions (National Cancer Institute 2000, Chriqui et al. 2000). After two federal reports about the problems of enforcement of youth access laws, the DHSS in 1990 issued a *Model Sale of Tobacco Products to Minors Control Act* for states and localities, presaging some of the FDA provisions in 1996 (US Department of Health and Human Services 2000b: 34).

It is more difficult to separate provincial and federal policies in Canada because of extensive consultation and cooperation among the relevant actors. Usually this means provincial support of federal tobacco-control initiatives, both in regulation and taxation. Despite the fact that Canada has one of the most decentralized federal systems in the world, federal and provincial actors have tended largely to behave in concert except on matters of litigation. British Columbia's attempts to get other provinces to engage in litigation against the tobacco companies have progressed only slowly even though they may have influenced the federal government to pursue such litigation in a limited fashion. There also has been some competitive federalism from Quebec, which passed its own bill, with stricter controls on tobacco company sponsorship, after the federal *Tobacco Act*.

Unlike Canada, the US states did not look to the federal government to dominate tobacco regulation in the early twentieth century. Various regulatory statutes, including outright bans on the manufacture, sale, and possession of cigarettes, were enacted in 21 states by the 1920s, while nothing similar was done on the federal level. In the United States, states were more active, especially in taxation, from the 1920s, but it took until the 1980s for regulatory activities to become well established. States have positioned themselves differently, although with some convergence in regard to tobacco regulation, but vary widely in terms of taxation. Compared to other separately taxed items such as gasoline and alcohol, tobacco taxation has extremely wide variation, even more so in recent years as some states have raised rates substantially, others not at all. The state lawsuits leading to the National Settlement and the MSA, remarkable episodes in that they showed much greater unity of purpose among US states than is the norm, were also part of competitive federalism.

In his book *Trading Up*, Vogel (1995) posits the existence of a "California effect" in economic and environmental regulatory policies, namely that instead of a "race to the bottom" among political jurisdictions in an attempt to lure economic enterprises, more will follow the example of California in stringent regulation of businesses, especially on environmental grounds. This will not chase business away, but in fact will lead to more uniform regulation elsewhere as businesses learn to incorporate these regulatory practices. In effect, California's actions in this respect will constitute a standard to which other jurisdictions can adhere. Vogel has extended this argument to the realm of economic globalization as well. Is a similar phenomenon of "trading up" observable, especially among states, provinces, and municipalities, in tobacco-control policies, whether they come from California or elsewhere? In short, is there a convergence in policies, and is that convergence toward the more restrictive rather than the less restrictive?

As one might expect in a federal system, especially one with so many states, there is wide variation in both taxes and regulatory policies on tobacco products in the United States. Nevertheless, there does seem to be a general tendency toward more restrictiveness, in effect, a "California effect" in operation. This is even more evident if one excludes the major tobacco agriculture states from the analysis. Over time, but especially in the 1990s, states were taxing tobacco at higher and higher rates and passing more regulations on tobacco. Similarly, local levels were more active in this area in the 1990s although these results varied widely.

Canada is a more puzzling case because, considering the small number of provinces and the federal leadership role, there remain relatively wide variations in regulations and taxes at the provincial level. The provinces stronger on taxes are largely in the West, but those are also, with one exception (British Columbia), the provinces that are weakest on regulating tobacco. At present, only British Columbia has a leadership position in both realms; other Western provinces may be using taxes more for revenue purposes. Provincial taxes have had more variation, not less, since 1994 although they can be grouped into two patterns. Provincial and local regulations, while showing some tendency toward being more restrictive, again demonstrate wide variation. After some delay, more provinces appear to be following in the footsteps of the legal challenges to tobacco companies pioneered in Canada by British Columbia. Notwithstanding federal financial equalization payments, Canadian provinces vary considerably in governmental resources because of their great range of population and assets. There is even evidence of cross-border "trading up" through lesson drawing, as discussed in Chapter Six.

With the proliferation of "best practices" documentation (US Department of Health and Human Services 1999; "World's Best Practice in Tobacco Control" 2000; Ontario Tobacco Research Unit 2000a), "trading up" practices will continue, although at a highly variable rate, among US states and Canadian provinces. There will remain considerable variation among states and provinces, but the general regulatory and taxation pressure on tobacco can be expected to continue for the foreseeable future as long as the dangers of tobacco consumption remain a massive public policy problem.

In both countries, it is difficult to separate federal and state/provincial policies on tobacco because of federal incentive policies, whether it be taxes in Canada or community development programs in the US, as well as authoritative research reports from federal agencies, primarily the US Surgeon General's Report. Still, even within this "marble cake" federalism, the episodes of the National Settlement, the MSA, and the four other individual state lawsuits stand out as "bottom up" policy in a concerted effort across all 50 US states to make federal tobacco-control policy. This only reinforces the impression that the process of tobacco-control policy is more "top-down" in Canada and more "bottom-up" in the US.

5

Political Processes and Tobacco Control

"Allowing the tobacco manufacturers to promote tobacco use now, given the evidence, is like allowing the promotion and sale of rats at the height of the bubonic plague, had officials of the time known the source of the plague." (Mahood 1997)

"In the United States, action beyond words was possible because the authoritative actors were partly independent of the elected public officials...While the Canadian system appeared to facilitate higher level consideration of the problem, and even possibly broader investigation, government response in Canada has not been markedly quick or effective." (Friedman 1975: 155)

"One of Canada's leading antismoking campaigners, Mr. Garfield Mahood of the Canadian Non-Smokers' Rights Association, says governments only deliver reforms 'when pummelled into submission by health agencies, professionals and the media.'" (*Irish Times*, May 30, 2001)

Introduction

This chapter considers the evidence for several of the theories which might explain tobacco-control policy in Canada and the United States. Which theory or combination of theories can provide a superior explanation of policy over both time and space, in Canada and the United States over a period of more than a third of a century? Some theories may be better at explaining similarities while others contribute more to explaining differences. The six examined here are (1) agenda setting, (2) interest groups/social movements, (3) ideology/parties/elections, (4) political institutions, (5) political culture, and (6) policy typologies. Chapter Six focuses solely on lesson drawing. The major question involving this theory is this: does it offer additional explanatory power not provided by other theories?

Agenda Setting

Since tobacco control has waxed and waned on the political agendas of both countries over the past forty years, agenda-setting theories appear to hold considerable promise in helping explain policy. But, as outlined in Chapter Two, agenda-setting theories come in several varieties, and all of them are heavily dependent on how policy issues are defined and what actors are involved in setting the agenda.

Public opinion is a major component of agenda-setting theories. Opinion on the health risks of tobacco use has undergone a major shift over the past third of a century. While the effects of different government policies in affecting smoking are difficult to disentangle (Licari and Meier 1997), two Surgeon General's reports, 1964 and 1986, had medium-term effects on both the decline in smoking and the increased willingness to tolerate restrictions on tobacco use (Viscusi 1992: 47-59). Although the exact questions differ, it appears that in both countries over time there is increasing public recognition of the health hazards of smoking and a willingness to countenance more restrictive measures of tobacco control (US Department of Health and Human Services 1989; Morin 1996; National Population Health Survey Highlights 1999). Studies usually also show that even smokers favour most regulations (Janofsky 1994; Viscusi 1992; Bull, Pederson and Ashley 1994). As tobacco control has made greater inroads on the public agenda, it has penetrated the governmental agenda as well. In many instances public opinion on tobacco control appears to be ahead of governmental action (US Department of Health and Human Services 1986, 2000b).

Public opinion, however, is not uniformly in favour of all tobacco restrictions. The Canadian smuggling crisis of 1994 was an episode where pro-tobacco forces were able to mobilize a winning coalition, but it took a particular confluence of circumstances. Without a burgeoning supply of Canadian cigarettes being shipped over the Canada-US border, negative opinion from smokers and vendors about the high price of cigarettes would have been ineffective. In that instance there was the opportunity to link tobacco-control issues to other concerns—the forthcoming Quebec election, aboriginal rights, and law and order—which made pressure to reduce taxes effective.

Derthick (2001: 55-57) argues that the US public is not particularly sympathetic to tobacco restrictions. She cites polls done at the time of the National Settlement and MSA in 1997-98 that showed only lukewarm public support for specific policies within those measures, especially tobacco-company legal and financial compensation for smoking-related illnesses. These surveys represent a specific point in time, however, and the results also may reflect the long and expensive tobacco-industry campaign against the National Settlement as it emerged in the McCain Bill. She acknowledges, however, that the public is not very intense in its views. This is probably also true of their knowledge of specific proposals.

There has been neither a great public demand for tobacco regulation and taxation nor much resistance to it. Public opinion has evolved into what analysts call a "permissive consensus" on tobacco control, that is, a willingness to accept greater government regulation of tobacco, usually including increased taxes (Mathematica Policy Research 1995), even if most people are not intensely interested in the issue. Tobacco control as a policy issue engages the active attention of only a small portion of the public, what might be termed the "attentive public." Aside from those economically dependent on tobacco growth, production, and sales, members of the attentive public include public-health practitioners and anti-tobacco activists.

In Kingdon's (1995) terms, the Surgeon General's reports of 1964, 1986, and 1988 were "focusing events." These changed the politics stream enough to allow a policy window to emerge that put tobacco control on the political agenda and allowed consideration, and in some cases adoption, of policies that few had considered seriously in previous times. In the 1990s, the public and medical consensus about the dangers of tobacco usage and the questionable behaviour of its promoters became so pervasive that dramatic Surgeon General's reports were no longer necessary to get and keep tobacco control on the agenda. Instead, other events—court cases, testimony from whistle-blowers, newly discovered internal tobacco company documents, and activities by anti-tobacco entrepreneurs—served this purpose.

Baumgartner and Jones (1993: 117) contend that only one side of a complex issue tends to dominate public discourse at a time, which in turn influences policy outcomes; this is what they refer to as the "tone" of the issue, while Nathanson (1999) refers to this as "ownership" of an issue. Certain dimensions of a multi-dimensional policy assume prominence in media coverage and become dominant in the minds of policy-makers and the public. In tobacco control, there has been a persistent struggle over issue definition, largely, as one might expect, between the groups concerned. For a long time in mid-century, tobacco restrictions were not an issue on the public or governmental agenda—instead, promotion of an economically valuable, culturally favoured product was the norm. The health concerns publicized in the 1950s gave tobacco restrictions an opportunity for re-entry onto the public agenda and made it a potential issue for the governmental agenda, but one that no government anywhere readily seized. By the mid-1960s, however, the agenda had shifted. The combination of policies of both promotion and restriction that governments have pursued since then through different agencies indicates the difficulties they have had in adopting consistent definitions of the issue.

But after a flurry of federal tobacco-restrictive activities in both the United States and Canada in the late 1960s and early 1970s, this dimension of the issue receded again. The Reports of the US Surgeon General on various aspects of tobacco use continued to be issued on a regular basis but without major political impact. According to Baumgartner and Jones (1993), the media were inattentive and anti-smoking groups lacked unity and focus. Research continued, some lower jurisdictions acted, but it was not until over a decade later that tobacco restrictions again became prominent on the federal level in both countries.

In Canada, the federal government gave the issue new prominence through its tax increases on cigarettes and investigative work within Health and Welfare Canada. Furthermore, aided by the stimulus of Lynn McDonald's private member's bill and more organized anti-tobacco groups, the federal government introduced Bill C-51, which eventually became the *Tobacco Products Control Act*. In the United States, there was increasing elite concern which led to a strengthening of the warning labels in 1984. But again it was a report from the US Surgeon General, this time on second-hand smoke in 1986, that prompted widespread public concern and propelled tobacco control to the more prominent and persistent position on the political agenda. However relatively small the damage caused by inhaling second-hand smoke in comparison to first-hand smoking, findings that exposure was dangerous meant that tobacco use was no longer only an individual choice, but a social problem, especially in light of the emerging preventive health policy agenda.

The 1986 report of the Surgeon General legitimized fears about second-hand smoke that had been voiced for years by interest groups such as GASP and the Non-Smokers' Rights Association. There had also been concern over this issue expressed by professional organizations. The coupling of the Surgeon General's public endorsement of the scientific evidence with groups eager to seize the opportunity resulted in a large amount of executive and legislative action on all levels of government, further enhanced by the 1993 EPA classification of tobacco smoke as a carcinogen (Berridge 1998; Nathanson 1999). In short, reducing environmental tobacco smoke was a solution that needed to be joined to the right problem. The struggle over defining the tobacco-control issue became more highly contested. Tobacco companies are interested in arguments that provide them with legal protection and allow delays in the imposition of regulations or taxes. In such a profitable industry, time is literally money. A regulation delayed for a period of time, even a year or two, results in more profits for that time period.

The tobacco industry and its allies have tried several different issue definitions, depending on the circumstances, with varying success. One persistent definition has been the economic benefits of tobacco production and the detriments of regulation. Companies also attempt to get the taxation of tobacco defined as a "taxation issue" rather than a health issue or a revenue question. This has been more successful in the United States than in Canada except when the taxation issue could be coupled with other concerns in 1994. But in the United States, the major public argument employed by the companies in a massive advertising campaign against the McCain version of the National Settlement was that it was a "tax grab" by politicians. Not satisfied with defeating the bill, the companies continued their advertisements even after its demise, possibly attempting to inculcate the association of financial penalties against tobacco companies with tax increases in the minds of the public (Kurtz 1998; Torry and Dewar 1998).

Another long-standing issue definition preferred by the industry has been commercial freedom of speech, which had a considerable impact on the Supreme Court decision overturning the TPCA in Canada. This concept appears to be one more readily argued based on the Charter of Rights and Freedoms than on the Bill of Rights in the US. Since 1942 the US Supreme Court has constructed rights to commercial free speech relatively narrowly, although recent decisions, including the 2001 Massachusetts tobacco-advertising case, have expanded it (Kluger 1996: 628-33). Individual free choice to consume tobacco, whatever its attendant risks, is an argument that is appealing to some (Viscusi 1992; Sullum 1998). Evidence that nicotine is highly addictive damages the "freedom of choice" definitions of tobacco usage. According to tobacco supporters, making tobacco products more expensive through taxation threatens law and order through smuggling. The 1994 Canadian experience was cited by tobacco companies in arguing against the increases in their costs contained in the McCain Bill.

Another definition regularly employed by the industry is that regulations are the "slippery slope" leading to eventual prohibition of cigarettes and that a similar fate may await other health-damaging products such as fast foods. Anti-tobacco advocates are often portrayed as prohibitionists in disguise. A successful use of the prohibition argument would benefit the industry because there is a general unwillingness to repeat the experience of alcohol prohibition in both Canada and the United States in the early twentieth century (Smart and Ogborne 1996). Apparently the industry was successful in recruiting other businesses to its fight against the McCain Bill in 1998 by arousing fears of potential litigation and financial penalties against them as well (Torry 1998).

The "doubts about health consequences" argument was an effective delaying tactic for many years, but this argument has faded in recent years in view of the overwhelming scientific evidence to the contrary and widespread public acceptance of it. The struggle for issue definition on the grounds of health effects lingers, however, in the debate over the health effects of second-hand smoke (Gori and Luik 1999; Non-Smokers' Rights Association 1999).

Anti-tobacco advocates, on the other hand, have generally tried to get the tobacco-control question defined as one of public and individual health. Since the mid-1980s, they have been more successful in impressing these definitions upon policy-makers and the public. Especially successful has been the focus on underage smoking, which has become the dominant part of the tobacco-control policy definition in the US in the 1990s (e.g., Center for Tobacco-Free Kids) and a large part of the definition in Canada (Forster and Wolfson 1998). Underage smoking has a "motherhood and apple pie" quality, hard for tobacco companies to oppose publicly, however much they may balk at effective enforcement of such policies (Hilts 1996). Some companies have decided to join in the public chorus against youth smoking, on their own terms. In testimony before a committee of the Senate in 2000, the chief executives of major tobacco companies in Canada gave qualified endorsement to Senator Kenny's bills to set up a foundation to combat teenage smoking with revenue from a levy on tobacco-company sales.

The recent tobacco company assertion that they do not want young people to smoke is an attempt to reclaim some of the legitimacy lost from the public exposure of internal company documents. The companies are aware that definition of the tobacco-control issue is very important to their standing with policy-makers and the general public. Tobacco-company studies of appeals to underage consumers of cigarettes have been some of the evidence most damaging to the companies' credibility. Much of the early evidence on this point came from Canadian documents (Hilts 1996: 91). This has put tobacco companies on the defensive in terms of issue definition. It has also given ammunition to those who argue that the real, underlying problem is the behaviour of the companies themselves. In this view, tobacco companies are not simply a private business selling a legal product but rather an outlaw industry that needs not only to be countered but to be "denormalized" or "delegitimized" in the public mind (Non-Smokers' Rights Association 1993; Glantz and Balbach 2000).

If there is not yet a consensus among anti-tobacco advocates that a strategy for denormalization is desirable, this is partly because what it would entail is not exactly clear. Is the aim to delegitimize the industry as well as the product it makes? At the broadest level, anything that limits smoking and the promotion of tobacco products might qualify. Thus, according to Gregory Connolly (Plenary Session 1996), even laws controlling environmental tobacco smoke constitute denormalization because such regulations create an environment that says "smoking is objectionable." On the other hand, the leading Canadian proponent of denormalization, Garfield Mahood of the NSRA, recommends focussing on the dangers to children, litigation, warning labels, and counteradvertising (Non-Smokers' Rights Association 1996; Mahood 1997).

Some date the beginning of this new phase—characterizing tobacco as a social menace, even to the extent of demonizing, delegitimizing, or denormalizing the industry as well as the product—to use of the term "merchants of death" by a spokesman for the American Cancer Society on television in 1988 (Nathanson 1999). But a book with the same title was published that year (White 1988). Even before the Surgeon General's Report of 1986, the first successful national campaign of the NSRA against joint tobacco company-government sponsorship of Canadian amateur skiing events had already occurred in 1984-85; that was also the first campaign by the newly formed PSFC, which had been formed to help conduct the effort (Rosser 1985). By 1986, even the prestigious *Journal of the American Medical Association* was using pejorative terms to describe the consequences of tobacco consumption. Also in that year, ideas for the "second wave" of anti-tobacco litigation in the United States were being

Table 5-1: Chronology of Books on the Politics of Tobacco

Phase 4 Books on the Politics of Tobacco, 1963-1983

1963: Neuberger, *Smokescreen: Tobacco and the Public Welfare*
1969: Fritschler, *Smoking and Politics: Policy Making and the Federal Bureaucracy*, 1st ed.
1971: Wagner, *Cigarette Country: Tobacco in American History and Politics*
1971: Whiteside, *Selling Death: Cigarettes and the Public Health*
1975: Friedman, *Public Policy and the Smoking-Health Controversy*
1978: Sobel, *They Satisfy: Cigarettes in American Life*
1979: Doron, *The Smoking Paradox: Public Regulation in the Cigarette Industry*
1983: Troyer and Markle, *Cigarettes: The Battle over Smoking*

Phase 5 Books on the Politics of Tobacco, 1984-2001

1984: Whelan, *A Smoking Gun: How the Tobacco Industry Gets Away with Murder*
1984: Taylor, *Smoke Ring: The Politics of Tobacco*
1985: Taylor, *The Smoke Ring: Tobacco, Money, and Multinational Politics*, revised ed.
1986: Wilkinson, *Tobacco*
1986: Tollison and Wagner, *Smoking and the State: Toward a More Balanced Assessment*
1988: White, *Merchants of Death: The American Tobacco Industry*
1989: Ferrence, *Deadly Fashion: The Rise and Fall of Cigarette Smoking in North America*
1989: Goodin, *No Smoking: The Ethical Issues*
1992: Viscusi, *Smoking: Making the Risky Decision*
1993: Rabin and Sugarman: *Smoking Policy: Law, Politics, and Culture*
1996: Cunningham, *Smoke and Mirrors: The Canadian Tobacco War*
1996: Kluger, *Ashes to Ashes: America's Hundred-Year Cigarette War, the Public Health, and the Unabashed Triumph of Philip Morris*
1996: Hilts, *Smokescreen: The Truth Behind the Tobacco Industry Cover-Up*
1996: Glantz et al., *The Cigarette Papers*
1997: Sullum, *For Your Own Good: The Anti-Smoking Crusade and the Tyranny of Public Health*
1998: Pringle, *Cornered: Big Tobacco at the Bar of Justice*

Table 5-1 continued: Chronology of Books on the Politics of Tobacco

1998: Mollenkamp et al., *The People vs. Big Tobacco: How the States Took on the Cigarette Giants*

1998: Phelps et al., *Smoked: The Inside Story of the Minnesota Tobacco Trial*

1999: Obey, *Assuming the Risk: The Mavericks, the Lawyers, and the Whistle-Blowers Who Beat Big Tobacco*

1999: Tate, *Cigarette Wars: The Triumph of the "Little White Slaver"*

1999: Males, *Smoked: Why Joe Camel Is Still Smiling*

2000: Glantz and Balbach, *Tobacco War: Inside the California Battles*

2000: Zegart, *Civil Warriors: The Legal Seige on the Tobacco Industry*

2001: Kessler, *A Question of Intent: A Great American Battle with a Deadly Industry*

2001: Parker-Pope, *Cigarettes: Anatomy of an Industry from Seed to Smoke*

developed at Northeastern University in a faculty symposium entitled "Selling Death: Individual and Organizational Responsibility and the Tobacco Industry" (Daynard et al. 1986).

The titles of the growing number of books on tobacco politics produced over the years are an indication of the change in tone over the tobacco-control issue (see Table 5-1). British journalist Peter Taylor made films about the tobacco industry in the mid-1970s called "Licenced to Kill" and "Death in the West: The Marlboro Story." Distribution of the latter was limited by legal action from Philip Morris in British courts (Kluger 1996: 470-72). After the mid-1980s, graphic, mordant titles involving death, war, and deception became more common, indeed almost *de rigueur*, for authors in this area, unless their work was sympathetic to the industry.

Increasingly, the problem was seen by anti-tobacco groups as the economic and political power of the tobacco industry. This viewpoint was encouraged by revelations about the contents of internal tobacco-company documents, first through leaked documents provided by whistle-blowers (Glantz et al. 1996; Hilts 1996), and later through the "discovery" process in US lawsuits, especially the Minnesota lawsuit against the tobacco industry (Collishaw 1999).

By attacking the credibility of the industry directly, anti-tobacco advocates aim to damage the industry's reputation and its status as a legitimate stakeholder to be consulted by governments. The language of such attacks has become confrontational. Tobacco companies have been characterized as "murderers," "killers," "merchants of death," "drug dealers," an "outlaw" industry responsible not only for a tobacco "epidemic," but also for a "pandemic" and a "holocaust." The industry itself is a "disease vector" (Sweanor 1998a; Koop 1998).

Even some official programs in California and Canada have added delegitimization or denormalization of the tobacco industry as a fourth goal, in addition to the older triumvirate of prevention, cessation, and protection. In California, one of the four priority areas for the 1993 Tobacco Control Program was "revealing and countering tobacco industry influence"; this has subsequently been reaffirmed and endorsed as "vigorously exposing tobacco industry tactics" in sponsorships and advertising (US Department of Health and Human Services 2000b: 388; *Toward a Tobacco-Free California* 2000). In Canada, denormalization became an official part of government policy in the 1999 National Tobacco Control Strategy. The Annual Report on the Ontario Tobacco Strategy from the Ontario Tobacco Research Unit (2000b) argued that the tobacco companies' "unethical and dishonest activities" ought to be publicized. Explicit targeting of the tobacco industry, however, remains controversial in both countries.

In terms of public agenda setting, however, the image of the tobacco executives testifying before Congress in 1994 and denying the dangerous nature of tobacco at this late date has been one of the signal events of the recent era, perhaps matching the landmark Surgeon General's reports. These images have been played repeatedly on television and prominently featured in the film "The Insider." Although revelations from documents may have been more important in lawsuits, the hearings had a more public impact. "Big Tobacco" became the appellation of the cigarette companies thereafter. In many ways, the recent "charm offensive" of the tobacco industry has been an attempt to overcome his image.

Tobacco companies themselves adopted defensive self-descriptions, such as their being "a responsible company making a legal product in a controversial industry," in the words of Nick Brookes (2000), Chairman and Chief Executive Officer of Brown and Williamson. In response to the negative tone established in recent years, by the late 1990s the companies were presenting a more acceptable face of tobacco, admitting some of the problems, posting some internal company documents on their Web sites, and offering to cooperate with those concerned about teenage smoking. Philip Morris especially has been pursuing this approach. At the same time, however, they continued to mount legal challenges to regulation and formidable defences against government and individual lawsuits. Outside the courtroom, however, the public face of tobacco was remade into a reasonable, discursive one, often abetted by having women as public affairs spokespersons.

Some anti-tobacco advocates have objected to tobacco companies sponsoring school-based programs on the dangers of smoking for young people because it allows the companies to present themselves as responsible members of the community. The issue is similar to the question of tobacco-company sponsorship of arts, sports, and charitable activities. Should tobacco companies be banned from doing "good works" because the company needs to be isolated from civil society as much as possible?

Anti-tobacco advocates, however, also faced a dilemma over definitions of the tobacco-control agenda. Should the tobacco industry be viewed as a stakeholder in the process or as a pariah? Following a denormalization strategy suggests the latter. If so, then how can one consider negotiating with such disreputable people? This led to serious internal divisions over the National Settlement in 1997-98. Some health groups endorsed it, but others did not. Matthew L. Myers of the Center for Tobacco-Free Kids became a controversial figure within his own coalition for participating in the discussions as the sole representative of public-health groups. Director-General Gro Harlem Brundtland of the WHO has compared tobacco companies to mosquitos carrying malaria and has refused to allow them to participate in negotiations over the FCTC. They are only to be allowed to submit written and oral testimony. This has generated controversy, especially since the United States initially favoured allowing the tobacco companies to participate in the negotiations ("The Tobacco War Goes Global" 2000; Joosens 2000).

Denormalization also divides anti-tobacco forces inside and outside government. Those outside government, having helped shape much of the agenda and to some degree the content of policy over the past two decades, want to push for further reductions in tobacco consumption. Thus a strategy of denormalization, identifying tobacco as a drug and its manufacturers as miscreants, is appealing. To those inside government—cabinet ministers, public-health officials, and even legislators—this approach is less appealing because, however vast the health problems raised by tobacco may be, the industry does represent an important economic and political force. It can be regulated and taxed, but can it be delegitimized? Denormalization suggests that policy-makers need not consult companies nor pay heed to their arguments and concerns. Such a strategy goes against the inclinations of policy-makers to allow all voices with a stake in the issue at hand to be heard and to construct necessary compromises in formulating policy. Significantly, the major governmental official arguing for denormalization while in office has been Surgeon General Koop, whose administrative responsibilities did not involve political negotiations with tobacco companies. How far to pursue denormalization, both in terms of defining the issue on the public agenda and within anti-tobacco groups, will be a critical consideration in the next decade.

The stasis that tobacco control has reached in the United States after the MSA, further encouraged by the Supreme Court decision against FDA authority, indicates why denormalization may be a critical dimension in defining tobacco control. As Michael Pertschuk (1997) predicted, any major negotiated settlement over tobacco issues might lead to a period in which tobacco control recedes on the public and governmental agendas because the problems are widely assumed to have been resolved. This helps explain why tobacco control was not an issue in the 2000 Presidential election. The incoming Bush Administration also was able to nominate two cabinet members, including the Secretary of Health and Human Services, who were on-record supporters of the tobacco industry, without major controversy over tobacco-control policy emerging in Senate confirmation proceedings. As some tobacco stock analysts and lobbyists suggested, the elite consensus in the United States at the time appeared to be that "tobacco has paid its dues in the last few years" (Chartier 2000). But that plateau of indifference toward further tobacco control may not last.

Political entrepreneurship—the ability to take advantage of circumstances to push an issue onto the public and governmental agenda—is an important part of several theories, including agenda setting, interest groups/social movements, and diffusion/lesson drawing. However, it has been incorporated most extensively into agenda setting. Kingdon (1995) especially argues that it takes individuals committed to an issue to push it forward at propitious moments. Recent work (Mintrom 1997a, 1997b; Mintrom and Vergari 1996) on diffusion has emphasized entrepreneurship, arguing that, in effect, policy innovations do not spread very far without committed, individual champions for the ideas. These authors also make a useful distinction between entrepreneurs and advocates, with the former being more creative in exploiting political opportunities for their favoured policy.

Similarly, within tobacco-control policy, one can point to particular individuals, sometimes governmental and sometimes nongovernmental, who have played important roles in placing and maintaining tobacco restrictions on the political agenda. Hays et al. (2000a, 2000b) have extended Kingdon's (1995) perspective to tobacco control at the local level in the United States, as has Studlar (2000) for the Canadian provinces. Most politicians and bureaucrats who become prominent on tobacco-control issues deal with it only for a time; legislators have a greater choice of interests to pursue than do bureaucrats. Nevertheless, in the United States and Canada there are some governmental officials who have achieved prominence through persistent efforts in tobacco-control policy. On the federal level in the United States these include Surgeon General C. Everett Koop, FDA Commissioner David Kessler, and US Senators and Representatives Maurine Neuberger, Henry Waxman, Richard Durbin, and Mike Synar. US state-level entrepreneurs include Gregory Connolly of the Massachusetts Tobacco Control Program and the attorneys general of several states, such as Mike Moore of Mississippi, Hubert H. Humphrey III of Minnesota, and Scott Harshbarger of Massachusetts.

In Canada, there are fewer legislators or ministers with this kind of long record, but for shorter periods of time on the federal level legislators Barry Mather, Lynn McDonald, and Colin Kenny and health ministers Jake Epp and David Dingwall achieved widespread recognition. Some analysts consider that Alan Rock has built a similar record as Health Minister. On the provincial level health ministers Joy McPhail and Penny Priddy in British Columbia and Jean Rochon in Quebec have been instrumental in pushing tobacco restrictions forward. In their usually quiet ways, some bureaucrats also may act as entrepreneurs although they might more properly be designated as advocates. Donald Shopland in the US worked on tobacco control for the federal government in various capacities for almost 40 years (Kluger 1996: 440-41). The longest-serving administrative official consistently working on tobacco issues in Health Canada is Murray Kaiserman. The expertise of both Shopland and Kaiserman has long been recognized on the other side of the border; in fact, Shopland was presented with an "unsung hero" award at the WCTOH in Chicago in 2000, shortly before his retirement from the US federal government. Michael Eriksen presided over the CDC during a time of mission and budgetary expansion for the agency under the Clinton Administration.

Even more internationally active bureaucrats might be termed "entrepreneurs." John Garcia has held several influential positions in tobacco control on both sides of the border. In a ten-year span, Garcia moved from the Toronto municipal government, where he became involved with the Canadian wing of the US COMMIT program, to the Ontario Ministry of Health, where he helped initiate the Ontario Tobacco Control Strategy under the NDP government on principles of community involvement adapted from COMMIT and ASSIST, to the private Prospect Associates, which monitored the ASSIST program in the United States; he then returned to Canada to serve with Cancer Care Ontario, also playing a role as an adviser to the Ontario Tobacco Control Strategy, now under the Conservative government. Beginning in the late 1970s, Neil Collishaw did the first ongoing investigations on various dimensions of tobacco for Health and Welfare Canada. He later was a key player in developing the *Tobacco Products Control Act* and then spent six years coordinating tobacco-control programs for the World Health Organization in the 1990s before returning to Canada to work with the lobby group Physicians for a Smoke-Free Canada. The careers of the latter two illustrate the fact that tobacco control has become an international issue, with cross-border bureaucrats as well as cross-border nongovernmental entrepreneurs.

Garcia and Collishaw also are examples of former government officials who moved to private anti-tobacco organizations. Others in the US include former Surgeon General Koop; former Massachusetts Attorney General Harshbarger, who subsequently worked for the Center for Tobacco-Free Kids; Michael Pertschuk, formerly a Congressional aide and an FTC Commissioner before heading the Advocacy Institute; and Matthew L. Myers, formerly on the staff of the FTC, then with COSH, and more recently with the Center for Tobacco-Free Kids.

In addition, many of the prominent entrepreneurs and advocates have remained in nongovernmental organizations, often with cross-border ties of varying strength. David Sweanor and Garfield Mahood of NSRA are undoubtedly entrepreneurs. Ken Kyle and Rob Cunningham of CCS, Michael Perley of OCAT, John Banzhaf of ASH, and Scott Ballin, formerly with COSH and now with the Center for Tobacco-Free Kids, may also fit into this category. A journalist such as Morton Mintz, who researched and wrote stories on tobacco issues in the late 1980s and early 1990s when few others in his profession gave this issue continuing attention, is at least an advocate. There are academic-activist entrepreneurs as well, such as Stanton Glantz of the University of California, San Francisco, and Richard Daynard of the Tobacco Litigation Center at Northeastern University in Massachusetts. Another who may become recognized as an entrepreneur is Allyn Taylor of Yale University, who was instrumental in developing the idea for a Framework Convention on Tobacco. Further consideration of the importance of some of these political, bureaucratic, and academic entrepreneurs and advocates will be offered in Chapter Six.

Another major contribution of agenda-setting theory to understanding tobacco control is the extensive venue switching that has occurred among critics and proponents of tobacco in both countries. Both groups have sought venues thought to be favourably disposed toward their definitions and policy alternatives. In Canada, the industry has sought judicial relief from both federal and provincial restrictions. Anti-tobacco activists increasingly have sought to bring legal actions against the companies. In the United States, the best venues for tobacco growers and industry have been Congress, certain federal agencies, and the federal courts, while anti-tobacco advocates have had better results with state legislatures, municipal governments in certain states, and state courts. Until the Clinton Administration, the US federal executive, with the exception of DHHS, was largely indifferent or hostile to restrictions on tobacco.

As a general explanation of changes in tobacco-control policy over time and between the two countries, agenda setting offers more similarities than differences. Both countries have had entrepreneurs who have been instrumental in pushing the issue forward. But restrictive tobacco control began in the 1980s rather than the 1960s. The entrepreneurs were able to take advantage of favourable circumstances in the general culture, namely the decline of smoking among the public and greater consciousness of healthy public policy, which aided receptivity to their arguments about the need for government action to regulate and tax tobacco.

Even if Canada had more cigarette regulation and taxation in the 1980s than did the United States, the agenda configuration of the tobacco-control issue in the two countries was similar, and appears to have converged even more, subsequently. Canada had to move further in policy, however, because of previous lack of government action. In the US, similar proposals to those in Canada were largely ignored until the mid-1990s and only sporadically adopted since then, indicating that it is easier in the US to get problems put on the agenda than to get policies adopted.

Interest Groups

Higher agenda status and more restrictive government policy actions during the fifth phase of tobacco control also have been attributed to the role of anti-tobacco interest groups and social movements in the latter period (Nathanson 1999; Glantz and Balbach 2000). There are more anti-tobacco groups now, encompassing more activists, and their degree of commitment and organization appears to be greater as well. As the focus of discontent shifted from the smoker to the environment that supports the habit, more people became willing to be involved. Grassroots activism appears to be especially important on the local level to sustain efforts at controlling environmental tobacco smoke in the face of business resistance, often financed by tobacco companies.

On the federal and state/provincial levels, the organization and commitment of leaders becomes even more important. Despite the accumulated scientific evidence in recent years of the dangers of cigarette smoking, without anti-tobacco political organizations to support appropriate legislation from governments, the situation might be similar to what it was in the third and fourth phases, with the tobacco lobby able to block practically any proposal.

However reluctant some Canadian health organizations, such as the CMA and the CCS, were to engage in political activities against tobacco, a comparative view indicates that they were actually more proactive against tobacco use after 1964 than their US counterparts. The ACS became less assertive on the issue, and the AMA did not endorse the findings of the 1964 Surgeon-General's Report for 14 years (Nathanson 1999). Kluger (1996: 465) calls this episode "a flagrant dereliction of the organization's professional responsibility." Once the AMA was brought into the anti-tobacco coalition, its support of tobacco-control measures remained lukewarm in comparison to higher-priority organizational concerns about government controls on medical practice and limits on civil lawsuits (Wolinsky and Brune 1994; Glantz and Balbach 2000).

Stimulated by the new perspectives on public health that emphasized a healthy lifestyle within a healthy environment, a more aggressive movement for restrictive tobacco control has arisen and flourished in both countries since the 1970s. The professional medical and health organizations opposing tobacco have joined since the 1980s in Canada and to a lesser degree in the United States with what might be called a "social movement" wing. Social movement organizations would be those such as

NSRA and PSFC in Canada and ANSR and DOC in the US, as described in Chapter One. Several authors (Chapman 1985; Wilson 1991; Nathanson 1999) have argued that such dedicated "splinter" groups were essential for the development of a politically powerful, confrontational attitude toward tobacco, not simply one based on disease treatment, persuasion, and education. In that sense, they have played a similar role as other "disease advocacy" groups such as those for AIDS and breast cancer in the United States (Fintor, Alciati and Fischer 1995).

In order to affect policy, attention to both public objectives and political lobbying is needed. This is where the role of nongovernmental political entrepreneurs with media savvy and governmental connections becomes important. As mentioned previously, several of the prominent entrepreneurs in tobacco control in both countries have been outside government. Beginning in the mid-1980s, the more radical, publicity-conscious anti-tobacco groups began to cooperate with the more established, mass-membership voluntary health organizations as the latter pursued a more active agenda of political advocacy (McGowan 1995: 35; Nathanson 1999). Indeed, some of the voluntary groups were re-energized. In both countries, even members of normally conservative professional groups dominated by the medical model of disease became motivated to send black-bordered messages with names of their constituents who had died from tobacco-related diseases to legislators, in support of tobacco-restrictive legislation.

One difference, perhaps a critical one, has been the relative unity of Canadian public-health interest groups on tobacco-control issues, in contrast to the United States. The Canadian Council on Smoking and Health, an umbrella organization, was established in 1974; its counterpart in the United States, the Coalition on Smoking OR Health, originated only in 1981. Some Canadian advocacy groups do receive government subsidies as public-interest lobbies, but they also can have their disbursements reduced or eliminated. The US pioneered in public subsidies to anti-tobacco groups, although more recently this has occurred on the local level through ASSIST, IMPACT, and NTCP.

There is always a certain amount of competition and rivalry among related interest groups, based on their differing missions, priorities, and leadership, but there seems to be more of this among anti-smoking groups in the United States than in Canada. In both countries, the major thrust for tobacco control has come from a trio of public-health organizations — usually labelled Cancer, Heart, and Lung Associations, but in Canada this has been abetted by the strong leadership of the Non-Smokers' Rights Association, which has no federal counterpart in the United States. These groups have pursued political advocacy against tobacco since the mid-1980s.

Overall, the more radical anti-tobacco groups have garnered support from the more traditional ones, but more so in Canada than the United States. This was evident in the battles over the *Tobacco Products Control Act* in 1987-88. A new, more concerted and aggressive political lobbying effort was created. Pross and Stewart (1994) argue that the intensity of lobbying on the TPCA was possibly unprecedented for Canada (see also Ondrick 1991; Wilson 1991). But this was not due solely to the anti-tobacco groups. Having lost its privileged access to cabinet, the CTMA also engaged in a major public lobbying effort against the bill (Callard 2000).

For interest groups to be successful, they must capitalize upon whatever windows of opportunity arise. Californians for Nonsmokers' Rights had some success at the local level in the late 1970s and early 1980s, but the main impact of the more radical groups occurred once "healthy public policy" became a more widespread outlook and other events and reports focussed concern, which political entrepreneurs then seized. NSRA, for instance, is especially oriented toward the healthy public policy perspective (Lachance, Kyle and Sweanor 1990: 4).

Kagan and Vogel's (1993) claim that interest-group explanations do better across time in one country than comparatively across space depends on interest-group activity being confined within borders. As the years went by, anti-tobacco groups developed international linkages to rival those of tobacco companies, as discussed more extensively in Chapter Six. Interest-group developments over the past two decades help account for changes in tobacco-control policy in both Canada and the United States. In both countries, increasing numbers of anti-tobacco groups may affect policy on different levels, but it is the *nature* of interest-group activity, especially organizational coherence and public appeal, which is critical.

Although similar interest-group developments might help account for some of the convergence of policy in the two countries, remaining variations in interest-group configurations also have led to differences. Specifically, Canadian groups appear to be more coherently organized and mutually supportive, and have a more aggressive strategy, especially on the federal level. This might help account for the more comprehensive and federally-oriented policies in Canada. Groups in the US remain less organizationally united and often have disproportionate strengths in

selected states, such as California. This helps explain the less comprehensive federal policy compared to policies in some states.

Parties, Ideology, and Elections

As the health problems of tobacco use have become more widely
recognized, defenders of the tobacco interests have come to rely more
heavily on lobbyists, lawyers, and legislators. Public opinion has shifted
toward greater tolerance for restrictive measures, especially as the number
of smokers has dropped by roughly half in the past 30 years. Even in that
group, many blame tobacco companies for their health problems; some
are unable to quit because they are addicted. This is further indication that
the hopes of tobacco interests lies increasingly in politics, not public
opinion.

Nevertheless, in the United States there has been no particular electoral advantage for individuals and parties taking strong tobacco-restrictive
stances. Attorneys General Scott Harshbarger in Massachusetts and
Hubert H. Humphrey III in Minnesota, both prominent in state lawsuits
against tobacco companies, lost their subsequent bids for election as governor. Mike Moore in Mississippi continued as attorney general rather
than run for an open gubernatorial position after his own lawsuit success.
A private attorney prominent in the Minnesota lawsuit, Mike Cerisi, lost a
bid to be the Democratic nominee for US Senator against a vulnerable
Republican incumbent in 2000. Tobacco control became a campaign
issue in the US presidential race in 1996 when Republican candidate Bob
Dole denied the addictive nature of tobacco and promised to fire FDA
Commissioner David Kessler, while President Clinton and Vice-President
Gore were critical of the industry. But tobacco control was not an issue in
the 2000 election despite one of the presidential debates being staged in
North Carolina. In Canada, some parties, such as the federal
Conservatives, Ontario NDP, and British Columbia NDP, introduced
greater tobacco regulation and taxation, and lost subsequent elections.
However, their losses were not attributed to their positions on this issue.
Other parties with strong tobacco-restrictive records, such as the federal
Conservatives in 1988, the federal Liberals in 1997, and the Parti
Québécois in 1998, have won. In short, tobacco has not been a major issue
in electoral politics among the public at large.

In the United States, there is considerable evidence that Republicans tend to inhibit stronger tobacco-control initiatives at the state level. Studies of the process by which states joined the lawsuit that eventually led to the MSA have consistently shown that Republican attorneys general, especially elected ones, were slower than their Democratic counterparts (Chard and Howard 2000; Hager and Gabel 2000; Spill, Licari and Ray 2001). Similarly, Chriqui (2000) finds that Republican control of a state legislature hindered tobacco-control innovation. In a survey of legislators in three states (Vermont, Texas, and North Carolina), Goldstein et al. (1997) found that Republicans were less likely to intend to vote for tobacco-restrictive measures; Flynn et al. (1997) discovered that in Vermont Republicans were not only less likely to vote for a tobacco tax increase tied to expanding low-income health insurance coverage, but were also less likely to signal that intention, i.e., they had a greater gap between expressed attitudes and actions. In Canada, although cohesive party voting usually occurs in legislatures, political party affiliation has been found to be slightly related to policy opinion on tobacco control (with New Democrat legislators being most favourable and Progressive Conservatives the least) (Cohen et al. 2000).

Although it is difficult to generalize from a limited number of cases, Progressive Conservative governments in the provinces have been reluctant to initiate or innovate in tobacco control, unlike at the federal level, where the PC government of 1984-93 passed the measures that made Canada temporarily a world leader in tobacco control. Provincial governments where the Progressive Conservatives recently have been in charge—Prince Edward Island, Alberta, New Brunswick, Manitoba, and Ontario—have not witnessed major legislation under their leadership. In Manitoba, the *Non-Smokers Health Protection Act* (1990) was the result of a private member's bill by the NDP leader rather than Conservative government legislation. In Ontario, the Progressive Conservative government inherited a strong tobacco-restrictive regime. Although it did not alter these policies radically, it substantially reduced funding for them.

While other parties contain individuals and groups with convictions to act in this area, the NDP, with its ingrained suspicion of business arguments and its willingness to use government to pursue the public interest, has been more inclined to adopt and implement strong tobacco restrictions and to commit the necessary resources to support them. As part of the preventive public-health agenda arising in recent years, tobacco control offers leftist governments a cause that does not incur the heavy public expenditures for which they are often criticized. Of the five recent New Democratic governments in Canada (two in British Columbia), as of mid-2001 only those in Saskatchewan and Manitoba have failed to adopt more stringent tobacco-control regulations, and Saskatchewan is considering such legislation. In their times, the NDP governments in Ontario and British Columbia instituted the most stringent provincial tobacco-regulatory regimes in Canada. The Parti Québécois, often accused of losing its social democratic roots, legislated the Quebec *Tobacco Act* of 1998 despite the importance of tobacco companies and the cultural significance of smoking in the province. The Liberals, as one might expect, are neither as aggressively anti-tobacco as the NDP nor as reluctant as the PC to act. The Liberal government in Newfoundland has indicated a willingness to litigate, but those in Nova Scotia and New Brunswick have wavered on tobacco restrictions. The one in Prince Edward Island did relatively little.

On the federal level, the influence of partisan, ideological, and electoral factors appears to be more limited. One electoral rule in the United States, which may be more important for interest-group access than elections *per se*, is the campaign finance system. The enormous financial clout of Big Tobacco has been applied to support the campaigns of its allies, which buttresses the high return rate of incumbent Congressmen. In Canada, there is less opportunity for such spending on behalf of individual candidates because of spending limits (Smith and Bakvis 2000). Support of an agreed party line is reinforced by the capacity of party leaders to intervene in parliamentary candidate selections, and election outcomes are heavily dependent on the relative popularity of parties, not individual candidates.

The decline of the Democratic party in the US South has allowed business-oriented interests and anti-regulatory attitudes of the Republican party to coalesce with the regional economic interests of tobacco growers and manufacturers. The Republican Congressional leadership in recent years also has been overwhelmingly from the South and has engaged in manoeuvres, especially on budget questions, to ease taxes and litigation costs borne by tobacco companies (Jacobson and Warner 1999). However, the Republican party does not always want its efforts to protect tobacco manufacturers publicized because of their poor public image.

Partisan patterns occur in Congressional voting on tobacco-related bills, legislative hearings on tobacco issues, and, most tellingly, the pattern of political contributions, in which 80 per cent of tobacco company donations go to Republicans. Even if tobacco-company political contributions do not influence the votes of legislators, they certainly reinforce the ideological inclinations of conservative legislators in the US (Moore et al. 1994; Wright 1998). Nevertheless, the loose party cohesion in the US Congress also has allowed some Republicans, such as Senator John McCain, to become leaders in the fight against Big Tobacco, along with such executive-level Republican anti-tobacco icons as C. Everett Koop and David Kessler.

Ironically, these partisan and electoral factors have led to greater partisan polarization on tobacco issues in the United States than in Canada. In the latter country, partisan and electoral factors have rarely been involved in tobacco policy. Operating under rules of party discipline and cohesion unthinkable to their counterparts in the United States, even Canadian MPs from tobacco regions are insulated from constituency complaints. For a party in government, once the Prime Minister and Cabinet decide policy, then the legislative party is expected to follow, at least with their votes. One exception to this occurred when a Liberal MP from a tobacco-farming constituency in Ontario introduced a successful amendment to the *Tobacco Act* compelling the Executive to submit new tobacco regulations to the House of Commons Committee on Health for scrutiny before they were enacted, an unusual process for executive regulations in Canada. Thus the new cigarette package warning labels were submitted and endorsed by the Committee in 2000.

Perhaps more interestingly, however, opposition parties in Canada have not made tobacco into a partisan issue, except the Bloc Québécois in a limited way; the BQ has acted sporadically to defend the interests of tobacco manufacturers, retailers, and the "champion smokers" of its home province. But despite fuming verbally at some aspects of tobacco-control legislation, the BQ lacks the power to block legislation in view of near unanimity among the other parties about the broad principles underlying tobacco regulation. In contrast to its many policies similar to those of US Republicans, the former Reform Party, with a physician as its health spokesperson, was critical of the Liberal government during passage of the *Tobacco Act*, and of subsequent amendments, for not pursuing even stronger restrictive measures in tobacco control.

There is no recent evidence of tobacco becoming an issue in federal elections. Canadian campaign finance rules limit the impact of contributions from the tobacco industry, especially on the local level. Thus, whatever divisions exist between and within parties over tobacco have tended to be blurred in public, especially at election time, with the exception of the Liberals' espousal of tax reductions to combat the smuggling crisis in anticipation of the Quebec election in 1994. In summary, then, there has been less evident partisanship in recent years on the tobacco-control issue in Canada than in the United States, which is at least partially attributable to the opportunities for interest groups to wield financial power in political campaigns.

Overall, the influence of partisanship, ideology, and electoral politics on tobacco-control policy is more behind-the-scenes than public because of the disapprobation in which tobacco companies have been held in recent years. Campaign finance rules in the US especially allow tobacco manufacturers to reinforce and reward the conservative inclinations of Republican legislators and executives, especially those from tobacco-growing regions. In Canada, tobacco influence is even more likely to be behind-the-scenes rather than overt because there are fewer opportunities for directly partisan and electoral influence. Redoubts of support for tobacco remain, however, especially in some sections of the federal Liberal Party, which dominates Ontario seats, and the Bloc Québécois. No party, however, has made tobacco control a major electoral issue, on either the provincial or federal level.

Parties, ideology, and elections show both similarities and differences between the two countries, but more of the former. Ideology operates as expected in both countries, with individuals and parties further to the left generally more favourable toward tobacco control. But this is muted by some figures on the right strongly supporting greater restrictions on tobacco, and parties being generally unwilling to make defence of tobacco a campaign issue. Somewhat surprisingly, legislative partisanship on tobacco is greater in the United States than in Canada.

Political Culture

Political culture also seems more suited to explaining similarities between the two countries than differences. Whatever general cultural distinctions remain between the US and Canada do not seem to have affected tobacco-control policy. As political culture differences have shrunk over time, the similarities in tobacco control have become stronger. Even when Canada was reluctant to impose legal restrictions on tobacco in the late 1960s, a memorandum from the Health Minister to the Cabinet expressed regret over Canada's not being a leading country in this area of health policy, as it had been on others (Government of Canada 1970). There is the same range of opinions and arguments on tobacco-control measures in both countries today.

Some have argued that Canadians still exhibit greater security consciousness and less "risk inclination" than residents of the United States, which might help account for their more comprehensive federal measures over time in tobacco control (Banting, Hoberg and Simeon 1997). But that does not explain why Canada and the US have converged on tobacco control in recent years, why Canadians tend to look to the federal level for action while in the US more policies have developed at the state and local levels, and, especially, why such a "risk-averse" orientation did not manifest itself earlier, in the 1960s and 1970s, when cultural differences from the United States presumably would have been greater.

The changes in Canadian interest group behaviour over the past quarter-century can also be considered changes in political culture brought about, at least in part, by changes in political institutions. Making lobbying on public policy more publicly visible has benefitted anti-tobacco groups more than the tobacco industry. This is a change that has moved Canada toward US practices and that might help account for the convergence of policies in tobacco control.

Similarly, the shift toward a "healthy public policy" stemming from the Lalonde Report in 1974 has had a cross-national impact for convergence in the two countries, starting in the bureaucracy but spreading more widely. In response to criticism that this was a "blaming the victim" approach that allowed governments to spend less on health care, proponents of this approach emphasized increasingly that reports showed how environmental as well as individual behaviour influences health. In the case of tobacco use, that environment was the still powerful cultural and political role of the tobacco industry, even more evident as domestic tobacco agriculture declined in both the US and Canada. Thus the emphasis on healthy public policy is a force for convergence as well.

In short, both the shrinking general cultural differences between the United States and Canada, and especially their shared embrace, over time, in the second revolution in public health, are forces for convergence. There may remain some cultural differences, however, in the tendency of the United States to see itself as a different and superior country, a leader for others but not a follower. This leads it to be sceptical of whether policies adopted in other countries can be successfully applied in the US as well.

Political Institutions

Despite the counter-intuitive findings of Friedman's (1975) earlier study, a broader inquiry finds that the variations observable between the US and Canada over time and across levels in tobacco control are at least partially due to the effects of political institutions (Weaver and Rockman 1993). In the US presidential system, there are more potential veto points than in the Canadian parliamentary one, which allows groups to seek more favourable venues for their interests.

In Canada, once tobacco control is placed on the formal parliamentary agenda, any legislation or budget proposals are highly likely to pass in a form closely resembling the original unless the Cabinet chooses to accept changes or allow the bill to die. Thus policy responsibility is clearly in the executive even though the tobacco constituency linkages of federal MPs are very similar to those in the US. Twelve per cent of the members of the House of Commons had an industry or agriculture presence in their district in 1996, almost identical to the rate in the US House of Representatives (Ashley et al. 1997). The Senate is not a co-equal body, as shown by the fate of Senator Kenny's bills. This same institutional responsibility for tobacco control obtains in provincial unicameral legislatures. When tobacco-control legislation has been allowed to wither, as on the federal level in 1971 and in Nova Scotia in the mid-1990s (the latter was never formally introduced), this is due to insufficient commitment by the executive of the governing party although it may be influenced by its legislative party caucus behind closed doors.

There are few democratic parliamentary systems in the world that enforce party discipline on the floor of a legislature as rigorously as does Canada's. A government committed to legislation, as was the federal Conservative government in 1988 and the Liberal government in 1997, can usually get its way, based on fusion of powers and majority party discipline. In the US, presidents and legislative leaders can propose, but party discipline usually cannot be relied upon to pass their proposals.

A similar situation occurs in finance. Despite the tax reductions in Canada in 1994 and the tax increases in the United States in 1984, 1989, and 1997, over the long term the Canadian federal government has imposed larger tax increases on tobacco products. This is facilitated by the fact that budgets are imposed by the executive relatively quickly through party voting in the legislature and cannot be delayed and "cherry picked" by affected interests, as in the United States. Some coordination of federal and provincial budgets also often occurs, again unlike the United States. Cunningham (1996:122) contends that Michael Wilson, Finance Minister under the Progressive Conservative government of Brian Mulroney (1984-93) did more to limit smoking than any other individual in Canada. On the other hand, if the government decides to change policy through the budget, it can readily do that as well, as shown by the 1994 tax reductions.

Tobacco interests can modify, postpone, and, in the run-up to an election, possibly even stifle legislation through delaying tactics by extending debate and offering amendments. They may also, as with the *Tobacco Act*, persuade the government to amend legislation and/or delay implementation. But in all these instances, they have to lobby the executive to support them rather than relying exclusively on the legislature. Tobacco companies have many powerful friends in high places in Canada, but once the battle in the executive is lost, the judiciary, rather than the legislature or the public, is their main venue.

Operating practices in the Canadian bureaucracy also have changed in ways detrimental to tobacco interests. Tobacco-company executives testifying before a Senate committee in 2000 complained that the government had adopted a US-type confrontational style toward them. As Harrison and Hoberg (1994) put it, Canada leans to a European regulatory framework of a closed, informal, and cooperative nature, but with tendencies toward US practices of more openness and therefore public conflict. The US system is more open, adversarial, formal, and legalistic, more publicly accountable but also more antagonistic; it possibly involves less expertise, since legislators and judges, two groups not necessarily having substantive knowledge of particular policies, often become involved. In tobacco control in recent years, Canada has moved toward a more US regulatory style. Previously, the voluntary code of the tobacco companies allowed by the Canadian government was notable for its extreme informality. There was no formal agreement between the tobacco companies and the government; the industry unilaterally changed the code several times (Non-Smokers' Rights Association 1986; Mitchell 1996).

This change in bureaucratic principles is still not complete. The *Tobacco Act* of 1997 was held up for some months by an official, familiar with consumer protection legislation, who still preferred that some type of voluntary arrangement be worked out with the companies. Thus the decline of voluntary arrangements in Canada may be not so much a change in general bureaucratic practice as a reflection of the fact that tobacco increasingly has been viewed as different from other consumer products; in other industries, producers take extraordinary steps, such as removing products from shelves, to avoid being labelled as makers of a dangerous product.

Institutions in the United States pose several problems for the adoption of restrictive tobacco-control policies. These include the separation of powers, the lack of party cohesion in favour of temporary and compromised majorities, strong bicameralism, the decentralization of party control in Congress giving considerable authority to senior legislators who are often from the few large tobacco-producing Southern states, and the need to finance political campaigns with contributions from wealthy private organizations such as tobacco companies.

In the US Congress, there is no overriding necessity for party cohesion to keep tobacco-state legislators from protecting their district's perceived economic interests. If one considers only the top six tobacco-producing states, there are 12 US Senators (12 per cent of the total), in a body fully co-equal with the House of Representatives; if this is expanded to the 17 significant tobacco-growing states, there are 34 Senators with ties to tobacco. Because of more frequent use of the filibuster rule (unlimited discussion), increasingly it takes 60 Senators to end debate and pass legislation. The co-equal US House of Representatives also has had many powerful legislators able to protect and advance the interests of tobacco growers and producers, even if that body is substantially larger. Although some of these characteristics, such as the one-party South and allocation of committee chairs through seniority in the House of Representatives, have been altered, others, such as lack of near-uniform party cohesion (although party voting has increased) and the importance of serving local constituency interests, have continued.

Some older studies (Pertschuk 1969; Wagner 1971) contend that the US House of Representatives protects tobacco interests even better than the Senate, but in recent years, especially with the rejection of the National Settlement, the Senate has become more prominent (Torry 1998). In the late 1980s tobacco was grown in only 51 of the 435 Congressional districts (11.7%), but in 27 of these districts (6.2%) it was the main crop (White 1988: 48). Such figures underestimate the power of the tobacco lobby because they do not take into account the hierarchical nature of Congress, especially the power of committee chairs, and the fact that the tobacco-industry network extends far beyond agriculture into constituencies without an obvious tobacco connection.

Despite the relatively low number of tobacco districts, the lack of party discipline means that log-rolling (vote-trading) occurs among legislators. This phenomenon plus institutional blockages make it more difficult to pass legislation restricting tobacco directly. Even when pressed, tobacco interests in Congress have typically held out until the last minute for compromise and have often obtained specific exemptions for the industry from other federal regulatory agencies, drug laws, and state action (Kluger 1996). The tobacco agenda in Congress may have changed, but the process and results have been similar.

Within the federal government, the serious regulatory and tax initiatives on tobacco in the United States have all come from the executive branch, either the semi-independent regulatory agencies such as the Interstate Commerce Commission, Federal Trade Commission, and the Federal Communications Commission, or other agencies such as the Surgeon General, the Food and Drug Administration, the National Cancer Institute within DHHS, or the Treasury Department (taxes). Only under the Clinton administration did the President put his own prestige on the line for tobacco control.

Tobacco interests exercise considerable power in the US executive branch. The Secretary of Agriculture, for instance, has normally acted to protect tobacco farm subsidies, notably in the Carter Administration when HEW Secretary Joseph Califano suggested that they be phased out. As Califano (1981:196) comments, "The anti-smoking campaign generated more political opposition than any other effort I undertook at HEW." The Commerce Department and cabinet-level Office of the US Trade Representative have also acted to promote markets for US tobacco products abroad, especially in less economically developed countries, irrespective of the state of tobacco in other parts of the executive branch (Mintz 1991; Frankel 1996). Although such practices have also occurred in Canadian trade missions, US export markets are much larger. The refusal of the otherwise tobacco-restrictive Clinton Administration to pursue a long-delayed Occupational Health and Safety (OSHA) rule limiting smoking in workplaces indicates that the financial clout of business and trade unions may affect the executive as well as inhibiting the government from embracing a comprehensive public-health perspective on tobacco control.

It is more difficult to generalize about how institutional factors affect US state tobacco control policy. But in 49 states the legislatures are similar to Congress in having two equal houses separate from the executive and party unity well short of complete on most votes. The executive and the judiciary are also co-equal branches, allowing venue switching and institutional conflict.

With the enactment of the Canadian Constitution and the Charter of Rights and Freedoms in 1982, the possibility of using the courts in a policy role increased. As in the US, tobacco companies have been able to employ their financial resources and legal acumen in this venue to oppose policy initiatives, notably the *Tobacco Products Control Act* and the *Tobacco Act*. Nevertheless, the Canadian policy process on tobacco regulation has been relatively straightforward compared to that in the United States. If federal officials consider that they have sufficient information and commitment about a policy problem to act, there are few obstacles to a statute reaching the books. Even if a judicial decision overturns a law, as has happened to both federal and British Columbia statutes, unified party government allows a recrafted law to be adopted if the government wishes, as occurred in both of these cases. In the United States, it is much more difficult to negotiate the legislative process once, much less a second time.

Largely blocked at the federal executive and especially legislative levels, US tobacco-control advocates have pursued their objectives through the courts, states, and local municipalities, a clear case of venue switching. This fragments regulatory initiatives, however, and, in the case of court cases, can lead to long delays. Furthermore, the courts, especially federal courts with increasingly large numbers of conservative jurists, have served as a major venue in which tobacco companies can successfully challenge regulations from both federal and state authorities.

Possibly one reason that anti-tobacco groups in Canada are more coherently organized than in the United States is that they can focus their efforts at the federal cabinet and bureaucracy, especially Health Canada, for maximum impact, both regulatory and financial. In contrast, in the United States it is much harder to identify an institution that is the key to policy change. As events since 1995 have shown, even strong leadership by a US president does not ensure a more comprehensive tobacco-control policy.

The question arises as to how the relative policy leadership positions in tobacco control could have shifted so much over the past 20 years. Friedman's early study (1975) found little evidence that would presage

Canada's emerging leadership role only a little over a decade later. David Sweanor of the Nonsmokers' Rights Association agrees that Canada neglected to deal seriously with tobacco control until the early 1980s (Plenary Session 1996). By the late 1990s, moreover, Canada and the United States had, through different institutional routes, arrived at similar tobacco-control regimes. But the operation of federal institutions in the US has also prevented even greater convergence, as Chapter Six demonstrates.

One complicating factor for any institutional explanation of policy differences is that political institutions have varied little in the two countries over time. Changes in policy style in the Canadian bureaucracy have facilitated more restrictive tobacco control policies, but the emergence of a Supreme Court willing to use judicial review to override parliamentary legislation potentially constitutes a continuing hindrance to such policies.

In short, the institutional framework of the US federal government has allowed even an interest group on the defensive over a long period of time to prevent comprehensive federal legislative or executive action against its product, despite a widespread public perception, buttressed by almost a half-century of scientific studies, that smoking is both addictive and a serious danger to the public health. The structure of political institutions, then, was and is more conducive to tobacco control in Canada, but the political commitment for a strong regulatory regime first had to develop. In the United States, federal institutions can frustrate greater tobacco restrictions even when they are high on the political agenda.

In both countries, shared responsibility for health care between the two levels of government has led to a process of competitive federalism. Thus tobacco-control policies have varied across both countries depending on the willingness of states, provinces, and municipalities to enact such legislation. Because there are more jurisdictions and less federal coordination of policies in the United States, tobacco-control policy varies more widely there.

Policy Typologies

Do policies determine politics in tobacco control? Are policy similarities between the two countries due to the nature of the policy rather than the institutions, and are policy differences similarly due to inherent or perceived differences in the nature of the issue itself? As indicated earlier, this explanation is difficult to evaluate, both because tobacco control has never been categorized in a policy typology, and because theoretical construction of these typologies differs. Nevertheless, some analysis will be offered concerning what policy typology theory contributes to an explanation of Canadian and US similarities and differences in this policy area. For the greater part of the twentieth century, at least since the 1920s, tobacco-control policy was "distributive" in Lowi's sense of the term, largely hidden from public view. Beginning in the 1960s, however, it developed a higher profile, involving more conflict. In both countries, the nature of tobacco-control policy has changed in the past two decades, in both taxation and regulation. Rather than taxation being primarily for revenue purposes, it has become valued for its potential impact in reducing tobacco use. Similarly, self-regulation by the companies in Canada and relatively light regulation in the US have been superseded by more restrictions. These developments suggest that tobacco control has characteristics of "regulatory" policy. The stridency of the anti-tobacco movement and the attempt of some elements within it to denormalize the tobacco industry, however, gives the issue features of "social regulatory" or "morally redistributive" policy as well. Because of the lack of broad categories of ideologically-engaged groups, it would probably not qualify as redistributive

Similar to environmental policy, tobacco control might be a mixed case of "economic" and "social" regulatory policy because there are both tangible material benefits at stake as well as collective public-health benefits and moral concerns. The tobacco companies and their network see the issue as primarily, if not exclusively, economic, while anti-tobacco advocates view it primarily as public health. In the absence of a widely agreed issue definition, it is difficult to argue that policy constitutes a particular type. Nevertheless, this mixture of characteristics of different policy types appears to apply equally in the two countries. This suggests that policy typology explains convergence better than divergence of policy. While policy typology analysis may help explain why institutional differences have not prevented convergence of policies between Canada and the United States, its relationship to agenda setting and political institutions remains to be demonstrated.

Conclusion

In summary, although elements of several of these theoretical perspectives may help explain how tobacco-control policy has developed in Canada and the United States, some are more useful than others, especially in explaining similarities and convergence in recent years. Agenda setting emphasizes the struggle over issue definitions and how political actors, especially entrepreneurs in the broader sense employed here, have employed strategic opportunities to push forward their preferred policies on tobacco control. Venue switching, also an important part of agenda-setting theory, has been employed by both sides in tobacco control. Broadly, the agenda of tobacco control has shifted over the years in similar ways in the US and Canada. Partly this has been because of the attention given to focussing events, especially those in the United States, such as the Surgeon General's reports and the 1994 Congressional hearings on tobacco.

Interest-group theory, especially in conjunction with agenda-setting theory, helps explain the lull in tobacco control in both countries in the 1970s and its resurrection in the 1980s. Moreover, anti-tobacco interest groups have been more coordinated and aggressive in Canada than the US, especially on the federal level. This helps account for the Canadian surge in tobacco control, compared to its past, since the 1980s. As the opportunities for "outside" interest groups became more facilitative in Canada, anti-tobacco groups took advantage of this. The general structure of the interest-group configuration in the US has changed much less, despite the rise of more radical anti-tobacco groups and better organization since 1981.

Political culture, including how change has occurred, also helps explain similarities to a degree because Canadian political culture on both elite and mass levels has more closely resembled that of the US in recent years. Furthermore, in both countries the healthy public policy orientation, more of an elite than a mass change, has facilitated health-oriented policies and more explicit government control of tobacco company behaviour. But there remain cultural differences, explored more extensively in Chapter Six, that continue to inhibit more restrictive US tobacco control policies. Partisan, electoral, and ideological factors allow opportunities for interest-group influence but only provide partial explanations of policy in recent years in the United States.

It is still unclear exactly where tobacco control fits in policy typologies, which makes this theoretical perspective less useful. Broadly, however, tobacco control seems to have moved from distributive to regulatory and, if anti-tobacco advocates have their way, will eventually become redistributive policy in both countries. But both in the early days of concern about cigarette use and more recently, there also are moral overtones. Once the struggle over definition of the issue on the agenda is settled, then policy typologies may become more useful.

Finally, political institutions, while not providing a complete explanation, do help in understanding differences in policies over time. US institutions are particularly ill-suited to having a comprehensive federal tobacco-control policy. In Canada, the parliamentary system has allowed more comprehensive policies to be constructed once the executive of the governing party developed the political commitment to pursue the issue. In both countries, competitive federalism has allowed provincial and state governments to take action beyond what the federal government has done. The presence of a strong judicial role in policy-making in both countries has facilitated venue shifting.

If agenda-setting, interest-group, and political-culture changes, especially in the form of healthy public policy, offer the best explanations for changes over time, and political institutions and interest groups offer the best explanations for continuing differences between Canada and the United States, then what does lesson-drawing theory have to contribute? The next chapter addresses this question.

6

Tobacco-Control Lessons Across the Border?

"Paul Paré and Leo Laporte have kept me advised of the latest developments on the health situation in Canada. We are very disturbed at
the situation and feel that whatever happens in Canada will have a
direct bearing on what may happen in this country." L.P. Finch,
President of Brown and Williamson Tobacco Company, in a letter
to Richard P. Dobson of British-American Tobacco Company, Ltd.,
December 11, 1968. (Cunningham 1996: 54)

"I think we have to have an equally comprehensive package (as the
USFDA regulations) addressing a variety of different aspects of the
smoking issue." David Dingwall, Canadian Minister of Health,
Montreal *Gazette*, August 28, 1996.

"In fact, many of the features of the proposed U.S. settlement are
already in place in Canada and have been for some time." Joe
Heffernan, President of Rothmans, Benson and Hedges, Inc, in a
public letter of June 26, 1997, to Joy McPhail, Minister of Health,
Province of British Columbia.

Introduction

This chapter surveys the evidence for lesson drawing between Canada and
the United States during phases four and five of tobacco control, since the
Surgeon General's report of 1964. It attempts to answer the question of
what each country learned from the other, how and when they did so, and,
from a theoretical perspective, whether lesson drawing helps explain
policy in the two countries. If convergence occurred, was this due to lesson
drawing or other, similar internal factors?

First, this chapter examines the question of how much lesson drawing
has occurred and when, by looking at the comparative course of policy
development, primarily at the central level but with some attention to

Table 6-1: *De Facto* Federal Laws and Regulations
Concerning Tobacco, by Type, Country, and Year

(1) Advertising	United States	Canada
Regulatory Restrictions on Specific Practices	1938-1971 (25+ times)	
Broadcasting Banned	1970	1971 (voluntary)
Broadcasting Counter-Advertising Allowed	1967	1967
Health Warnings on Advertisements	1972 (billboards, periodicals)	1975 (text, voluntary) 1984 (billboards, voluntary)
Advertising Banned	1988(X)	
Advertising Restricted	1996 (X), 1998 (S)	1997
Sponsorship Restricted	1998 (S)	1988
Sponsorship Banned	1996 (X)	1997
Only Pre-existing Company Logos Allowed	1996 (X)	
Trademarks on Non-nicotine Products Banned	1996 (X)	1988 (X)
Trademarks on Non-nicotine Products Restricted	1998 (S)	1997
Cartoon Characters Banned	1998 (S)	1997
Real or Fictional Persons and Animals Banned		1997
Lifestyle Advertising Banned		1997
Material Misrepresentations Banned	1998 (S)	1997
Paid Film Promotions Banned	1998 (S)	1997
Black and White Ads Only (Partial)	1996 (X)	

(2) Sales

Age 18 and Above Sales Only	1996(X)	1993
Vending Machines Restricted	1996 (X)	1993
Vending Machines Banned		1997
Kiddie Packs Banned	1996 (X), 1998 (S)	1993
Single Cigarette Sales Banned		1997
Free Samples Banned	1996 (X),	1988, 1997
Free Samples Restricted	1998 (S)	
Mail Order Sales Restricted		1997
Discounts and Prizes Banned		1971 (voluntary) 1988, 1997

(3) Environmental Tobacco Smoke

Airline No-Smoking (Domestic)	1987 (2-hour flights, partial) 1989 (comprehensive)	1987 (2-hour flights) 1988 (comprehensive)
Airline No-Smoking (International)	1994 (partial)	1994
Comprehensive, Federal Government Facilities	1997	1989

(4) Residual Regulatory Authority, Contents Disclosure

Broad Executive Authority over Tobacco	1996 (X)	1997
Tar and Nicotine Levels on Packages	1970 (voluntary)	1975 (voluntary)
Toxic Contents on Packages		1988, 1993, 2000
Tar and Nicotine Contents on Ads	1970 (voluntary), 1984	1975 (voluntary)
Additives Reported to Government Agency	1984	1988

Table 6-1: *De Facto* Federal Laws and Regulations
Concerning Tobacco, by Type, Country, and Year

	United States	Canada
(5) Taxation		
Taxation Increased	1983, 1990, 1997	1981-1989, 1991, 1996, 1999, 2001
Taxation Reduced due to Smuggling		1952, 1953, 1994
Special Levies on Tobacco Companies	1998(S)	1992, 1994, 1997, 2001
Taxation on Purchases in Duty-Free Shops		2001
(6) Agricultural Alternatives		
Transitional Funds for Tobacco Farmers	1998 (S)	1987
(7) Litigation Against Tobacco Companies		
Smuggling	1999	1999
Health Care Cost Recovery	1998 (S), 2000	
(8) Federally Funded Program for		
Community Action	1987, 1991, 1998	1994 (X), 2001
(9) Health Warning Labels		
First Warning Labels	1965	1971(voluntary), 1988
Attribution of Warning	1964	1971 (voluntary), 1997

Warning Labels Language Strengthened	1970, 1985, 1996 (X)	1989, 1990, 1993, 1997, 2000
Rotating Warning Labels	1985	1989
Warning Labels on Front of Packages		1989
Black and White Warning Labels Only		1993
Graphic Warnings on Packages		2000
Federal Preemption Laws on Warning Labels	1965, 1970	
Package Warnings No Liability Protection		1988
Warning Labels on Non-cigarette Products	1986 (smokeless only)	1988 (all)
	2000 (cigars)	
Package Insert Warnings		1988 (authorized)
		2000 (implemented)

(10) Education

(11) General Learning Tools

First Official Expression of Tobacco-Health Concern	1957	1963
First Legislative Committee Investigation and Hearings	1958	1969
Subsequent Major Legislative Investigation and Hearing	1994	2000
Chief Medical Officer Reports	1964-2000 (26 times)	1964
Other Major Agency Reports	1993	1983
Healthy Public Policy	1980	1974

(X)=overturned by court ruling or otherwise abandoned; (S)=national-policy results of state lawsuits.
Except where noted, dates are based on passage of legislation, not implementation dates, which vary.

lower levels. This will allow a more focussed, analytical assessment of which instruments were transferred, in which direction, when, and through what agents. Chapter Seven will take up the question of whether lesson drawing adds to other explanations of tobacco-control policy in these two countries.

Policy Convergence

Have both governmental and nongovernmental actors in Canada and the United States taken account of the experience of the other country, either positively or negatively, in formulating their own positions and policies? Table 6-1 lists dates when similar policy actions have been taken by the federal governments, and in one instance (the MSA) a coordinated effort of states, in the two countries.

Table 6-1 indicates that there has been an increasing range of instruments in tobacco control over the years. While some differences exist, in general the US and Canada have tended to employ similar instruments at about the same time, at least on the federal level. This tendency has accelerated over the past two decades. This is clear evidence of policy convergence, although not necessarily policy transfer, since the instruments could have been developed from similar internal sources. The evidence for policy transfer will be assessed in three ways below: first, through a narrative of policy developments in the two countries; second, through an analysis of how specific instruments came to be adopted; and third, through an examination of the agents and directions of lesson drawing for certain instruments.

DEVELOPMENT OF TOBACCO-CONTROL POLICY
TRANSFER BETWEEN CANADA AND THE UNITED STATES

When governments faced the problem in the mid-1960s, restrictions on tobacco consumption constituted unfamiliar territory. In such circumstances, it is common to search for lessons from abroad. But few other countries had dealt with the issue either, especially in terms of regulation rather than finance. Even taxation of tobacco was viewed in revenue terms rather than primarily from a public-health perspective. Once US policies and those of a few other countries were in place, however, other jurisdictions deliberating about tobacco-control policies could study these experiences. In the late 1960s and early 1970s, Canada carefully considered experience abroad, especially policies in the United States and United Kingdom, before settling on allowing the tobacco companies to regulate themselves by an informal, written voluntary code. Nevertheless, even though they were somewhat weaker than the proposed legislation, the specific provisions of this code had been influenced through legislative testimony, the Isabelle Report, and cabinet deliberation over its abortive bill (Mitchell 1996).

Why did Canada not follow US policies even more closely by choosing government regulation of tobacco? Even though the US was in the forefront of tobacco regulation and continued to be among the leaders until the 1980s (Licari 2000a), there was extremely limited evidence of how effective the policies would be. Thus lessons were drawn about the content of policies on advertising restrictions and broadcasting bans, which were similar in the US and Canada even if the processes of adoption and enforcement were different. Canadian officials congratulated themselves that their approach was more in line with Canadian cultural values than the more strident, abrasive conflict seen across the border (Friedman 1975: 102), even if it compromised Canada's self-image as a leader in world health matters.

Canadian governments and legislators were paying close attention to developments in the United States. The circumstances of the tobacco control problem were slightly different in the two countries; for instance, in Canada there was proportionately less spending on advertising by the companies and more effort put into gifts and discounts. Later, tobacco company sponsorship became a more controversial issue in Canada than in the US. Canadian tobacco companies used sponsorships to promote lifestyle associations with their products in ways similar to what US companies used in advertising. Nevertheless, tobacco-control issues such as health effects, taxes, and advertising were so comparable overall that many of the policy decisions made were similar to what was done, usually first, by the United States.

During the 28 formal meetings of the Standing Committee on Health, Welfare and Social Affairs (Isabelle Committee), various testimony was offered about US developments, including Health Minister John Munro noting favourably the "free time" for counteradvertising of the FCC in the US; Canada had already embarked on a similar small program, mainly in children's programming (Friedman 1975). Daniel Horn, Director of the National Clearinghouse for Smoking and Health in the US, testified before the committee on US policies (Friedman 1975: 91). Paul Paré, President of Imasco Ltd. (the forerunner of Imperial), was chair of the CMTC and very attentive to policy developments elsewhere. In officially announcing the industry's voluntary code as a response to the government's Bill C-248, Paré said, "the revised code brings the Canadian industry into line with the situation existing in the United Kingdom and the United States" (Friedman 1975: 94). In at least one respect— limiting total advertising expenditures—it went beyond them. Furthermore, even "voluntary action" by the companies in Canada, already attempted in the US in 1964, was really a pre-emptive response to anticipated regulatory action (Mitchell 1996).

The Canadian federal government's acceptance of this code followed British rather than American proclivities but was not especially unusual for the time (Roemer 1993; Licari 2000a). Few other governments mandated warning labels or limited advertising; if they did, it was by voluntary agreement with the tobacco companies. But the Canadian arrangement was different in that it was self-enforcing by the industry.

After the initial flurry of activity in each country in the years following the 1964 Surgeon General's Report, there were periodic reports from the respective health departments but little evidence of lesson drawing. By the mid-1980s, however, evidence of Canadian borrowing from the US does appear. Although much of this involved incorporating US research on the economic effects of tobacco price increases or health findings, such as the 1986 and 1988 Surgeon General's reports (see below), some were policy recommendations. In the TPCA, Canada followed the US in adopting rotating health warnings, atlhough the cautionary language was not the same (Liston n.d.) By the time the TPCA was in preparation, tobacco advertising bans in Norway and Finland had also gained the attention of Canadian officials. Under the regulatory discretion allowed by the TPCA, within a few years larger, more direct warnings were printed on the front of the pack, a form which the US only approached in the abortive National Settlement of 1997.

As the federal legislation that made Canada one of the most stringent tobacco-regulatory regimes in the world was being passed, Canadian developments received more attention in the United States. In 1987, Health Minister Jake Epp and Deputy Health Minister Maureen Law wrote letters to Health and Human Services Secretary Otis Bowen and US Surgeon General C. Everett Koop, respectively, informing them of the contents of Bill C-51, which was then going through Parliament, and inviting their cooperation in tobacco regulation efforts (Epp 1987b; Law 1987). Canadian organizations such as CCS and NSRA kept their US counterparts, especially the ACS and the Advocacy Institute, apprised of the bill's progress, and the latter touted similar legislation for the US (Advocacy Institute 1988). Washington journalist Morton Mintz, long interested in health matters, wrote in the *Washington Monthly* about the success of the health lobby in Canada, urging that similar legislation be considered in the US (Mintz 1990). In the week before the advent of the Seventh World Conference on Smoking or Health in Perth, Australia, in 1990, the Advocacy Institute sponsored a forum in Virginia for American and Canadian tobacco-control advocates. This led to further consultations, described below, as nongovernmental organizations began to collaborate across the border, first on tax issues, later across a wider range of regulatory issues. When a large US conference on tobacco and health, involving both governmental and nongovernmental groups, was held in Washington early in 1993, several of the presenters referred to Canada's example in regulation, taxation, and lobbying cohesion (*Tobacco Use: An American Crisis* 1993). In general, there was more recognition of the fact that international comparisons might have useful lessons for US tobacco control.

While US advocacy groups were learning from Canada about the TPCA and tax matters, the bureaucracy was engaging in some cross-border shopping, too. Brantford and Peterborough, Ontario, were included as study communities in the US NCI COMMIT study, 1987-93. Initially from his position as Health Planner, Health Protection and Promotion for the Metropolitan Toronto District Health Council, John Garcia was closely involved in the portion of the US COMMIT program in Canada and took ideas from this program with him when he later became one of the two advisers on tobacco policy in the Health Ministry during the NDP government in Ontario from 1991 to 1994. With modifications, the perspective of the COMMIT and ASSIST (1991-98) programs were adopted into the Ontario Tobacco Reduction Strategy, an executive plan that predated the Ontario *Tobacco Control Act* (1994) (Ontario Tobacco Research Unit 1995b: 7). This was the first well-financed attempt in Canada to build community support for institutionalizing programs of tobacco control (Taylor, Goldsmith and Best 1994; Mitchell and Garcia 1995).

In using financial instruments for tobacco restrictions, Canada was ahead of the US on the federal level. On the state/provincial level, Canada trailed until the 1980s, but it then took the lead there, too. Even in the late

1960s, the Canadian government was contemplating the possibility of sponsoring alternative endeavors for tobacco growers (Friedman 1975: 91); such a program was eventually implemented in 1987. In the US, it has received only sporadic consideration after COSH actively began promoting it in the early 1990s, citing Canada as an example ("Saving Lives and Raising Revenue: The Case for Major Increases in State and Federal Tobacco Taxes" 1993); it still lacks implementation aside from a modest program negotiated between tobacco growers and industry as an afterthought to the MSA.

The connection between taxation and tobacco control was first discussed by the Isabelle Committee in 1969, which considered the economic importance of tobacco, including the dependence of the federal government on tobacco tax revenues (Friedman 1975). From at least the mid-1970s, the issue of using taxation as a potential instrument for tobacco control was periodically raised within Health and Welfare Canada.

The study by economists Thompson and McLeod on demand for cigarettes in Canada and the United States (1976) had first been commissioned by Health and Welfare Canada. In 1977, Health and Welfare Canada produced an interrnal document, later released (1979), which surveyed the potential impact of different forms and levels of taxation on public health. It cited the experience in New York City with differential taxation of tobacco by ingredients and estimated the social costs of cigarette consumption. By the early 1980s, even though the switch to *ad valorem* taxes with its resulting tax spiral was not initiated on health grounds, by 1983 Health Minister Monique Bégin was advocating even greater taxes on tobacco (Health and Welfare Canada 1983), but to little avail.

Some US research contended that tobacco consumption, while largely inelastic, could be affected by tax increases (Lewit and Coate 1982; Lewit, Coate and Grossman 1981). This academic research was incorporated first into Canadian tobacco-control advocacy through the initiative of the Non-Smokers' Rights Association, which used it, largely successfully, to lobby for federal and provincial tax increases (Sweanor 1991). Several years later, the US Surgeon General's Report of 1989 (US Department of Health and Human Services 1989) as well as a report from the US General Accounting Office in the same year (US General Accounting Office 1989) reviewed the economic literature on the relationship between price and cigarette consumption among adults and teenagers, respectively, and came to similar conclusions, which provided a more fertile environment for tobacco restrictions through taxation.

As Canadian taxes soared far beyond their US counterparts, the NSRA and CCS in Canada began to coordinate with their US counterparts, especially ACS, AI, and COSH, to provide information for the latter groups to use to lobby for tax increases in the US. In 1990 NSRA and AI produced, with the assistance of CCSH for Canadian distribution, *Death or Taxes: A Health Advocate's Guide to Increasing Tobacco Taxes* (Non-Smokers' Rights Association and The Advocacy Institute 1990). Ken Kyle of CCS made some appearances in the US to discuss taxation in Canada and distributed his remarks to interested officials and advocates (Kyle 1992). The most frequent visitor, however, was David Sweanor of NSRA. By the early 1990s Sweanor was consulting extensively with US governments on federal and state levels as well as with nongovernmental organizations. In fall 1991 he was the sole Canadian to present a report to the Subcommittee on Tobacco Policy Research (1991), a joint private-public US group attempting better coordination of research and policy advocacy. In 1993 COSH cited Canada as "the clearest example"of the health benefits of higher taxation policies ("Saving Lives and Raising Revenue: The Case for Major Increases in State and Federal Tobacco Taxes" 1993: 19). An "expert panel" convened by the US National Cancer Institute in the same year included only two non-Americans, Canadians Sweanor and Murray Kaiserman, among a group of some two dozen academics, bureaucrats, and activists from the US. They reaffirmed the case for increased taxes as a tobacco-control measure by, among other things, citing comparative evidence (National Cancer Institute 1993). At an address to the first national conference on Tobacco or Health in Ottawa in 1993, Garfield Mahood of NSRA hailed Sweanor's activities:

> I regret that David Sweanor, NSRA's Senior Legal Counsel, is out of the country and not yet here. His financial analysis and his leadership on tobacco taxation, on both sides of the border, is enormous. Some day, more of the story of David's work to encourage United States governments to raise their tobacco taxes may be told. (Mahood 1993)

As concern about smuggling into Canada rose in 1993, representatives from COSH and the Advocacy Institute held a joint press conference with the NSRA and CCS in Ottawa. The conference had three purposes: to commend Canada for its tax increases and general leadership in tobacco control, to ask Canadian governments to hold the line on taxes, and to promise that the US would undertake similar action to alleviate the smuggling problem ("Cross-Border Health Coalition" 1993). Alan C. Davis (1993), Chairman of the Steering Committee of the Coalition on Smoking OR Health, stated, "The United States is at long last poised to follow Canadian footsteps in tobacco control. For the first time in history, we have a President and an Administration committed to improving public health by reducing tobacco related disease." Later David Sweanor wrote a letter to the *Wall Street Journal* (1993), asserting that "[v]irtually all of Canada's tobacco smuggling problem is due to the low tobacco taxes in the United States." But these efforts could not prevent the smuggling crisis and tax cuts of 1994 (Sweanor and Martial 1994: 17).

The separation of cigarette regulation from the economic aspects of tobacco in the United States is an indication of the fragmentation of policy debate there. While at the same time engaging in health education initiatives from the 1960s through the 1980s, the US federal government allowed tobacco to become more affordable by not raising the cigarette tax for 32 years, between 1950 and 1982; furthermore, despite some increases in the past 20 years, US taxation is still far below the world average (see Table 3-7). Despite the efforts of advocacy groups, Canada's early 1990s example in taxation never fully convinced US officials. The lesson was further damaged by the Canadian tax rollback in 1994. Despite joint conferences of advocacy groups in the two countries affirming the power of taxation even after the rollback (*Tobacco Taxes: What's Next?* 1995) and an extensive analysis of what happened in the smuggling crisis prepared by NSRA and SHAF for its US counterparts (Sweanor and Martial 1994), federal governments on both sides of the border became reluctant to raise taxes on cigarettes other than incrementally.

Even under President Clinton, agricultural and commercial tobacco promotion programs continued. Similarly, in US states, Master Settlement money has been eagerly accepted and used largely for expenses other than tobacco control. Some of the recipient states have not raised their own tobacco taxes in years. Even though the Canadian federal government made the connection between economics and health aspects of tobacco earlier, they too have had difficulty in maintaining a coherent policy, especially since 1994. Moreover, since Canadian governments are, if anything, even more reluctant than those in the US to have dedicated taxes, increased revenues from cigarette taxes were only directed at long term tobacco-control projects in 2001.

THE HIGH TIDE OF CANADIAN-US
FEDERAL POLICY TRANSFER, 1994-1998

The 1994-1998 period featured the most intense efforts at policy transfer between Canada and the US on the federal level, which affected the FDA regulations, the *Tobacco Act*, and the proposed US National Settlement. The FDA was building a case to justify its authority over tobacco. Ever since the TPCA passed in 1988, journalists, advocacy groups, and other agents had made the US policy community aware of Canadian policies and their impacts. This became an important element in the attempts to generate a comprehensive federal tobacco-control policy in the US. On the other side of the border, with the court defeat of the TPCA in 1995, Canadians could point to what was being proposed or adopted in the United States as worthy of consideration for their new federal legislation on tobacco control.

In fact, the policy transfer during this period would have been even greater if the US Congress had adopted President Clinton's Health Security Plan, which relied on a large increase in tobacco taxes to finance it. Nevertheless, there were several indications of cross-border borrowing during this extraordinary period. In 1994 and 1995 there were two separate public announcements by the health ministers of the two federal governments, after joint meetings in Washington and Vancouver, that they would work together on anti-smoking strategies through the relevant officials in Health Canada, OSH, and FDA (Health Canada 1994, 1995). Early in 1995, NSRA initiated a project with COSH involving public lobbying for Canadian-style warning labels in the US through the media and letters to Congress. The major participants in the project were Garfield Mahood of NSRA, Scott Ballin of COSH, Michel Perley of OCAT, and Tom Houston of AMA. This was an explicit attempt to strengthen FDA Commissioner David Kessler's hand in the expected battle concerning FDA authority over tobacco. NSRA believed that enhanced regulatory authority over tobacco in the US would strengthen the position of tobacco-control advocates in Canada.

The culmination of this lobbying process was a press conference at the National Press Club featuring representatives of NSRA, AMA, and COSH ("Canadian Warnings Go to Washington" 1995). Once the President formally declared in August 1995 that the FDA would accept public comments on the provisions of a specific proposal for its jurisdictional claim over tobacco, the public-health community in Canada not only sent comments to the FDA (*In Support of Public Health* 1995) but domestically began to clamour that in some respects the US was moving ahead of Canada in tobacco control (Morris 1995; Selin 1995; Evenson 1997; McCarthy 1998). In short, there was widespread recognition that tobacco control in the two countries was converging.

At the time, an article in *Business Week* argued that Canada had "field-tested virtually all of the Administration's proposals" (Symonds 1995). After the TPCA was overturned, Health Canada's document presaging new legislation, *Tobacco Control: A Blueprint to Protect the Health of Canadians* (1995: 13), commented diplomatically that "many components of the US initiative mirrored the Canadian experience." Both US and Canadian media featured stories about the implications of the other country's tobacco-control policies. For instance, there were at least two stories on US National Public Radio (NPR) on "lessons for President Clinton from Canada," reiterating the history and effects of tobacco control in Canada since the late 1980s, including an interview with the Canadian Health Minister. More significantly, in preparing its regulations on tobacco the FDA formed two working groups, one of which studied the potential effectiveness of new policies, including examination of the experiences of other countries (Hilts 1996: 190-91).

Upon promulgation of the final FDA Rule, Canadian Health Minister David Dingwall publicly promised an equally stringent set of regulations for Canada in the forthcoming *Tobacco Act*. Policy advisers within the Canadian bureaucracy were kept appraised of developments in the United States and sought evidence from the US and elsewhere in crafting their own legislation (Winsor 1997).

The elements of the 1988 TPCA, 1992 TSYPA, 1996 FDA regulations, 1997 National Settlement, 1997 *Tobacco Act*, and 1998 MSA, as shown in Chapter Three and in Table 6-1, exhibit some striking resemblances. The FDA regulations were not solely or perhaps even principally based on Canadian policy. However, in contrast to the usual US avoidance of careful scrutiny of the policy experience of other countries, in this case there was systematic and substantial interest among policy-makers in the United States in the nature and effects of Canadian policy (Hilts 1996). A nearby, similar country from which information could readily be obtained served, in effect, as an FDA laboratory to test proposed policies.

The Second Canadian Conference on Tobacco or Health, held in Ottawa in October 1996, signified this mutual respect for each other's efforts in tobacco control. In contrast to the first conference in 1993, there were many references to practices as well as research from the United States; for example, David Sweanor indicated that the NSRA was receiving an increasing number of inquiries about Canadian policy from the United States. The clearest indication of the mutual attraction that tobacco-control policy, especially at this particular juncture, held for activists and governmental officials in the two countries was that a plenary session at the conference was devoted to a comparison of US and Canadian policy, including lesson drawing. This panel was composed of Sweanor of NSRA and two influential policy-makers from different levels in the United States: Gregory Connolly of the Massachusetts Tobacco Control Program, and Mitchell Zeller, Associate Commissioner of the FDA. The US commentators praised Canada's leadership role in tobacco control. Sweanor indicated that the US and Canada were "leapfrogging" in tobacco-control leadership in various areas (Plenary Session 1996).

In addition to describing the main purposes of the new regulations, Zeller commented on the ways in which the FDA had learned from the Canadian policy experience. In its search for ways to combat these problems in the US, the FDA was attracted by the fact that Canada's regulatory policies at the time (TPCA and TSYPA) were comprehensive and dealt with such important dimensions as access (sales), advertising, and education. Zeller discussed several FDA policies, implying that the provisions were related to previous Canadian policies. These included severe restrictions on vending and self-service displays, altering the imagery and colour of ads to make them less appealing to the young (plain advertising if not plain packaging), and allowing only corporate names, images, and logos on merchandise and event sponsorship. On the latter policy, Zeller specifically noted that the US had learned one negative lesson from Canada. After the 1988 TPCA, tobacco companies registered some of their best-selling brand names, such as du Maurier and Players, as new "corporations," in effect dummy corporations, in order to retain these cigarette names before the public. To prevent a similar occurrence in the US, the FDA regulations would allow only existing corporate logos, not new ones (Plenary Session 1996).

Sweanor, the internationally active NSRA lawyer, agreed that tobacco control is one of the few areas in which the US does pay attention to Canada. He argued along similar lines as this book, that there were three eras of US-Canada relations in tobacco control. Initially the US led through research, the Surgeon General's reports, the 1965 Congressional hearings documenting the need for health warnings, the ban on broadcast advertising, and the package health warnings. Canada was slow to follow, but learned both positive and negative lessons from observing the US; two negative lessons incorporated into the TPCA were the dangers of federal pre-emption of lower-level policies and the problems of weak warning labels on the sides of packages. By 1986, the start of Sweanor's second era, Canada began taking the lead by leapfrogging US policies in such areas as taxes, warning labels, second-hand smoke, and access to cigarettes. Over a ten-year period Canada had the largest declines in smoking among industrialized countries, confirmation of its leadership position. Canada and the US have influenced other countries, especially in warning labels and regulation of advertising. By the start of the third era in 1996, the US, through both state and federal FDA action, was returning to the forefront of tobacco-restrictive countries. Massachusetts spent substantially more on tobacco control for its six million people than Canada spent for 30 million. Litigation and local ordinances were also stronger in the US (Plenary Session 1996).

Sweanor noted that by fall 1996, Canada had fallen behind; therefore, the new federal legislation (what became the*Tobacco Act*, 1997) needed to be comprehensive. British Columbia was contemplating major initiatives, and ordinances on second-hand smoke were being strengthened in some cities, mainly Toronto and Vancouver. Point-of-sale restrictions in New Brunswick and Nova Scotia were also seen as promising provincial initiatives (Plenary Session 1996).

Gregory Connolly, a frequent visitor to Canada and other international sites in the cause of tobacco restrictions, commented that the NSRA and the Canadian Council on Smoking and Health provided "inspiration" for Massachusetts to tackle the tobacco industry. He indicated that the Massachusetts dollar allocation for tobacco control from its successful 1992 referendum vote followed the NCI model of money for control, local development, and cessation, a case of internal top-down lesson drawing. He contended that well-financed tobacco-control campaigns can work, which resonated with Canadian anti-tobacco advocates who envied the greater long-term, dedicated funding from federal and state sources that US programs have. He concluded by commending Canada for being a model for the rest of the world to follow in combating internationally the problems posed by multinational tobacco companies, especially those that were US-based (Plenary Session 1996).

While the 1994-1998 period was exceptionally intense and bi-directional in terms of policy transfer between the US and Canada, especially on the federal level, such lesson drawing has continued even as Canada and the US have since diverged subsequently somewhat in policies on the federal level. More recently, Canadian governments, both federal and provincial, increasingly have looked to US states for policies to emulate rather than to the US federal level.

Shortly after the *Tobacco Act* passed through parliament in 1997, the National Settlement between the US states and tobacco companies to settle healthcare cost claims presented a mixture of provisions already enacted in Canada and others, especially huge cash payments, unavailable there (Evenson 1997). Canadian anti-tobacco forces were attracted to US state and private litigation activity against tobacco companies for financial compensation as well as the capacity of some states to impose taxes dedicated to tobacco-restrictive measures (Sweanor 1997; LeGresley 1998a). "Canadian politicians are surely aware that multi-billion dollar settlements and altered industry practices have been attained in the US, and that the relative stakes in Canada are dramatically higher for the provinces due to Canada's entirely publicly-funded health care system. Many Canadians are wondering why cost recovery is being ardently pursued in the United States but not in Canada." (LeGresley 1998a). At the end of the 1990s, British Columbia explicitly developed policies based on its studies of the US experience, especially state litigation for healthcare cost recovery and state revenue dedicated to local tobacco-control efforts. The Canadian federal and Ontario governments litigated against tobacco companies, with other provinces examining the option.

The outcome of these US initiatives was less effective than anticipated, however, since Congress rejected the National Settlement in 1998 and the US Supreme Court in 2000 ruled that the FDA had no legal authority to regulate tobacco. The replacement settlement between 46 US states and tobacco companies, the MSA, was not as far-ranging as its predecessor but it became the *de facto* comprehensive tobacco-control policy in the US. While the MSA did not directly impose taxes, cigarette companies soon raised prices by US$0.45 per pack in order to cover the costs of that settlement as well as the four separate settlements with individual states; some considered this a *de facto* tax (see Table 3-4). By 1999, the prices of cigarettes in Canada and the United States were closer than they had been for years, a similar outcome through different processes. But overall, Canada had a more comprehensive federal tobacco-control policy than the US did.

By 2000, Canadian-US lessondrawing experiences had become so ingrained through both governmental and nongovernmental channels that occasional references to Canadian policy became more explicit in official US publications and declarations. At the eleventh World Conference on Tobacco Or Health in Chicago, Surgeon General David Satcher released the 2000 Surgeon General's Report on Smoking, the second in six years, with a press conference at which he praised Canadian package warning labels and suggested something similar should be done in the United States. In the 2000 Surgeon General's Report itself, for the first time there were two sections referring to Canadian policy developments. One concerned health warnings, including how the 1988 *Tobacco Products Control Act* had incorporated and implemented a policy that the US Secretary of Health, Education and Welfare had proposed in 1965, namely that changing warning labels be done at executive discretion without having to pass new legislation (US Department of Health and Human Services 2000b: 164-65, 169). A second discussed tax policy in Canada (US Department of Health and Human Services 2000b: 349). While hardly evidence of a full-scale move toward a more comprehensive US policy, this is an indication that Canada still serves as a reference point for US officials, perhaps increasingly so as they become more aware of Canadian policy and the international dimensions of tobacco control.

Overall, it appears that policy transfer between Canada and the United States on tobacco control has increased since the mid-1980s. In phase four, almost all of the policy transfer that occurred was from the United States to Canada. Then, once Canada became a world leader in federal-level tobacco control in the mid-1980s, the US began to pay attention to its neighbour. As a greater degree of federal control over tobacco began to seem possible in the US, Canada was a natural place from which to borrow, especially as the policies were associated with a reduction in smoking.

The period immediately preceding and following promulgation of the FDA Rule in 1996 was exceptional in terms of how much policy transfer occurred between the US and Canada. If the FDA Rule had been allowed to stand or the National Settlement had been adopted, then Canadian and US tobacco-control policies would resemble each other even more than they do now. Overall lesson drawing has increased between the two countries. If one examines specific specialist policy agendas rather than policies adopted, then increased lesson drawing would be even more evident. Whether this will continue in the future will be examined in the next chapter.

The Transfer of Policy Instruments

There are several policy instruments (tools) that governments have employed in an attempt to control tobacco use. Several ways have been developed to categorize policy instruments. One of the most frequently utilized is a five-fold differentiation, largely based on the degree of coercion exercised by government: (1) authority, (2) inducements and sanctions, (3) capacity-building, (4) exhortation, and (5) learning (Schneider and Ingram 1990; 1997). Authority means using the law in the form of command and control to compel obedience to official rules. Inducements and sanctions are mainly economic but also may involve coercion. Capacity-building tools provide training and information relevant to policy actions. Hortatory tools involve government exhortations to engage in desired behaviour. Finally, learning tools are more open-ended, leaving targeted groups to choose strategies.

A similar distinction among policy instruments has been applied in simplified form in tobacco-control policy research (Pal and Weaver 2002, forthcoming; Licari 2000a). Their trifold categorization is regulation (command and control), taxation, and education. The major form of regulation is advertising restrictions. Taxation serves both as a revenue source and as a mechanism for attempting to reduce consumption, two goals which may come into conflict. Education mainly concerns health warning labels on cigarette packages.

The more elaborate examination of tobacco-control policies in Canada and the United States that follows distinguishes more carefully among instruments that governments have used in tobacco-control policy and how these have been transferred between countries. The eleven categories are as follows:

I. Regulation (authority) includes four areas: (1) advertising; (2) sales; (3) environmental tobacco smoke; (4) regulation of ingredients.
II. Finance (economic incentives) includes three dimensions: (5) taxation and other levies; (6) agricultural incentives; and (7) litigation against tobacco companies for financial recovery of health care costs and lost taxation through smuggling.
III. Capacity building refers to (8) funding for community development programs to combat tobacco use.

IV. Education (exhortation) has two categories: (9) health warning labels and (10) general anti-smoking and anti-tobacco use campaigns.

V. (11) Learning tools are a more diffuse category, but include legislative hearings and executive reports.

The lesson-drawing influences on policy in the two countries in these eleven categories are listed in Table 6-1 and discussed below. The discussion also includes material from states and municipalities not listed in the table.

Policy Instruments for Tobacco Control

I. REGULATION

(1) Regulation of advertising

Regulation of advertising showed a strong initial US policy lead, with some transfer to Canada in the early years, followed by Canada assuming a leadership role in the 1980s and mutual policy transfer from the mid-1990s. Although Canada's federal cabinet in 1971, upon the recommendation of the health minister, even considered banning advertising, there was an explicit reluctance to get ahead of the United States (Government of Canada, Cabinet Minutes, May 6, 1971). There was some counteradvertising done in Canada, at first on children's programs only, but it was not as extensive as that in the United States (Friedman 1975: 82). The restrictions on advertising in the 1971 voluntary code closely resembled those in the US that had been legislated for broadcasting except that Canadian companies voluntarily withdrew from their expensive discount competition and also pledged to limit their total advertising budget. In contrast, after the broadcast ban in the US, other forms of advertising, especially on billboards and in magazines, increased tremendously (Miles 1982). The Canadian voluntary code was also the first instance in these two countries of advertising being limited near schools, although enforcement was lacking.

A similar dynamic applied to health warnings on advertising, primarily print and billboard. In the US this occurred in 1972 when the Federal Trade Commission negotiated an agreement with the tobacco companies to print the same warning as on the packages, but in black and white and scaled to the size of the ad (Whelan 1984; Kluger 1996: 372). Ironically, this is a stronger warning in terms of colour contrast and placement than has ever appeared on US cigarette packages. Health warnings on print advertising were added to the industry's voluntary code in Canada in 1975, but they were only put on billboard advertising in 1984 (Mitchell 1996: 17). Although similar bills to severely restrict tobacco advertising had been proposed in the United States, Canada took the lead in this area in the TPCA in 1988, by banning advertising. Many of these provisions were later incorporated into the FDA Rule in 1996; some also survived in the MSA agreement. Regulation of advertising was a major issue during the period of intense policy transfer between Canada and the United States in the mid-1990s.

Although the advertising problems were similar in the two countries, there were some differences. Resources that might have gone into product advertising in the United States were channelled into sponsorships in Canada, especially after the broadcast ban. This also may be due to the fact that there are more widespread general restrictions on the amount of billboard advertising allowed to take up space in Canada. In the United States, it was estimated that cigarettes were the single most advertised product on billboards in the mid-1980s (White 1988: 120). After the TPCA ban on advertising was overturned by the Supreme Court of Canada, policy in both countries concentrated on more legally defensible moves attempting to restrict or eliminate "lifestyle advertising" associated with tobacco.

After the demise of the FDA Rule in favour of the MSA and passage of the federal *Tobacco Act* in Canada, in most instances Canada had a more restrictive regulatory framework (O'Neill 1999b). On the other hand, US states such as California, Massachusetts, and Florida have engaged in more counteradvertising in recent years, which has been studied and in some instances emulated by provinces such as British Columbia and Ontario, as well as by Health Canada, and incorporated explicitly into the proposed Canadian Senate legislation in bills S-13, S-20, and S-15.

(2) *Regulation of sales*

This is another area in which similar problems have led to considerable policy transfer, especially on the federal level. Several of the policy transfers occurred in the mid-1990s, as discussed below. There was no federal regulation of sales to minors in the US before the FDA Rule in

1996, three years after the Canadian federal law of 1993. However, unlike Canadian provinces, all states had a minimum age for sales. Vending machine restrictions, point-of-sale restrictions, and bans on kiddie packs and free samples, first in Canada and subsequently in the US, were designed to combat underage smoking. Some policy instruments, however, have not transferred. Discounts and prizes were more of a concern in Canada because of intense industry competition in this area in the 1960s, although companies voluntarily gave up the practice in 1971. The US has still not successfully addressed the issues of single cigarette sales, mail-order sales, or discounts and prizes, although both the FDA Rule and the National Settlement attempted to deal with them.

In both countries, many of the sales restrictions have been left to lower levels of government, especially the states and provinces. On this level, one noticeable difference is that some Canadian provinces have banned pharmacy sales of tobacco products and presented textual warnings at the point of sale. Only two US states, however, have an age of purchase of 19 (in fact two others reduced their age to 18), which four Canadian provinces legislated in 1994, followed by two thereafter; Newfoundland proposed it in 2001. In general, as pointed out earlier, innovative policies in Canadian provinces have not generally transferred across the border, in contrast to policies pursued by leading tobacco-restrictive states in the United States.

(3) Regulation of Environmental Tobacco Smoke

In limiting environmental tobacco smoke, the United States has generally been the leader through the activities of selected state and local governments although their policies vary considerably. The first major initiatives were taken in the 1970s by a few states and municipalities, followed by a larger group in the 1980s and an ever-expanding number thereafter. In Canada, there was even more limited activity in this area until the 1990s, as Chapter Four indicates. On the federal level, however, the *Non-Smokers' Rights Act* of 1988 was a more comprehensive policy for federal buildings than anything in the United States until the arrival of President Clinton. While the US has been stalled on a federal workplace smoking rule, this is an area of provincial jurisdiction in Canada. The attempt to have a workplace ban in British Columbia, acting through the Workers Compensation Board, was overturned by the courts, but renewed efforts have been made. Policy transfer is difficult to establish in this area because of the many jurisdictions involved. However, there is evidence that some early Canadian ETS limitations were patterned after existing statutes in US cities (Lachance, Kyle and Sweanor 1990: 9). There also is general recognition in Canada that US state and local levels have been engaged in more ETS regulation, perhaps attributable to greater grass-roots political activism.

The two countries were able to cooperate on two international agreements to provide for the reduction of ETS on international flights, as described below. This built on what each country had done in progressively limiting smoking on domestic flights, first in the US in the 1970s and subsequently in Canada in the 1980s. Once again, from initially a lagging position, Canada became the leader in this policy area. Canada initiated nonsmoking on all domestic airline flights in 1987, followed closely by the United States.

Even if the more restrictive policies in each country may be a case of similar internal developments, by the late 1980s the improved cross-border coordination of NGOs allowed the movement to expand into the international arena, led by Canada. In 1991 the first international summit for smoke-free skies, "Rendez-vous '91," was organized in Ottawa and Montreal by the Canadian Cancer Society. Other groups in attendance included the NSRA, HSFC, ACS, and ALA, as well as others from France and Belgium and a representative of US flight attendant unions. This established an international network for lobbying on this question, which soon produced results. Canada was the first country in the world to ban smoking on all of the international flights of its carriers in 1994. This was followed by an international treaty among Canada, the US, and Australia for flights between those countries and pressure being placed on the International Civil Aviation Organization (whose headquarters are in Montreal) to make the ban universal by 1996. While this formal goal was not reached, the pressure for such an international regime has resulted in an estimated 80 per cent of international flights being smoke-free (Kyle and DuMelle 1994; Kyle 1996). The development of convergent internal policy regimes from domestic sources within each country led to policy transfer on the international level.

(4) Regulation of ingredients

Apparently the Canadian federal government drew another important lesson from US federal policy-making. The 1997 *Tobacco Act* established executive powers to regulate tobacco products progressively as science and the market evolved, giving the Canadian executive similar powers to those the FDA had claimed in 1996. The government of Canada would not need to enact additional specific legislation involving such matters as sales, advertising, and even design of the product through parliamentary procedures. Such regulations would, however, have to be submitted to the scrutiny of the Standing Committee on Health of the House of Commons. Such executive regulatory authority was one of the major points of controversy in the FDA claiming jurisdiction over tobacco in the United States, and, in a concession to the tobacco companies, the abortive National Settlement limited FDA authority over tobacco products. Although no governments have yet regulated tobacco ingredients, as research on nicotine replacements for tobacco and the effects of the various ingredients in cigarettes on the human body continues, there is some prospect that cigarettes and other tobacco products could be re-engineered, by either government consent or order (Sweanor 1998a).

Governments have, in various ways, however, attempted to gain knowledge of and in some instances make public the ingredients, especially toxic ones, in cigarettes. These policies have been controversial. Friedman (1975) commends the voluntary code of Canadian tobacco companies because, unlike its counterparts in the US, it limited the tar and nicotine content of cigarettes. Under the *Tobacco Products Control Act* (1988), the companies were required to list on the side of the package average yields of toxic ingredients in their products, usually tar, nicotine, and carbon monoxide. The expanded package-warning legislation of 2000 adds formaldehyde, benzene, and hydrogen cyanide to this list. The earlier legislation also mandated that manufacturers report additives to the government. In 1998, the province of British Columbia became the first jurisdiction in the world to require cigarette manufacturers to report all ingredients, including those in papers and filters, to the health ministry.

In the United States, tar and nicotine yields have been printed in tobacco advertising (but not on packages) since 1986, and lists of additives (but not amounts or product-specific information) are provided to the government. These lists are not revealed publicly, with the exception of one voluntary instance in 1993 (US Health and Human Services 2000b: 179). Since 1967 the FTC has published tables, based on machine-smoking tests of tar and nicotine delivery and, since 1980, carbon monoxide levels, of cigarettes. These values have been printed on the packages only selectively and voluntarily, mainly for low-tar brands (US Health and Human Services 2000b: 179). Tobacco companies have so far resisted stronger government regulation in this area as an invasion of their individual trade secrets, although this has been challenged by the states of Massachusetts, Texas, and Minnesota (US Health and Human Services 2000b: 183; Phillips 2000).

None of these ingredient-disclosure provisions has been considered particularly effective although some have only recently been put into place. Tar (a general term covering several different particulates) and nicotine yields depend on the technique the smoker uses in consuming the cigarette. More specific listing of toxic ingredients might cause some alarm to smokers and others, but many also tend to think of smoking in terms of relative rather than absolute danger. In short, ingredients have proven to be difficult to regulate because of industry resistance, the complexities of tobacco mixtures, and the phenomenon of "compensatory smoking," whereby consumers absorb different amounts of chemicals depending on how they smoke.

II. FINANCE

(5) *Taxation*

It has been more difficult to transfer policies on taxation than on regulation, especially government-to-government, despite the fact that these are supposedly more fungible economic matters (Rose 1991) and also despite ideological similarities in governing parties. Although the first major increases in federal and provincial taxation of cigarettes in the early 1980s in Canada were for revenue reasons, health advocates began to make the link between increased taxes and reducing tobacco use. By the mid-1980s the connection was clear, and it was made an explicit part of federal government justification for tax increases in 1989 and 1991 (Cunningham 1996). Even though much of the research that led to tobacco-control advocates in Canada recommending further tax increases in the 1980s had been done in the United States, similar arguments in the US for huge tax increases to finance health care and reduce smoking, although advocated by the Coalition on Smoking OR Health from the late 1980s, did not become politically viable until the early 1990s. By then the economic arguments had made a circuitous route back to the US primarily though David Sweanor, who was then developing an international reputation as an expert advocate on tobacco taxation.

After the widely acclaimed success of Canada in reducing tobacco usage through increases in taxation (Kaiserman and Rogers 1991), this part of Canadian policy received greater attention in the US as well. The US Surgeon General's Report of 1992 (US Department of Health and Human Services 1992: 129-31) reviewed 15 studies from various countries on the relationship between price and consumption of cigarettes (price elasticity of demand), including two from Canada, and concluded that higher taxes could deter smoking. When President Clinton proposed a substantial increase in cigarette taxes as a method of financing his proposed Health Security Act, health advocates redoubled their efforts on taxation, only to see the amount of the tax reduced and eventually lost when the whole bill collapsed in Congress in 1994.

Meanwhile, the early 1994 smuggling crisis in Canada showed how vulnerable Canadian taxing policies on tobacco were to the low-tax policies of its larger neighbour. The Canadian federal government declined to petition the US federal government or nearby states to raise their taxes. Unlike Canada, US budgetary processes can be protracted and not subject to rapid change, and there is no federal-state coordination of budgetary timing and taxes. With these structural obstacles, complaints from US and Canadian health advocates that the underlying problem was the low US tax rates were ultimately fruitless (Sweanor 1993; Davis 1993; "Cross-Border Health Coalition" 1993). The limits of even successful convergence in taxation are indicated by the fact that when cigarette prices later rose in nearby US states due to state legislation and the MSA, Canada remained reluctant to increase its taxation except in small amounts. Ultimately, governments have been more sensitive to their own internal concerns on taxation than to international coordination.

(6) Agriculture

Although there has been much rhetoric about governments finding alternative crops or employment for tobacco farmers, more has been done in Canada than in the US. In Canada some financial incentives for tobacco farmers to leave this economic sector were part of the original attempt at tobacco-use reduction in the late 1980s. Similar policies have only recently reached the US political agenda. The only US federal governmental policy coming close to adoption was the abortive McCain Bill. As an addition to the MSA, tobacco companies agreed to provide funds to farmers to alleviate economic distress generated by the increase in prices from the agreement. Even in a market in which they must sell their product to oligopo-listic producers and in which increasingly US producers seek leaf from abroad, there are few crops that bring the financial return that tobacco does, especially for small family farmers. Although most tobacco-control advocates wish to end government price supports, only recently have some initiatives begun to explore alternatives. A few tobacco-growing states have used their MSA money for this purpose, and Maryland is even purchasing and retiring tobacco acreage (Final Report of the Advisory Commission on Tobacco Policy and Public Health 1997; *Show Us the Money* 2000; Gibson 2000). In 2000 President Clinton appointed a Presidential Commission on Improving Economic Opportunity in Communities Dependent on Tobacco Production While Protecting Public Health. Nevertheless, there is no indication that the federal government will soon follow the Canadian government's attempt to ease the transition to other employment for tobacco farmers (Lindblom 1999).

(7) Litigation against tobacco companies

Because of different legal cultures, especially the difficulty of getting large tort awards in Canada, pursuing tobacco-control policy through the courts originally had poor prospects for cross-border transfer. Governments in the US pursued legal action against tobacco companies largely because legislative and administrative venues for policy were persistently blocked, especially at the federal level. Government lawsuits have been of two types: recovery of health care costs, and recovery of taxes lost to smuggling. There have also been criminal sanctions for smuggling cigarettes into Canada. Litigation also has had regulatory implications when tobacco companies have been willing to agree in out-of-court settlements to policies limiting some of their practices.

Government and individual lawsuits against tobacco companies have occurred only recently in Canada, but Canadian observers had been following US developments for years previously (Gray 1988). These US court cases—including individual and class action lawsuits claiming tobacco-company liability for health problems, the suits of US states and the federal government for Medicaid and Medicare costs, the federal criminal court action against smuggling, and associated documents through revelations of tobacco-company whistleblowers and the process of legal "discovery" in court—have been widely covered in Canadian media. Canadian interest groups and government officials closely followed developments in the US (Sweanor 1997; LeGresley 1998a; Ouston 1998). A US state government official, involved in a major lawsuit against tobacco companies, claimed that all the international experience he had was an invitation to speak to a conference in Canada on tobacco litigation.

In the United States, courts often serve as a venue for policy if actors are disappointed by decisions in other institutions. In the state lawsuits, a novel theory of responsibility for governmental healthcare costs was combined with the hiring of private attorneys who were pursuing individual lawsuits against the tobacco companies. This led not only to the discovery of many embarrassing internal company documents concerning their practices, but also to a concerted attempt to make national-level public-health policy through the National Settlement (Pringle 1998; Mollenkamp et al. 1998). But with the defeat of the National Settlement and its replacement by the MSA, the outcome was well short of comprehensive. Furthermore, only a small portion of the revenues from tobacco companies to the states under the MSA money went to tobacco control. Some of the states also took legislative action to guard their revenues against a punitive class action claim in Florida (the *Engle* case). Tobacco settlement money became, in effect, a diversion from tobacco restrictions as some states tried to protect the tobacco companies as their "cash cows."

Using litigation as an instrument both to regulate the industry and to extract revenue from it spread from the United States to Canada. The government of British Columbia assiduously sought information from the US experience before crafting its own policy: first a law allowing it to sue tobacco companies, and then the lawsuit itself. While British Columbia wanted other provinces to follow in a more united effort, this was hindered by ideological and resource differences among them. Ontario sued US and Canadian companies as well as the CTMC in a US court, but that suit was disallowed. After the US federal government criminally prosecuted individuals associated with Northern Brands, an affiliate of RJR, for smuggling across the Canadian border, the Canadian government followed suit with a civil court action for recovery of tax revenue lost to smuggling, again in a US court. The federal government has not laid any criminal charges against tobacco companies, however. At a meeting in Montreal in 2000, the government of Quebec consulted experienced health-care cost litigants, including representatives from British Columbia, US states, and Professor Daynard of Northeastern University. Garfield Mahood of NSRA has advocated that Canadian governments pursue litigation as part of a strategy of denormalization of the tobacco industry. Mahood also hailed the *Engle* verdict as an inspiration that Canadians should follow in their own class-action suits ("Tobacco Opponent Predicts Similar Legal Action in Canada" 2000). Thus far, however, individual and class-action lawsuits in Canada have made little headway.

There is no doubt that in the use of this particular instrument to further both regulatory and financial goals of tobacco-control strategy, the US has been the leader (Ackerman 1997). But it is difficult to make a comprehensive tobacco-control policy from lawsuits alone. The sole attempt to do so, the National Settlement, foundered on the basis that it needed the legal endorsement of the more broader policy branches of government to make comprehensive regulatory policy.

III. CAPACITY BUILDING

(8) Capacity building through targeted funding

Both Canada and the United States have developed federally-funded programs to help provinces, states, and municipalities reduce smoking. The US had ASSIST funds from the National Cancer Institute and the IMPACT program of the Centers for Disease Control and Prevention, now amalgamated into one under the auspices of the CDC. Canada had provincial aid as part of its Tobacco Demand Reduction Strategy, and more recently in the Federal Tobacco Control Strategy. US programs have been more specifically oriented toward youth access and were, prior to the FDA Rule, the major federal effort at greater tobacco regulation in the fifth phase. In Canada, on the other hand, funding under the TDRS was less targeted, in both jurisdictions and policy, and largely short-term (Pechmann, Dixon and Layne 1998).

US state programs, funded either through dedicated tax revenues such as those in California and Massachusetts or through allocation of litigation settlement revenues, as in Florida and a few other states, have also stimulated local anti-tobacco programs. This level of funding, much higher in California and Massachusetts on a long-term basis than either the US or Canadian federal efforts (Plenary Session 1996), have been enviously viewed in Canada. Senator Kenny's abortive bills took the US state programs as models. Similarly, Ontario and British Columbia have adopted US models of directed spending on tobacco-control programs although financed from different sources. While the British Columbia licensing program for tobacco companies to sell in the province is unique, the use of these funds to pay for anti-tobacco health campaigns borrows the concept from similar programs in the United States. The recent best practices report from the Ontario Tobacco Research Unit (2000a) not only discusses relative tobacco-control financing levels of Canadian provinces and US states, but also evaluates in detail the purposes for which US states have used their dedicated revenues.

A community-oriented program judged to be successful in one country can be emulated by other jurisdictions both within the country and across the border. As noted previously, Brantford, in Ontario was included in the COMMIT (Community Intervention Trial for Smoking Cessation) program of the US National Cancer Institute, the forerunner to the ASSIST program (Ontario Tobacco Research Unit 1995a: 10). The Ontario Tobacco Strategy, one of the first provincial ones, was based on revised ASSIST principles and included a component of aid to community projects (Garcia and Mitchell 1994). In turn the Ontario Strategy influenced the later Canadian federal Tobacco Demand Reduction Strategy (Ontario Tobacco Research Unit, 1995a: 7). According to Gregory Connolly, the ASSIST approach also has influenced some state programs in the US (Plenary Session 1996).

IV. EDUCATION

(9) Health warning labels

Warning labels are a publicly visible issue, and developments in these two countries, as well as in others, have generated considerable cross-border interest. The Health and Social Affairs Committee deliberations in 1969 included consideration of the US innovation of warning labels, at that time opposed by the Canadian tobacco industry. The Committee recommended warnings that also carried tar and nicotine levels, and Health Minister Munro also advocated it in Bill C-248. But it was left to the tobacco industry to put a health warning on packages and advertising "voluntarily" in 1971; the warning was changed after its introduction, and attributed to the Department of National Health and Welfare.

When the question of tobacco control was revisited in the 1980s, the US was still a reference point for warnings, albeit a diminished one. Canadian officials noted the rotating US warnings legislated in 1984. By then, however, other countries had warning labels as well, including rotating texts in Sweden and drawings in Iceland. Canada adopted the rotation principle and later, in the regulations for the TPCA, put the warnings on the front and back tops of the packages, in black and white, in both official languages, after discovering that coloured warnings blended into package designs (Tamburri 1990).

Although the warnings in Canada were stronger than in the US, Canada deliberately rejected the attribution of the warning to a government agency or official in favour of an unattributed one, ironically from other USFDA research suggesting that this made the warning more convincing. This rebounded against the government since one of the objectionable features that the Supreme Court found in the TPCA in 1995 was the lack of attribution on warning labels, despite the fact that the companies still had legal liability for their products. In this instance there were two conflicting lessons from the US on the question of attribution, and the federal government chose the wrong one, according to the Supreme Court. Subsequently Canadian packages have carried warnings attributed to Health Canada, even in the time between the demise of the TPCA and the enactment of the *Tobacco Act* when the companies voluntarily placed warning labels on the packages.

As previously noted, the Canadian federal government adopted graphic warnings in 2000. Package insert information about the health effects of cigarettes, authorized since 1988, were included for the first time. In addition, there have been studies of plain packaging by both the federal executive (Health Canada) and legislature (House of Commons Standing Committee on Health) as well as authorization for package alterations in the Ontario *Tobacco Act*. Furthermore, Canadian warning labels since the early 1990s have used the words "kill," "fatal," and "addiction," never mentioned in any US federally-imposed warnings. Although NSRA coordination with US anti-tobacco NGOs (COSH and AMA) in an attempt to interest US federal officials in Canadian warnings failed to elicit much comment ("Canadian Warnings Go To Washington" 1995), it may have led to their incorporation into the abortive National Settlement (see below). It is clear is that Canada sees a role for itself as part of the international front line on package warnings, irrespective of what the US does. This is something a small country can do without incurring smuggling problems as long as Canadians continue to prefer domestically-made cigarettes.

In comparison to other countries, US labels are still relatively small and obscure, often askew on the sides of packages and with their colours readily blending into those of the packages (Aftab, Kolben and Lurie 1999). "Death" and "Addiction" are not on any package even though the

FTC proposed a warning containing the former word as far back as 1964. The package warnings in place since 1965 in the US ironically have become a tobacco company defence in individual and class-action lawsuits. According to David Sweanor (Plenary Session 1996), Canada learned from the US experience of tobacco companies claiming immunity from legal liability for smokers' health problems because of the warnings on cigarette packages. Therefore the 1988 *Tobacco Control Act* included a provision specifically stating that Canadian companies were not legally protected in the same way. Furthermore, while Canada's 1988 legislation was comprehensive, including warnings on practically all tobacco products for internal consumption, the US has required health warnings only on smokeless tobacco products (1986) and cigars (2000).

The US has been attracted to Canada's lead, but the actual policy adoptions have been slight. The FDA Rule of 1996 did mandate a new warning label, never implemented because of the lawsuit of the companies, that cigarettes were a nicotine-delivery device, and since 1998 Liggett tobacco company has voluntarily placed a warning label on its packages noting that cigarettes are addictive. The abortive National Settlement would have imported Canadian-style warnings into the United States. The Settlement document (Mollenkamp et al. 1998: 272-73) explicitly refers to Canadian improvements in warning labels: eight of the nine specified rotating warnings are the same as the Canadian ones, covering 25 per cent of the upper front of the panel, in black and white, and "would be printed in line with current Canadian standards" (e.g., with 17-point type). This may have been due to the influence of Matthew Myers, who had taken part in NGO meetings with Canadian anti-tobacco groups (Pringle 1998: 306). But these provisions were lost with the defeat of the National Settlement in the US Senate. Upon learning of the graphic Canadian package warnings in 2000, some US Senators also expressed the desire to have the US adopt a similar policy, but none has resulted.

There may have been some lesson drawing on the more general question of black and white, "tombstone" text material. The FDA and MSA attempts to have black and white text only for some tobacco advertising may have borrowed from the Canadian package warnings, including the discussions at the federal and Ontario legislative levels about plain packaging, but there is no direct evidence for this.

In summary, there were some initial policy transfers from the US to Canada in the area of warning labels. More recently, despite considerable desire among US anti-tobacco advocates to follow Canada's leadership in this area, warning labels have been a policy instrument in which Canada has continued to innovate without the US following in policy adoption.

(10) *Educational campaigns*

Educational campaigns of various sorts, either narrowly or broadly targeted, have been a feature of tobacco-control policy since the mid-1960s. These campaigns are not separately delineated in Table 6-1 because they are so numerous and overlap with some of the other instruments.

"Educational campaigns" refer to programs primarily aimed at spreading information about the dangers of smoking to a broad section of the public, including indirectly through voluntary or professional groups. In the broader sense, regulatory policy instruments also have educational components, as, for instance, counteradvertising. Educational campaigns are sometimes part of a more comprehensive tobacco-control strategy, usually under the strategies of "prevention" and "cessation." Educational campaigns can be sustained, like the early governmental ones in both Canada and the US, on relatively small budgets, although the results are often questionable. In its evaluation of the initial 1964-66 program, Health and Welfare Canada (1983: 43) comments, "While it would be difficult to single out the federal program of health education from other influences upon the public—notably the impact of US-based news wire services and television broadcasting—the immediate goals of the program were being met."

In the US, educational programs have been mainly at the state and local levels, while in Canada they have tended to be federal programs coordinated with the provinces and private organizations. There have been countrywide educational campaigns in the US, however, especially through DHHS in 1986 and more recently, with state variations, through the establishment of the Youth Smoking Foundation with MSA revenues. One might even argue that the abolition of the lobbying and research arm of the tobacco industry, the Tobacco Institute, as a result of the MSA constituted an educational program. Invariably these campaigns have drawn lessons from each other. Canadian educational programs, for instance, have acknowledged borrowing from the United States and Sweden in the 1970s (Health and Welfare Canada 1983: 59, 93). Posters from Minnesota and Massachusetts have appeared in campaigns in other US states, British Columbia, and Ontario. Canadian campaigns also have resembled those in the US in that one of their main goals has been to reduce the appeal of cigarettes to youth.

Since 1980, Health Canada has coordinated four major educational campaigns involving federal-provincial and public-private cooperation, commencing in 1980, 1985, 1994, and 1999. A fifth was announced in 2001. By the early 1980s, however, professional and governmental opinion began to shift away from nearly exclusive reliance on educational campaigns for tobacco reduction. In the words of the Ontario Advisory Committee on Smoking and Health, "Governmental actions will be most effective if they include a mix of educational, economic, legislative, research, and organizational measures. Early work suggested that an educational approach might be sufficient. Recent research makes it clear that variety of initiatives is required." (Ontario Council of Health 1982, quoted in Health and Welfare Canada 1983: 82). In recent years, health education has become "health promotion," including goals of healthy public policy and a more direct, confrontational posture about tobacco-related problems (Forster and Wolfson 1998; US Department of Health and Human Services 2000a). Since the late 1980s the Canadian strategy has been to restrict tobacco promotion to complement the credibility of health-promotion campaigns.

V. GENERAL LEARNING TOOLS

(11) *General learning through hearings and reports*

The most difficult policy instrument to assess is general learning tools. These include government documents and events, such as testimony before legislative committees, which affect policy largely in an indirect and diffuse manner, without a focussed educational or promotional campaign. By a narrow definition, this may not even qualify as "policy" except as agenda setting, since it is not legislation, executive orders, or judicial decisions directed at particular ends. But in a broader sense, it is "policy" since it affects how policy-makers and the public think about tobacco control. In some instances, it is the major instrument that certain government officials, most prominently the Surgeon General of the United States, possess. Because they are so diffuse, the lessons from these instruments are particularly amenable to cross-border learning, especially for agenda setting.

In the *Federal Cigarette Advertising and Labeling Act of 1965* and its successor in 1970, Congress mandated periodic public reports from the

Table 6-2: US Surgeon General's Reports, 1964-2000

1964	Smoking and Heath: Report of the Advisory Committee to the Surgeon General of the Public Health Service, 1964
1967	The Health Consequences of Smoking: A Public Health Service Review
1968	The Health Consequences of Smoking: 1968 Supplement to the 1967 Pubic Health Service Review
1969	The Health Consequences of Smoking: 1969 Supplement to the 1967 Public Health Service Review
1971	The Health Consequences of Smoking: A Report to the Surgeon General
1972	The Health Consequences of Smoking: A Report to the Surgeon General
1973	The Health Consequences of Smoking: A Report to the Surgeon General
1974	The Health Consequences of Smoking, 1974
1975	The Health Consequences of Smoking, A Report to the Surgeon General
1976	The Health Consequences of Smoking: Selected Chapters from 1971 through 1975 Reports
1978	The Health Consequences of Smoking, 1977-1978
1979	The Health Consequences of Smoking: A Report to the Surgeon General
1980	The Health Consequences of Smoking for Women: A Report of the Surgeon General
1981	The Health Consequences of Smoking – The Changing Cigarette: A Report of the Surgeon General
1982	The Health Consequences of Smoking – Cancer: A Report of the Surgeon General
1983	The Health Consequences of Smoking – Cardiovascular Disease: A Report of the Surgeon General
1984	The Health Consequences of Smoking – Chronic Obstructive Lung Disease: A Report of the Surgeon General
1985	The Health Consequences of Smoking – Cancer and Chronic Lung Disease in the Workplace: A Report of the Surgeon General
1986	The Health Consequences of Involuntary Smoking: A Report of the Surgeon General
1988	The Health Consequences of Smoking: Nicotine Addiction, 1988
1989	Reducing the Health Consequences of Smoking – 25 Years of Progress: A Report of the Surgeon General
1990	The Health Benefits of Smoking Cessation: A Report of the Surgeon General
1992	Smoking in the Americas: A Report of the Surgeon General
1994	Preventing Tobacco Use Among Young People: A Report of the Surgeon General
1998	Tobacco Use Among U.S. Racial/Ethic Minority Groups, 1998
2000	Reducing Tobacco Use: A Report of the Surgeon General

Surgeon General on smoking and health. These publications have become the principal means for the Surgeon General to influence public behaviour and more specific policy on tobacco control, not only in the United States but throughout the world. There have been 26 Surgeon General's reports on tobacco-related subjects since the first one in 1964. These documents are generally compilations and summaries of research on particular topics, including policy activities by governments in regard to tobacco. A full list of these reports is provided in Table 6-2.

The one-way mirror operates in this realm. There is no Canadian equivalent of the US Surgeon General, whose major responsibility is to be a public-health advocate. Furthermore, legislative committees usually play more limited roles than in the US, with less publicity for their hearings. Canada pays considerably more attention to such general learning instruments as the 1964, 1986, and 1988 Surgeon General's reports, the 1993 report of the Environmental Protection Agency (EPA) on the health effects of ETS, and the 1994 House Subcommittee on Health and Environment hearings than does the United States to Canadian government investigations and legislative hearings. Health Canada documents from the mid-1980s testify to the effects on Canadian policy deliberations not only of the 1986 Surgeon General's Report on involuntary smoking, but also to Surgeon General Koop's use of the term "addiction" in published interviews (Somers n.d.; Cook 1986; Collishaw 1986b).

Similar Canadian general learning tools—such as the 1983 report of Health and Welfare Canada in conjunction with the World Conference on Tobacco or Health in Winnipeg, or the 2000 Senate committee hearings involving the subpoenaed testimony of tobacco company executives (which some Canadian observers compared to the 1994 legislative hearings in the United States)—were significant mainly or, in the latter case, exclusively within Canada. Even if the 1983 report had some international impact, it was more likely to be in countries other than the United States. Nevertheless, if one considers the concept of healthy public policy as a general learning tool, it clearly originated, at least in terms of government support of the idea, in Canada and rapidly spread to the United States. The US applied the concept more specifically to tobacco control and has more consistently documented this linkage in periodic reports. This complements the general US tendency for being the leader in public education and the dissemination of general learning tools, even if other countries have often gone further in implementing the lessons of such tools into more concrete policies.

Comparing Policy Tools Across Countries: A Summary

There is considerable evidence that lesson drawing is occurring between these two countries, across jurisdictions as well as over the international border. Regulatory policies seem to be more susceptible to policy transfer than are financially-based policies; even though finance is fungible, economists have few qualms about limiting the applicability of their findings to specific countries, and research on the effects of taxation is readily available. Despite considerable effort, federal cigarette taxation policies in the two countries have not been close. States and provinces in the same region sometimes have diverse taxation policies regardless of the threat of smuggling. The US has made little effort to duplicate Agriculture Canada's policy of financial incentives to help move farmers out of tobacco growing. Perhaps because financial matters generally are one of the principal issues of concern to political leaders, they see themselves as more conversant in these policies and are more reluctant to adopt policy instruments used in other countries when they have the option.

When it comes to financial instruments of both revenue and spending, politicians are reluctant to make major, or synoptic, changes. The exception, of course, is the lawsuits for smuggling and healthcare cost recovery, but even these were initially selective among jurisdictions and had the potential of huge payoffs for the amount of government effort invested. The US lawsuits for healthcare cost recovery have been more admired than emulated by tobacco-control policy-makers in Canada thus far, largely because of differences in the legal systems. But these differences are shrinking, and more legal actions can be expected in Canada as well. In the US, success in lawsuits has not resulted in the financial gains accruing proportionately to tobacco control. Despite the integration of regulation and finance through the MSA in the US and in British Columbia, there continue to be differences in the transferability of these two broad types of tobacco-control policy.

Even though several similar policies and instruments have been adopted, differences remain. Canada has targeted some restrictions, in packaging, principally by health warnings, and in reduced-price schemes such as discounts, coupons, and free samples, more prominently than has the United States. Canada was the first country to put TPCA warning labels on cigars; the United States did not undertake a similar policy until 2000. Some provinces have adopted bans on pharmacy sales, something never enacted and rarely even mentioned in the United States.

Sponsorship has been a particular dilemma for Canada, due to the heavy tobacco investment in it. The alliances such promotions have built with affected groups in the arts and sports communities have made it more difficult for the federal government to forbid such sponsorships, especially since it was unwilling to offer compensatory funds in return.

Two areas in which the United States has engaged in more regulation than Canada are at the local level. The first is environmental tobacco smoke; the second is the construction of a local infrastructure of tobacco control across the country through federal and private support. In Canada there has been considerably less sustained and systematic effort devoted to this (Pechman, Dixon and Layne 1998). There were two problems with the Canadian funding: there was little systematic planning, and funding was substantially reduced through general federal government budget cuts. Local initiatives have varied considerably from province to province, despite federal coordinating committees.

If one considers the tobacco-control specialist agenda as well as adopted policy, then the realm of lesson drawing between the United States and Canada is potentially much larger. Some ideas, such as Canadian-style warnings, large tax increases, and more comprehensive regulation through the FDA, have come close to becoming policy in the US; others may be more remote but continue to generate interest in specialist circles. Some of these are described in Chapter Seven. In the years ahead, there could be more policy transfer between the two countries. Whether the intense borrowing of the 1994-98 period will recur, however, is unlikely.

It is not only policies that are transferred between countries, however; it is also political techniques useful for tobacco-control policy. Some of them also involve particular policies, for instance, local capacity building and litigation against companies for financial compensation. But others are not entirely captured by the discussions of policy above; for instance, the spread of more aggressive forms of anti-tobacco advocacy from Canada to the United States. The diffusion of these forms of behaviour may have general effects on a wide range of policies.

Directions and Agents of Policy Transfer

Although a pattern of cross-border lesson drawing between these two countries, and indeed even wider internationally, does exist, it is not necessarily a simple one of an inevitable leader and follower. Table 6-3 summarizes some of the major policy instruments subject to policy transfer, both positive and negative, for all levels of Canadian and US government by eras. Within each, consideration is given to whether there were indications of lesson drawing, whether the type of lesson was positive, negative, or "mixed," which country provided the lesson, and the major agents of transfer. This table covers only policies that were in effect for at least a brief period of time. Proposals that were part of the active political agenda but never adopted, for instance those in the US National Settlement, are not considered.

In the first period, 1964-84, the direction of lesson drawing was entirely from the United States to Canada, and the lessons were generally positive. The instruments were limited to those used in the United States at the time. The major agents were the media, bureaucracy, and legislative testimony from US officials and Canadians who had studied US developments. Yet similar Canadian legislation was not forthcoming, although some executive actions were taken and some elements were incorporated into the 1971 voluntary code. This was usually done in a manner less inhibiting to tobacco companies than what had been proposed by the Isabelle Committee or cabinet deliberations (Mitchell 1996).

During the second period, 1984-94, the dominant direction of information was still from the United States to Canada, but transfer occurred in the opposite direction as well, in both taxation and regulation. Canada assessed lessons from the US more critically, for instance in having stronger health warnings. Even though Canada gained its reputation as a major tobacco-control country during this period, the lessons from Canada, while being absorbed in the United States, resulted in only minimal policy changes there because only at the end of this period did the US federal government move in a concerted fashion toward a more stringent tobacco-control policy. The number of instruments remained limited. Advocacy groups as well as the bureaucracy became the main transfer agents, with the media continuing to play a role.

The third period, 1994-2000, shows that the number of policy instruments transferred became greater and the relationship between Canada and the US became more complex. Most of the lessons were positive. There were more two-way transfers using the same instruments (leapfrogging). If anything, the table may underestimate Canada's leadership role in some areas because, as in the second period, the US was absorbing more lessons from Canada than it could get adopted as policy. Advocacy

Table 6-3: Policy Transfer by Phase, Direction,
Policy Instrument, Nature of Lesson, and Agents (All Levels)

1964-1984

Direction	Policy Instrument	Nature	Agent
US→C	(11) General Learning Tools (Surgeon General's Report)	(+)	Bureaucracy, media, legislative testimony
	(1) Warnings on ads	(+)	Media, legislative testimony
US→C	(1) Counter-advertising	(+)	Media, legislative testimony, bureaucracy
US→C	(1) Banning broadcast ads	(+)	Media, legislative testimony
US→C	(10) Educational campaigns	(+)	Bureaucracy, media

1984-1994

Direction	Policy Instrument	Nature	Agent
US↔C	(11) General learning tools (Surgeon General's reports, EPA report, Congressional hearings, Healthy Public Policy)	(+)	Bureaucracy, media, advocacy groups
US→C	(10) Rotating warning labels	(+)	Media, bureaucracy
US→C	(2) Age sales restrictions	(+)	Media, bureaucracy, advocacy groups
US→C	(3) ETS (local)	(+)	Media, advocacy groups
US↔C	(3) ETS (domestic and international airlines)	(+)	Advocacy groups, bureaucracy
US→C	(5) Special taxes/ levies for health	(+)	Advocacy groups, media, bureaucracy
US↔C	(5) Heavy taxes on cigarettes	(±)	Academics, bureaucracy, advocacy groups
US→C	(8) Funds for local capacity building	(+)	Bureaucracy, personnel
US→C	(4) Federal pre-emption	(−)	Advocacy groups, bureaucracy

Table 6-3 continued: Policy Transfer by Phase, Direction, Policy Instrument, Nature of Lesson, and Agents (All Levels)

1994-2000 Direction	Policy Instrument	Nature	Agent
US←C	(9) Stronger warning labels	(+)	Bureaucracy, advocacy groups
US↔C	(1) Sponsorship restrictions	(±)	Media, advocacy groups, bureaucracy
US↔C	(1) Advertising restrictions	(+)	Media, advocacy groups, bureaucracy
US→C	(1) Counter-advertising	(+)	Advocacy groups, bureaucracy
US←C	(2) Minimum sales age of 18	(+)	Bureaucracy, Media Groups
US↔C	(2) Sales restrictions— vending machines, self-service displays, kiddie packs, free samples	(+)	Bureaucracy
US→C	(3) ETS (local)	(+)	Media, Advocacy Groups
US↔C	(3) ETS (international)	(+)	
US→C	(5) Special levies on tobacco industry	(+)	Media, Advocacy Groups, Executive
US←C	(5) Heavy taxes on cigarettes	(±)	Legislative testimony, Academics, Advocacy Groups, Media
US→C	(7) Litigation against smuggling	(+)	Judicial Decisions, Media, Advocacy Groups, Executive, Bureaucracy
US→C	(7) Litigation for healthcare costs	(+)	Media, Executive, Bureaucracy
US→C	(10) Educational campaigns	(+)	Advocacy Groups, Bureaucracy
US→C	(4) Executive discretionary authority	(+)	Bureaucracy

+ = positive lesson   – = negative lesson
± = mixed positive and negative lessons
→← = lesson drawing from one country to the other
↔ = mutual lesson drawing

groups, the bureaucracy, and the media continued to be the major transfer agents, but the political executive and the judiciary also became more involved than previously. As the range of instruments under consideration broadened, the number of actors involved became larger, too. Tobacco control became a higher profile issue. Over the course of the three periods, the growing role of advocacy groups as transfer agents is especially striking.

Processes of Policy Transfer

There have been several attempts to develop explanations of policy transfer categorized not by content, but by process. Dolowitz and Marsh (1996, 2000) present elaborate typologies based largely on two major underlying principles: the degree of voluntariness or coercion and an evaluation of the rationality/appropriateness of the transfer. The most parsimonious and relatively consistent categorization, however, has been used by Bennett (1991a, 1991b, 1992, 1997), initially in a study of data protection (privacy information) policy and more recently encompassing freedom-of-information and ombudsman laws. For data protection laws, originally this was a five-fold typology. Lessons could be transferred through (1) technological determinism, (2) emulation (imitation or adaptation of government policies elsewhere), (3) elite networking (an international policy community or an epistemic community), (4) harmonization (authoritative action by international organizations), and (5) penetration (international coercion). More recently, Bennett (1997) argues that, in addition to convergence occurring through growth of government and democratization, policy transfer can occur through three processes: lesson drawing, "a quasi-rational attempt to search for solutions to common problems across space and time"; legitimation, using foreign evidence to support arguments developed first from domestic sources; and harmonization, where international standards affect state policies (Bennett 1997: 228). In a general theoretical essay on policy convergence, Seeliger (1996: 301) offers four possible explanations of convergence through policy transfer, in addition to general diffusion of knowledge: media, policy entrepreneurs, epistemic communities, and harmonization through international cooperation.

In tobacco control, growth of government and democratization do not appear to be factors for convergence. Technological determinism is of some importance, in the sense that the scientific evidence about the dangers of cigarette smoking is the same on both sides of the border.

Nevertheless, what governments can do is limited by the widespread social acceptance and economic significance of cigarettes in each country. Therefore, regulation is the preferred policy mechanism, but that still leaves wide leeway for choices and priorities. Harmonization through international organizations is at a formative stage through the Framework Agreement on Tobacco Control. Penetration is a force favouring international tobacco companies, especially when their business activities are endorsed by powerful governments such as those in the US. No international governmental regime coercive on tobacco restrictions has been constructed. From the remaining list of possible processes of policy transfer in tobacco control between the US and Canada, four categories seem especially important: epistemic communities, those based more on the generation and dissemination of specific knowledge rather than on political advocacy; nongovernmental policy communities, consisting of interest groups and political entrepreneurs attempting to influence policy; media; and government agencies. Within these general categories, there can be different specific agents of transfer, such as the bureaucracy, political executive, or judiciary within the government.

Epistemic Communities

Although it may be difficult to trace their influence on specific policies, published research on tobacco may influence policy across borders, especially when the researchers themselves are not only read but also consulted by governments and activist groups. This is not "technological determinism," but it does show that scientific knowledge can affect public policy, even if the process may be contested, slow, and uneven. Governments and anti-tobacco groups in Canada and the United States generally have high regard for research on tobacco control conducted in the other country. Some well-known researchers in the field of tobacco control, such as Americans Kenneth Warner, James Repace, and Richard Pollay (now resident in British Columbia), and Canadian Lynn Kozlowski (now resident in Pennsylvania), are recognized authorities on both sides of the border and often called upon, either by bureaucracies or judiciaries, for their expertise (Kluger 1996; Cunningham 1996).

Hoberg (1991) found that in health and safety regulations for drugs and pesticides, the superior scientific research capacity of the United States often plays a significant role in Canadian policy formation. The difference is not only one of scale. The US federal government funds health research, through such organizations as the National Cancer Institute within the National Institutes of Health, at a higher level proportionately than does the Canadian federal government. In fact, there was little government-funded research on tobacco outside the agencies themselves until the National Research Initiative on Tobacco in 1997, co-sponsored by Health Canada and the National Cancer Institute of Canada within the Canadian Cancer Society. In such circumstances, it is only logical for Canada to look to the United States for much of the physical-science evidence on which to base its health regulations. Since the population structures of the two countries are similar, U.S-generated behavioural research also is often used by Canadians. In tobacco control this process began early, with Health Canada's citation of research from the United States (primarily) and Britain (secondarily) in its initial 1964 publication. Subsequent Health Canada documents contain references to US medical and behavioural research as well as to that in other countries (Cook 1986; Collishaw 1986b; Sweanor 1991; 1998b).

Because of majority use of the same language and physical proximity to the United States, as well as the fact that most Canadian libraries purchase considerable amounts of US material, it is relatively easy for Canadian policy advocates and officials to acquire this information. This is the classic free-rider approach, which many Canadians are pleased to acknowledge. An official of a voluntary health organization has stated, "We are a small country; we'll steal ideas from anyone."

On the other hand, the huge resources in skills and finances available for research on tobacco-related topics in the United States make it considerably less dependent on Canadian work. In fact, the Surgeon General's reports only occasionally employ contributors from outside the United States, and of these, more are from Britain than Canada. Nevertheless, increasingly the Surgeon General and other US agencies have become interested in developments in other parts of the world (US Department of Health and Human Services 1992; Pan-American Health Organization 1992). The 1964 Surgeon General's Report pooled seven major studies on the relationship between tobacco use and disease, including a prospective study of 92,000 Canadian veterans from 1956 to 1963. Some major literature reviews on health behaviour topics also have surveyed Canadian as well as US studies (Schwartz 1969; Schwartz and Ryder 1977; Schwartz 1987). A project of international cooperation on tobacco control was launched in 1988 by Surgeon General Koop and resulted in two 1992 publications, both issued in conjunction with the Pan-American Health Organization, a regional body of WHO. The Surgeon General's report of that year, *Smoking and Health in the Americas* (1992), focussed on general patterns while a companion report, *Tobacco or Health: Status in the Americas*, issued under the auspices of the Pan-American Health Organization, described the situation in individual countries in the Americas, excluding the United States, in more detail. Canada has also been a source of some important information from company files, especially on targeting underage smokers (Hilts 1996: 91). As previously mentioned, the 2000 Surgeon General's report had more Canadian-specific information than any previously, with Canadian researcher and activist David Sweanor as one of the contributors. Many of the researchers most frequently cited and consulted by governments are also policy activists, sometimes with anti-tobacco NGOs. US interest in Canada peaks when the latter innovates in policy, although that does not mean that the US will necessarily adopt the same policies.

Professional conferences and journals also provide opportunities for the broad, if often diffuse, sharing of ideas. The journal *Tobacco Control*, a product of a discussion among activists at the World Conference on Tobacco Or Health in 1990, was established to convey both academic and popular information on tobacco-control issues in a more systematic fashion than other journals. The National Clearinghouse on Tobacco and Health, part of the Canadian Council on Smoking and Health in Ottawa, has gathered a large library of information relevant to tobacco control around the world, partially supported by the federal government and mainly for the use of anti-tobacco groups and government programs in Canada but available to others. The NCTH directory of organizations and personnel concerned with tobacco control, on all sides of the issue, includes many people in the United States and elsewhere in the world as well. There is no equivalent central information bureau for tobacco control available to both governments and the public in the United States.

Nongovernmental Policy Communities

There also is more policy-focussed contact between these two countries. Interest groups increasingly developed cross-border links, some specifically devoted to lesson drawing. The Canadian and American Cancer societies have been especially active in these connections. Since 1991 the joint

Borderline Committee of the two Cancer societies has regularly met in an attempt to coordinate public positions and lobbying efforts in their respective countries. Based on its evaluation of both the Canadian and US experience, the CCS submitted a long position paper, including 18 appendices on Canadian policy, to the FDA during its consideration of the proposed regulation of tobacco (*In Support of Public Health* 1995). Public Issues Director Ken Kyle of the CCS was instrumental in working with Fran DuMelle of the American Lung Association, other NGO leaders, and bureaucrats in both countries in developing international regulations for ETS on air transport. The Canadian Cancer Society also distributed many videotaped copies of an invited lecture in Canada by a police officer from Woodridge, Illinois, on preventing underage tobacco sales through licensing, undercover inspections, fines, school-based educational programs, and strict enforcement. Woodridge is a community often cited in both countries for its efforts on this issue (Feder 1996).

In addition to the other elements for policy transfer, policy entrepreneurs are often essential (Keck and Sikkink 1998). Within the anti-tobacco community, some of the more prominent individuals are from nongovernmental organizations, perhaps because they are less constrained in pursuing tobacco restrictions on a continuing basis. Some are much more active on the international level than others, but even those who begin with a local focus are often consulted by groups and governments in other countries.

Leading anti-tobacco activists are not inhibited by the border; they frequently cross it, physically or virtually, in an attempt to influence policy in the other country. David Sweanor of the Non-Smokers' Rights Association has been especially active in the United States, testifying as an expert witness before legislative committees in the United States on the federal and state level, serving on committees reviewing research grant applications for US health agencies, and leading workshops for tobacco-control training sessions. Within one year alone he visited some 20 US states. In testimony on issues in the McCain Bill before the US Senate Democratic Task Force on Tobacco in 1998, Sweanor (1998b) identified some of the US and international bodies with which he had worked: the American Cancer Society, the National Cancer Institute, the American Medical Association, the World Bank, the Pan American Health Organization, and the World Health Organization. Similarly, US anti-tobacco leaders such as Michael Pertschuk of the Advocacy Institute and Gregory Connolly of the Massachusetts Tobacco Control Program have visited Canada, including appearances before parliamentary committees and in the media. They also regularly interact with Canadian representatives in conferences and through other means of communication. Most US tobacco-control conferences now include at least one representative from a Canadian NGO. At the New England and Eastern Canada Tobacco Control Conference in 1999, six Canadians, from both governments and NGOs, gave presentations, along with some two dozen from the US.

Such cross-border links are not limited to anti-tobacco groups, of course. Tobacco companies, too, have international links through joint ownership schemes, professional trade organizations, and conferences (Hilts 1996; Cunningham 1996). Although Canadian tobacco companies claim to operate independently of their American affiliates and deny that their behaviour can be considered equivalent to that of their US counterparts, they admit to paying attention to developments in the United States and how tobacco companies there respond. Stoffman (1987) reports that tobacco executives in North Carolina were well aware of the progress of Bill C-51 as it passed through the Canadian parliament. The cross-border lesson drawing in which companies engage has become more evident with the public release of tobacco company documents in recent years.

Tobacco industry arguments from one country to another are familiar. As Friedman's (1975: 98) comparative study indicates, tobacco-company representatives in both the United States and Canada rely on similar, sometimes identical, arguments and evidence. More recently, tobacco companies in both countries have attempted to shift the arguments from public-health considerations to a focus on individual rights, including commercial free speech in advertising and the individual's freedom of choice to smoke. Ontario activist Michael Perley ("Understanding and Countering the Tobacco Industry"1996) found many common features of industry strategies at the local level in Canada and the United States. Investigations into cross-border smuggling have also revealed international cooperation among affiliated tobacco companies (Marsden 1999).

Tobacco-control lessons from other countries often are interpreted to reinforce the previous positions of those citing them (Robertson 1991), what Bennett (1997) calls "legitimation." In its ultimately successful fight against advertising restrictions before the Supreme Court, Canadian tobacco companies made occasional references to US court cases. US tobacco companies, in their submission to the FDA on its proposed regulations, also cited Canadian studies. The 1994 Canadian smuggling episode has been widely cited by tobacco-company representatives and apologists as demonstrating the dangers of heavy taxation (Sullum 1998). After they turned against the McCain Bill in 1998, the companies hired the former mayor of Cornwall, Ontario, as well as a former RCMP officer, to testify before Congress on the problems of law enforcement resulting from high tobacco taxes and smuggling (Moon 1997).

Despite their small share of the Canadian cigarette market, US tobacco companies had former US trade representative Julius Katz testify on their behalf before a House of Commons Committee in 1994. Katz claimed that plain packaging for cigarettes in Canada, including imported brands, could lead to a lawsuit by US companies under NAFTA, based on claims of interference with commercial sales through trademark infringement. Nevertheless, NSRA's Mahood (2000) claims that plain packaging would survive a legal challenge under international trade rules.

Through electronic mail and the Internet, it is now even easier for interested parties to follow developments in other countries. Both tobacco companies and anti-tobacco groups have been active participants in establishing Internet sites (Davis 1997). The Advocacy Institute took a major role by establishing SCARC-Net, covering North America, and eventually GlobaLink, a worldwide site for the exchange of information among tobacco-control activists. There are several other anti-tobacco subscription services in the United States. Since 1995, Montreal-based Stan Shatenstein has provided a daily summary of press items on tobacco, "Tobacco News Online," especially from the US, Canada, and the United Kingdom, most recently under the sponsorship of SHAF. The Ontario Tobacco Research Unit maintains OTRU-Net for the public-health community, mainly in Canada, and also provides access to Shatenstein's reports. In 1999 the CDC hosted a multilateral conference in Atlanta to launch its international Web site of information on tobacco control for governments ("Global Information Management and Surveillance Systems for a Tobacco-Free World" 1999). While cross-border communication for anti-tobacco groups has become easier in recent years, it is more difficult to document specifically how information through these channels influences policy.

Media

Through the massive penetration of US media across the border, Canadian elites as well as the public can follow major US developments in tobacco control. Some 80 per cent of the Canadian population live within 150 miles of the US border, making media access, especially television, readily available, even more so now with the rise of cable and satellite television. The situation is much different in the US, where the population is more scattered, movement in recent years has been away from the northeastern part of the country which abuts the major population centres of Canada in Ontario and Quebec, and most of the US population and leaders, no matter how close they may be to Canada, are ignorant of Canadian developments. Except in cities bordering Canada, such as Detroit and Buffalo, it is unusual for US cable television companies to carry any Canadian channels. Only a few major US newspapers provide coverage of Canadian tobacco control, mainly the *New York Times, Washington Post,* and the *Wall Street Journal.* These publications do, however, tend to reach much of the policy-making elite audience in Washington and other political centres across the US. Media now include some of the sources noted above, such as electronic mail and the Internet, insofar as these are capable of general, diffuse information flow as well as toward more specialized policy audiences.

Government Agencies

Not all lesson drawing is done through nongovernmental intermediaries. Sometimes it is done directly government-to-government, especially through bureaucracies. As previously noted, Health Canada has links with the Department of Health and Human Services, the Office of Smoking and Health in the Centers for Disease Control and Prevention, and the Food and Drug Administration in the United States. These communications channels were extensively utilized during the most intense period of lesson drawing in the mid-1990s (Hilts 1996; Winsor 1997). In considering the McCain Bill on the National Settlement, Congress not only heard testimony from various interests about Canadian policy, but also commissioned a report from the US General Accounting Office concerning Canadian tax policies, smuggling, and underage smoking (US General Accounting Office 1998). In its deliberations over whether or not to include this in its National Tobacco Strategy, Health Canada invited US proponents of a "denormalization of the industry" strategy to make presentations and take part in a roundtable discussion of this approach in Quebec during National Non-Smoking Week in 1999. The invited participants were nongovernmental policy advocate and researcher Stanton Glantz of California, Gregory Connolly of Massachusetts, and Chuck Wolfe, formerly an official in the Florida governor's office. Litigation and financial compensation strategies have spread from the United States to Canada through direct contacts at the provincial and federal levels. The Canadian Senate Committee on Energy, the Environment and Natural Resources invited officials from US states to testify before it in hearings on Senator Kenny's bill S-20 in 2000.

At the provincial level, governments have sometimes been involved in direct, publicly recognized communications with officials in the US. British Columbia, in particular, has consciously and explicitly based its tobacco-control strategy on close examination of state policies and consultations in the United States by health ministers and attorneys general. Particular attention was devoted to Florida's law change to enable a lawsuit to be filed against tobacco companies, dedicated anti-tobacco funds and advertising campaigns in California and Massachusetts, the Minnesota lawsuit against tobacco companies, and the National Settlement (McPhail 1997). In preparation for a possible lawsuit, Quebec consulted with Florida officials. Even Alberta, a late entrant into provincial regulation, conferred in 2000 with officials from Oregon about tobacco regulation. Ontario and Manitoba maintain formal links to some US states through participation in the Great Lakes Tobacco Control Coalition, but so far this group has not been a major communication channel for lesson drawing. The New England and Eastern Canada Tobacco Control Conference is a second cross-border inter-provincial and inter-state meeting.

Less public, but perhaps of equal or even greater importance, are the personnel transfers among health care professionals between the two countries, which can also be multi-level and between governmental and nongovernmental organizations. At least four Canadian healthcare officials prominent in research or policy advocacy—John Garcia, Heather Selin, Lawrence Green, and Linda Pedersen—have also held positions in US agencies or with organizations closely associated with governmental agencies. John Garcia's activities in private and public bodies on both sides of the border have previously been described in Chapter Five. Selin moved from NSRA in Canada to the Office on Smoking and Health in the CDC, then to the Pan-American Union in Washington, DC, to work on hemispheric tobacco issues. Green went from the British Columbia Ministry of Health in 1999 to the OSH-CDC, where he became Acting

Director upon Michael Erickson's departure in 2000, while Pedersen transferred from a public-health position at the University of Waterloo to OSH-CDC.

While there may be more opportunities for upward mobility in careers in tobacco control in the United States, having a Canadian background does not appear to be a handicap to advancement. Knowledge of Canadian research and policies, federal and provincial, affords one an opportunity to gain a foothold in the US bureaucracy as well. Personnel returning to Canada, such as Garcia, then also have increased knowledge of US policies. In short, these bureaucratic personnel transfers show the ease of operating in a cross-border public-health environment with shared values.

In this multi-level issue, cross-border policy transfer has occurred on several levels. Although lower levels of government in each country are more likely to engage in lesson drawing from other jurisdictions in the same country, in Canada in particular they are not immune to lessons from states and even municipalities in the United States. Despite considerable evidence of lesson drawing from Canada to the United States on the federal level, there appears to be little transfer from the Canadian provinces to the United States on either the federal or state level (Studlar 1999a). For instance, there has been no concerted attempt in the United States to emulate some of the more innovative provincial policies, such as a ban on pharmacy sales or raising the age for sales to 19. There is still a partial one-way mirror.

Summary

While Bennett (1992) found convergence in policy content among countries developing freedom-of-information policies but considerable divergence in the policy instruments they utilized, this study makes an even stronger case for lesson drawing as a contributing explanation for policy convergence. The analysis in this chapter has revealed a "double similarity," in both content and instruments, between Canada and the United States in tobacco-control policy. In fact, now there may be an even closer relationship among the instruments used in the two countries than in policy content since some attempts at adoption of similar policies, for instance through the National Settlement and the FDA Rule, have been frustrated.

The relationship between content and instruments has changed over the years. When more restrictive tobacco-control was being formulated in the 1960s and early 1970s, Canada and the United States established similar policy content but varying policy instruments. The major difference was that in Canada the tobacco companies had responsibility for enforcement and could also unilaterally revise the policies, an approach that had been rejected in the US.

Policy transfer has become more prevalent, in either direction and across several levels of government, with the notable exception of provinces and municipalities in Canada not transferring policies to the United States. While federal-level government-to-government lesson drawing occurred especially when both were attempting to develop comprehensive policies in the mid-1990s, the activities of nongovernmental and state/provincial governments have become more persistent. Currently there is a worldwide search for "best practices" in tobacco control (see Chapter Seven). With the publicity given to Canadian regulatory and tax policies by US journalists and advocacy groups in the late 1980s and early 1990s, there has been an increased thickening of relations among groups and sometimes government officials dedicated to tobacco control in both countries. NSRA and the CCS in Canada have been key organizations for these cross-border contacts, and the Advocacy Institute, ACS, and increasingly the Tobacco Products Litigation Project have served a similar function in the US. Provincial governments and federal institutions, ranging from the Canadian Senate to the US Office on Smoking and Health, have made attempts to learn what is occurring in the other country. Transfer of expert anti-tobacco personnel between the US and Canada, both between governments and NGOs, and, as will be explored in Chapter Seven, even extending to the World Health Organization, have facilitated the transfer of policies.

An international tobacco-control network has developed, an "advocacy coalition" beyond Sabatier's (1999) description, organized around an issue and working across multiple levels of government within one country as well as across country borders. Canada and the United States are not the only members of this coalition, but they have been principal reference points for each other's development of policy. Since the late 1980s, there has been more policy coordination, especially among anti-tobacco groups. Geographic proximity, similar social and economic standing, and a common language have facilitated this cross-border lesson drawing. The availability of professional conferences, intergovernmental meetings, specialist journals, media reports, and electronic information sources between the two countries has provided opportunities for lesson drawing. Within that international advocacy coalition, policy entrepreneurs share their ideas and experiences broadly with other countries.

The impact of lesson drawing, however, depends on both institutional and cultural configurations in each country. As David Kessler (2001) indicates in his book, the FDA's main concern was to get cigarettes persuasively identified as a drug delivery device, which would allow it to regulate tobacco. Using a legislative rather than an executive process, Canada did not have to characterize cigarettes as drugs in order to change policy.

Culturally, the US is, perhaps more than any other country, reluctant to acknowledge lesson drawing from other countries, even when it occurs. Lesson drawing from abroad is considered inappropriate for the "city on the hill." This idea maintains that the US is different and better than other countries, a beacon rather than a reflection. Thus the FDA proposals do not specifically mention their Canadian counterparts, and US books on tobacco control politics have few references to Canada. Nevertheless, tobacco-control policy networks in the two countries have grown closer, both formally and informally. Both governmental and nongovernmental bodies have increased linkages with their counterparts and other organizations. In contrast to normal expectations, the smaller country, Canada, may serve at least partially as a model for policy formulation in the larger country, the United States. Lesson drawing is a two-way street; sometimes the mouse leads, and the elephant follows.

7

Canada and the United States in the Global Politics of Tobacco Control

"Is the Tobacco Epidemic Being Brought Under Control, or Just Moved Around?—An International Perspective." (Collishaw 1994)

"The tobacco epidemic is now recognized as a political rather than a medical problem....We have not, as one British minister put it, changed emphasis from addressing tobacco diseases at the surgical table to prevention by decisions at the cabinet table." (Mahood 1997)

"Increasingly, national social policies are being affected by transnational forces. With the advent of global markets 'social policy activities traditionally analysed within and undertaken within one country now take on a supranational and transnational character.'" (Yach and Bettcher 2000, quoting Deacon, Hulse and Stubbs 1997).

"Our lack of greater progress in tobacco control is more the result of our failure to implement proven strategies than it is the lack of knowledge about what to do." (US Surgeon General David Satcher, commenting on the release of the 2000 US Surgeon General's Report)

Introduction

This concluding chapter will do three things. First, it will provide an overall evaluation of the theories possibly explaining tobacco-control policy in Canada and the United States. Second, it will suggest some possible short-term future developments for tobacco control in both countries. Finally, it will consider tobacco control in Canada and the United States in relation to the developing international level of tobacco control, principally exemplified by the attempt to adopt a Framework Convention on Tobacco

Control (FCTC) under the auspices of the World Health Organization, and the role of international governmental organizations (IGOs) and non-governmental organizations (NGOs) in that process.

There are four major arguments in this book. First, tobacco control operates on several different levels in each country, with significant policy struggles occurring at the local, state/provincial, and federal levels in both countries. Increasingly, tobacco control even is becoming an international issue. Second, in the process of constructing more restrictive regulatory regimes toward tobacco consumption, the United States and Canada have adopted more convergent policies. Although some of this is the result of similar internal processes, cross-border lesson drawing also has played a substantial role. Third, policy has developed in some unusual ways: the identity of the policy leader has changed over time, both between countries and by levels of government; the smaller country (Canada) has led the larger country in most dimensions of federal level tobacco control policy since the 1980s, in contrast to the usual pattern; there has been a process of leapfrogging, whereby different jurisdictions have become policy leaders on particular dimensions at different times; even though Canadian federalism is generally considered more decentralized than that in the United States, in tobacco restrictions the Canadian federal government has led the provinces while in the US lower levels of government have been, overall, more restrictive than the federal government. Fourth, despite starting from a self-imposed status as a policy laggard in tobacco control, overall Canada has developed a more comprehensive tobacco-control policy.

Summary Evaluation of Theories of Tobacco Control

Table 7-1 presents summary findings, on a macro-level, of how well the theories perform in explaining tobacco-control policy on all three levels of government in Canada and the United States since 1964. These judgments about the relative explanatory power of the theories are based on how well they explain policy in the United States alone, policy in Canada alone, changes in policy in both countries over time, and the process of convergence. The relative strength of the theory in explaining policy is indicated by a mark (+), ranging from zero to two. In this comparative analysis, the major question to be answered is how well the theories explain developments over both time and space. Theories which might

Table 7-1: Explanatory Power of Theories, 1964-2001

Theory	Canada	United States	Change Over Time (both countries)	Convergence	Divergence
1. Agenda Setting	++	++	++	++	–
2. Interest Groups	++	+	++	+	+
3. Political Institutions	+	++	+	+	+
4. Parties/Elections/Ideologies	–	+	+	–	+
5. Political Culture					
a. General	+	–	+	+	+
b. Healthy Public Policy	++	++	++	++	–
6. Policy Typologies	+	+	+	+	–
7. Lesson Drawing	++	+	++	++	+

++ = explains policy well   + = some explanation of policy
– = does not explain policy

perform well in one country or even across both countries within a limited time period may be less successful when tested more elaborately. Some of the theories seem to perform better in explaining within-country variation, others in explaining between-country variation. Some are better at explaining similarities over time, others at explaining the remaining differences.

As portrayed in Table 6-1, there have been many similarities in tobacco-control policies in the two countries, especially in recent years. Accordingly, it is more difficult to choose among theories that explain similarities than those that can help account for differences. Of the seven theories of tobacco-control policy outlined and discussed in previous chapters, the major ones that help to explain similarities over time are agenda setting, healthy public policy as a form of political culture, and lesson drawing. Political institutions and parties, ideology, elections, and general political culture appear to make a larger contribution to explaining remaining differences rather than similarities. Interest groups help explain both similarities and differences. Yet explaining tobacco-control policy at different levels of government also varies somewhat. Lesson drawing, especially of the cross-border variety, is less of a factor on the US state and local levels than on the same levels in Canada. Interest groups, agenda setting, and political institutions appear to be superior explanations of policy below the federal level in the US. The role of policy typologies in explaining policy is still unsettled, but the issue does appear to have moved through similar policy types in both countries.

Why did Canada not have a consistently more restrictive tobacco-control policy from earlier times? Changes in interest-group structure and strategies, along with changes in political institutions, have complemented changes in the political agenda and the growth of healthy public policy, leading to transformations in tobacco-control policy. In the United States, changes in policy transfer on the federal level, especially increased willingness to accept lessons from abroad on policy questions, and changes in partisan, ideological, and electoral configurations have interacted with other factors, leading to some changes in policy.

Even though Canadian and US tobacco-control policies have converged in recent years, they have done this through somewhat different influences. Policy transfer, however, has led to greater convergence than otherwise might be expected by making each country aware of what is occurring in the other. Convergent policy change that might have taken place not at all or more slowly has been accelerated, even more so if one considers the policy agenda rather than adopted policy alone. As compared to the 1960s, 1970s, or even the 1980s, US and Canadian policy became more convergent in the mid-1990s.

Agenda-setting theories mainly help explain similarities because the policy agendas in the two countries have broadly coincided over the years, with some specific differences, such as federal taxation increases in Canada in the 1980s and early 1990s, earlier and more pervasive litigation in the United States, especially from the states, and stronger health warning labels in Canada since 1988. As described in Chapters One and Five, the struggle over issue definition has been generally similar in the two countries, but there have been two notable differences: the greater emphasis on protection against underage smoking in the US and the greater Canadian orientation toward denormalization.

Interest-group/social-movement theories contribute to explaining changes over time in each country and thus help account for convergence. But they also help explain differences between the countries. The similarities include the early dominant role of the tobacco industry and their affiliated groups and the rise of more confrontational anti-tobacco groups in both countries since the 1980s. The tobacco companies themselves as an interest group have remained powerful over time despite losing much of their public image and support. They still wield influence through their economic impact and capacity for broad coalition building (Pertschuk 1997). What has arisen in both Canada and the United States is a more aggressive, politically savvy set of anti-tobacco actors, ranging from established groups to more loosely organized social movements, not only willing to challenge tobacco, but indeed relishing the opportunity. Even though some of these groups were organized in the 1970s, it was not until the mid-1980s that they began to make their mark on the political agenda. The political commitment of the more radical anti-tobacco groups has allowed them to help set the agenda, often with support from more established, conservative groups. As pointed out earlier, there has been considerable cross-border fertilization of the groups.

Even though anti-tobacco groups in both countries have become more unified in the past twenty years, Canadian groups are more cohesive and aggressive on the federal level than their counterparts in the United States. They have been aided by the more public form of lobbying that has developed in Canada since the 1970s. On the other hand, there are more active and better-funded (partially by federal revenues) activist groups at the state and local levels in the United States. This helps explain the relative differences observed in policy activity at these levels in the two countries.

Political institutions are largely responsible for differences in tobacco-control policy across these countries. Changes in institutions also help explain similarities and how policies have changed in each country over time. As Friedman (1975) noted, on the surface it would seem that restrictive tobacco-control policies would be easier to legislate in a Canadian central government with unified partisan control through a parliamentary system, but this did not occur until the 1980s. Tobacco company connections to the executive in Canada, less publicly observable in those times, help explain this tardiness. Once lobbying became more public, there were greater opportunities for broader sections of the public to mobilize in support of restrictive tobacco-control legislation. Thus, in Canada it is the interaction of changes in lobbying style with political institutions that made the first anti-tobacco legislation possible.

Changes in the role of the judiciary in Canada have been a two-edged sword for combatants in this struggle. A stronger policy role for the judiciary has enabled tobacco companies to defend themselves against government actions by changing venues and claiming protection under the Canadian Charter of Rights and Freedoms; however, it has allowed more scope for government and individual litigation against tobacco companies. Anti-tobacco activists, however, have not pursued this venue as assiduously as their counterparts in the US because of continuing differences in liability law between the two countries. As the role of the Canadian judiciary in policy has become more important, the US and Canada have developed increasingly similar policies in tobacco control.

Within the bureaucracy, voluntary arrangements to regulate affected industries still exist to a greater degree in Canada than in the US. But tobacco has become generally recognized as a case where this procedure does not work well.

Canadian federalism has allowed tobacco-control activity to take place on provincial and local levels as well, although the central government still provides leadership on most issues. Although there have been regular attempts at federal-provincial coordination in tobacco-control policy, policy agreement across the provinces has been limited. On the other hand, in the United States there have been fewer institutional changes. Federalism has been a major instrument for tobacco control, and the availability of a wide range of venues has enabled both sides, pro- and anti-tobacco, to carry on struggles over specific legislation for an extended time period. On the central level, however, established institutions, especially the structure of Congress, have allowed tobacco interests to protect themselves. In response, "federal" tobacco-control policy has been made by the unconventional processes of the National Settlement and the MSA. The US institutional structure allows tobacco-control issues access to the political agenda, where they often remain unresolved for years despite extensive and ongoing policy learning.

In summary, even though the rise of the judiciary has allowed for venue switching and delay, overall Canadian institutions still facilitate the resolution of issues. On the other hand, US institutions, especially at the central level, favour the status quo, which in turn induces activists toward alternative, creative ways of trying to enact public policy. These have focussed on the state and local levels as well as litigation. Political culture also may help explain similarities in policy and some differences as well. Changes in Canadian political institutions and interest group behaviour, as delineated above, have coincided with changes in political culture, for instance the development of what Cairns (1990) calls "Charter Canadians," sensitive to claims of individual and group rights. In short, Canadian political culture has changed in ways that are, more often than not, favourable toward interests challenging the status quo. The political culture in the United States has changed less. That means attitudes of US exceptionalism, including resistance to lesson drawing, still exist. Why then has there been a convergence of policy, but one which features leapfrogging and different policy leaders at various times?

The most favourable cultural converging force for anti-tobacco interests has been the move toward healthy public policy. This shift in outlook, while hardly complete in either country, has led to more interest in measures that can be taken to prevent illness. The relative scale of the health problems generated by tobacco use makes it an obvious target for inclusion in HPP. Emphasis on the social environment of disease leads some to the conclusion that the overriding problem is the practices of the profit-seeking multinational companies. There is no reason to believe that the HPP outlook will decline in the years ahead. With an aging population in both countries, it may only be reinforced.

Generally, the influence of parties, ideology, and elections has led to similar policies, although changes in the US have interacted with interest-group activity to make these factors more important in explaining differences between the US and Canada. Parties in both countries, especially the major ones, have traditionally acted as "brokerage" parties, not far apart in ideology. Rarely have they made tobacco an election issue. Especially in earlier times, party differences on tobacco control were minimal in both countries. This has continued in Canada, despite the traditional affiliation between the Liberals and tobacco interests; only the Bloc Québécois has ever voted against a federal tobacco-control bill. But in the US, these factors have played a more prominent role, especially in recent years as partisan ideological differences have increased, pro-tobacco interests have shifted more strongly into the Republican party, and elections, while rarely involving major policy differences on tobacco control, have presented opportunities for large-scale industry financial support for Republican candidates. Much of this influence is hidden from public view, however, and is subject to some variability because of the lack of party discipline in the US. Nevertheless, the operation of partisan factors has led to more divergence than convergence in tobacco control between these two countries.

Dominant perceptions of the nature of the tobacco-control issue, important for policy typologies, seem to have moved similarly in the two countries. In both, the early anti-tobacco movements were more directed at morals than at health; then tobacco became a distributive, largely promotional issue, little regulated and sometimes subsidized, until finally greater restrictive initiatives led to more conflict over regulation. Taxation also moved similarly in the two countries, from sin taxes on tobacco as a source of revenue to consideration of taxes as punitive, compensatory measures for the damage that tobacco does to health. Nevertheless, the nature of the issue at different levels of government varied between the two countries. In Canada, the provinces were remarkably slow in taxation until the 1980s, while in the US the federal government has lagged behind the states most of the time since 1950. In both countries, the nature of the issue remains somewhat mixed and problematic because of policy hangovers from earlier times and the lack of coordination among different agencies of government at the same level, much less different levels. But there are not discernible differences in classifying the issue between the two countries, and the nature of the issue has shifted largely at the same time in both.

Lesson drawing between the two countries also helps explain the convergence of policies in the 1990s and, because of some negative evaluations of policies in the other country, even may aid the explanation of policy differences. In the 1960s there was considerable attention in Canada to the ground-breaking research findings and political debates over the regulation of cigarettes that occurred in the United States, even as Canada settled for less governmentally mandated regulation. By the mid-1980s, Canada largely looked elsewhere for inspiration for its federal tobacco legislation but there was still attention to US developments, such as rotating warning labels and US research findings, especially as incorporated in the US Surgeon General's Reports. As Canada took more stringent action, this in turn provoked attention from journalists, health groups, executive officials, and legislators in the United States. Ground-breaking US state actions, especially the adoption of dedicated funding for statewide tobacco-control campaigns and the advertising techniques utilized in these endeavours, received attention in Canada. As tobacco-control measures multiplied, especially on the federal level in both countries and on the US state level, and as interest-group connections across the border grew, lesson drawing became even more common. Sometimes these lessons could not be applied in the other country, but they were still posited as goals—for instance, dedicated healthcare funding in Canada, or the graphic nature of Canadian tobacco warnings. By 2000, "best practices" were being offered from a variety of jurisdictions (US Department of Health and Human Services 1999; "World's Best Practice in Tobacco Control" 2000). There was one remnant of the "one-way" mirror, however. Innovative practices from Canadian provinces, such as point-of-sale warnings and bans on sales of tobacco in pharmacies, were not seriously considered in the US. Nevertheless, the increasing leapfrogging and convergence observable across many jurisdictions in Canada and the United States was due in no small part to awareness of what was going on elsewhere, both within and outside the country.

Each country has learned valuable lessons from the policies of the other. Obviously this is not the only source of tobacco-control policy, but it has been an important one. This policy transfer has been carried out across several different levels of government and by non-governmental groups. Policy emulation has not always been between governments operating on the same level or top-down. It has also involved bottom-up vertical borrowing as well as horizontal lesson drawing among interest groups.

For Canada, what the US does in similar policy areas will always be noticed and evaluated, even if not copied. While the US is more reluctant to take lessons from others, at least explicitly, there is somewhat more willingness to do this in unfamiliar areas. Thus in the debate over President Clinton's healthcare policy, the experience of other countries with national insurance-based systems, including Canada, became an important consideration. In tobacco control, when new policies are being considered, the experience of a similar country that has employed such policies can become an important reference point. Just as the United States seems to be replacing Britain as a general reference point for Canada, Canada appears to be replacing Britain as a reference in health policy for the United States. The breakdown of trade barriers through the North American Free Trade Agreement may have increased that inclination, and perhaps will do so even more in the future. In short, general patterns of influence within "families of nations" are not fixed.

There are strong relationships indicating policy transfer. When one country gave attention to the other's policies in tobacco control, whether that was Canada looking to the US in the late 1960s, the US looking to Canada in the early and mid-1990s, or the two countries closely watching each other thereafter, policies did tend to converge. When one country gave less attention to the other's policies, as Canada did to the US in the 1980s, then policies diverged. General underlying social trends in each country cannot completely explain why Canada moved ahead of the United States in the 1980s and then the two converged in the 1990s.

Furthermore, as Seeliger (1996) suggests, intra-country variations in a policy affected by federalism can also indicate policy transfer in tobacco control. Borrowing has occurred primarily on the central level, especially in the United States. There is still wide variation in polices among US states and municipalities and precious little indication that US states have looked to Canada for direct policy guidance, although they may have absorbed some more diffuse lessons. On the other hand, the Canadian central government clearly has learned lessons from the more active tobacco-control policies of certain US states. While there is still considerable policy variation even among the ten provinces of Canada, the more restrictive tobacco-control governments among them have borrowed from US state government policies. In short, federalism in both countries shows both the possibilities and limits of policy transfer within such systems. Some states and provinces can engage in lesson drawing, while others do not.

In summary, of the seven major explanations for the course of tobacco control in Canada and the United States over the past two phases, and especially the past twenty years, agenda setting, the healthy public policy version of political culture, and lesson drawing best account for the convergence of policies over time. Policy typologies may also help explain convergence. The interest-group/social-movement theory also contributes to the explanation of convergence, although there remain some differences in how interest groups are organized, their strategies, and their goals in the two countries. Similarly, political institutions have affected both similarities and differences in policy between the two countries. Insofar as institutions, especially in Canada, have changed to become more like those in the US, they have a convergent effect. But insofar as they have not changed, as in the US, largely they are a force for difference.

While these theories help account for the direction and convergence of tobacco-control policy in both countries, their contributions have not occurred at the same time. Formation of more cohesive and aggressive anti-tobacco interest groups in both countries was instrumental in helping bring about policy change in the 1980s as they seized opportunities presented by the changing definition of the issue. This policy change was greater at the time in Canada than in the US, however. The example of Canadian policy, assimilated through lesson drawing, was an additional, possibly critical, ingredient in changing US policy in the 1990s. Even if anti-tobacco activists and politicians in the US did not know the details of the Canadian experience, the knowledge that changes in regulatory and tax policy could be successfully implemented in a nearby, largely English-speaking country with a similar democratic tradition and social makeup made Canada a convenient example for the US. But US political culture still inhibits lesson drawing, especially its public acknowledgment. When Canada was forced to reformulate its policy after the 1995 Supreme Court decision, it, too, had a ready reference in addition to its own experience. This encouraged further policy borrowing later, as in tobacco litigation and counter-advertising.

Overall, tobacco control has become an interactive process, with no one theory dominating. Changes in the political culture in both countries, especially the increased emphasis on healthy public policy, have facilitated the rise of tobacco control as an issue on the policy agenda. The social movement against tobacco use has become more organized into interest groups, with the aid of political entrepreneurs who seize opportunities, often provided by scientific findings, to push tobacco control higher on the agenda and toward their favoured solutions. Public opinion has become increasingly favourable, although hardly intense, toward measures to punish and limit tobacco companies. The power of well-financed and politically connected tobacco-company representatives is more likely to hold sway in the closed quarters of cabinet meetings, bureaucratic agencies, party caucuses, and party fund-raising than in more open forums. Increasingly it has become a public liability, although rarely an electorally disabling one, for a legislator or executive outside a US "tobacco state" to be perceived as being a spokesperson for tobacco companies. But, especially in the US system of multiple institutional hurdles to pass any public policy, it is still difficult for anti-tobacco interests to mobilize their resources in a sufficiently steady manner to establish a comprehensive tobacco-control policy. That is why the strongest anti-tobacco policies in the US tend to be on lower levels, often endorsed through referenda rather than the usual legislative-executive process.

Over time, as Canada and the United States have become more aware of policies within the other country, some jurisdictions have attempted to improve their own policies through a process of leapfrogging. Policies have become generally transferable, perhaps because, aside from some institutional differences and local variation in other factors (political culture, tobacco growing, interest group strength, public support, etc.), most of the other influences on policy are similar across the two countries.

Prospects for the United States and Canada

The 1990s witnessed a policy convergence on tobacco control. Despite the continuing influence of factors that brought this about, including similar political agendas, cultural shifts toward healthy public policy, more organized anti-tobacco interest groups, and lesson drawing, there is at least some prospect that the US and Canada may diverge again. The next few years may witness a lull in federal and possibly even state action in the US. There are already signs that the federal Republican administration will not disappoint its campaign supporters, as its positions on the Justice Department lawsuit, federal aid for tobacco growing, and the WHO negotiations indicate (Hunt 2001). The largest US company, Philip Morris, has indicated a willingness for the FDA to have authority over cigarettes if the right terms could be negotiated. An attempt at legislation involving a narrow remit for the FDA, similar to pre-emption on the state level, would be unlikely to get through Congress but could also stimulate another internal conflict within the anti-tobacco organizations.

The Economist (1998) asked, "Can Lawsuits Make Policy?" (see also Jacobson and Warner 1999; Derthick 2001). The answer is "yes, but they cannot make *comprehensive* tobacco control policy." Lawsuits have become a major, possibly even dominant, part of tobacco-control policy in the United States and have increased in Canada as well. Overall, this is advantageous to the industry since lawsuits inevitably take time, and tobacco companies have huge resources to fight such suits, even if they cannot win them all. Even a large punitive damage award in the US, such as the *Engle* verdict in 2000, can lead to years of appeals. As the actions of some US states have shown, there will be attempts to protect tobacco company assets from the effects of such awards to individuals and groups other than states. Dependence on tobacco-company revenues, either through taxes or agreed financial compensation, is a two-edged sword. Lawsuits, and economic approaches more generally, cannot, in the final analysis, substitute for a comprehensive tobacco-control policy from the executive and legislature.

There has been more agenda change than policy change in the US, especially at the federal level. The Surgeon General's reports, Congressional hearings, tobacco document leaks, and other phenomena have led to tobacco becoming a mainstay of the political agenda, but in terms of policies, there has been only incremental rather than large-scale change. While change in Canada has also been largely incremental, especially since 1994, there has been more policy change at the federal level there. Incremental change might be expected with a powerful, entrenched industry with an enormous capacity to create allies. Nonetheless, given the demonstrable dangers of tobacco, especially cigarette consumption, and compared to the degree of alarm and policy change used to combat much lesser threats to the public health in recent years (Foreman 1994), the similarity of the issues being debated today to those raised in early hearings in the US and Canada in the aftermath of the first Surgeon General's Report in 1964 is remarkable.

What would constitute a comprehensive tobacco-control policy has evolved over the years since the World Health Assembly called for such a policy in 1986. All versions, however, emphasize multiple approaches, including legislative and regulatory. In reviewing five US state programs, Wakefield and Chaloupka (1998: 177-86) define comprehensive tobacco-control strategies as those involving a range of coordinated and coexisting strategies, reinforcing and complementing each other in a synergistic manner. The key is to change smoking behaviour through affecting the social environment in which uptake and cessation occur. Both the COMMIT and ASSIST programs, while more limited than others in some ways, still had multi-channel interventions on the local level. California's program after passage of the referenda for cigarette tax increases was based on a federal model developed by the National Cancer Institute for comprehensive smoking prevention and control, but with more focus on attacking the industry (*A Model for Change: The California Experience in Tobacco Control* 1998: 5). The Ontario Tobacco Strategy in 1993 had five components: legislation, media campaign and public education, community support, research, and coordinating mechanisms (Mitchell and Garcia 1995: 341).

According to the CDC (US Department of Health and Human Services 1999: 3, 7-9), the goal of comprehensive tobacco-control programs is to reduce disease, disability, and death related to tobacco use by preventing the initiation of use among young people, promoting quitting, eliminating ETS, and identifying and eliminating disparities in tobacco use among population groups. Nine components of such a program are community programs to reduce tobacco use, chronic disease programs to reduce the burden of tobacco-related diseases, school programs, enforcement, statewide programs, counter-marketing, cessation programs, surveillance and evaluation, and administration and management. The two best examples cited of such programs are those in California and Massachusetts.

The 2000 Surgeon General's Report (US Department of Health and Human Services 2000b) endorses the idea of having a comprehensive program: an attempt to reduce tobacco use through a multistage, multimedia approach in which it is recognized that individual behaviour occurs in a complex social, economic, physical, governmental, and legal environment. Cunningham (2000: 239) offers a more extensive, specific, and future-oriented list of policies, including nicotine replacement, high taxation, anti-smuggling, smoking restrictions, strict advertising and promotion bans, intensive education through mass media, youth access controls, package warnings inside and covering 80 per cent of the outside of the package, plain packaging, point of sale anti-tobacco counter-advertising, tobacco-control funding, eliminating deceptive cigarette labelling, banning sales in pharmacies, sales only from government stores, eliminating agricultural subsidies and other economic support, ingredient disclosure, disclosure of all industry research and documentation, effective enforcement, control of manufacturer prices and profits, and product modification.

Even if Canada's world leadership position in tobacco control has been compromised by its tax problems over the past decade, it still has a more comprehensive federal policy than the US. Table 6-2 shows Canada to have a more far-ranging policy covering taxes, health warnings, ETS, reduction of tobacco agriculture, advertising, sales, and other dimensions in 2001. If the federal government and the provinces east of Manitoba could ever agree on the re-establishment of a regime of substantially increased taxes, then Canada could reclaim its international leadership position.

The US has had two opportunities to institute such a comprehensive federal policy, the National Settlement and the FDA Rule, but both were lost because of tobacco-company opposition, the first in Congress, the second in the Supreme Court. The MSA is the *de facto* comprehensive policy in the US, but, in comparison to either of the above, it covers fewer policy areas, has large loopholes, and relies on state attorneys general for enforcement. In short, it would be difficult to argue that the US truly has a comprehensive national tobacco-control policy, and only a few states can lay claim to such a policy. The CDC's efforts to get states to adopt "best practices" through use of the MSA money was largely ignored; less than ten per cent of the MSA funds went to tobacco-control programs in the first two years of the program (DeBarros 2001).

The strength of US efforts, acknowledged on both sides of the border, is the vitality of selective local and state programs. Some of this is due to federal funding, but the bottom-up nature of such programs gives them both advantages and disadvantages. The strength is that they are more difficult for the tobacco industry to oppose because they are hydra-headed. The weakness, however, is that comprehensive programs at the state level are rare, and local levels usually focus on ETS. The limited diffusion of "best practices" at the state level means that there is no comprehensive tobacco-control policy covering even an appreciable portion of the US states, nor is there likely to be such a far-ranging policy in the foreseeable future.

If there is a lull in tobacco-control policy on the federal level in the United States, Canada may increasingly look to the international level, especially the Framework Agreement on Tobacco Control of the WHO, as a buttress for its own tobacco-control program. Canada has always had more of an international orientation than has the United States. If Canada can no longer count on the US, especially on the federal level, for policies which serve to leapfrog its own and therefore provide a basis for even more restrictive policies, then there is more reason to work cooperatively with other countries, to both sustain and spread Canadian initiatives and to find ideas that might work domestically.

Canada and the United States in Comparative Context: Toward a Global Politics of Tobacco Control

Comparatively, the policy actions against tobacco taken by the United States in the 1960s were pace-setting and remained so for a considerable time thereafter. Other advanced industrial countries took little action on tobacco except to tax it heavily. When Canada began to consider stronger measures in the late 1980s, there were surprisingly few countries with warning labels on cigarettes or other restrictions on smoking (Sasco, Dalla-Vorgia, and Van der Elst 1992; Corrao et al. 2000). Although these policies have spread subsequently, with warning labels promoted by the European Union, and Australia and New Zealand developing several restrictive policies, taxation remains the instrument of choice for most governments in advanced industrial democracies (Licari 2000a). In that respect, the United States and Canada are still notable for the number of policy instruments other than taxation that governments in these countries are willing to employ to combat tobacco usage.

Tobacco control now operates on the international level as well as on the domestic one. Tobacco companies themselves, of course, are part of multinational conglomerates, and they buy tobacco from several countries. The fact that tobacco control is becoming increasingly recognized as a public-policy problem of global dimensions has led to increasing "internationalization" of the tobacco-control movement, culminating in recent years in the attempt by the World Health Organization at an International Framework Convention on Tobacco Control.

Like other public-health problems, there is considerable technical and scientific information that can be transmitted across country borders relatively easily, thus facilitating lesson drawing and perhaps even international agreements (Rose 1993). The health dimensions of the problems do not vary greatly, and "best practices" are increasingly shared across political jurisdictions, both within and across borders. One might expect that policies addressing this problem should be readily transferable as well, but, as Leichter (1991) points out, tobacco control as an issue presents barriers to lesson drawing across countries. It is not solely a technical health question, but it also involves other dimensions such as individual rights and the immense economic power of the industry.

The trends of the past decade indicate, however, that some of these difficulties are being overcome. The increased concern about controlling healthcare costs has led to a worldwide search for better methods of controlling health risks. Thus health questions related to tobacco have assumed a more prominent role in the debate and have led to more attempts at international coordination and lesson drawing, including greater prominence for a worldwide strategy of tobacco reduction advocated for over 30 years by the World Health Organization.

Tobacco is both a health and an economic problem. Despite the trends in the US and Canada, tobacco use worldwide is growing, not shrinking. There has been a steady increase in the number of cigarettes smoked daily worldwide, especially in developing countries. Today there are an estimated 1.1 billion smokers, 80 per cent of them in developing countries, and tobacco is estimated to become the leading cause of death in the world by 2030. If tobacco did not have a powerful industry behind it and were not such a widely accepted consumer product, it would likely be treated as a drug and banned. But with tobacco's widespread availability and continuing popularity, anti-tobacco forces face an uphill battle in trying to regulate it.

International tobacco control is literally a matter of life or death. The international movement against tobacco consumption resembles earlier campaigns over value-related issues such as those over slavery, women's suffrage, and land mines (Keck and Sikkink 1998). Paradoxically, questions predominantly involving values, often thought more difficult for policy transfer than those largely based on economics (Rose 1993; cf. Studlar 1993), seem to be especially suitable for international cooperation among nongovernmental groups, eventually leading to international governmental action. This may be due to the frustrations of country-to-country lesson drawing. For international agenda setting, if tobacco control is framed largely as a public health/human rights issue, it is more likely to lead to stronger international action than if tobacco companies can persuade governments to think of it largely in economic and trade terms.

If the problem can be raised to a higher level, then in principle an agreement binding on all countries could be achieved. Issues such as women's rights in the modern era undoubtedly have benefitted from international sponsorship by both IGOs and NGOs in an increasingly interconnected world (True and Mintrom 2001). More of these issues are likely to arise in the future. With rapid transmission, international public-policy campaigns are more readily undertaken, although their success may be variable.

Aside from WHO guidelines and recommendations appearing regularly since 1971, one of the first international efforts at a multilateral agreement on tobacco control was the 1994 treaty among the United States, Canada, and Australia specifying nonsmoking on almost all international flights between these three countries. This treaty also served as a model for an attempt at a broader international agreement through the International Civil Aviation Organization, which also involved WHO (Kyle and Du Melle 1994; Kyle 1996). While adoption and enforcement of nonsmoking provisions on airlines has largely been left to individual countries, the international pressure has been a significant force.

Other international bodies that have concerned themselves with tobacco to some extent are the European Union, the World Bank, and the United Nations Children's Fund (UNICEF). The EU has attempted tobacco regulation through its competence in the internal trade of its members, and, since the Maastricht Treaty, in cross-border social policy. In 1989 the EU Commission received permission from the Council of Health Ministers of the individual countries to issue a directive banning tobacco advertising near schools and requiring common health warnings in advertisements and cigarette packages, with stark messages such as "Smoking Kills." As with many EU matters, not all members have complied. Subsequently the EU Commission proposed to ban all tobacco promotion, including product advertising and sponsorship, by 2006, but this was overruled by the European Court of Justice in 2000 on the grounds that it was a health matter beyond the legal competence of the EU Commission. After long ignoring tobacco as an issue, since 1993 the World Bank has issued reports emphasizing the pitfalls of tobacco-based economies; its most recent report suggested that increased production of tobacco constituted a "development risk" for countries (World Bank 1999). UNICEF, with its mission of advancing children's protection, also began supporting international and national tobacco-control initiatives in the 1990s ("Protect All Children from Tobacco, says UNICEF" 1997).

The major organization attempting to develop a global tobacco-control policy, however, is the World Health Organization. Since 1971, WHO has issued 16 voluntary tobacco reduction targets for its members. Beginning in 1975, WHO also began publishing periodic Expert Committee reports, which recommended more stringent government tobacco-control measures (Skirrow and Edwards 1986: 8). In 1986, the World Health Assembly of WHO unanimously passed a resolution calling upon governments to adopt comprehensive strategies to combat tobacco usage.

WHO's Tobacco or Health Program on Substance Abuse in Geneva, Switzerland, was directed from 1992 to 1998 by Neil Collishaw, a former

Canadian federal official who had a major role in the formation and defence of the TPCA. Despite staff reductions, Collishaw pursued tobacco restrictions on a regional and global basis through publications, conferences, and expert missions to countries faced with new challenges in tobacco control, especially the developing democracies of Eastern Europe (World Health Organization 1997, 1998). Collishaw brought Canadian expertise into WHO projects, including such tobacco-control experts as former Ontario health official Brenda Mitchell, Physicians for a Smoke-Free Canada's chief lobbyist Cynthia Callard, and Eric LeGresley of the Non-Smokers Rights' Association. Jean Rochon served under Collishaw at WHO and later successfully pursued the adoption of tobacco-control legislation as health minister in Quebec.

In recent years WHO has given higher priority to tobacco control. In 1996 the World Health Assembly adopted a resolution requesting that the Director General of WHO initiate a Framework Convention on Tobacco Control (FCTC). Upon her accession to the post in 1998, the new Director-General, Gro Harlem Brundtland, a public-health physician and former prime minister of Norway, established a Tobacco Free Initiative (TFI) as one of her two priority areas. The centrepiece of the TFI is the development of an International Framework Convention on Tobacco Control, to be finalized by 2003.

The goal of the FCTC is to curb tobacco use through strengthening transnational controls on tobacco; to improve individual governments' health policies through international coordination on issues such as prices and taxes, smuggling, duty-free tobacco products, advertising and promotion, testing and reporting of tobacco constituents, package design and labelling, agricultural policy, and general information sharing (Taylor 1996). Specific protocols to be agreed within the convention will address cigarette pricing policies, anti-smuggling measures, advertising and promotion (including promotion on the Internet), and cigarette labelling.

This marks the first time that WHO has used its constitutional mandate to negotiate the creation of an international treaty on public health. An intergovernmental committee is negotiating the convention. The World Health Assembly of WHO would have to approve any agreement, and then it would be presented to countries for ratification. A series of preliminary planning meetings were held, including two in Canada, in Nova Scotia in 1997 and British Columbia in 1998. Then, in fall 2000, the formal negotiations commenced. The negotiating committee is made up of government representatives, not only from health ministries but also from trade, finance, and agriculture ministries.

While anti-tobacco NGOs and other groups are full participants, tobacco companies have been invited only to present testimony, not to participate in decision making. (Brown 1999; Yach and Bettgen, 2000; "The Tobacco War Goes Global" 2000). Despite US financial support for WHO, cooperation with it in establishing the Global Information Management and Surveillance system (see below), and the presence of Michael Eriksen, former Director of the Office on Smoking and Health of the CDC, as a consultant in the process, the United States has been viewed by anti-tobacco groups within the US and in other countries as being insufficiently committed to strong measures in the treaty. Initially the US government supported voluntary enforcement of any treaty only, inclusion of tobacco industry representatives in the discussions, and targeting advertising bans only at children (Joossens 2000). At the initial negotiating session among governments in fall 2000, however, the US took a stronger-than-expected stance ("International Effort Begins for Anti-Smoking Accord" 2000). By the spring 2001 meeting, the US, under the new Republican administration, was widely perceived as having reverted to being an awkward partner in the discussions, raising objections to many key provisions (Fairclough and Lueck 2001). The chief US negotiator abruptly resigned, possibly because of differences with the new administration's positions (Kaufman 2001).

On the other hand, Canada has been pushing for a strong global tobacco treaty that will serve as a legal instrument to stop the growth of tobacco consumption ("Canada to Play Key Role in Second Round of Talks on International Tobacco Control Convention" 2001). Garfield Mahood of NSRA has a straightforward position on the FCTC: "The document should be similar to the Control of Narcotics Treaty. Countries should sign a powerful document to combat the worldwide spread of tobacco products, tobacco use, and tobacco related disease by enforcing common standards on taxation, smuggling, and international trade of tobacco" (Toma 2000).

Earlier, Nadelman (1990) predicted that tobacco was a likely target for an attempt at what he calls an "international prohibition regime" based on moral objections to parts of international commerce that demonstrably affect humans across the globe in an overwhelmingly negative fashion. The proponents of the Framework Convention deny that they are attempting to prohibit all legal uses of tobacco, but rather only to regulate it in a more comprehensive and coordinated manner. But in Nadelman's terms, this is a "prohibition regime" similar to the ones he discusses concerning piracy, slavery, prostitution, extradition, the killing of whales and elephants, counterfeit money, alcohol, and psychoactive substances.

Nadelman (1990) argues that prohibition regimes are based on five stages of development. In the first stage, most societies view the activity as legitimate and even aid it; limitations are of prudence and bilateral treaties, rather than moral and international norms. During the second stage, the activity is redefined as a problem and an evil—generally by international legal scholars, religious groups, and other moral entrepreneurs—and explicit government involvement in the activity is gradually delegitimized, although many individual governments continue to tolerate or even sponsor the involvement of private groups and individuals in the activity. During the third stage, regime proponents begin to agitate actively for the suppression and criminalization of the activity by all states and the formation of international conventions. The regime proponents include governments, typically those able to exert hegemonic influence in a particular issue-area, as well as transnational moral entrepreneurs. Their agitation takes many forms, ranging from the diplomatic pressures, economic inducements, military interventions, and propaganda campaigns of governments to domestic and transnational lobbying, education, organization, and proselytizing efforts of individuals and nongovernmental organizations (Nadelman 1990: 485).

At present the international movement to regulate and even eliminate tobacco use is somewhere between the second and third stages, with recognition of tobacco use as a problem and an evil, leadership mainly from a few countries in the economically developed world, but lots of disarray and qualms, especially economic ones, from both developed and other countries. The galvanizing moral leadership is coming largely from nongovernmental organizations, which increasingly are developing their international linkages and now, through WHO, have an international forum through which to engage the attention of governments and legal scholars. The major mechanisms heretofore have been lobbying, education, and proselytization, but economic inducements and diplomatic pressures are in nascent development as well.

Nadelman (1990) goes on to describe the fourth and fifth stages of international prohibition regimes. In the fourth stage, the activity becomes a target of criminal laws and police actions, with international institutions and conventions playing a coordinating role. Given the vagaries of international behaviour, however, there is a need for constant vigilance to enforce the norms against deviant states, weak states unable to control violations, and dissident individuals and criminal organizations. This is obviously the critical stage for an international prohibition regime to reach, and some, such as those on drugs, have had considerable problems at this stage, while others, such as alcohol prohibition, foundered even earlier.

If the prohibition regime is largely successful in the fourth stage, there is still a fifth stage, in which the proscribed activity is reduced to a small scale at remote outposts. Nadelman (1990: 485) sees this stage as similar to what happens with successful public-health campaigns to eradicate infectious diseases. The prospects for reaching the fifth stage in tobacco control are questionable. The difficulties of prohibiting tobacco consumption, at least in the medium term, are so daunting that tobacco reduction rather than prohibition is the official goal. Although successful global prohibition regimes have also encountered vested economic interests and recalcitrant governments, the multinational tobacco companies of today are powerful on both domestic and international levels, so much so that even states that might stake a claim as moral leaders in the international prohibition regime still cooperate to some extent with tobacco companies. Achieving an International Framework Convention on Tobacco Control, especially one with strong norms of regulation, will be a formidable task.

But even if a strong treaty emerges, the difficulties of enforcing it are likely to be considerable. Nadelman (1990: 486) argues that a critical test in getting from the fourth to the fifth stage of an international prohibition regime is the susceptibility of the targeted activity to ready enforcement of criminal laws: "Criminal laws and international prohibition regimes are particularly ineffective in suppressing those activities which require limited and readily available resources and no particular expertise to commit, those which are easily concealed, those which are unlikely to be reported to the authorities, and those for which the consumer demand is substantial, resilient, and not readily substituted for by alternative activities or products" (486). He goes on to argue that the global drug enforcement regime is unlikely ever to achieve this level of success and, in fact, may join the previous global alcohol prohibition campaign in legalizing a regulated trade in these products.

The problems with a tobacco-control regime are similar. They have the same characteristics as Nadelman describes above and, of course, are often already claimed to be legal drugs. The problems of extensive international regulation, not to mention prohibition, can be summarized in one word:

smuggling. As Nadelman points out, psychoactive drugs have been the subject of a problematic prohibition regime, not because they are more dangerous than alcohol and tobacco, but because the latter two substances became well integrated into society before an attempt at an international prohibition regime got under way. If there are problems with controlling illegal drugs, under these circumstances, then the difficulties facing a tobacco prohibition regime are even greater. Advocates of denormalization are, in effect, arguing for the eventual establishment of just such a prohibition regime.

Governments can provide legal frameworks, but NGOs may provide a critical element in an emergent international tobacco control regime. Democratic governments are not renowned for reacting rapidly to policy problems; indeed, their very institutional mechanisms are often cumbersome. Since one of the major interests of tobacco companies is delay in policy implementation, they take advantage of these traits. Any international agreements on tobacco control will take years to negotiate, are likely to be weighed down with compromises and loopholes, and may be difficult to enforce.

International nongovernmental networks, regardless of their state's commitment to international norms more generally, can be an important element in policy transfer. The United Nations forums on women's rights have acted as international nongovernmental stimuli leading countries with groups attending them to be more likely to adopt state bureaucracies for the advancement of women (True and Mintrom 2001). This is supported by other findings that the United Nations Fourth World Conference on Women in China in 1995 had an important regional effect in advancing the cause of women's legislative representation in Latin America (Htun and Jones 2001). This is a contemporary manifestation of international policy transfer through nongovernmental policy networks, a phenomenon that Keck and Sikkink (1998) found to extend back to the nineteenth century for anti-slavery and women's rights movements and more recently for environmental movements.

Similarly, NGOs may be a key element for an international tobacco-control regime because they are problem-oriented and flexible, like their opponents in the tobacco industry. NGOs also can provide some prominent policy entrepreneurs. WHO has recognized the role of NGOs with similar goals across countries and attempted to bring a wide array of NGOs into the process of developing the FCTC at an early stage (*Together Against Tobacco* 1999). NGOs with extensive connections abroad such as the Canadian ones can help facilitate a WHO Treaty through what amounts to an "inside-outside" process on the international level, as has been done domestically in some circumstances.

As tobacco control becomes a more international issue, how will this affect policy in both the US and Canada, especially lesson drawing between them? Canada has always been more internationally minded on tobacco control than has the United States, perhaps because it is a small country without the same sense of "specialness." From the earliest consideration of tobacco control during the late 1960s through the development of the *Tobacco Products Control Act* in 1988, and later involvement in WHO and other international tobacco-control activities, Canada has tried both to learn from the rest of the world and to teach it.

The House of Commons committee investigating tobacco control in 1968-69 considered information from several other countries in its deliberations, although there was a clear orientation toward Britain and the United States. Both witnesses and committee members made abundant references to the findings and experiences of other advanced industrial democracies in dealing with this unfamiliar issue. Comments from the most indefatigable Commons campaigner for tobacco control in this period, Barry Mather, NDP MP from British Columbia, showed him to be especially well-versed in what had occurred up to this point in the US in the areas of warning labels, counteradvertising, and restrictions on advertising—all policies that he wanted to see adopted in Canada as well.

In the wake of the first World Conference on Smoking and Health in New York City in 1967, more interest arose in gathering information about what other countries were doing. In 1969, the health ministries of both countries produced summaries of tobacco-control policies elsewhere in the world (Department of National Health and Welfare 1969; United States Public Health Service 1969). Subsequent Canadian executive deliberations, in both the cabinet and the bureaucracy, frequently considered policies employed abroad. This trend accelerated in the 1980s as investigations concerning possible legislation and the hosting of the fifth WCTOH in Winnipeg allowed Canadian officials to become more aware of policies elsewhere (Health and Welfare Canada 1983). In 1985, Health and Welfare Canada and the Alberta Alcohol and Drug Abuse Commission hosted a small workshop of participants in Calgary considering comparative and international strategies for reducing tobacco use (Skirrow and Edwards 1986).

In developing what became the *Tobacco Products Control Act* in 1988, the Canadian government considered the policies of several other advanced industrial countries, as well as those of the United States, and WHO guidelines. Health Minister Epp mentioned some of these in justifying advertising restrictions (Epp 1987a). Behind the scenes, Neil Collishaw and other officials in the ministry had done extensive analytical comparisons of regulations, taxes, and smoking rates in other countries; some of this work was published or presented at public meetings (Rogers, Myers and Collishaw 1985; Collishaw 1986a, 1990; Collishaw, Rogers and Kaiserman 1990; Collishaw and Galbraith 1992). In contrast, despite its role in founding the World Conference on Smoking and Health and other early attention to the international realm, the United States revived an interest in the importance of tobacco control in other parts of the world only in the mid-1980s, first at the nongovernmental International Summit of Smoking Control Leaders in Washington in 1985, and subsequently in meetings of the Interagency Task Force on Tobacco (US Department of Health and Human Services 1990: 52). The latter primarily focussed on the activities of transnational tobacco companies rather than regulatory and tax policies of other countries. Unlike in Canada, WHO guidelines for tobacco control were rarely mentioned in US government communications until the late 1990s.

Canada has continued to be relatively more internationally minded than the US in tobacco-control efforts, notably through financial and program aid to developing countries through the Ottawa-based International Development Research Centre and other international agencies. The director of the IDRC is Linda Brigden, formerly chief Tobacco Control Officer in the Ministry of Health of British Columbia. The recent Canadian National Tobacco Strategy incorporates an international dimension as part of Canadian tobacco-control policy. In addition to Canada's sponsorship of two early WHO "expert meetings" for development of the FCTC, there have been informal contacts and monitoring of developments across countries among government officials in Canadian health ministries as well as such US organizations as the National Cancer Institute and the Centers for Disease Control and Prevention. Some personnel transfers between Canadian and US organizations, both public and private, were discussed in Chapter Five. The Non-Smokers' Rights Association also works extensively with groups in Africa and Southeast Asian countries, a major target for an expanded tobacco market.

No US policy ever explicitly acknowledged the incorporation of lessons from abroad until the FDA Rule and the National Settlement, although President Clinton's abortive National Health Security Act did attempt to include Canadian tax lessons. The Surgeon General's Report of 1992, as indicated earlier, reported on tobacco in the Americas, but the next report with any international focus did not appear until eight years later. In releasing the 2000 report at the WCTOH in Chicago, Surgeon General David Satcher gave more prominence to the need for the US to cooperate with WHO in the TFI and to follow the lead of Canada in package warnings. On the other hand, US policies have tended to export problems through trade aid to tobacco companies. The US endured considerable criticism when the state attorneys general initially called their negotiated agreement with the tobacco companies a "Global" Settlement, even though it directly concerned only US operations of the industry. Despite an appeal from an international committee of 19 tobacco-control advocates, including Garfield Mahood of Canada, the attorneys general bowed to resistance from the companies and drew back from any provisions extending outside the US ("Statement by International Tobacco Control Advocates" 1997; Mollenkamp et al. 1998).

Subsequently the US government and tobacco-control groups have become more internationally oriented. However, this is still largely focussed on regulating the trade of US tobacco companies and exporting US tobacco-control policies rather than on learning from other countries. The Koop-Kessler Committee report in response to the National Settlement called for US support for international action on tobacco control, including support for WHO, UNICEF, and the FCTC, the regulation of tobacco in international trade agreements, and for exporting what it hoped would be a model comprehensive US tobacco-control policy. However, it had only two references to practices in other countries which the US should adopt; both were from Australia. The major section of the report dealing with international issues was from the Task Force on the Future of the Tobacco Industry and Tobacco Control Efforts, chaired by Michael Pertschuk of the Advocacy Institute, which, along with the American Cancer Society and to an increasing degree the Campaign for Tobacco-Free Kids, is the most internationally-sensitive of US anti-tobacco groups. The Task Force on the Regulation of Nicotine and Tobacco Products, chaired by John Seffrin of the American Cancer Society, also touched on international questions, including taxation and the funding of international information exchange, later incorporated into CDC and

ACS policy (*Final Report of the Advisory Committee on Tobacco Policy and Public Health* 1997).

By the time the National Settlement reached Congress in 1998, there were several bills on tobacco control that incorporated such international provisions as including public-health findings as a required element of US trade policy, extending US regulations to overseas sales, assessing fees on companies for international tobacco-control programs, preventing smuggling, supporting tobacco control in established international agencies, and establishing a tax-supported NGO focussing on international tobacco control (Bloom 1998). But all of these provisions were lost with the defeat of the McCain Bill, and the MSA did not attempt to address international issues.

While initially reluctant to tackle tobacco control internationally, President Clinton eventually provided some leadership for the US federal government in this area. The US has both recognized tobacco-control activities in other countries and taken part in international forums to a greater degree in recent years. Two days before he left office, President Clinton emphasized the international dimensions of tobacco control in an Executive Order, including generalized support for WHO, the involvement of DHHS in international trade decisions on tobacco, and limited financial assistance and research to support other countries' tobacco-control efforts (Clinton 2001).

The CDC also has engaged in more international work recently and has been named a WHO Collaborating Center on Tobacco and Health. It supported the dissemination of the WHO publication *Guidelines for Controlling and Monitoring the Tobacco Epidemic* (1998: viii), and cooperated with international agencies (WHO, UICC, and the World Bank) as well as the ACS to establish an international equivalent of the CDC US STATE tracking system on tobacco control, whereby governments could readily obtain information on what other jurisdictions were doing through the Internet ("Global Information Management and Surveillance Systems for a Tobacco-Free World" 1999). The potential for lesson drawing obviously grows with such developments. Whether the more international orientation of the US Surgeon General's Report in 2000 will persist remains to be seen.

As LeGresley (1998b) indicates for tobacco control and as Castles (1993) has elaborated for other policies, some countries are more important exemplars than others, irrespective of "best practices" on a world basis. Writing shortly after the National Settlement was negotiated,

LeGresley argues that a potential C+ for the US in tobacco control would carry more weight in the world than an A+ for Australia, simply because of the relative international importance of each. A country's general place in the world power hierarchy and its specific policies both help determine its influence in tobacco control elsewhere in the world. By that measure, a Canadian A+ probably would rate more highly in international esteem than an Australian A+, but possibly still less than a US C+.

In short, Canadian governmental and nongovernmental organizations view international cooperation as necessary for tobacco control. The United States, a larger and more self-centred country, has traditionally seen international cooperation and organizations as less essential, but this slowly may be changing. Whatever the US does, however, will have an influence on the rest of the world because of its general international power and prestige.

Endgame for Tobacco Control?

If tobacco is being subjected to a pincer movement, with decreasing public consumption and approval in industrialized countries, and subject to increasing regulation and taxation by governments ranging from local to even possibly international, what hope does it have of surviving? The answer is four-pronged. First, there is the difficulty of getting international agreement on regulating tobacco, especially a strong normative regime. Second, while the public in Western societies is increasingly composed of non-smokers, who tolerate a much higher level of governmental taxation and regulation of tobacco than smokers (Green and Gerken 1989), the issue has not achieved the degree of intensity among a wide enough public to overcome entrenched forms of resistance. The public does not yet view tobacco as the equivalent of an infectious disease or a major public-health epidemic. Hence governments have wide leeway for action on tobacco, ranging from the promotional to the restrictive.

To a large degree, the struggle over tobacco-control policy today is a struggle over the agenda, especially issue definitions. Until the 1980s, the pro-tobacco lobby largely "owned" the agenda, casting doubts on health studies and arguing for individual choice. The scientific establishment and political promotion of the dangers of second-hand smoke, aided by other findings of addiction and embarrassing revelations of tobacco industry documents about the differences between what the companies knew in private and what they admitted in public, meant that the producers lost control of the agenda and were put on the defensive. Public opinion, even in its relatively passive mode as a political actor on this issue, shifted against them in the 1980s. Subsequently, the companies have attempted to redefine the issue, first by denying the second-hand smoke and addiction findings and later by attempting to portray themselves as responsible companies willing, within limits, to admit past errors and to cooperate with anti-teen-smoking programs. In short, the tobacco companies are trying to get the public to consider them a "normal industry" again, while some anti-tobacco advocates, the moral entrepreneurs necessary for a global prohibition movement, have embarked on a campaign of denormalization of the industry, showing how tobacco companies differ from responsible companies, especially in continually selling and promoting a lethal product with no known safeguards for its use.

Governments are in the middle of this struggle over the agenda. Even those governments that regulate and tax tobacco restrictively are reluctant to denormalize the industry. Cooperation makes for more efficient regulation, but how does one cooperate with drug pushers and criminals? Furthermore, tobacco taxes are still a "cash cow" for governments and tobacco production is important to local communities. Thus, even though denormalization was initially one of the four goals of the 1999 National Tobacco Control Strategy in Canada, it was later suspended. The struggle is over the definition of the public and governmental tobacco-control agenda. Keeping the public less attentive to tobacco restrictions would help tobacco companies prevent government action. Some observers see this as having occurred in the US since the MSA gave the illusion of a comprehensive tobacco-control policy (Pertschuk 1997; Chartier 2000). With a *de facto* national policy in place and FDA authority frustrated, the media and politicians have lost interest in further tobacco-restrictive measures.

Third in an assessment of the assets tobacco producers have against further restrictions is maintenance of the network of affiliated organizations and groups economically dependent upon the industry—vendors, the hospitality industry, farmers, arts, sports, and charitable organizations. Political controversy continues over the economic impact of smoking bans, especially in restaurants and bars. As tobacco companies have used more imported tobacco in the United States, it has become more difficult for companies to keep tobacco growers completely in their corner. The tobacco network may be fraying at the edges, but it is still substantial, buttressed by the economic importance of tobacco and the deep coffers of tobacco companies.

The fourth, and in many ways most formidable, asset the tobacco companies still possess is their political influence in the councils of government. Both US and Canadian studies argue that legislators who are smokers believe and act in more pro-tobacco ways than do nonsmokers. But smokers are likely to become a smaller portion of legislators and those in key leadership positions (Burden 2000; Cohen et al. 2000). More significant are the lobbying efforts that tobacco interests can mount, especially their willingness to donate large sums to election campaigns in the United States, and their party leadership and cabinet connections in Canada. As both the domestic and international political environments become less hospitable for tobacco interests, increasingly they will have to rely even more on political lobbying, institutional blockages, and venue shifting in order to block policy challenges. This can be abetted by differing priorities and disunity in the anti-tobacco ranks.

An international regulatory regime may be necessary in order to maintain an effective tobacco-control policy against companies that are transnational actors and whose future markets lie much more in developing than in developed countries. Such a regime, properly constructed, could complement rather than undermine domestic efforts at tobacco restrictions. It would also incur challenges from the tobacco industry. For instance, restrictive regulations on tobacco advertising or packaging would probably result in complaints about violations of the rules of the World Trade Organization (WTO).

It is not up to governments alone, however, to construct such a regime. In many international activities, especially on behalf of weak groups, nongovernmental activists have constructed linkages across borders and have proven effective by their greater political flexibility and capacity to focus on particular issues. The role of cross-border interest groups in facilitating lesson drawing between the US and Canada suggests that they may be equally important in the attempt to construct a global prohibition regime against tobacco.

There will be no quick, easy solution to the problem of tobacco control. The protracted conflict will continue for the foreseeable future.

Appendix: List of Persons Interviewed

Scott Ballin, American Heart Association
D. Douglas Blanke, Office of the Attorney General, State of Minnesota
John L. Bloom, National Center for Tobacco-Free Kids
Alan Blum, Doctors Ought to Care
Cynthia Callard, Physicians for a Smoke-Free Canada
Neil Collishaw, Physicians for a Smoke-Free Canada
Gregory N. Connolly, Office of Tobacco Control, State of Massachusetts
Rob Cunningham, Canadian Cancer Society
Richard A. Daynard, Tobacco Products Liability Project, Northeastern
    University
Zahir Din, Ministry of Health, Province of Ontario
Joy Epstein, Prospect Associates
Roberta Ferrence, Ontario Tobacco Research Unit
Janice Forsythe, Canadian Council on Smoking and Health
John M. Garcia, Prospect Associates; Cancer Care Ontario
John Giglio, American Cancer Society
Maurice Gingues, Canadian Cancer Society; Canadian Council on
    Smoking and Health
Stanton A. Glantz, University of California, San Francisco
Richard S. Hamburg, American Heart Association
Jay F. House, Canadian Council on Smoking and Health
Bill Howard, Department of Health and Community Services, Province
    of New Brunswick
Murray J. Kaiserman, Office of Tobacco Control, Health Canada
Ken Kyle, Canadian Cancer Sociey
Jeffrey MacLeod, Ministry of Health, Province of Nova Scotia
William Maga, Health Canada
Garfield Mahood, Non-Smokers' Rights Association
Alan Mills, American Cancer Society

Morton Mintz, *Washington Post*
Brenda Mitchell
Michael O'Neill, Justice Canada
Robert Parker, Canadian Tobacco Manufacturers Council
Jessica Z. Parris, American Cancer Society
Michael Perley, Ontario Campaign Against Tobacco
Christine Reshitnyk, National Clearinghouse on Tobacco and Health
Byron Rogers, Health Canada
Donald Shopland, National Cancer Institute
Eric Solberg, Doctors Ought to Care
David Sweanor, Non-Smokers' Rights Association
Kenneth E. Warner, University of Michigan
Elinor Wilson, Heart and Stroke Foundation of Canada
Merv Ungurain, Tobacco Control Unit, Nova Scotia Department of
    Health
Mitchell Zeller, United States Food and Drug Administration

References

Abramson, Jill. 1998. "Tobacco Industry Gave Big to Parties in States Where It Faced Attack." *New York Times*. June 8.

Ackerman, Gwen. 1997. "Anti-tobacco Activists Abroad Emboldened by U.S. Settlement." *Pittsburgh Post-Gazette*. June 24.

Advisory Commission on Intergovernmental Relations. 1977. *Cigarette Bootlegging: A State and Federal Responsibility*. Washington: Advisory Commission on Intergovernmental Relations.

Advisory Commission on Intergovernmental Relations. 1985. *Cigarette Taxes and Tax Avoidance: A Second Look*. Washington: Advisory Commission on Intergovernmental Relations.

Advocacy Institute. 1988. "Issue: Canadian Tobacco Control Legislation." SCARC Action Alert. June 14.

Advocacy Institute. 1998. *Smoke and Mirrors: How the Tobacco Industry Buys and Lies Its Way to Power and Profits*. Washington: Advocacy Institute.

Aftab, Macksood, Deborah Kolben, and Peter Lurie. 1999. "International Cigarette Labeling Practices." *Tobacco Control* 8: 368-372.

Alciati, Marianne H., Marcy Frosh, Sylvan B. Green, Ross C. Brownson, Peter H Fisher, Robin Hobart, Adele Roman, Russell C. Sciandra, and Dana M Shelton. 1998. "State Laws on Youth Access to Tobacco in the United States: Measuring Their Extensiveness with a New Rating System." *Tobacco Control* 7: 345-52.

Alexander, Dianne L., Joanna E. Cohen, Roberta G. Ferrence, Mary Jane Ashley, David A. Northrup, and John S. Pollard. 1997. "Tobacco Industry Campaign Contributions in Ontario, 1990-95." *Canadian Journal of Public Health* 88 (4): 230-31.

Ashley, Mary Jane, Ted Boadway, Roy Cameron, Josie d'Avernas, Roberta Ferrence, Andrew Pipe, Richard Schabas, and Peter Thomsen. 1999. *Actions Will Speak Louder Than Words: Getting Serious About Tobacco Control in Ontario*. Toronto: Expert Panel on the Renewal of the Ontario Tobacco Strategy.

Ashley, Mary Jane, Roberta Ferrence, David Northrup, Joanna Cohen, John Pollard, and Dianne Alexander. 1997. *Survey of Federal, Provincial and Territorial Legislators Regarding Tobacco and Tobacco Control Policies*. Report submitted to National Health Research Development Program, Health Canada.

Ayres, Jeffrey M. 1998. *Defying Conventional Wisdom: Political Movements and Popular Contention against North American Free Trade*. Toronto: University of Toronto Press.

Bachrach, Peter, and Morton Baratz. 1962. "The Two Faces of Power." *American Political Science Review* 56: 947-52.

Backhouse, Constance, and David H. Flaherty (eds.). 1992. *Challenging Times: The Women's Movement in Canada and the United States*. Montreal and Kingston: McGill-Queen's University Press.

Badger, A.J. 1980. *Prosperity Road: The New Deal, Tobacco and North Carolina.* Chapel Hill: University of North Carolina Press.

Banting, Keith, George Hoberg, and Richard Simeon (eds.). 1997. *Degrees of Freedom: Canada and the United States in a Changing World.* Montreal: McGill-Queen's University Press.

Baumgartner, Frank R., and Bryan D. Jones. 1993. *Agendas and Instability in American Politics.* Chicago: University of Chicago Press.

Begos, Kevin. 2000. "Most States Neglect Intent of Tobacco Deal, Report Finds." *Winston-Salem Journal.* October 6.

Bennett, Colin J. 1990. "The Formation of a Canadian Privacy Policy: The Art and Craft of Lesson Drawing." *Canadian Public Administration* 33: 331-370.

Bennett, Colin J. 1991a. "How States Utilize Foreign Evidence." *Journal of Public Policy* 11: 31-54.

Bennett, Colin J. 1991b. "Review Article: What Is Policy Convergence and What Causes It?" *British Journal of Political Science* 21: 215-33.

Bennett, Colin J. 1992. *Regulating Privacy: Data Protection and Public Policy in Europe and the United States.* Ithaca, NY: Cornell University Press.

Bennett, Colin J. 1997. "Understanding Ripple Effects: The Cross-National Adoption of Policy Instruments for Bureaucratic Accountability." *Governance* 10: 213-33.

Bennett, Colin J. and Michael Howlett. 1992. "The Lessons of Learning: Reconciling Theories of Policy Learning and Policy Change." *Policy Sciences* 25: 275-294.

Bennett, John Sutton. 1996. *History of the Canadian Medical Association, 1954-94.* Ottawa: Canadian Medical Association.

Berridge, Virginia. 1998. "Science and Policy: The Case of Postwar British Smoking Policy." In S. Lock, L.A. Reynolds, and E.M. Tansey (eds.), *Ashes to Ashes: The History of Smoking and Health.* Amsterdam: Rodopi.

Berry, Francis Stokes, and William D. Berry. 1990. "State Lottery Adoptions as Policy Innovations: An Event History Analysis." *American Political Science Review* 84: 395-416.

Biener, Lois, Jeffrey E. Harris, and William Hamilton. 2000. "Impact of the Massachusetts Tobacco Control Programme: Population Based Trend Analysis." *British Medical Journal* 321: 351-54.

Bloch, Michele, Richard Daynard, and Ruth Roemer. 1998. "A Year of Living Dangerously: The Tobacco Control Community Meets the Global Settlement." *Public Health Reports* 113: 488-97.

Bloom, John L. 1998. "International Interests in U.S. Tobacco Legislation." *Health Science Analysis Project.* Advocacy Institute. http://www.advocacy.org/hsap/international.htm

Bomberg, Ian, and John Peterson. 1993. "Prevention from Above? The Role of the EC." In Mike Mills (ed.), *Prevention, Health and British Politics.* Brookfield, VT: Ashgate.

Brandt, Allan M. 1992. "The Rise and Fall of the Cigarette: A Brief History of the Antismoking Movement in the United States." In Lincoln C. Chen, Arthur Kleinman, and Norma C. Ware (eds.), *Advancing Health in Developing Countries.* New York: Auburn House.

Brandt, Allan M. 1998. "Blow Some Smoke My Way: Passive Smoking, Risk and American Culture." In S. Lock, L.A. Reynolds, and E.M. Tansey (eds.), *Ashes to Ashes: The History of Smoking and Health.* Amsterdam: Rodopi.

Brokaw, Jeanne. 1996. "The War in the States." *Mother Jones* May/June: 56-57.

Brookes, Nick. 2000. "A New Spirit of Openness in the Tobacco Industry." Speech at National Press Club. January 11. http://npc.press.org/who/luncheonspeakers.htm.

Brooks, Stephen.1993. *Public Policy in Canada.* 2nd ed. Toronto: McClelland and Stewart.

Brown, Phyllida. 1999. "WHO Agrees Measures to Stop Global Spread of Tobacco Use." *British Medical Journal* 318: 1437.

Bull, Shelley B., Linda L. Pederson, and Mary Jane Ashley. 1994. "Restrictions on Smoking: Growth in Population Support Between 1983 and 1991 in Ontario, Canada." *Journal of Public Health Policy* 15 : 310-28.

Burden, Barry C. 2000. "Representation versus Self-Interest in U.S. Politics: The Cases of Tobacco Regulation and School Choice." Paper presented at American Political Science Association, Washington.

Burns, James MacGregor. 1963. *The Deadlock of Democracy: Four-Party Politics in America*. Englewood Cliffs, NJ: Prentice-Hall.

Cabinet Memoranda and Minutes. 1967-1971. Government of Canada.

Cairns, Alan. 1990. "Citizens (Outsiders) and Governments (Insiders) in Constitution Making: The Case of Meech Lake." In Douglas Williams (ed.), *Disruption: Constitutional Struggles from the Charter to Meech Lake*. Toronto: McClelland and Stewart.

Califano, Joseph A. 1981. *Governing America: An Insider's Report from the White House and the Cabinet*. New York: Simon and Schuster.

Callard, Cynthia. 1997. "The Canadian Set-Back: Tobacco Use in Canada 1986-1997." Paper presented at 10th World Conference on Smoking Or Health, Peking, China.

Callard, Cynthia. 2000. "The Golden Years of the CTMC, 1962-1987." World No-Tobacco Day on Industry Documents. Ottawa: Physicians for a Smoke-Free Canada.

Came, Barry. 1997. "Elbows Fly in Smoking Wars." *Macleans* April 14.

Campion, Frank D. 1984. *The AMA and U.S. Health Care Policy Since 1940*. Chicago: Chicago Review Press.

"Canadian Warnings Go To Washington." 1995. *Indoorair* June: 1, 4.

Castles, Francis G. (ed.). 1993. *Families of Nations*. Aldershot: Dartmouth.

Castles, Francis G. 1998 *Comparative Public Policy*. Northampton, MA: Edward Elgar.

Centers for Disease Control and Prevention. 1990. "State Coalitions for Prevention and Control of Tobacco Use." *Morbidity and Mortality Weekly Report* 39 (28): 476-77, 483-85.

Centers for Disease Control and Prevention. 1996. *State Tobacco Control Highlights—1996*. Atlanta: Centers for Disease Control and Prevention, National Center for Chronic Disease Prevention and Health Promotion, Office on Smoking and Health.

Chaloupka, Frank J. 1999. "Macro-Social Influences: The Effects of Prices and Tobacco-Control Policies on the Demand for Tobacco Products." *Nicotine and Tobacco Research* 1: S105-S109.

Chandler, Marsha, and William Chandler. 1979. *Public Policy and Provincial Politics*. Toronto: McGraw-Hill Ryerson.

Chapman, Simon. 1985. "Competing Agenda in Smoking Control Agencies: 'Those Who Pay the Piper...'" *New York State Journal of Medicine* 85: 287-89.

Chard, Richard, and Robert M. Howard. 2000. "Not Just Blowing Smoke: An Analysis of the Politics of the Tobacco Settlement." Paper presented at Midwest Political Science Association, Chicago.

Chartier, John. 2000. "Tobacco Lights Up for Bush." CNN. http://cnnfn.com/sooo/10/23/companies/election_tobacco. October 23.

Chriqui, Jamie F. 2000. "Restricting Minors' Access to Tobacco Products: How Do State Laws Measure Up?" Poster presented at American Political Science Association, Washington.

Chriqui, Jamie F., Michelle L. Avril, Lisa Lineberger, and Regina el Arculli. 2000. "Assessing the Nature and Extent of State Tobacco Control Laws." Poster presented at World Conference on Tobacco Or Health, Chicago.

Clinton, William J. 2001. Executive Order: Federal Leadership on Global Tobacco Control and Prevention. Washington: The White House, Office of Press Secretary. January 18.

Cobb, Roger, and Charles D. Elder. 1972. *Participation in American Politics: The Dynamics of Agenda-Setting.* Boston: Allyn and Bacon.

Cobb, Roger, Jennie Keith-Ross, and Marc Howard Ross. 1976. "Agenda Building as a Comparative Political Process." *American Political Science Review* 70: 126-38.

Cohen, Joanna E., Adam O. Goldstein, Brian S. Flynn, Michael C. Munger, Nell H. Gottlieb, Laura J. Solomon, and Greg S. Dana. 1998. "State Legislators' Perceptions of Lobbyists and Lobbying on Tobacco Control Issues." *Tobacco Control* 6: 332-36.

Cohen, Joanna E., Nicole A. de Guia, Mary Jane Ashley, Roberta Ferrence, David A. Northrup, and Donley T. Studlar. 2000. "Predictors of Canadian Legislators' Support for Tobacco Control Policies." Poster presented at 11th World Conference on Tobacco Or Health Chicago.

Coleman, James D. 1957. *Community Conflict.* New York: Free Press.

Collier, David, and Richard E. Messick. 1975. "Prerequisites Versus Diffusion: Testing Alternative Explanations of Social Security Adoption." *American Political Science Review* 69: 1299-314.

Collishaw, Neil. 1986a. "Approaches to Tobacco Control." Presentation to Meeting of the Royal College of Physicians and Surgeons of Canada.

Collishaw, Neil. 1986b. Memorandum: The Meaning of the Term Addiction. Health and Welfare Canada. June 9.

Collishaw, Neil E. 1990. "Monitoring Effectiveness of Canada's Health-Oriented Tobacco Policies." Paper presented to the National Workshop on Smoking and Health, Halifax.

Collishaw, Neil E. 1994. "Is the Tobacco Epidemic Being Brought Under Control, or Just Moved Around?—An International Perspective." Paper presented to Conference on the Reduction of Drug-Related Harm, Toronto.

Collishaw, Neil E. 1999. "From Montreal to Minnesota: Following the Trail of Imperial Tobacco's Documents." Physicians for a Smoker-Free Canada.

Collishaw, Neil E., and John W. Galbraith. 1992. "Tobacco Consumption and the Relative Effects of Advertising Restrictions in OECD Countries." National Health and Welfare Canada.

Collishaw, Neil, and Ian Mulligan. 1984. "Recent Trends in Tobacco Consumption in Canada and Other Countries." *Chronic Diseases in Canada* 4: 52-54.

Collishaw, Neil E., and Byron Rogers. 1984. "Tobacco in Canada." *Canadian Pharmaceutical Journal* 117: 147-50.

Collishaw, Neil E., Byron Rogers, and Murray J. Kaiserman. 1990. "Legislative Control of Tobacco in Canada." Ottawa: Department of National Health and Welfare.

Cook, Denys. 1986. Memorandum: Meaning of the Term "Addiction." Health and Welfare Canada. May 22.

Corrao, Marlo Ann, G. Emmanuel Guindon, Namita Sharma, and Dorna Fakhrabadi Shokoohi (eds). 2000. *Tobacco Control Country Profiles.* Atlanta: American Cancer Society.

Coutts, Jane. 1996. "New Hope for Canadian Regulations." *Globe and Mail.* March 23.

"Cross-Border Health Coalition Challenges Tobacco Industry Deception on Contraband Tobacco." 1993. April 13.

Cunningham, Rob. 1995. "An Evaluation of Federal and Provincial Legislation to Control Tobacco, 1994." Unpublished paper.

Cunningham, Rob. 1996. *Smoke and Mirrors: The Canadian Tobacco War.* Ottawa: International Development Research Centre.

Cunningham, Rob. 1999. "A Summary of Canadian Tobacco Legislation." Unpublished paper.

Cunningham, Rob. 2000. "Comprehensive Tobacco Control Strategy Needed." *Tobacco Control* 9: 239.

Dahl, Robert. 1956. *A Preface to Democratic Theory*. Chicago: University of Chicago Press.

Davis, Alan C. 1993. "Statement of Alan C. Davis." Ottawa: Coalition on Smoking Or Health. April 13.

Davis, Ronald M. 1992. "The Slow Growth of a Movement—and Finally a Journal." *Tobacco Control* 1:1-3.

Davis, Ronald M. 1997. "Web Watch: Tracking Tobacco on the Internet." *Tobacco Control* 6: 81.

Daynard, Richard A., Clive Bates, and Neil Francey. 2000. "Tobacco Litigation Worldwide." *British Medical Journal* 320: 111-13.

Daynard, Richard A. *et al.* 1986. "Selling Death: Individual and Organizational Responsibility and the Tobacco Industry." Conference at Northeastern University, Boston, Massachusetts.

de Groh, Margaret, and Thomas Stephens. 2000. "Ten Natural Experiments in Tobacco Control: Assessing Canadian Outcomes." Poster presented at 11th Conference on World Tobacco Or Health. Chicago.

de Guia, Nicole A., Joanna E. Cohen, Mary Jane Ashley, Roberta Ferrence, David A. Northrup, and John S. Pollard. 1998. "How Provincial and Territorial Legislators View Tobacco and Tobacco Control: Findings from a Canadian Study." *Chronic Diseases in Canada* 19 (2): 57-61.

Deacon, Bob, Michelle Hulse, and Paul Stubbs. 1997. *Global Social Policy: International Organizations and the Future of Welfare*. London: Sage.

DeBarros, Anthony. 2001. "Anti-Smoking Funds Sparse." *USA Today*. January 30.

Della Porta, Donatella, Hanspeter Kriesi, and Dieter Rucht (eds.). 1999. *Social Movements in a Globalizing World*. New York: St. Martin's Press.

Delducci, Don. 1996. "OSHA Should Rewrite Its Workplace Smoking Plan." *Pittsburgh Post-Gazette*. October 16.

Department of National Health and Welfare. 1969. "Smoking and Health Enquiry of Countries Outside North America."

Derthick, Martha. 2001. "Federalism and the Politics of Tobacco." *Publius* 31: 47-63.

DiFranza, Joseph R. 1999. "Are the Federal and State Governments Complying with the Synar Amendment?" *Archives of Pediatric and Adolescent Medicine* 153:1089-97.

Dolowitz. David.1998. *Learning from America: Policy Transfer and the Development of the British Workfare State*: Sussex: Sussex Academic Press.

Dolowitz, David, and David Marsh.1996. "Who Learns What from Whom: A Review of the Policy Transfer Literature." *Political Studies* 44: 343-57.

Dolowitz, David P., and David Marsh. 2000. "Learning from Abroad: The Role of Policy Transfer in Contemporary Policy-Making." *Governance* 13: 5-24.

Doron, Gideon. 1979. *The Smoking Paradox: Public Regulation in the Cigarette Industry*. Cambridge, MA: Abt Books.

Downs, Anthony. 1972. "Up and Down with Ecology: The Issue-Attention Cycle." *The Public Interest* 28: 38-52.

Drew, Elizabeth Brenner. 1965. "The Quiet Victory of the Cigarette Lobby: How It Found the Best Filter Yet—Congress." *Atlantic Monthly* (September): 76-79

Dunn, Christopher (ed.). 1996. *Provinces: Canadian Provincial Politics*. Peterborough, ON: Broadview Press.

Durant, Robert F., and Paul F. Diehl. 1989. "Agendas, Alternatives, and Public Policy: Lessons from the U.S. Foreign Policy Arena." *Journal of Public Policy* 9: 179-205.

Dyck, Rand. 1997. "The Socio-Economic Setting of Ontario Politics." In Graham White (ed.), *The Government and Politics of Ontario*. 5th ed. Toronto: University of Toronto Press.

Eisner, Marc Allen, Jeffrey Worsham, and Evan J. Ringquist. 2000. *Contemporary Regulatory Policy*. Boulder, CO: Lynne Rienner.

Epp, Jake. 1987a. "Health Initiatives Related to Tobacco Control." Speaking Notes for Address to the Progressive Conservative Party Caucus. March 25.

Epp, Jake. 1987b. Letter to Otis Bowen. May 8.

The Erosion of Federal Cigarette Taxes Over Time. 2000. Washington: Campaign for Tobacco-Free Kids.

Evenson, Brad. 1997. "U.S. Outdoes Canada with New Tobacco Deal." *Ottawa Citizen*. July 6.

Eyestone, Robert. 1977. "Confusion, Diffusion and Innovation." *American Political Science Review* 71: 441-47.

Fairclough, Gordon, and Sarah Lueck. 2001. "U.S. Draws Back on Cigs Treaty." *The Age*. May 8.

Feder, Barnaby J. 1996. "Battle on Youth Smoking Brings Hope and Caution." *New York Times*. November 29.

Federal-Provincial Priorities Planning Committee. 1977. "Smoking and Health Strategies."

Ferrence, Roberta G. 1989. *Deadly Fashion: The Rise and Fall of Cigarette Smoking in North America*. New York: Garland Publishing.

Ferrence, Roberta. 1996. "Using Diffusion Theory in Health Promotion: The Case of Tobacco." *Canadian Journal of Public Health*, 87 (Supplement 2): S24-S27.

Final Report of the Advisory Committee on Tobacco Policy and Public Health. 1997. July.

Finger, William R. (ed.). 1981. *The Tobacco Industry in Transition*. Lexington, MA: Lexington Books.

Fintor, Lou, Marianne Haenlein Alciati, and Ruth Fischer. 1995. "Legislative and Regulatory Mandates for Mammography Quality Assurance." *Journal of Public Health Policy* 16: 81-107.

Fishman, Julia A., Harmony Allison, Sarah B. Knowles, Burke A Fishburn, Trevor A. Woollery, William T. Marx, Dana M. Shelton, Corinne G. Husten, and Michael P. Eriksen. 1999. "State Laws on Tobacco Control–United States, 1998." *Morbidity and Mortality Weekly Report* 48 (SS-3): 21-62.

Fleenor, Patrick. 1996. The Effect of Excise Tax Differentials on the Interstate Smuggling and Cross-Border Sales of Cigarettes in the United States. Background Paper #16. Washington: Tax Foundation.

Flynn, Brian S., Greg S. Dana, Adam O. Goldstein, Karl E. Bauman, Joanna E. Cohen, Nell H. Gottlieb, Laura J. Solomon, and Michael C. Munger. 1997. "State Legislators' Intentions to Vote and Subsequent Votes on Tobacco Control Legislation." *Health Psychology* 16: 401-404.

Foreman, Christopher. 1994. *Plagues, Products and Politics: Emergent Public Health Hazards and National Policy-making*. Washington: Brookings Institution.

Forster, Jean L., and Mark Wolfson. 1998. "Youth Access to Tobacco: Policies and Politics." *Annual Review of Public Health* 19: 203-35.

Frankel, Glenn. 1996. "The Tobacco Pushers: How the U.S. Government Helped Recruit New Cigarette Smokers Overseas." *Washington Post* (Weekly Edition), November 25-December 1.

Freeman, Aaron. 1999. *Cashing In: Money and Politics in Canada*. Toronto: McLelland and Stewart.

Freeman, Gary P. 1986. "National Style and Policy Sectors: Explaining Structured Variation." *Journal of Public Policy* 5: 467-95.

Friedman, Kenneth M. 1975. *Public Policy and the Smoking-Health Controversy*. Lexington, MA: Lexington Books.

Fritschler, A. Lee. 1969. *Smoking and Politics: Policy-Making and the Federal Bureaucracy*. Englewood Cliffs, NJ: Prentice-Hall.

Fritschler, A. Lee, and James M. Hoefler. 1996. *Smoking and Politics: Policy Making and the Federal Bureaucracy.* 5th ed. Upper Saddle River, NJ: Prentice-Hall.

Galbraith, John W., and Murray Kaiserman.1997. "Taxation, Smuggling and Demand for Cigarettes in Canada: Evidence from Time-Series Data." *Journal of Health Economics* 16: 287-301.

Garcia, John, and Brenda Mitchell. 1994. "Post COMMIT in Ontario: The Ontario Tobacco Strategy—The First Three Years." *Health and Canadian Society* 2: 339-47.

Gibson, Ed. 2000. "Smoke and Mirrors: Contrasting Policies for the Tobacco Settlement Allocation Money in Two Southern States." Paper presented at Southern Political Science Association, Atlanta.

Givel, Michael S., and Stanton A. Glantz. 2000. "Failure to Defend a Successful State Tobacco Control Program: Policy Lessons from Florida." *American Journal of Public Health* 90: 762-67.

Glantz, Stanton A., John Slade, Lisa A. Bero, Peter Hanauer, and Deborah E. Barnes. 1996. *The Cigarette Papers.* Berkeley: University of California Press.

Glantz, Stanton A. 1996. "Editorial: Preventing Tobacco Use—The Youth Access Trap." *American Journal of Public Health* 86: 156-58.

Glantz, Stanton A., and Ethel Balbach. *Tobacco War: Inside the California Experience.* Berkeley: University of California Press, 2000.

Glick, Henry R. 1992. *The Right to Die.* New York: Columbia University Press.

Glick, Henry R., and Scott P. Hays. 1991. "Innovation and Reinvention in State Policymaking: Theory and the Evolution of Living Will Laws." *Journal of Politics* 53: 835-50.

"Global Information Management and Surveillance Systems for a Tobacco-Free World." 1999. A Joint WHO-UICC-CDC-World Bank Project. Atlanta, March 24-26.

Gloeckler, Wally. 2000. "20 Years On, Same Debate About Smoking." *Edmonton Journal.* October 9.

Godshall, William T. 1999. "Giving 10% to Gain Eternity." *Tobacco Control* 8: 437-39.

Goldstein, Adam O., and Nathan S. Bearman. 1996. "State Tobacco Lobbyists and Organizations in the United States: Crossed Lines." *American Journal of Public Health* 86: 1137-42.

Goldstein, Adam O., Joanna E. Cohen, Brian S. Flynn, Nell H. Gottlieb, Laura J. Solomon, Greg S. Dana, Karl E. Bauman, and Michael C. Munger. 1997. "State Legislators' Attitudes and Voting Intentions Toward Tobacco Control Legislation." *American Journal of Public Health* 87: 1197-2000.

Goodin, Robert E. 1989. *No Smoking: The Ethical Issues.* Chicago: University of Chicago Press.

Goodman, Jordan. 1998. "Webs of Drug Dependence: Towards a Political History of Tobacco." In S. Lock, L.A. Reynolds, and E.M. Tansey (eds.), *Ashes to Ashes: The History of Smoking and Health.* Amsterdam: Rodopi.

Gori, Gio B., and John C. Luik. 1999. *Passive Smoke: The EPA's Betrayal of Science and Policy.* Vancouver: Fraser Institute.

Gorovitz, Eric, James Mosher, and Mark Pertschuk. 1998. "Preemption or Prevention? Lessons from Efforts to Control Firearms, Alcohol, and Tobacco." *Journal of Public Health Policy* 19: 36-50.

Gottsegen, Jack J. 1940. *Tobacco: A Study of Its Consumption in the United States.* New York: Pitman.

Government of Canada. 1970. "Confidential Memorandum to Cabinet." April 27.

Gow, James Iain. 1994. *Learning from Others: Administrative Innovations Among Canadian Governments.* Toronto: Institute of Public Administration in Canada.

Gray, Charlotte. 1988. "Passage of Antismoking Bills Provides a Lesson in Lobbying." *Canadian Medical Association Journal* 139 (July 15): 153-54.

Gray, Virginia. 1973. "Innovation in the States: A Diffusion Study." *American Political Science Review* 57: 1174-1185.

Gray, Virginia. 1994. "Competition, Emulation, and Policy Innovation." In Lawrence C. Dodd and Calvin Jillson (eds.), *New Perspectives on American Politics*. Washington: CQ Press.

Gray, Virginia, Russell L. Hanson, and Herbert Jacob (eds.). 1999. *Politics in the American States: A Comparative Analysis*. 7th ed. Washington: CQ Press.

Green, Donald Philip, and Ann Elizabeth Gerken. 1989. "Self-Interest and Public Opinion toward Smoking Restrictions and Cigarette Taxes." *Public Opinion Quarterly* 53: 1-16.

Grodzins, Martin. 1966. *The American System: A New View of Government in the United States.* Chicago: Rand McNally.

Grossman, Michael, and Philip Price. 1992. *Tobacco Smoking and the Law in Canada*. Toronto: Butterworths.

Hager, Gregory L., and Matthew J. Gabel. 2000. "Money for Nothing and Check for Free: States, Attorneys General, and the Tobacco Settlement." Paper presented at Midwest Political Science Association, Chicago.

Hahn, Harlan. 1968. "Voting in Canadian Communities: A Taxonomy of Referendum Issues." *Canadian Journal of Political Science* 1: 462-69.

Hall, Peter A.(ed.). 1989. *The Political Power of Economic Ideas: Keynesianism Among Nations*. Princeton: Princeton University Press.

Hall, Peter A. 1993. "Policy Paradigms, Social Learning, and the State." *Comparative Politics* 25: 275-96.

Hamilton, Vivian H., Carey Levinton, Yvan St.-Pierre, and Franque Grimard. 1997. "The Effect of Tobacco Tax Cuts on Cigarette Smoking in Canada." *Canadian Medical Journal* 156: 187-91.

Harris, Richard A., and Sidney M. Milkis. 1996. *The Politics of Regulatory Change: A Tale of Two Agencies*. 2nd ed. New York: Oxford University Press.

Harrison, Kathryn, and George Hoberg. 1994. *Risk, Science and Politics*. Montreal: McGill- Queen's University Press.

Harrop, Martin (ed.). 1993. *Power and Policy in Liberal Democracies*. New York: Cambridge.

Hartz, Louis (ed.). 1964. *The Founding of New Societies*. New York: Harcourt Brace.

Hays, Scott P. 1996. "Influences on Reinvention During the Diffusion of Innovations." *Political Research Quarterly* 49: 631-50.

Hays, Scott P., Carol E. Hays, John Vinzant, and Kathleen Gary. 2000a. "Factors That Facilitate the Adoption of Municipal Ordinances for Tobacco Control." Paper presented at Midwest Political Science Association, Chicago.

Hays, Scott P., Carol E. Hays, John Vinzant, and Kathleen Gary. 2000b. "Change Agents, Policy Entrepreneurs, Focusing Events and the Adoption of Municipal Ordinances for Tobacco Control." Paper presented at American Political Science Association, Washington.

Health and Welfare Canada. 1964. *Smoking and Health*. Health and Welfare Canada.

Health and Welfare Canada. 1974. *A New Perspective on the Health of Canadians*. Ottawa: Health and Welfare Canada.

Health and Welfare Canada. 1979. "Smoking, Health and Tax Policy." Non-Medical Use of Drugs Directorate, Health and Welfare Canada.

Health and Welfare Canada. 1983. *Canadian Initiatives in Smoking and Health*. Ottawa: Health and Welfare Canada.

Health Canada. 1986. *Achieving Health for All: A Framework for Health Promotion*. Ottawa: Health Canada.

Health Canada. 1994. "Canada-U.S. to Cooperate on Anti-Smoking Strategies" News Release. September 29

Health Canada. 1995a. "Canada-U.S. Reaffirm Joint Commitment to Anti-Smoking Strategies." News Release. May 31.

Health Canada. 1995b. "Minister Marleau Congratulates President Clinton for His Anti-Tobacco Initiative." News Release. August 10.

Heclo, Hugh. 1978. "Issue Networks and the Executive Establishment." In Anthony King (ed.), *The New American Political System*. Washington: American Enterprise Institute.

Heidenheimer, Arnold, Hugh Heclo, and Nancy Adams. 1990. *Comparative Public Policy*. 3rd ed. New York: St. Martin's Press.

Hiebert, Janet. 1999. "Wrestling with Rights: Judges, Parliament and the Making of Social Policy." *Choices* 5 (3): 1-36.

Hilts, Philip J. 1996. *Smokescreen: The Truth Behind the Tobacco Industry Cover-up*. Reading, MA: Addison-Wesley.

A History of the Vote in Canada. 1997. Ottawa: Minister of Public Works and Government Sources.

Hoberg, George.1991. "Sleeping with an Elephant: The American Influence on Canadian Environmental Regulation." *Journal of Public Policy* 11: 107-32.

House of Commons Standing Committee on Health, Welfare and Social Affairs. 1968-69. Minutes of Proceedings and Evidence.

Howlett, Michael. 1997. "Issue-Attention and Punctuated Equilibria Models Reconsidered: An Empirical Examination of the Dynamics of Agenda-Setting in Canada." *Canadian Journal of Political Science* 30: 3-29.

Howlett, Michael. 1998. "Predictable and Unpredictable Policy Windows: Institutional and Exogenous Correlates of Canadian Federal Agenda-Setting." *Canadian Journal of Political Science* 31: 495-524.

Howlett, Michael. 1999. "Rejoinder to Stuart Soroka, 'Policy Agenda-Setting Theory Revisited: A Critique of Howlett on Downs, Baumgartner and Jones, and Kingdon.'" *Canadian Journal of Political Science* 32: 773-79.

Htun, Mal N., and Mark P. Jones. 2001. "Engendering the Right to Participate in Decision-Making: Electoral Quotas and Women's Leadership in Latin America." In Nikki Craske and Maxine Molyneux (eds.), *Gender, Rights and Justice in Latin America*. New York: Macmillan.

Hunt, Albert R. 2001. "Going into the Tank for Tobacco." *Wall Street Journal Interactive Edition*. August 2.

In Support of Public Health: A Submission to the United Sates Food and Drug Administration Respecting Proposed Tobacco Regulations under the Food, Drug and Cosmetic Act. 1995. Canadian Cancer Society. December.

Inglehart, Ronald F., Neil Nevitte, and Miguel Basanez. 1996. *The North American Trajectory: Cultural, Economic, and Political Ties among the United States, Canada, and Mexico*. Hawthorne, NY: Aldine De Gruyter.

"International Effort Begins for Anti-Smoking Accord." 2000. *Baltimore Sun*. October 22.

Isabelle, Gaston. 1969. *Report of the Standing Committee on Health, Welfare and Social Affairs on Tobacco and Cigarette Smoking*. Ottawa: Queen's Printer.

Jacob, Herbert. 1988. *Silent Revolution: The Transformation of Divorce Law in the United States*. Chicago: University of Chicago Press.

Jacobson, Peter D., and Kenneth E. Warner.1999. "Litigation and Public Health Policy Making: The Case of Tobacco Control." *Journal of Health Politics, Policy and Law* 24: 769-804.

Jacobson, Peter D., and Jeffrey Wasserman. 1997. *Tobacco Control Laws: Implementation and Enforcement*. Santa Monica: RAND.

Jacobson, Peter D., Jeffrey Wasserman, and John R. Anderson. 1997. "Historical Overview of Tobacco Legislation and Regulation." *Journal of Social Issues* 53: 75-95.

Jacobson, Peter D., Jeffrey Wasserman, and Kristiana Raube. 1993. "The Politics of Antismoking Legislation." *Journal of Health Politics, Policy and Law* 18: 787-819.

Janofsky, Michael. 1994. "Majority of American Say Cigarettes Spur Addiction." *New York Times*. May 1.

Johnson, Paul R. 1984. *The Economics of the Tobacco Industry*. New York: Praeger.

Joossens, Luk. 2000. "The Big Disappointment: U.S.A. Weak on Convention." *Tobacco Control* 9: 134-35.

Kagan, Robert A., and David Vogel. 1993. "The Politics of Smoking Regulation: Canada, France, the United States." In Robert L. Rabin and Stephen D. Sugarman (eds.), *Smoking Policy: Law, Politics, and Culture*. New York: Oxford University Press.

Kaiserman, Murray J., and Byron Rogers. 1991. "Tobacco Consumption Declining Faster in Canada Than in the U.S." *American Journal of Public Health* 81: 902-04.

Kaplan, Sheila. 1996. "Tobacco Dole." *Mother Jones* May/June: 38-41.

Kaufman, Marc. 2001. "Negotiator in Global Tobacco Talks Quits." *Washington Post*. August 2.

Keck, Margaret E., and Kathryn Sikkink. 1998. *Activists beyond Borders*. Ithaca, NY: Cornell University Press.

Kelder, Graham E., Jr., and Richard A. Daynard. 1997. "Judicial Approaches to Tobacco Control: The Third Wave of Tobacco Litigation as a Tobacco Control Mechanism." *Journal of Social Issues* 53: 169-86.

Kenny, Colin. 1999. "Smoking Out Smugglers." *Montreal Gazette*. February 10.

Kerr, Clark. 1983. *The Future of Industrial Societies*. Cambridge: Harvard University Press.

Kessler, David A. 2001. *A Question of Intent: A Great American Battle with a Deadly Industry*. New York: Public Affairs Press.

King, Anthony. 1973. "Ideas, Institutions and the Policies of Governments: A Comparative Analysis, Parts I and II, III." *British Journal of Political Science*. 3: 291-313; 409-23.

Kingdon, John W. 1995. *Agendas, Alternatives, and Public Policies*. 2nd ed. New York: HarperCollins.

Kinney, Joseph A. 1981. "Tobacco's Global Economy: Is North Carolina Losing?" In William R. Finger (ed.), *The Tobacco Industry in Transition*. Lexington, MA: Lexington Books.

Klase, Rebecca. 1999. "Policy Transfer Among State Bureaucracies: The Role of Professional Networks." Poster presented at American Political Science Association, Atlanta.

Klein, Richard. 1993. *Cigarettes are Sublime*. Durham: Duke University Press.

Klingeman, Hans-Dieter, Richard I. Hofferbert, and Ian Budge. 1994. *Parties, Policies, and Democracy*. Boulder, CO: Westview Press.

Kluger, Richard. 1996. *Ashes to Ashes: America's Hundred-Year Cigarette War, The Public Health, and the Unabashed Triumph of Philip Morris*. New York: Alfred A. Knopf.

Knopf, Rainer, and F.L. Morton. 1992. *Charter Politics*. Scarborough: Nelson Canada.

Koop, C. Everett. 1998. "The Tobacco Scandal: Where Is the Outrage?" *Tobacco Control* 7: 393-96.

Kurtz, Howard. 1998. "Tobacco Shows Senate It Can Still Sell." *Washington Post*, June 19.

Kyle, Ken. 1992. Letter on "Tobacco Tax Coalitions." Canadian Cancer Society. November 25.

Kyle, Ken. 1996. "Engineering an International Coup—Smoke-Free Skies in 1996." Speaking notes for presentation at Tobacco-Free Canada: Second National Conference on Tobacco or Health, Ottawa.

Kyle, Ken, and Fran Du Melle.1994. "International Smoke-Free Flights: Buckle Up for Take-Off." *Tobacco Control* 3: 3-4.

Lachance, Victor, Kenneth Kyle, and David Sweanor. 1990. "Tobacco Control in Canada." Paper presented at 7th World Conference on Tobacco Or Health, Perth, Australia. April.

Laroche, Andree. 1992. "The Politics of Tobacco: A Study of the Making of Bills C-204 and C-51." Ph.D. Dissertation, Carleton University.

Lascher, Edward L., Jr. 1998. "Loss Imposition and Institutional Characteristics: Learning from Automobile Insurance Reform in North America." *Canadian Journal of Political Science* 31: 143-64.

Law, Maureen. 1987. Letter to C. Everett Koop. May 8.

Leary, Warren E. 1994. "A 30-Year Report Card on Smoking Prevention." *New York Times.* January 12.

LeGresley, Eric. 1998a. "Recovering Tobacco-Caused Public Expenditures from the Tobacco Industry: Options for Provincial Governments." Smoking and Health Action Foundation. March.

LeGresley, Eric. 1998b. "Session Four: Foreign Impact." *Proceedings of the Conference on the So-Called Global Tobacco Settlement: Its Implications for Public Health and Public Policy.* Madison: Institute for Legal Studies, University of Wisconsin Law School.

Leichter, Howard M. 1991. *Free to Be Foolish: Politics and Health Promotion in the United States and Great Britain.* New York: Cambridge University Press.

Lemco, Jonathon (ed.). 1994. *National Health Care.* Ann Arbor: University of Michigan Press.

Lewis, Charles and the Center for Public Integrity. 1998. *The Buying of the Congress.* New York: Avon Books.

Lewit, Eugene, and D. Coate. 1982. "The Potential for Using Excise Taxes to Reduce Smoking." *Journal of Health Economics* 1: 121-45.

Lewit, Eugene, D. Coate, and M. Grossman. 1981. "The Effects of Government Regulation on Teenage Smoking." *Journal of Law and Economics* 24:545-69.

Licari, Michael J. 2000a. "Comparative Policy Effectiveness: Smoking Regulation in 13 OECD Countries." Poster presented at American Political Science Association, Washington.

Licari, Michael J. 2000b. "Regulatory Instrument Effectiveness: Testing the Meier-Licari Model." Poster presented at American Political Science Association, Washington.

Licari, Michael J., and Kenneth J. Meier.1997. "Regulatory Policy When Behavior Is Addictive: Smoking, Cigarette Taxes and Bootlegging." *Political Research Quarterly* 50: 5-24.

Lijphart, Arend. 1984. *Democracies: Patterns of Majoritarian and Consensus Government in Twenty-One Countries.* New Haven, CT: Yale University Press.

Lindblom, Eric N. 1999. *False Friends: The U.S. Cigarette Companies' Betrayal of American Tobacco Farmers.* Campaign for Tobacco-Free Kids. December.

Lipset, Seymour M. 1990. *Continental Divide: The Values and Institutions of the United States and Canada.* New York: Routledge.

Liston, A.J. n.d. Recommendations. Health and Welfare Canada.

Lockwood, Frank E. 2001. "U.S. May Promote Tobacco Overseas." *Lexington Herald-Leader.* July 31.

Lowi, Theodore H. 1964. "American Business, Public Policy, Case Studies and Political Theory." *World Politics* 16: 677-715.

Lugar, Richard G. 1998. "A Good Time to End Tobacco Quotas." *New York Times.* April 7.

Lutz, James M. 1989. "Emulation and Policy Adoptions in the Canadian Provinces." *Canadian Journal of Political Science* 22: 147-54.

MacLeod, Jeffrey J. 1996. *Health Care Reform in Nova Scotia: A Study in Pressure Group Politics, 1993-1996.* Unpublished M.A. thesis, Acadia University.

McCarthy, Shawn. 1998. "Canada Slow on Tobacco Front." *Globe and Mail.* June 4.

McEwen, E. Duncan. 1979. "Whatever Happened to the Lalonde Report?" *Canadian Journal of Public Health* 70: 13-16.

McKinley, John B., and Lisa D. Marceau. 2000. "Upstream Health Public Policy: Lessons from the Battle of Tobacco." *International Journal of Health Services* 20: 49-69.

Mahood, Garfield. 1993. "The Politics of Tobacco Control in Canada: An Assessment of the Issues, Strategies Which Work, and Challenges in the Future." Paper presented at Tobacco Free Canada: First National Conference on Tobacco Or Health. Ottawa. October 21.

Mahood, Garfield. 1995. "Canadian Tobacco Package Warning System." *Tobacco Control* 4: 10-14.

Mahood, Garfield. 1997. "Legislation: A Key Component of a Comprehensive Tobacco Control Plan." Plenary Address to the 10th World Conference on Smoking or Health. Beijing, China. August 27.

Mahood, Garfield. 1999. "Warnings That Tell the Truth: Breaking New Ground in Canada." *Tobacco Control* 8: 356-62.

Maioni, Antonia. 1998. *Parting at the Crossroads: The Emergence of Health Insurance in the United States and Canada.* Princeton: Princeton University Press.

Males, Mike A. 1999. *Smoked: Why Joe Camel Is Still Smiling.* Monroe, ME: Common Courage Press.

Manfredi, Christopher. 1990. "The Use of United States Decisions by the Supreme Court of Canada Under the Charter of Rights and Freedoms." *Canadian Journal of Political Science* 23: 499-518.

Manley, Marc, William Lynn, Roselyn Payne Epps, Donna Grande, Tom Glynn, and Donald Shopland. 1997. "The American Stop Smoking Intervention Study for Cancer Prevention: An Overview." *Tobacco Control* 6 (supplement 2): S5-S11.

Marotte, Bertrand. 1997. "Big Tobacco Still Smoking." *Ottawa Citizen.* July 9.

Marsden, William.1999. "Tobacco Insider Talks." *Montreal Gazette.* December 18.

Mathematica Policy Research. 1995. *Public Opinion Surveys on Tobacco Control Policies for the Robert Wood Johnson Foundation SmokeLess States Program.* Princeton, NJ: Mathematica Policy Research, Inc.

Matland, Richard E., and Donley T. Studlar. 1995. "Determinants of Legislative Turnover: A Cross-National Analysis." Paper presented at European Consortium of Political Research, Bordeaux, France.

Mayhew, David. 1974. *Congress: The Electoral Connection.* New Haven, CT: Yale University Press.

McAdam, Doug, and Dieter Rucht. 1993. "The Cross-National Diffusion of Movement Ideas." *The Annals,* 528 (July): 56-74.

McElroy, Helen. 1990. "Break Free: Towards a New Generation of Non-smokers." *Health Promotion* 28 (4): 2-7.

McGowan, Richard. 1995. *Business, Politics, and Cigarettes.* Westport, CT: Quorum Books.

Meier, Kenneth J. 1994. *The Politics of Sin.* Armonk, NY: M E. Sharpe..

Miles, Robert H. 1982. *Coffin Nails and Corporate Strategies.* Englewood Cliffs, NJ: Prentice-Hall.

Mills, Mike (ed.). 1993. *Prevention, Health and British Politics.* Brookfield, VT: Ashgate.

Mintrom, Michael. 1997a. "Policy Entrepreneurs and the Diffusion of Innovation." *American Journal of Political Science* 41: 738-70.

Mintrom, Michael. 1997b. "The State-Local Nexus in Policy Innovation Diffusion: The Case of Social Choice." *Publius* 27: 41-59.

Mintrom, Michael, and Sandra Vergari. 1996. "Advocacy Coalitions, Policy Entrepreneurs, and Policy Change." *Policy Studies Journal* 24: 420-34.

Mintz, Morton. 1990. "No Ifs, Ands, or Butts." *Washington Monthly* 22 (6-7): 30-37.

Mintz, Morton. 1991. "Tobacco Roads: Delivering Death to the Third World." *The Progressive* 55 (5): 24-29.

Mintz, Morton. 1996. "Blowing Smoke Rings Around the Statehouses." *Washington Monthly* 28 (5): 20-22.

Mitchell, Brenda. 1996. *Voluntary Codes for Tobacco Advertising and Promotion.* Health Canada.

Mitchell, Brenda, and John Garcia. 1995. "Post COMMIT in Ontario: The Ontario Tobacco Strategy—The First Three Years." *Health and Canadian Society* 2: 339-47.

A Model for Change: The California Experience in Tobacco Control. 1998. California Department of Health Services, Tobacco Control Section. October.

Mollenkamp, Carrick, Adam Levy, Joseph Menn, and Jeffrey Rothfeder. 1998. *The People vs. Big Tobacco: How the States Took on the Cigarette Giants.* Princeton: Bloomberg Press.

Moon, Peter. 1997. "High Taxes Make Good Smuggling." *Globe and Mail.* July 28.

Mooney, Christopher Z. 2000. "Modeling Regional Effects on State Policy Diffusion." *Political Research Quarterly* 54: 103-24.

Moore, Stephen, Sidney M.Wolfe, Deborah Lindes, and Clifford E. Douglas. 1994. "Epidemiology of Failed Tobacco Control Legislation." *Journal of the American Medical Association* 272: 1171-75.

Morin, Margaret. 1996. *Canadian Survey Data.* Health Canada.

Morris, Aldon. 1993. "Centuries of Black Protest: Its Significance for America and the World." In Herbert Hill and James E. Jones, Jr. (eds.), *Race in America: The Struggle for Equality.* Madison: University of Wisconsin Press.

Morris, Chris. 1995. "Critics Hope We'll Follow U.S. Anti-Smoking Rules." *Ottawa Citizen.* August 11.

Morrison, A.B. 1977. Letter to Paul Paré, Chairman, Canadian Tobacco Manufacturers Council. April 18.

Mossberger, Karen. 2000. *The Politics of Ideas and the Spread of Enterprise Zones.* Washington: Georgetown University Press.

Nadelman, Ethan A. 1990. "Global Prohibition Regimes: The Evolution of Norms in International Society." *International Organization* 44: 479-526.

Nathanson, Constance A. 1999. "Social Movements as Catalysts for Policy Change: The Case of Smoking and Guns." *Journal of Health Politics, Policy and Law* 24: 421-88.

National Cancer Institute. 1993. *The Impact of Cigarette Excise Taxes on Smoking Among Children and Adults: Summary Report of a National Cancer Institute Expert Panel.* Washington: National Cancer Institute, Division of Cancer Prevention and Control, Cancer Control Science Program.

National Cancer Institute. 2000. *State and Local Legislative Action to Reduce Tobacco Use. Smoking and Tobacco Control Monograph No. 11.* Bethesda, MD: U.S. Department of Health and Human Services, National Institutes of Health, National Cancer Institute, NIH Pub. No. 00-4804.

National Clearinghouse on Tobacco and Health. 1995. *Federal and Provincial Tobacco Legislation in Canada: An Overview.* Ottawa: National Clearinghouse on Tobacco and Health.

National Clearinghouse on Tobacco and Health. 1999. *Canadian Law and Tobacco.* http://www.cctc.ca/ncth/docs/legislation.

National Population Health Survey Highlights. 1999. *Smoking Behaviour of Canadians: Cycle 2, 1996/97.* Ottawa: Health Canada.

Nelson, Barbara. 1984. *Making an Issue of Child Abuse: Political Agenda Setting for Social Problems.* Chicago: University of Chicago Press.

Neuberger, Maurine. 1963. *Smoke Screen: Tobacco and the Public Health.* Englewood Cliffs, NJ: Prentice-Hall.

Neustadt, Richard. 1966. "White House and Whitehall." *The Public Interest* 2: 55-69.

Nevitte, Neil. 1996. *The Decline of Defer-ence: Canadian Value Change in Cross-National Perspective*. Peterborough: Broadview Press.

New England and Eastern Canada Tobacco Control Conference. 1999. Agenda. Boston. September 21-22.

Nielsen, A.C. 1999. *Measurement of Retailer Compliance with Respect to the Tobacco Act and Provincial Tobacco Sales-to-Minors Legislation*. Final Report. Ottawa: Health Canada, Health Protection Branch, Office of Tobacco Control.

Non-Smokers' Rights Association. 1986. *A Catalogue of Deception: The Use and Abuse of Voluntary Regulation of Tobacco in Canada*. Toronto: Non-Smokers' Rights Association.

Non-Smokers' Rights Association. 1996. *Denormalizing Tobacco: A Response to Tobacco Control: A Blueprint to Protect the Health of Canadians*. Toronto: Non-Smokers' Rights Association.

Non-Smokers' Rights Association. 1999. *The Fraser Institute: Economic Think Tank or Front for the Tobacco Industry?* Toronto: Non-Smokers' Rights Association.

Non-Smokers' Rights Association and the Advocacy Institute. 1990. *Death or Taxes: A Health Advocate's Guide to Increasing Tobacco Taxes*. Ottawa: Canadian Council on Smoking and Health.

Norr, Roy. 1952. "Cancer by the Carton." *Reader's Digest*. December: 35-36.

Oliver, Daniel. 1987. Prepared Statement of Daniel Oliver, Chairman, Federal Trade Commission on Cigarette Adver-tising Bans Before the Transportation Subcommittee, Committee on Energy and Commerce, U.S. House of Repre-sentatives. April 3.

Ondrick, James J.S. 1991. "The Erosion of Elite Accommodation and the New Sys-tem of Lobbying and Decision Making in Canadian Government." Unpub-lished M.A. thesis, Concordia Univer-sity.

O'Neill, Michael A. 1999a. "Evaluating the Scope and Future Prospects of Interna-tional Co-operation and Regulation: A Discussion of the Proposed Framework Convention o Tobacco Control." Paper presented at Canadian Political Science Association, Sherbrooke.

O'Neill, Michael A. 1999b. "United States Tobacco Settlement Agreement—Mea-sures and Analysis." Unpublished paper.

Ontario Council of Health. 1982. *Smoking and Health in Ontario: A Need for Bal-ance*. Report of the Task Force on Smok-ing Submitted to the Ontario Council of Health. Toronto: Ontario Council of Health.

Ontario Tobacco Research Unit. 1995a. *A Review of Evaluations of Anti-Smoking Interventions in Countries Other than Canada*. Toronto: Ontario Tobacco Research Unit.

Ontario Tobacco Research Unit. 1995b. *Monitoring Ontario's Tobacco Strategy: Progress Toward Our Goals*. October.

Ontario Tobacco Research Unit. 1996. *Monitoring the Ontario Tobacco Strat-egy: Progress Toward Our Goals* 1995/1996. 2nd Annual Report. October.

Ontario Tobacco Research Unit. 1998a. *Monitoring the Ontario Tobacco Strat-egy: Progress Toward Our Goals* 1996/1997. 3rd Annual Report. April.

Ontario Tobacco Research Unit. 1998b. *Monitoring the Ontario Tobacco Strat-egy: Progress Toward Our Goals* 1997/1998. 4th Annual Report. Novem-ber.

Ontario Tobacco Research Unit. 2000a. *Comprehensive Tobacco Control Pro-grams: A Review and Synthesis of Evalu-ation Strategies in North America*. June.

Ontario Tobacco Research Unit. 2000b. *Monitoring the Ontario Tobacco Strat-egy: Progress Toward Our Goals* 1999/2000. 6th Annual Monitoring Report. October.

O'Reilly, Patricia. 2000. "The Federal/Provincial/Territorial Health Conference System." Unpublished paper.

Orey, Michael. 1999. *Assuming the Risk: The Mavericks, the Lawyers, and the Whistle-Blowers Who Beat Big Tobacco.* Boston: Little, Brown and Company.

Ouston, Rick. 1998. "Dosanjh to Monitor U.S. Tobacco Lawsuit." *Vancouver Sun.* September 28.

Pal, Leslie. 1993. *Interests of State: The Politics of Language, Multiculturalism and Feminism in Canada.* Montreal and Kingston: McGill-Queen's University Press.

Pal, Leslie A., and R. Kent Weaver (eds.). 2002 (forthcoming). *The Politics of Pain: Political Institutions and Loss Imposition in Canada and the United States.*

Pan-American Health Organization. 1992. *Tobacco or Health: Status in the Americas.* Washington: Pan American Health Organization, Pan American Sanitary Bureau, Regional Office of the World Health Organization.

"Panel Urges Tobacco Regs, Cigarette Tax Hike." 2001. Morgantown *Dominion-Post.* May 13.

Parker-Pope, Tara. 2001. *Cigarettes: Anatomy of an Industry from Seed to Smoke.* New York: New Press.

Pear, Robert. A. 1998. "Health Agency Is Urged to Re-evaluate Spending Priorities." *New York Times,* July 9.

Pechmann, Cornelia, Philip Dixon, and Neville Layne. 1998. "An Assessment of US and Canadian Smoking Reduction Objectives for the Year 2000." *American Journal of Public Health* 88: 1362-67.

Pertschuk, Michael. 1970. "A Look Backward and a Glance Forward." In National Interagency Council on Smoking and Health, *National Conference on Smoking and Health.* New York: National Interagency Council on Smoking and Health.

Pertschuk, Michael. 1986. *Giant Killers.* New York: Norton.

Pertschuk, Michael. 1997. "We've Come a Long Way–Maybe; Assessing the Strengths and Weaknesses of the Tobacco Control Movement Today." Keynote Address for "Entering a New Dimension: A National Conference on Tobacco and Health," Houston.

Pertschuk, Michael, and the Advocacy Institute Staff. 1994. *New Opportunities, New Threats: Some Strategic Implications of the Changing Public Policy Environment for Tobacco Control: A Work in Progress.* Washington: Advocacy Institute.

Phelps, David, Deborah C. Rybak, Tom Mason, and Mark Luinenburg. 1998. *Smoked: The Inside Story of the Minnesota Tobacco Trial.* Minneapolis: MSP Communications.

Phillips, Frank. 2000. "Tobacco Firms Say They May Sue State." *Boston Globe.* November 15.

Pierce-Lavin, Candace, Alan C. Geller, Jim Hyde, and Jack Evjy (eds.). 1998. "Robert Wood Johnson Foundation and Boston University School of Medicine Working Group: Creating Statewide Tobacco Control Programs after Passage of a Tobacco Tax." *Cancer* 83 (12: Supplement) December 15.

Plenary Session. 1996. Tobacco-Free Canada. 2nd National Conference on Tobacco or Health. Toronto: Audio Archives International.

Poel, Dale H. 1976. "The Diffusion of Legislation among the Canadian Provinces: A Statistical Analysis." *Canadian Journal of Political Science* 9: 605-626.

Poland, Blake D. 1998. "Smoking, Stigma, and the Purification of Public Space" In Robin Kearns and Wil Gester (eds.), *Putting Health into Place: Landscape, Identity and Well-Being.* Syracuse: Syracuse University Press.

Presthus, Robert. 1973. *Elite Accommodation in Canadian Politics.* Toronto: Macmillan.

Pringle, Peter. 1998. *Cornered: Big Tobacco at the Bar of Justice.* New York: Henry Holt.

Pritchard, R. 1986. "Tobacco Industry Speaks with One Voice, Once Again." *U.S. Tobacco and Candy Journal.* July 17-August 6.

Proctor, Robert N. 1995. *Cancer Wars: How Politics Shapes What We Know and Don't Know About Cancer.* New York: Basic Books.

Proctor, Robert N. 1999. *The Nazi War on Cancer.* Princeton: Princeton University Press.

Promoting Health, Preventing Disease: Objectives for the Nation. 1980. Atlanta: Public Health Service.

Pross, A. Paul 1992. *Group Politics and Public Policy.* 2nd ed. Toronto: Oxford University Press.

Pross, A. Paul, and Iain S. Stewart. 1994. "Breaking the Habit: Attentive Publics and Tobacco Regulation." In Susan Phillips (ed.), *How Ottawa Spends, 1994-95.* Ottawa: Carleton University Press.

"Protect All Children From Tobacco, Says UNICEF." 1997. *UNICEF Newsline.* July 28.

Rabe, Barry G. 1994. *Beyond NIMBY: Hazardous Waste Siting in the United States and Canada.* Washington: Brookings Institution.

Rachlis, Michael, and Carol Kushner. 1989. *Second Opinion: What's Wrong with Canada's Health-Care System and How to Fix It.* Toronto: Collins, 1989.

Read, Melvyn D. 1996. *The Politics of Tobacco.* Aldershot: Avebury.

Reich, Robert A. 1997. *Locked in the Cabinet.* New York: Alfred A. Knopf.

Report of the Kessler-Koop Advisory Committee on Tobacco Policy and Public Health. 1997. Washington.

Richardson, J.J., and Grant Jordan (eds.). 1982. *Policy Styles in Western Democracies.* Boston: Allen and Unwin.

Rienzo, David A. 1998. "About-Face: How FDA Changed Its Mind, Took on the Tobacco Companies in the Their Own Back Yard, and Won." *Food and Drug Law Journal* 53: 243-66.

Ripley, Randall B. 1985. *Policy Analysis in Political Science.* Chicago: Nelson-Hall.

Robertson, David Brian. 1991. "Political Conflict and Lesson-Drawing." *Journal of Public Policy* 11: 55-78.

Robertson, David Brian, and Jerold L. Waltman. 1993. "The Politics of Policy Borrowing." In David Finegold, Laurel McFarland, and William Richardson (eds.), *Something Borrowed, Something Learned?* Washington: Brookings Institution.

Roemer, Ruth. 1993. *Legislative Action to Combat the World Tobacco Epidemic.* 2nd ed. Geneva: World Health Organization.

Rogers, Byron, Gordon Myers, and Neil E. Collishaw. 1985. "Trends in Tobacco Consumption in Seven Countries." Paper presented to International Congress on Alcoholism and Drug Dependence, Calgary.

Rogers, Everett M. 1995. *Diffusion of Innovations.* 4th ed. New York: The Free Press.

Rose, Richard (ed..). 1974. *Lessons from America.* New York: Halsted/Wiley.

Rose, Richard. 1976. "On the Priorities of Citizenship in the Deep South and Northern Ireland." *Journal of Politics* 38: 247-91.

Rose, Richard. 1982. *Do Parties Matter?* 2nd ed. Chatham, NJ: Chatham House.

Rose, Richard. 1991. "Lesson-Drawing Across Nations." *Journal of Public Policy* 11: 3-30.

Rose, Richard. 1993. *Lesson-Drawing in Public Policy.* Chatham, NJ: Chatham House.

Rose, Richard, and Philip Davies. 1994. *Inheritance in Public Policy: Change Without Choice in Britain.* New Haven, CT: Yale University Press.

Rosenau, Pauline V., Russell D. Jones, Julie Reagan Watson, and Carl Hacker. 1995. "Anticipating the Impact of NAFTA on Health and Health Policy." *Canadian-American Public Policy* 21 (January).

Rosenblatt, Roger. 1994. "How Do Tobacco Industry Executives Live with Themselves?" *New York Times Magazine,* March 20: 34-41, 55, 73-74, 76.

Rosser, W.W. 1985. "Physicians for a Smoke-Free Canada." *Canadian Medical Association Journal* 133: 1115-16.

Rushefsky, Mark, and Kant Patel. 1999. *Health Care Politics and Policy in America.* 2nd ed. Armonk, NY: M.E. Sharpe.

Ryder, David. 1998. "The Analysis of Policy: Understanding the Process of Policy Development." In Jeffrey A. Schaler and Madga E. Schaler (eds.), *Smoking: Who Has the Right?* Amherst, NY: Prometheus Books.

Sabatier, Paul A. (ed.). 1999. *Theories of the Policy Process.* Boulder, CO: Westview.

Sancton, Andrew. 1998. "Introduction." In Donald N. Rothblatt and Andrew Sancton, *Metropolitan Governance Revisited.* Berkeley, CA: Institute of Governmental Studies Press.

Sasco, Annie J., Panagiota Dalla-Vorgia, and Pierette Van der Elst. 1992. *Comparative Study of Anti-Smoking Legislation in Countries of the European Economic Community.* Lyon: International Agency for Research on Cancer, IARC Technical Report No. 8.

Sato, Hajime. 1999. "The Advocacy Coalition Framework and the Policy Process Analysis: The Case of Smoking Control in Japan." *Policy Studies Journal* 27: 28-44.

Savage, Robert. 1985. "Diffusion Research Traditions and the Spread of Policy Innovations in a Federal System." *Publius.* 15 (4): 1-27.

"Saving Lives and Raising Revenue: The Case for Major Increases in State and Federal Tobacco Taxes." 1993. Coalition on Smoking Or Health. March.

Savoie, Donald J. 1999. *Governing from the Centre: The Concentration of Power in Canadian Politics.* Toronto: University of Toronto Press.

Sawatsky, John. 1989. *The Insiders: Power, Money and Secrets in Ottawa.* Toronto: McClelland and Stewart.

Schattschneider, E.E. 1960. *The Semi-Sovereign People.* New York: Holt, Rinehart and Winston.

Schneider, Anne, and Helen Ingram. 1990. "Behavioral Assumptions of Policy Tools." *Journal of Politics* 52: 510-29.

Schneider, Anne L., and Helen Ingram. 1997. *Policy Design for Democracy.* Lawrence: University Press of Kansas.

Schwartz, Jerome L. 1969. "A Critical Review and Evaluation of Smoking Control Methods." *Public Health Reports* 84: 483-506.

Schwartz, Jerome L. 1987. *Review and Evaluation of Smoking Cessation Methods: The United Staes and Canada, 1978-1985.* US. Department of Health and Human Services, Public Health Service, National Institutes of Health, Division of Cancer Prevention and Control.

Schwartz, Jerome L., and G. Rider. 1978. *Review and Evaluation of Smoking Control Methods: The United States and Canada, 1969-1977.* Bureau of Health Education, Center for Disease Control, Public Health Service, U.S. Department of Health, Education and Welfare.

Seeliger, Robert. 1996. "Conceptualizing and Researching Policy Convergence." *Policy Studies Journal* 24: 287-306.

Selin, Heather. 1995. "Canada Should Echo Clinton's Stand on Nicotine." *Globe and Mail.* September 4.

Shelton, Dana M., Marianne Haenlein Alciati, Michele M. Change, Julie A. Fishman, Liza A. Fues, Jennifer Michaels, Ronald J. Bazile, James C. Bridgers, Jr., Jacqueline L. Rosenthal, Lalitha Kutty, and Michael P. Eriksen. 1995. "State Laws on Tobacco Control—United States, 1995." *CDC Surveillance Summary, Morbidity and Mortality Weekly Report* 44 (1): 1-28.

Show Us the Money: An Update on the States' Allocation of the Tobacco Settlement Dollars. 2000. Campaign for Tobacco-Free Kids, American Cancer Society, American Heart Association, and the American Lung Association. Washington.

Showalter, Mark. 1998. "The Effect of Cigarette Taxes on Cigarette Consumption." *American Journal of Public Health* 88: 1118-19.

Shultz, James M., Michael E. Moen, Terry F. Pechacek, Kathleen C. Harty, Mark A Skubic, Steven W. Gust, and Andrew G. Dean. 1986. "The Minnesota Plan for Nonsmoking and Health: The Legislative Experience." *Journal of Public Health Policy* 7: 300-13.

Siegel, Michael, and Lois Biener. 1997. "Evaluating the Impact of Statewide Anti-Tobacco Campaigns: The Massachusetts and California Tobacco Control Programs." *Journal of Social Issues* 53: 147-68.

Skirrow, Jan, and Peggy Edwards. 1986. *Strategies for a Smoke-Free World*. Calgary: Alberta Alcohol and Drug Abuse Commission.

Skogstad, Grace. 1987. *The Politics of Agricultural Policy-making in Canada*. Toronto: University of Toronto Press.

Slade, John, and Scott Ballin. n.d. "Who's Minding the Tobacco Store? It's Time to Level the Regulatory Playing Field." Washington: Coalition on Smoking Or Health.

Smart, Reginald G., and Alan C. Ogborne. 1996. *Northern Spirits: A Social History of Alcohol in Canada*. Toronto: Addiction Research Foundation.

Smith, Jennifer, and Herman Bakvis. 2000. "Changing Dynamics in Election Campaign Finance: Critical Issues in Canada and the U.S." *Policy Matters* 1(4): 1-40.

Smith, T. Alexander. 1975. *The Comparative Policy Process*. Santa Barbara, CA: ABC-Clio.

Smith, T. Alexander, and Ray Tatalovich. 2002 (forthcoming). *Moral Conflicts in Western Democracies*. Peterborough: Broadview.

"Smoking: Just Say No." 2000. *Economist*. December 9: 36-37.

Sobel, Robert. 1978. *They Satisfy: The Cigarette in American Life*. Garden City, NY: Anchor/Doubleday Books.

Somers, E. n.d. Memorandum to A.J. Liston. Health and Welfare Canada.

Soroka, Stuart. 1999. "Policy Agenda-Setting Theory Revisited: A Critique of Howlett on Downs, Baumgartner and Jones, and Kingdon." *Canadian Journal of Political Science* 32: 763-72.

Spill, Rorie L., Michael J. Licari, and Leonard Ray. 2001. "Taking on Tobacco: Policy Entrepreneurship and the Tobacco Litigation." *Political Research Quarterly* 54

"Statement by International Tobacco Control Advocates on U.S. Tobacco Litigation Settlement Discussions." 1997. Essential Action. http://www.essential.org/action/tobacco/state.html. June 17.

Statistics Canada. 1995. *General Social Survey: Cycle 10*. Housing, Family and Social Statistics Division.

Statistics Canada. 1999. *Statistical Report on the Health of Canadians*. Ottawa: Statistics Canada.

Stoffman, Daniel. 1987. "Where There's Smoke." *Report on Business*. September: 20-28.

Stone, Diane. 1999. "Learning Lessons and Transferring Policy Across Time, Space and Disciplines." *Politics* 19: 51-59.

Stone, Diane. 2000. "Non-Governmental Policy Transfer: The Strategies of Independent Policy Institutes." *Governance* 13: 45-62.

Studlar, Donley T. 1993. "Ethnic Minority Groups, Agenda Setting and Policy Borrowing in Britain." In Paula D. McClain (ed.), *Minority Group Influence*. New York: Greenwood Press.

Studlar, Donley T. 1998. "The Tobacco War in West Virginia." *West Virginia Public Affairs Reporter* 15 (1): 2-10.

Studlar, Donley T. 1999a. "Diffusion of Tobacco Control in North America." *Annals of the American Academy of Political and Social Science*, No. 566 (November): 68-79.

Studlar, Donley T. 1999b. "The Mouse That Roared? The Interaction Between Canada and the United States on Tobacco Regulation." *Canadian-American Public Policy* 38: 1-64.

Studlar, Donley T. 2000. "Federalism and Public Policy: The Canadian Provinces and Tobacco Control," Paper No.14, *Occasional Papers Series*, Canadian Studies Center, Bowling Green State University.

Studlar, Donley T. 2002 (forthcoming). "Tobacco Control and Loss Imposition in Canada and the United States." In Leslie A. Pal and R. Kent Weaver (eds.), *The Politics of Pain: Loss Imposition in Canada and the United States.*

Studlar, Donley T., and Raymond Tatalovich. 1996. "Abortion Policy in the United States and Canada: Do Institutions Matter?" In Dorothy McBride Stetson and Marianne Githens (eds.), *Abortion Politics: Public Policy in Cross-Cultural Perspective.* New York: Routledge.

Subcommittee on Tobacco Policy Research. 1991. Washington, September 20.

Sullum, Jacob. 1998. *For Your Own Good: The Anti-Smoking Crusade and the Tyranny of Public Health.* New York: The Free Press.

Swan, Judith, and Karen Fraim Goss. 1994. "Lessons From Other Coalition-Based Programs of the National Cancer Institute." In Richard A. Couto, Nancy K. Simpson, and Gale Harris (eds.), *Sowing Seeds in the Mountains.* Washington: National Cancer Institute, Division of Cancer Prevention and Control, Cancer Control Sciences Program, the Appalachia Leadership Initiative on Cancer.

Sweanor, David T. 1991. "The Canadian Tobacco Tax Project, 1985-1991: A Review of a Major Public Health Success Story." Ottawa: Non-Smokers' Rights Association.

Sweanor, David T. 1993. Letter to the Editor. *Wall Street Journal.* June 7.

Sweanor, David T. 1997. "Government Action on Tobacco's Costs." Smoking and Health Action Foundation. July.

Sweanor, David T. 1998a. "The Regulation of Tobacco and Nicotine: The Creation, and Potential for Resolution, of a Public Health Disaster." *Drugs: Education, Prevention and Policy* 5 (2): 135-40.

Sweanor, David T. 1998b. "The Smuggling of Tobacco Products." Testimony Before the United States Special Senate Democratic Task Force on Tobacco. Smoking and Health Action Foundation. May 4.

Sweanor, David T., and Luc R. Martial. 1994. "The Smuggling of Tobacco Products: Lessons From Canada." Non-Smokers' Rights Association and Smoking and Health Action Foundation. August.

Symonds, William C. 1995. "Warning: Cigarette Bans Do Not Curb Teen Smoking." *Business Week.* August 28.

Tait, Lyal. 1968. *Tobacco in Canada.* Tillsonburg, ON: Ontario Flue-Cured Tobacco Growers' Marketing Board.

Tamburri, Rose. 1990. "Canada Proposes Tough New Warnings, Health Information on Cigarette Packs." *Wall Street Journal.* January 23.

Tatalovich, Ray, and Byron W. Daynes (eds.). 1988. *Social Regulatory Policy.* Boulder, CO: Westview.

Tatalovich, Ray, and Byron W. Daynes (eds.). 1998. *Moral Controversies in American Politics: Cases in Social Regulatory Policy.* Armonk, NY: M.E. Sharpe.

Tate, Cassandra. 1999. *Cigarette Wars: The Triumph of "The Little White Slaver."* New York: Oxford University Press.

Taylor, Allyn L. 1996. "An International Regulatory Strategy for Global Tobacco Control." *Yale Journal of International Law* 21: 257-304.

Taylor, Peter. 1984. *The Smoke Ring: Tobacco, Money, and Multinational Politics.* New York: Pantheon Books.

Taylor, Peter. 1985. *The Smoke Ring.* Rev. ed. New York: Viking.

Taylor, S. Martin, Charles H. Goldsmith, and J. Allan Best. 1994. "The Community Intervention Trial for Smoking Cessation (COMMIT)." *Health and Canadian Society* 2: 179-95.

Tennant, Richard B. 1950. *The American Cigarette Industry*. New Haven, CT: Yale University Press.

Thomas, David (ed.). 1993. *Canada and the United States: Differences That Count*. Peterborough, ON: Broadview.

Thomas, David (ed.). 2000. *Canada and the United States: Difference That Count*. 2nd ed. Peterborough, ON: Broadview.

Thompson, M., and I. McLeod. 1976. "The Effects of Economic Variables upon the Demand for Cigarettes in Canada." *Mathematical Scientist* 1: 121-32.

Tobacco Control: A Blueprint to Protect the Health of Canadians. 1995. Ottawa: Health Canada.

"Tobacco Fund for Farmers." 1999. *New York Times*. January 22.

Tobacco Institute. 1997. *The Tax Burden on Tobacco*. Volume 32. Washington: Tobacco Institute.

"Tobacco Opponent Predicts Similar Legal Action in Canada." 2000. *London Free Press*. July 15.

Tobacco Policy Options: Summary Report of ATRA Public Policy Committee. 2000. Edmonton: Alberta Tobacco Reduction Alliance.

Tobacco Tax Policy in Canada: A Health Perspective: A Submission to the Minister of Finance, the Honourable Michael Wilson. 1989. Canadian Cancer Society, Canadian Council on Smoking and Health, Canadian Heart Foundation, Canadian Lung Association, Canadian Medical Association, Non-Smokers' Rights Association.

"Tobacco Taxes in Industrialized Countries." 1990. *World Smoking and Health* 15 (3): 9.

Tobacco Taxes: What's Next. 1995. Ontario: Ontario Campaign for Action on Tobacco.

Tobacco Use: An American Crisis. 1993. Final Conference Report and Recommendations from America's Health Community. Washington, January 9-12.

"The Tobacco War Goes Global." 2000. *Economist*. October 12.

Together Against Tobacco. 1999. Proceedings, INGCAT International NGO Mobilisation Meeting. Geneva, May 15-16.

Tollison, Robert D., and Richard E. Wagner. 1988. *Smoking and the State*. Lexington, MA: Lexington Books.

Toma, Tudor. 2000. "Canada Pushes for Strong Global Tobacco Treaty." *British Medical Journal* 20: 1296.

Torry, Saundra. 1998. "Business Groups Fight Tobacco Bill Harder." *Washington Post*. May 19.

Torry, Saundra, and Helen Dewar. 1998. "Big Tobacco's Ad Blitz Felt in Senate Debate." *Washington Post*. June 17.

Toward a Tobacco-Free California: Strategies for the 21st Century 2000-2003. 2000. Tobacco Education and Research Oversight Committee.

Troyer, Ronald J., and Gerald E. Markle. 1983. *Cigarettes: The Battle over Smoking*. New Brunswick, NJ: Rutgers University Press.

True, Jaqui, and Michael Mintrom. 2001. "Transnational Networks and Policy Diffusion: The Case of Gender Mainstreaming." *International Studies Quarterly* 45: 27-57.

Tucker, David. 1982. *Tobacco: An International Perspective*. London: Euromonitor Publications.

Tuohy, Carolyn H. 1999. *Accidental Logics: The Dynamics of Change in the Health Care Arena in the United States, Britain, and Canada*. New York: Oxford University Press.

U.S. Department of Health, Education and Welfare. 1964. *Smoking and Health: Report of the Advisory Committee to the Surgeon General of the Public Health Service*. Princeton: D. Van Nostrand Co., Inc.

U.S. Department of Health, Education and Welfare. 1979. *Healthy People: The Surgeon General's Report on Health Promotion and Disease Prevention*. Public Health Service.

U.S. Department of Health, Education and Welfare. 1980. *Promoting Health, Preventing Disease: Objectives for the Nation.* Public Health Service, Centers for Disease Control, Center for Health Promotion and Education.

U.S. Department of Health and Human Services. 1986. *The Health Consequences of Involuntary Smoking: A Report of the Surgeon General.* Public Health Service, Centers for Disease Control, Center for Health Promotion and Education, Office on Smoking and Health.

U.S. Department of Health and Human Services, 1988. *The Health Consequences of Smoking: Nicotine Addiction.* Public Health Service, Centers for Disease Control, Center for Chronic Disease Prevention and Health Promotion, Office on Smoking and Health.

U.S. Department of Health and Human Services. 1989. *Reducing the Health Consequences of Smoking: 25 Years of Progress. A Report of the Surgeon General.* Public Health Service, Centers for Disease Control, Center for Chronic Disease Prevention and Health Promotion, Office on Smoking and Health.

U.S. Department of Health and Human Services. 1990. *Smoking and Health: A National Status Report.* A Report to Congress. 2nd ed. Rockville, MD.

U.S. Department of Health and Human Services. 1991. *Strategies to Control Tobacco Use in the United States: A Blueprint for Public Health Action in the 1990s.* Public Health Service, National Institutes of Health, National Cancer Institute.

U.S. Department of Health and Human Services. 1992. *Smoking and Health in the Americas: A 1992 Report of the Surgeon General, in Collaboration with the Pan American Health Organization.* Public Health Service, Disease Prevention and Health Promotion, Centers for Disease Control and Prevention, Office on Smoking and Health.

U.S. Department of Health and Human Services. 1999. *Best Practices for Comprehensive Tobacco Control Programs.* Centers for Disease Control and Prevention, National Center for Chronic Disease Prevention and Health Promotion, Office on Smoking and Health, August.

U.S. Department of Health and Human Services. 2000a. *Healthy People 2010.* Public Health Service, Centers for Disease Control and Prevention, Office of Disease Prevention and Health Promotion.

U.S. Department of Health and Human Services. 2000b. *Reducing Tobacco Use: A Report of the Surgeon General.* Public Health Service, Centers for Disease Control and Prevention, National Center for Chronic Disease Prevention and Health Promotion, Office on Smoking and Health.

U.S. Department of Health and Human Services. 2001. *Investment in Tobacco Control: State Highlights 2001.* Public Health Service, Centers for Disease Control and Prevention, National Center for Chronic Disease Prevention and Health Promotion, Office on Smoking and Health.

U.S. General Accounting Office. 1989. *Teenage Smoking: Higher Excise Tax Should Significantly Reduce the Number of Smokers.* United States General Accounting Office.

U.S. General Accounting Office. 1998. *Tobacco: Issues Surrounding a National Tobacco Settlement.* Report to the Honorable Richard M. Burr, House of Representatives. April.

U.S. Public Health Service. 1969. "Smoking and Health Programs in Other Countries: A Report of the National Clearinghouse for Smoking and Health."

Viscusi, W. Kip. 1992. *Smoking: Making the Risky Decision.* New York: Oxford University Press.

Vizzard, William. 1997. *In the Cross Fire: A Political History of the Bureau of Alcohol, Tobacco, and Firearms.* Boulder, CO: Lynne Rienner Publishers.

Vogel, David. 1986. *National Styles of Regulation*. Ithaca, NY: Cornell University Press.

Vogel, David. 1995. *Trading Up: Consumer and Environmental Regulation in a Global Economy*. Cambridge, MA: Harvard University Press.

Wagner, Susan. 1971. *Cigarette Country*. New York: Praeger.

Wakefield, Melanie E., and Frank J. Chaloupka. 1998. "Improving the Measurement and Use of Tobacco Control 'Inputs.'" *Tobacco Control* 7: 333-35.

Walker, Jack L. 1969. "The Diffusion of Innovations Among the American States." *American Political Science Review* 63: 880-99.

Walker, Jack. 1977. "Setting the Agenda in the U.S. Senate: A Theory of Problem Selection." *British Journal of Political Science* 7423-45.

Waltman, Jerold L. 1980. *Copying Other Nations' Policies*. Cambridge: Schenkman.

Waltman, Jerold L. 1987. "The Strength of Policy Inheritance." In Jerold L. Waltman and Donley T. Studlar (eds.), *Political Economy: Public Policies in the United States and Britain*. Jackson: University Press of Mississippi.

Waltman, Jerold L., and Donley T. Studlar (eds.). 1987. *Political Economy: Public Policies in the United States and Britain*. Jackson: University Press of Mississippi.

Warner, Kenneth E. 1981. "State Legislation on Smoking and Health: A Comparison of Two Policies." *Policy Sciences* 13: 139-52.

Warner, Kenneth E., Linda M. Goldenhar, and Catherine G. McLaughlin. 1992. "Cigarette Advertising and Magazine Coverage of the Hazards of Smoking: A Statistical Analysis." *New England Journal of Medicine* 336: 305-09.

Warner, Kenneth E., Frank J. Chaloupka, Philip J. Cook, Willard G. Manning, Joseph P. Newhouse, Thomas E. Novotny, Thomas C. Schelling, and Joy Townsend. 1995. "Criteria for Determining an Optimal Cigarette Tax: The Economist's Perspective." *Tobacco Control* 4: 380-86.

Weaver, R. Kent, and Bert A. Rockman (eds.). 1993. *Do Institutions Matter? Government Capabilities in the United States and Abroad*. Washington: Brookings Institution.

Weir, Margaret, and Theda Skocpol. 1985. "State Structures and the Possibilities for 'Keynesian' Responses to the Great Depression in Sweden, Britain, and the Untied States." In Peter B. Evans, Dietrich Rueschemeyer, and Theda Skocpol (eds.), *Bringing the State Back In*. Cambridge: Cambridge University Press.

Weissert, Carol S., and William G.Weissert. 1996. *Governing Health: The Politics of Health Policy*. Baltimore: Johns Hopkins University Press..

Welch, Susan, and Kay Thompson. 1980. "The Impact of Federal Incentives on State Policy Innovation." *American Journal of Political Science* 14: 715-29.

Whelan, Elizabeth.1984. *A Smoking Gun: How the Tobacco Industry Gets Away with Murder*. Philadelphia: Stickley.

"When Lawsuits Make Policy." 1998. *Economist*. November 21: 17-18.

White, Larry. 1988. *Merchants of Death*. New York: William Morrow.

White, Linda. 1999. "What Can Canada Learn from the United States? A Comparison of American and Canadian Child Care Policies." Paper presented at Midwest Political Science Association, Chicago.

Wigle, Donald T., Neil E. Collishaw, J. Kirkbride, Y. Mao, et al. 1987. "Deaths in Canada from Lung Cancer Due to Involuntary Smoking." *Canadian Medical Association Journal* 136: 945-51.

Wilkinson, James. 1986. *Tobacco*. Harmondsworth: Penguin Books.

Wilson, Maureen O'Hara. 1991. "The Politics of Tobacco in Canada: No Smoking: Sign of the Times." Unpublished M.A. thesis, Queen's University, Kingston, Ontario.

Winsor, Hugh. 1997. "Dingwall's Diligence Overcame Goliath." *Globe and Mail*. March 8.

Wolinsky, Howard, and Tom Brune. 1994. *The Serpent on the Staff: The Unhealthy Politics of the American Medical Association.* New York: Putnam.

Wolman, Harold. 1992. "Understanding Cross National Policy Transfers: The Case of Britain and the U.S." *Governance* 5: 27-45.

World Bank. 1999. *Curbing the Epidemic: Government and the Economics of Tobacco Control.* Washington: World Bank.

World Health Organization. 1986. *Ottawa Charter for Health Promotion.* Geneva: World Health Organization.

World Health Organization. 1997. *Tobacco or Health: A Global Report.* Geneva. World Health Organization.

World Health Organization. 1998. *Guidelines for Controlling and Monitoring the Tobacco Epidemic.* Geneva: World Health Organization.

"World's Best Practice in Tobacco Control." 2000. *Tobacco Control* 9: 228-36.

Wright, John R. 1998. "Tobacco Industry PACs and the Nation's Health: A Second Opinion." In Paul S. Herrnson, Ronald G. Shaiko, and Clyde Wilcox (eds.), *The Interest Group Connection: Electioneering, Lobbying, and Policymaking in Washington.* Chatham, NJ: Chatham House.

Yach, Derek, and Douglas Bettcher. 2000. "Globalisation of Tobacco Industry Influence and New Global Responses." *Tobacco Control* 9: 206-16.

"Your Move, Mr. Rock." 1998. *Montreal Gazette.* December 5.

Zahariadis, Nikolaos. 1999. "Ambiguity, Time, and Multiple Streams." In Paul A. Sabatier (ed.), *Theories of the Policy Process.* Boulder, CO: Westview Press.

Zegart, Dan. 2000. *Civil Warriors: The Legal Siege on the Tobacco Industry.* New York: Delacorte Press.

Index

aboriginal reserves, 121
Abramson, Jill, 54
Achieving Health for All: A Framework for Health Promotion (1986), 77
Ackerman, Gwen, 231
Action on Smoking and Health (ASH), 58
Adams, Nancy, 87
addiction, 38, 98, 100, 173, 238, 284
advertising, 37, 55, 90, 91, 93, 95, 98, 100, 106-07, 113, 115, 116, 133, 136, 137, 140, 149, 173, 178, 204, 209, 210, 217, 218, 220, 221, 222-23, 242-43, 249, 267, 270, 271, 274, 275, 276, 280, 281, 286
Advisory Committee of the US Surgeon General, 35-36
Advisory Committee on Intergovernmental Relations (ACIR), 51, 146
Advocacy Coalition Framework (ACF), 70, 254
advocacy groups. *See* anti-tobacco interest groups
Advocacy Institute (AI), 55, 58, 211, 213, 250, 254, 282
Africa, 281
Aftab, Marianne H., 233
agenda setting, 19-40, 64-69, 71, 89, 98, 125, 170-84, 200-01, 228, 236, 259, 260, 261, 263, 266, 267, 268, 269, 270, 271, 284-85
Agricultural Adjustment Act (1933), 30
agriculture, 28, 30-31, 39, 42-43, 62, 68, 97, 119-20, 124, 125, 130-32, 211-12, 214, 221, 228-29, 268, 270, 276, 285
Agriculture Canada, 239
AIDS, 47, 185

airline agreements, 99, 225, 273-74
Alberta, 141, 144, 150, 156, 164, 188, 252
Alberta Alcohol and Drug Abuse Commission, 280
Alciati, Marianne H., 62, 72, 185
alcohol, 28-30, 47, 78, 79, 80-81, 97, 174
Alcohol, Drug Abuse and Mental Health Agency Reorganization Act of 1992, 100, 148, 151
Allison, Harmony, 136-37, 143, 145
Amendment to *Tobacco Act*, 21
American Cancer Society (ACS), 33, 35, 58, 91-93, 99, 151, 154, 175, 184, 211, 225, 247, 248, 254, 282-83
American Civil Liberties Union (ACLU), 55
American Heart Association (AHA), 35, 58, 92, 154
American Legacy Foundation (ALF), 59
American Lung Association (ALA), 58, 92, 154, 225, 248
American Medical Association (AMA), 35, 56, 58, 152, 175, 184, 215, 248
American Public Health Association (APHA), 35
American Stop Smoking Intervention Study for Cancer Prevention (ASSIST), 20, 99, 151, 164, 166, 182, 185, 211, 231, 232, 269
American Tobacco Company, 24, 25, 26
Americans for Nonsmoker's Rights (ANR), 59
Anti-Cigarette League, 28
anti-slavery movement, 85, 273, 277, 279